REVOLUTIONARY BECOMINGS

INVESTIGATING VISIBLE EVIDENCE

STUDIES OF THE WEATHERHEAD EAST ASIAN INSTITUTE,
COLUMBIA UNIVERSITY

**INVESTIGATING VISIBLE EVIDENCE:
NEW CHALLENGES FOR DOCUMENTARY**

Jane Gaines, Faye Ginsburg, Michael Renov, Brian Winston, Series Editors

A new series addressing the most pressing questions for documentary studies today.

Kill the Documentary: A Letter to Filmmakers, Students, and Scholars, by Jill Godmilow

**STUDIES OF THE WEATHERHEAD EAST ASIAN INSTITUTE,
COLUMBIA UNIVERSITY**

The Studies of the Weatherhead East Asian Institute of Columbia University were inaugurated in 1962 to bring to a wider public the results of significant new research on modern and contemporary East Asia.

REVOLUTIONARY BECOMINGS

Documentary Media in Twentieth-Century China

YING QIAN

Columbia University Press
New York

Columbia University Press
Publishers Since 1893
New York   Chichester, West Sussex
cup.columbia.edu

Copyright © 2024 Columbia University Press
All rights reserved

Library of Congress Cataloging-in-Publication Data
Names: Qian, Ying, author.
Title: Revolutionary Becomings: Documentary Media in Twentieth-Century
    China / Ying Qian.
Description: New York : Columbia University Press, [2024] | Series:
    Investigating visible evidence: new challenges for documentary |
    Includes bibliographical references.
Identifiers: LCCN 2023008250 (print) | LCCN 2023008251 (ebook) |
    ISBN 9780231204460 (hardback) | ISBN 9780231204477 (trade paperback) |
    ISBN 9780231555555 (ebook)
Subjects: LCSH: Documentary films—China—History and criticism. |
    Motion pictures—Political aspects—China. | Motion pictures—
    China—History—20th century.
Classification: LCC PN1995.9.D6 Q25 2023 (print) | LCC PN1995.9.D6 (ebook) |
    DDC 070.1/80951—dc23/eng/20230803
LC record available at https://lccn.loc.gov/2023008250
LC ebook record available at https://lccn.loc.gov/2023008251

Cover design: Elliott S. Cairns
Cover image: Still from *The Shanghai Document* (1928)

For my parents, Min Fan and Zhenying Qian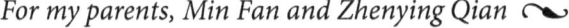

CONTENTS

Acknowledgments   ix

Introduction   1

1. Emergence: Colonial War, Nationalist Revolution, and Documentary's Beginnings   26
2. Bombs and Seafarings: Documentaries Hard and Soft   60
3. Winning Realities: Wartime Propaganda and Solidarity   102
4. When Taylorism Met Revolutionary Romanticism: Great Leap Temporalities   145
5. The Uncertainty of Political Knowledge: Documentary in Crisis   176
6. Rehabilitation: Documentary in the Post-Mao Decade   213

    Epilogue: Notes on Chinese Independent Documentary   248

Notes   255
Index   293

ACKNOWLEDGMENTS

This book is long in the making. I owe profound gratitude to many people and institutions that have supported and sustained me on this challenging and rewarding journey.

This book began as a doctoral dissertation at Harvard University. I am deeply grateful for the privilege to study with my adviser David Der-Wei Wang, who taught me to write with empathy, precision, and openness, and whose incisive guidance and mentorship nurtured this project from the very beginning. My committee members, Eileen Cheng-yin Chow, Eugene Yuejin Wang, and Markus Nornes, guided me with their wide-ranging scholarship, creative spirit, and deep compassion for students. Their discerning readings of the earliest draft chapters helped me find my voice and pushed me to do the best work I could. The interdisciplinary nature of an East Asian studies department allowed me to study cinema and literature alongside history, philosophy, and anthropology. I owe deep thanks to Peter Bol, Arthur Kleinman, Wai-yee Li, Stephen Owen, Elizabeth Perry, Michael Puett, Michael Szonyi, and Xiaofei Tian for showing me how questions of politics, ethics, epistemology, and aesthetics are interrelated, and how our scholarship must strive to explore the contradictions and predicaments facing historical actors at crossroads, thereby illuminating emergent opportunities and possible futures, while heeding lessons from the past. Outside my home department, I benefited enormously from studying with Giuliana Bruno, Dominique Bluher, Lucien Castaing-Taylor, Tom Conley, Alfred Guzzetti, Eric Rentschler and David Rodowick, whose inspiring seminars and scholarship encouraged me to think about cinema comparatively and as embedded in political and social lives. I'm also grateful to Jonathan Bolton at the Slavic Department, who guided me in my studies of Central and Eastern European literature and helped me place Chinese experiences in transnational and comparative perspectives.

During my graduate school years, I was also fortunate to gain experience in filmmaking and curation. Harvard's Film Study Center assisted me in making my first documentary films. The Fairbank Center for Chinese Studies supported Emergent Visions, a monthly film series showcasing Chinese independent documentary that I co-curated with fellow graduate students J. P. Sniadecki, Jie Li, and Benny Shaffer. These invaluable experiences brought me into communities of filmmakers, critics, and media activists, generating conversations and long-lasting friendships that have greatly enriched my understanding of cinema and media's embeddedness in both social movements and everyday life. It was while interning at the renowned filmmaker Carma Hinton's Long Bow Film Studio in Newton, Massachusetts, that I became fascinated by the Mao-era documentaries in Long Bow's impressive film archive. I'm deeply grateful to Carma and Long Bow filmmakers and scholars, Richard Gordon, Geremie Barmé, Dong Hua, and Nora Chang, for sharing their passions and insights with me and for their continued guidance and help through the years.

A great deal of revision and rewriting has taken place to expand the scope of the book and clarify its intellectual and political stakes. In doing so, I have benefited tremendously from the engaging and committed intellectual community at Columbia University where I teach. At my home department, ongoing collaboration and discussion with Lydia Liu has been very inspiring, and her discerning feedback on the manuscript brought further acuity to its analysis. Eugenia Lean's rigorous reading of draft chapters and incisive comments helped me better discuss media history in relation to political, social, and material histories. Takuya Tsunoda and Nicholas Bartlett have been wonderful collaborators and friends with whom to try out and clarify ideas. For the many stimulating and nurturing conversations that have shaped my continuous growth as scholar and educator, I am deeply grateful to Madeleine Zelin, Shang Wei, Gray Tuttle, Paul Anderer, Haruo Shirane, Tomi Suzuki, David Lurie, Theodore Hughes, Jungwon Kim, Zhaohua Yang, and Guo Jue. I also thank Chuck Wooldridge, Kristine Harris, Rebecca Karl, Yukiko Koga, Grace Shen, Laurence Coderre, and other members of the University Seminar on Modern China for reading and commenting on my draft chapter and for building such an engaged community for intellectual camaraderie.

Beyond my home department, I have found kindred spirits and invaluable interlocutors at Columbia's Center for Comparative Media. I am deeply grateful to Jane Gaines, Nico Baumbach, Zeynep Çelik Alexander, Noam Elcott, and Reinhold Martin for taking the time to read draft chapters and offer incisive feedback that improved the book. I learned so much from Brian Larkin's work on infrastructure and Debashree Mukherjee's work on cine-ecology; collaborating with them has influenced the book's trajectory. For vigorous discussions at the monthly University Seminar on Theory and History of Media, I also thank Stephen Andriopoulos, Alexander Alberro, Lucia Allais, Claudia Breger, Jonathan Crary, Felicity Scott, and Dennis Tenen. I am indebted to the late Thomas Elsaesser for his inspiring media-archaeological approach to thinking about film history.

Many other colleagues and friends have generously taken the time to read, critique, and support my work. My deep gratitude goes to Chris Berry, Weihong Bao, Carma Hinton, Jie Li, Jason McGrath, Charles Musser, and Laikwan Pang, who have read the manuscript in full at different stages and lent their insights and encouragement to the project. Rebecca Karl read multiple draft chapters, tested them out with her students, and provided invaluable editorial suggestions when I most needed them. Weihong Bao, Zhang Zhen, Jacob Eyferth and Arunabh Ghosh kindly invited me to lecture from or workshop parts of the book in their classes and offered wonderful feedback. Charles Laughlin and Jason McGrath generously shared films with me. For creating opportunities of exchange, or for feedback, advice and conversation that pushed me to think more expansively and precisely, I also thank Jennifer Altehenger, Nicholas Baer, Tani Barlow, Geremie Barmé, Peter Bloom, Yomi Braester, Francesco Casetti, Letty Chen, Tina Mai Chen, Gloria Davies, Rossen Djagalov, Victor Fan, Andrew Field, Geraldine Fiss, Evie Yi Gu, Nan Hartman. Belinda He, Margaret Hillenbrand, Denise Ho, Nicole Huang, Huang Wangli, Paola Iovene, Andrew Jones, Olivier Krischer, Charles Laughlin, Haiyan Lee, Jinying Li, Li Xiaofeng, Li Zhen, Shiqi Lin Nan Ma, Laliv Melamed, Avind Rajagopal, Claire Roberts, Luke Robinson, Carlos Rojas, Masha Salazkina, Salomé Aguilera Skvirsky, Marsha Siefert, Shi Ce, Shi Chuan, Mingwei Song, Christian Sorace, Wanning Sun, Luigi Tomba, Edward Tyerman, Ban Wang, Lingzhen Wang, Emily Wilcox, Felix Wemheuer, Sebastian Veg, Wen-Hsin Yeh, Yiman Wang, Winnie Wong, Jiwei Xiao, Guobin Yang, Jinghong Zhang, Zhang Jishun, Ling Zhang, and Chenshu Zhou.

It has been thrilling and rewarding to use draft chapters from the manuscript in my own teaching. Students in my undergraduate and graduate seminars read draft chapters, and I'm immensely grateful to their thoughtful responses, which helped me improve the clarity and rigor of the text, and make it more accessible to students of diverse backgrounds and interests. Yilun Li offered brilliant feedback on the book's multiple chapters. Yingchuan Yang shared with me research materials he found on *Chairman Liu Visits Indonesia*. Susanna Sun suggested research literature on the Yue opera. I have learned so much from wide-ranging discussions with Tenggeer Hao and Sam

Hellmann. I thank David Borgonjon, Harlan Chambers, Junnan Chen, Benjamin Kindler, Di Luo, Qi Hong, Wentao Ma, Yedong Sh-chen, Raymond Tsang, Siwei Wang, Chung-wei Yang, Xinyi Zhao, Jieming Zhu, and all my former and current students for sharing journeys of inquiry and learning with me.

This book's research and writing have been supported by fellowships and grants from Harvard Graduate School of the Arts and Sciences, the Fairbank Center for Chinese Studies, Australian Center on China in the World at the Australian National University, and the China Studies Center at University of Sydney. A Tsunoda Senior fellowship allowed me to spend research time at Waseda University in Japan. At Columbia I have been supported by the Lenfest Junior Faculty Development Grant, Provost's Diversity Grant, Provost's Global Humanity Projects Grant, and funding from the Department of East Asian Languages and Cultures and the Weatherhead East Asia Institute. I thank staffs at the Harvard-Yenching Library, the Fung Library (Harvard), the Shanghai Library, China Film Archive, Li Xianting Film Fund, Taiwan Film and Audiovisual Institute, Hong Kong Film Archive, National Film Archive of Japan and the National Diet Library (Japan) for research assistance. Columbia's Starr East Asian Library is any film scholar's dream library for its extensive holdings, and I'm so grateful to its director Jim Cheng and its capable Chinese librarian Chengzhi Wang for amazing support over the years. I thank Zheng Dali for generously sharing materials from his father Zheng Junli's papers with me and for ongoing conversations on everything to do with cinema. I thank collectors Liu Debao and Cao Guimin for making their collections available.

Many thanks to my editor at the Columbia University Press, Philip Leventhal, who has patiently shepherded this book from drafts to production. Jane Gaines, as the series editor for Visible Evidence, provided enormously helpful and comprehensive editorial suggestions on behalf of the editorial committee that improved the book. I thank Kenneth Ross Yelsea and Ariana King, former and current editors for Studies of the Weatherhead East Asia Institute, for support and encouragement. I thank Susan Pensak and Monique Laban at the Columbia University Press production for making the process so smooth. I'm grateful to Irene Pavitt, Eleanor Goodman, and Anita O'Brien for editorial assistance at various stages of the manuscript preparation, and Cynthia Col for her work on the indexes of the book.

A condensed version of chapter 4 appeared in *Critical Inquiry* 46 (spring 2020). An earlier treatment of *Victory of the Chinese People* (1950) appeared as "Crossing the River Twice–Cinematic Re-enactments and the Founding of PRC Documentary" in *Oxford Handbook for Chinese Cinemas* (2013). A brief treatment of Liu Shaoqi's fall from power and rehabilitation was published in *A New Literary History of Modern China* (2017). I thank editors Carlos Rojas, Eileen Chow, David Der-Wei Wang, Haun Saussy, and Christian Sorace for helpful feedback and editorial suggestions.

The making of a book is truly a marathon. I'm deeply grateful to my dear friends and family who have supported me through thick and thin. Mary Brooksbank and Brian Brophy welcomed me to their seaside cottage in Carrickalinga, South Australia, where I wrote substantial parts of the book. David Brophy tirelessly read drafts, offered editorial suggestions, and saw me through the lengthy writing process with patience, encouragement, and camaraderie. In Cambridge, Massachusetts, Ling Zhang and David Mozina are my rock and anchor. They consoled me at times of loss, and their delicious cooking replenished me with love and kept me going. As a single child, I am so fortunate to have Duan Wu, Kathleen Lau, Qi Wang, and Kris Ma, who know me forever and are as close to me as siblings can be. These friendships are sources of joy that have kept me strong in challenging times.

When writing this book, I often thought of my grandparents, Fan Xianqun and Yan Ruilan, with whom I spent my childhood and teenage years. They lived through the bombing of Shanghai in 1932 and many turns in history thereafter. Their storytelling, often aided by photographs, was among the first history lessons that I remember to this day. I wish they had lived to see the publication of this book. My parents, Fan Min and Qian Zhenying, have had their shares of aspirations, confusions and disappointments from China's turbulent twentieth century. Carrying many unresolved quandaries and wounds from their own pasts, they have nevertheless given me the sweetest and most unconditional love anyone could ask for. I dedicate this book to them.

REVOLUTIONARY
BECOMINGS

INTRODUCTION

On the evening of November 26, 1911, a crowd of more than one thousand gathered at the Michitaza Theater in Nagasaki, Japan, to attend the premiere of a film entitled *The Chinese Revolution*.[1] According to the local newspaper, about two hundred among the audience were Chinese. They waved revolutionary army flags, applauding and cheering in celebration whenever the army appeared on screen. At the end of the screening, a young Chinese student dashed to the front of the theater for an impromptu speech. Having concluded his studies in Tokyo, he was, like many Chinese in Japan, passing through Nagasaki en route to Shanghai to join the revolution. Announcing to great applause that he was no longer a Qing subject but a Chinese citizen and a revolutionary, the student thanked the Japanese for their kind support before he switched from Japanese to Chinese and delivered a rousing speech, stirring the Chinese audience into ecstatic hooraying, while the Japanese looked on with awe.[2]

What the excited audience watched that night was the first of a series of three films shot on-site in China documenting the development of the 1911 revolution, from the outbreak of insurgency in October in Wuchang to the inauguration of Sun Yat-sen, the tireless revolutionary organizer, as the provisional president in December.[3] These films were produced by M. Pathé, one of Japan's leading early film companies, founded in 1906 by the Japanese film pioneer Umeya Shōkichi. An enterprising pan-Asianist activist, Umeya had been a loyal supporter of Sun Yat-sen's revolutionary cause ever since the two first met in 1895 in Hong Kong. In fact, Umeya had entered the film business partly due to his involvement in Sun's revolution. Wanted by the authorities as a collaborator in Sun's scheming, Umeya fled Hong Kong in 1903 for Singapore as a fugitive. There, with the support of Sun's revolutionary networks in Southeast Asia, he took up film exhibition, a novel business that promised to generate fast cash and popular support for the revolution. Ordering film reels from Japan and Hong Kong, and exhibiting them in Southeast Asia, Umeya gained a windfall of profits during the Russo-Japanese War (1904–1905) by showing news films on the war to viewers enthused to witness the historic victory of a rising Asian power on screen. Founding M. Pathé upon return to Japan in 1906, he continued to fund Sun's revolutionary activities with hot cash from his film business, including supporting the *Minbao*, the party newspaper for Sun's Revolutionary Alliance, based in Tokyo.[4]

The Chinese Revolution was one of tens of thousands of films made in China in the twentieth century that would fall into a broadly defined category of documentary. The close involvement of Umeya, its producer, with Sun's activities and the surging energy at its Nagasaki premiere alert us to documentary's multifaceted engagement with revolutionary movements from the medium's earliest years. In this case, documentary not only recorded the eruption of a revolutionary insurgency but was integral to the revolutionary organizing that had led to the uprising and underpinned its success in the first place. The globetrotting revolutionary and the itinerant filmmaker shared infrastructures and networks, pooling financial, social, and symbolic resources and allowing them to be shared between the mass politics of revolution and the mass medium of cinema. Furthermore, while members of Umeya's camera crew were among the first responders to the momentous event of the uprising, the exhibitions of the complete film created further events of exhilarating mass participation, initiating the Chinese viewers present into new political imaginations, providing sources of pride to overseas Chinese communities amid rising racism, and encouraging popular support for the revolution and identification with China as a new modern nation-state.

This book studies the long and rich documentary tradition of China's twentieth century, treating it as a prism to investigate the entwined history of media and China's revolutionary movements. I begin my inquiry in 1895, a year marked not only by cinema's invention but also by a radical reconfiguration of power dynamics in East Asia and a fresh wave of revolutionary agitation in China in the wake of the Qing Empire's defeat in the First Sino-Japanese War (1894–1895). I end with television documentaries in China's post-Mao decade of reorientation and briefly comment on DV documentaries of the present day. With this long horizon, I treat twentieth-century Chinese revolutions not only as moments of explosive rupture but also as arduous, contingent, and contested processes of becoming, where existing fields of action and categories of meaning underwent radical destabilization and reconstitution, and revolutionary movements experienced not only growth and consolidation, but also predicaments and crises. By approaching documentary as "eventful media," attending to its attunement to, and reconfigurations of, relationships across and around the camera, and investigating documentary's embedment in other (re)productive activities in the society, this book asks how media and revolutions are mutually constitutive of each other: how revolutionary movements gave rise to media practices that reconfigured political relationality and revolutionary epistemology in specific ways, and how these media practices in turn informed and delimited the particular paths of revolutions' actualization.

Documentary cinema has had a long history of association with radical politics globally. It was the preferred form of filmmaking for radical film groups in the 1920s and 1930s, including the Workers Film and Photo League in the United States and Prokino in Japan. It also figured importantly in the militant film cultures of the 1960s and 1970s, as in works by the Dziga-Vertov Group in France, the Newsreel groups in the United States, and the Third Cinema of Latin America. As the internet and the mobile phone have made it easier to share video recordings from the front lines of struggle, moving images in the documentary mode have become an integral part of contemporary social movements as well. Documentary has many advantages as a revolutionary media: its fast and inexpensive production, close connection to the struggles on the ground, openness to people's testimonies from the thick of everyday life, and many affective and rhetorical strategies that have developed over time to mobilize emotions and advance arguments.

Revolutionary agitation and upheaval characterized a large part of China's twentieth century, from the 1911 revolution that toppled the Qing Empire, to the 1949 revolution that brought the Chinese Communist Party (CCP) into power, to the various campaigns that the CCP launched to effect radical social transformation and political reorientation. Emerging from distinct contradictions in society at specific historical moments, these revolutionary movements differed greatly from one another in their political agendas, ideologies, styles of leadership, and forms of mass engagement. With different proposals and visions, however, they all sought to modernize the country. All engaged with mass politics, though they saw the masses differently and conceived different organizational forms for them. All had ambitions to usher in a radical break with the past by reconfiguring the relationships on which society was organized; all sought to create political subjects by cultural transformation; and all emerged from China's confrontations with and participation in an evolving world order and drew from transnational circulation of ideas, movements, and resources.[5]

In the midst of it all, a large number of documentaries were made. From the transnational production of news films on the 1911 revolution, to educational films teaching backyard furnace construction during the Great Leap Forward in the 1950s, to reels of "documentary evidence" at the trial of the "Gang of Four" in the early 1980s, for most of the twentieth century in China, documentary films were produced and viewed on a large scale, circulating well beyond movie theaters into many arenas of social and political life.

To date, scholarly attention to Chinese documentary cinema has largely been focused on the independent documentaries that emerged around 1990 and flourished from the 2000s to the present.[6] The longer documentary traditions of the Republican period (1911–1949) and the first forty years of the People's Republic of China (PRC, 1949–1989) have not received comparable attention. There are a number of reasons for the neglect. For a long time, documentary film texts from these periods were unavailable or inaccessible, due either to wartime destruction or to state-enforced political obsolescence associated with regime change. This difficulty has now been overcome to an extent: access to some Mao-era documentaries has improved over the past decade or so.[7] Yet even when film texts are available, it has been unclear how these texts should be approached. As many of the films were made for explicit propaganda purposes in association with state, partisan, civic, business, or educational organizations, and as auteurist discourses on documentary as "film art," commonplace in Euro-American documentary traditions, rarely appeared in China prior to the rise of independent documentary in the late 1980s, there has been a general impression that this body of films were too "artless," didactic and dogmatic to deserve dedicated study.[8]

Documentary didacticism and dogmatism will indeed be reckoned with in this book; not universal traits to Chinese documentary as a whole, these were historical occurrences that marked the challenges and crises of knowledge formation and political relationality in the revolutionary process. More broadly, however, by excavating understudied films and production stories, and by examining documentary's historical embedment in radical social transformations, I show that, contrary to conventional impressions, the Chinese documentary tradition entailed rich, innovative, and diverse media practices, whose engagements in China's twentieth-century revolutions present us with an opportunity to reconsider our approaches not only to documentary and cinema but to revolution itself as well.

This book proposes to study documentary as an eventful media. It excavates documentary's multifaceted engagements— material, infrastructural, epistemic, and symbolic—in political and social lives, and argues for an understanding of documentary aesthetics as "situated," that is, integral to the specific mediation work it performs in a variety of situations from revolutionary financing to war mobilization, industrial and agricultural productions, diplomacy, class struggle sessions, court proceedings, and others. Close reading of film texts, the bread-and-butter of film studies, remain important here: it helps us discern continuous, and often astounding, innovations in documentary form and aesthetics throughout the twentieth century. Yet at the same time, documentary's productivity goes beyond the text. Documentary production and exhibition are events in themselves: they transform political relationalities, build networks, and give form to emergent possibilities that help propel the unfolding of revolutionary processes in certain directions. Indeed, it is when we attend to the nature of collaborations underlying the documentary event, focusing not just on the quality of *representation* but also on the process of *mediation* and extent of *participation*, that we can begin to assess the politics and ethics of documentary and, more broadly, revolutionary culture. Furthermore, it is when we take seriously documentary's capacity to work with what's too new to have a proper name that we can grasp media's epistemological importance to revolutionary processes, which were inherently open, contingent, and difficult to navigate, despite the efforts made to create stability and teleology for them.

What Is Documentary?

The question "What is documentary?" is a difficult one, as documentary comes in diverse forms. In the words of film scholar Bill Nichols, "Documentary as a concept or practice occupies no fixed territory. It mobilizes no finite inventory of techniques, addresses no set number of issues, and adopts no completely known taxonomy of forms, styles, or modes."[9] Documentary's diversity testifies to its historical contingency. This book takes the position that there is no universal documentary, but only historical constructions and actualizations of its possibilities. Chinese documentary emerged and developed in different historical circumstances from its counterpart in Euro-America and therefore had distinct concerns and strategies, even though the transnational exchange of ideas and practices carried on throughout the twentieth century and the Chinese documentary tradition was, without doubt, part of these exchanges.

Provincializing the Griersonian Documentary

Standard accounts of the history of documentary cinema attribute the term *documentary* to the British filmmaker and critic John Grierson, who first used the term in 1926 and later defined it as "the creative treatment of actuality."[10] Grierson's definition asserted documentary's photographic realism (actuality) and authorial control (creative treatment). Seemingly broad, this definition excluded "lower categories" of "factual films" such as newsreels, industrial and educational films, and travelogues, for their apparent lack of authorial creativity, as well as avant-garde experimental films, for their insufficient adherence to photographic realism.[11]

Grierson's definition has been provincialized; we now understand it as responding to the specific historical situations of interwar Britain in which he worked. His choice of the word *documentary*, according to film scholar Philip Rosen, drew from an existing reverence for the "document" as an evidentiary medium affording privileged access to historical reality.[12] This reverence had to do with a host of cultural formations that became dominant in nineteenth-century Euro-America, including the use of documents as proof in legal courts and in practices of modern historiography and the emergence of a scientific culture based on ideas of "objectivity" and "impartial" observation.[13] The technologies of photography and cinema, having emerged in the same milieu, were widely appreciated for the "document" quality of their images, understood to be connected to their referents not only iconically (by resemblance) but also indexically (the sign being caused by the referent). By promoting documentary's photographic realism, Grierson was able to carve out a special niche for documentary as a factual cinema suitable for public education in reformist interwar Britain. Meanwhile, by asserting filmmakers' authorial creativity, he further validated documentary's status as film art, at a time when Hollywood narrative films dominated the international film market.[14]

The historicization of Grierson's documentary concept has allowed new investigations into documentary's rich and multiple beginnings and later developments. Scholars now include a wide range of nonfiction films and screen practices, such as travel films, educational films, and illustrated lectures, in the documentary tradition.[15] Documentary's close connection to avant-garde experimental films has also been recovered.[16] Meanwhile, the Griersonian emphasis on documentary realism has been called into question. Louis Althusser's theorization of the ideological operations pervading our societies has led critics to consider cinema as an ideological apparatus, whose mimetic function at best creates a "reality effect" that must be critiqued and demystified.[17] Scholarship on visual technology has also shown that the photographic camera, once imagined to be neutral, transparent, and independent from human vision, in fact offers specific ways of seeing that prioritize monocular vision, Cartesian perspective, and the homogenization and geometrification of space.[18] Machine visions are not neutral, nor are human perceptions. The ways we look, listen, and sensorially engage with the world are cultivated techniques conditioned by our political, social, and technological environments.[19] In other words, photographic and cinematic images do not give direct access to reality. Behind their seeming transparency lie multiple processes of mediation that are often obscured: mediations by the camera, by interactions between the filmmaker and the filmed subject, and by the larger social formations in which these images are produced.

The untenability of the Griersonian documentary realism has brought new questions to the fore. Is documentary just fiction? What kinds of claims can documentaries make? How to approach documentary's engagement with the world now that we know its access to the world is heavily mediated? Given documentary's long-standing involvement in emancipatory movements, scholars interested in its political salience have also raised questions about how to retain documentary's power to expose injustices and call for action, while not resorting to a naive understanding of documentary images as factual. Mindful that "realism is often the first recourse of oppressed groups wishing to counter vicious stereotypes or lies," feminist scholars have proposed to consider the context for the deployment of realism: Who uses it, how, and for what purpose?[20] As Jane Gaines writes, "Much of the challenge of the new work on documentary has to do with finding a way to be both a champion of the critique of realism and a defender of the uses of realism."[21] These concerns would have resonated deeply with Chinese filmmakers of the early twentieth century.

Historical Formations of Chinese Documentary

The present-day Chinese term for "documentary film," *jilu dianying*, emerged in the mid-1930s as an imported term from the Japanese *kiroku eiga*, one of several literal translations of Grierson's term "documentary" in Japan.[22] In early twentieth-century China, nonfiction films went by various designations depending on the topics they covered, such as news films (*xinwen pian*), industrial films (*shiye pian*), educational films (*jiaoyu pian*), and scenery films (*fengjing pian*), and these designations remained in occasional use after "documentary" entered the Chinese lexicon. After the founding of the PRC, news films (*xinwen pian*), documentary (*jilu pian*), and science and educational films (*kejiao pian*) became the standard terminology. In the late 1970s and early 1980s, when television as the new media of the day began to transform documentary, we find new names, such as "special topic film" (*zhuanti pian*), for television documentaries. This book uses the word *documentary* capaciously and includes all these variously named films and TV programs in its discussion.

Chinese documentary emerged from historical conditions very different from those of Grierson's Britain, and over the course of the twentieth century it developed in tandem with China's specific political and social transformations. As I discuss in chapter 1, cinema arrived in China in the midst of intensifying colonialism and recurrent warfare. Having experienced China's defeat in colonial war and its disadvantageous incorporation into a globalized media circuit, Chinese political elites were intensely aware of the politics of media and took media production seriously as an essential part of their revolutionary agitation. Documentary had been connected to political endeavors from the very beginning. Chinese elites may have kept a distance to entertainment cinema in the first decades of the twentieth century, yet if we turn our attention to documentary, we immediately encounter all types of Chinese elites—political, cultural, scientific, military, business—who were interested and involved in documentary production, exhibition and discourse in the 1900s–1920s.[23]

Documentary's engagement with party politics was manifest early on. Umeya's filmmaking with Sun Yat-sen's Revolutionary Alliance, mentioned earlier, could be considered an early example of "party filmmaking." After the 1911 revolution, as political power fragmented in the country, the contending forces, including political parties, regional military power-holders (warlords), as well as the emergent political force of the working class, employed documentaries to articulate their political ideas and seek popular support. Besides engaging with partisan politics, early documentary in China also played important roles in modernizing industrial and agricultural production. Imported industrial and educational films sought to standardize Chinese production for the global market, while China's own educational film production—the earliest by the Commercial Press between 1917 and 1925—asserted local and national priorities for modernization. Documentary's engagements with political, educational and civic spaces demonstrate the historical malleability, flexibility, and ubiquity of cinema. This book's excavation of these engagements locates documentary in broader ecologies of media where mass politics, modern industry, and mass entertainment were deeply interconnected and contributes to debates on Chinese film genealogy as well as on cinema's participation in vernacular modernities and political modernizations.[24]

Intermingling with rivaling politicians and warlords, working for commercial film studios as well as for partisan, civic, and business organizations, and producing both documentary and fiction works, early Chinese filmmakers witnessed documentary's imbrication in colonial war and participation in partisan politics and nation building. They understood that viewing positions—who made the image, for what purpose, on which side, and supported by what kinds of power—mattered, and they saw photographic realism as heavily circumscribed by politics, positionality, and logistical and technical capacity. If John Grierson deemed factual films, made by simply pointing the camera at a scene on location, too lacking in auteurist creative vision to be considered documentary, Chinese filmmakers didn't take on-location filming as a given. Instead they saw access to location as a privilege supported by financial, infrastructural, and political advantage. Euro-American newsreel cinematographers enjoyed timely access to location shooting around the world, thanks to the political privilege of the colonizing powers, and the vast infrastructure of production and distribution put in place by their well-funded, vertically integrated film companies. In contrast, early Shanghai filmmakers had limited entrée even to parts of their own home city, as the semicolonial space of Shanghai was divided into a number of foreign concessions and a Chinese city governed by different jurisdictions, and gaining access to shoot on location was especially hard during political upheaval (e.g., workers' protest and massacre in 1925) and war (the Japanese bombing of Shanghai). These challenges prompted filmmakers to engage in formal innovations such as docu-fiction to call the "objectivity" of the camera apparatus into question. As I discuss in chapter 2, documentary, previously considered absent from Shanghai's left-wing film movement of the 1930s and the hard (Marxist) versus soft (non-Marxist) cinema debate, in fact provided a critical impetus to this period's experimentations with film form and strong media reflexivity. Meanwhile, filmmakers experienced the process of filmmaking and exhibition as meaningful acts of intervention where cinema's multiple productivities were manifested. The maneuver to put the camera on location, for example, could summon forth communities of supporters. The camera's intervention into, and inscriptions of, power contestations on the ground further encouraged these struggles and scaled up their impact at the film exhibition. Chen Jianran's filming of workers' protests and general strike in 1925, discussed in chapter 2, brought workers' and students' organizations, medical doctors, journalists, and charity organizations into networks of action to evade policing and enable on-location filming. These networks also helped exhibit the film in public meetings in Shanghai and other major industrial cities, spreading the workers' unrest and creating income to support workers on strike.

Certainly, this interventionist and reflexive approach to documentary was not unique to China. As filmmakers representing the oppressed often find themselves at a political, economic, and infrastructural disadvantage, experiences of early twentieth-century Chinese filmmakers—their problematization of photographic realism as well as their interventionist stance to filmmaking—readily resonated with other activist cinemas around the world. Historically, such shared experiences among filmmakers offered ground for solidarity and allowed insights and resources to travel between sites of struggle, as testified by a fruitful 1938 meeting between the progressive filmmaker Joris Ivens and the Shanghai filmmaker Yuan Muzhi, who was soon to found the CCP's first film unit in Yan'an. Documentary's engagement with partisan politics, industrialization, and institution and community building was also common in other parts of the world. Recent scholarship on educational, industrial and institutional films has brought attention to this previously overlooked, massive body of moving image and allowed us to think about cinema much beyond the movie theaters, in broader arenas of social life.[25]

This book's examination of the historical formations of Chinese documentary, therefore, does not claim its uniqueness but rather emphasizes its relevance to and exchange with practices elsewhere. What this book makes clear is that documentary's deep imbrications in China's revolutionary processes has allowed documentary's multifaceted productivity to manifest particularly strongly. Chinese filmmakers worked at historical conjunctures where revolutions were possible and with political forces capable of becoming the hegemonic power in the country. As vanguard cinema, documentary's prolonged and expansive engagement with political and social transformations urge us to go beyond compartmentalization of documentary as auteurist, activist, partisan, industrial, educational, or state filmmaking and instead search for a broader theorization of documentary as revolutionary media, operative across all these arenas undergoing reconstitution and transformation.

Documentary as Revolutionary Media

The Work of Media

In recent decades, with increasing saturation of media technologies in all arenas of life, there has been a surge of scholarly interest in media and mediation as foundational operations that underlie the political, social, epistemological, and experiential formations of our societies. The interest is not limited to the contemporary period or to digital media alone. Each era has had its own "new media." Digital media have alerted us to the pervasive material and technical acts of mediation that have made our existence and actions possible throughout history.[26]

Let us probe a bit into what *mediation* means and what is gained by highlighting it. Tracing the "genesis of the media concept," John Guillory observes that mediation, whose verb is *to mediate*, involves bringing into relationship entities that would have otherwise resisted such relationship. "If we think of mediation as a process whereby two different realms, persons, objects, or terms are brought into relation, the necessity for mediation implies that these realms, persons, objects, or terms resist a direct relation and perhaps have come into conflict."[27] Certainly, "resistance" may not characterize the full range of prior relations, or lack thereof, between the domains to be mediated. What's important to note here is that, first, mediation arises where there are potential contradictions and conflicts; and second, mediation transforms what gets mediated by reconfiguring their relationality, or, in other words, mediation creates *constitutive* relationships that not only connect entities but also change them. Compared to representation, another widely used concept in the study of cultural production, the concept of mediation highlights "a hidden complexity in the representational process."[28] It urges us to pay attention to the material, technical, and political maneuvers that accompany semiotic and discursive operations and take them seriously as part of the cultural productivity in question.

The "medial turn" has brought about a proliferation of research on a large variety of media objects, technologies, and institutions, from conventional mass media such as cinema, television, and the internet, to media infrastructures such as telegraph cables, filing systems, and cloud storage, to mediated and mediating environments such as the ocean and the air.[29] This capacious understanding of *media* has aroused some ontological anxiety: If all is media, then what is it exactly? In response, scholars have argued for a nonontological understanding of media, which helps to further clarify the implications of a medial approach. Media, as Eva Horn writes, are not ready-made and bounded objects; instead, they are events, processes, or "assemblages or constellations of certain technologies, fields of knowledge, and social institutions" that *become* media when they come together in specific historical situations to serve mediating roles.[30] In other words, mediation as a process not only transforms what's mediated by reconfiguring relationality but also gives rise to media itself: media and what's mediated are in a mutually constitutive relationship of co-becoming. This understanding of media's contingent formation in relation to the moment of its service underlies Thomas Elsaesser's reenvisioning of "film history as media archaeology," as he suggests to ask not *what* is cinema, but to ask where and why is cinema, and what good it is for. Cinema, he writes, has always been "embedded in other media practices, other technologies, other social uses."[31] A media view of cinema expands its location and acknowledges its entanglement with other media.

Among the various modes of cinema, documentary, for its collaborative production and its broad reach into many arenas of social life, is particularly amenable to a media approach. Scholars have long attended to documentary's reliance on, and creation of, relationships in its making. Moving away from the Griersonian paradigm, Brian Winston has proposed documentary witness and ethics as central concerns for documentary scholarship, foregrounding the specific relationships enabled by documentary among the filmed subject, the filmmaker, and the viewer.[32] Bill Nichols's classical taxonomies of documentary modes and gazes have offered valuable tools to discern and evaluate in documentary texts the modes of interaction and ethical relations inherent to its production process.[33] As documentary's mediating role becomes more apparent in the digital age, scholars of contemporary documentary have further conceptualized documentary in a medial direction. Daniel Marcus and Selmin Kara observe that documentary in the twenty-first century has "redefined" itself "as a type of connector or creative hub among vast fields of media activity."[34] Patricia Zimmermann and Helen De Michiel approach digital participatory documentary as open-space practices of "co-creation, collaboration, and community." Documentary filmmakers, they observe, have transformed from auteurs to "community designers who convene people around contradictory, suppressed, and unresolved issues. Documentary production became an ongoing process of community mobilization and renewal within provisional small-scale public spheres."[35]

These discussions of the relational and participatory nature of documentary offer inspiring insights into documentary's work of mediation in political activism and digital culture. This book expands on and contributes to this literature by arguing that documentary has performed such mediation work since its earliest days, and by considering the significance of mediation work in revolutionary processes.

Media and Revolution

If mediation refers to, broadly, a large variety of material, symbolic, and technical operations that create and alter relationships underlying our existence, then a revolution, aiming to transform power relations and create new categories of meaning and fields of action, necessarily entails complex and comprehensive processes of mediation.

Revolutionaries have long understood the importance of media to their endeavors. In his essay "Where to Begin" (1901), Lenin discussed the newspaper as the "starting point" toward revolutionary organization, "the main thread which, if followed, would enable us steadily to develop, deepen, and extend that organization." The newspaper would allow party activists to "follow political events carefully, appraise their significance and their effect on the various strata of the population, and develop effective means for the revolutionary party to influence these events." Its production and dissemination would also bring activists together in coordinated action. If we see the newspaper as part of revolutionary culture, Lenin's understanding of culture did not follow the conventionally understood, classical Marxist model that posited culture as the superstructure to the economic "base." Instead, Lenin saw the newspaper's role as providing infrastructure simultaneously for revolutionary organization as well as knowledge formation. The newspaper's role as a collective organizer, Lenin wrote, "may be likened to the scaffolding round a building under construction, which marks the contours of the structure and facilitates communication between the builders, enabling them to distribute the work and to view the common results achieved by their organized labor."[36]

Likewise, Chinese reformers and revolutionaries of the twentieth century had a keen awareness of media's importance in their endeavors for political and social change. Writing in 1896, the late Qing reformer Liang Qichao compared the newspaper, and the information flow it created, to blood circulation vital for the health of the body politic.[37] In association with the nationalist revolution of 1911–1912 and the May Fourth New Culture Movement of 1919, Chinese cultural elites of the early twentieth century relentlessly pursued reforms in language, literature, and the arts, understanding them as providing preconditions for modernizing political relationalities in the society.

Media played an even more foundational role in the Chinese Communist Revolution, as the Chinese Communist Party positioned itself as a mediator between Marxist theories and Chinese historical conditions and was constituted by the specific mediation work it engaged in. Founded in 1921 in Shanghai, the city of modern media technology and cinema, the Chinese Communist Party aimed to launch a Communist revolution in a country where, according to classical Marxist theories, the material preconditions for such a revolution scarcely existed. For this reason, the CCP engaged in substantial mediation work to mend the schism between Marxist revolutionary theory and China's historical circumstances, and to constitute itself through these acts of mediation. Writing on early CCP mobilization at the Anyuan coal mine, Elizabeth J. Perry argues that Communist activists served as mediators to adapt revolutionary ideologies into cultural forms more acceptable to local communities, and that the role of the messenger (the activists' mediation work) mattered as much as the message itself. This "cultural positioning," Perry argues, was crucial to the Communist success in the long run.[38] In 1927, in a major defeat (which contributed to the split between Stalin and Trotsky in the USSR), the CCP was forced out of China's industrial cities by the Nationalist Party's violent campaign of suppression and had to rebuild a revolutionary movement in rural China, where the proletariat as a class did not exist and peasant militancy still followed traditional forms.[39] In such a situation, the Maoist practice of the "mass line" posited the party explicitly as a mediator, who would take "incoherent" ideas and political demands from the masses and, with Marxist analysis, turn them into forms commensurate with socialist politics, before propagating these party-mediated ideas back to the masses. Hence the dictum, "from the masses to the masses."[40]

The "mass line" entailed complex processes of mediation between the party and the masses, placing the two in mutually constitutive relationships, with the extent of mutuality shifting through history. Ideally, neither the party nor the masses, neither revolutionary ideology nor "proletarian consciousness," should be external to this vital mediating activity: every essential aspect of the revolution, from ideology to policy, from the nature of the party to the nature of the masses, should be generated through it.[41] And needless to say, the ways in which these mediation processes took place—their structures of power, their modes of perception and knowledge, and the extent of openness, inclusivity, and exclusivity—matter a great deal to what the party and the masses could be, and to revolutionary outcomes in general.

It is in this capacity that revolutionary culture became particularly important because the "mass line" was implemented not only by cadres but also by cultural workers such as writers, dramatists, artists, and filmmakers, who, answering Mao Zedong's call at the Yan'an Forum on Literature and Art in 1942 and equipped with Marxist thought and the guidance of the party, went to live with the masses, educate and be educated by them, and create a revolutionary culture commensurate with both socialist politics and the concrete and changing historical conditions of the Chinese revolution. Revolutionary culture, then, must be understood and evaluated as important sites of mediation, not only textually but also in terms of production process, as where the most important aspects of the revolution were to be worked out.

The Eventfulness of Documentary

Nimble, responsive, shot on location, and produced rapidly, documentaries have historically been among the "first responders" to events large and small. Documentary cameras were present at the eruption of the 1911 revolution, the workers' protests in 1925, and the Japanese bombing of Shanghai in 1932. During the Sino-Japanese War (1937–1945) and the Civil War (1946–1950), documentaries recorded both battlefield conflict and wartime mobilization in wider society. After the PRC's founding in 1949, a nationwide infrastructure of documentary production took shape. Filmmakers staffed regional offices of the Central Newsreel and Documentary Film Studio (Zhongyang xinwen jilu dianying zhipianchang, or Xinying), supplying footage on new developments in the region every week to the headquarters in Beijing. Xinying filmmakers traveled overseas to follow international events such as the Korean War and the Bandung Conference. Domestically, documentary cameras were present at major political events from production campaigns such as those during the Great Leap Forward (1957–1960), to Red Guard rallies and struggle sessions during the Cultural Revolution. In April 1976, when millions filled Tiananmen Square to mourn the passing of Premier Zhou Enlai, Xinying filmmakers went with their cameras and sound recorders on their own accord, despite the ban on the movement by the party at that time. In short, capturing events as they unfolded constituted a great deal of documentary's mediation work analyzed in this book.

Events, in sociologist William Sewell's terms, are "a relatively rare subclass of happenings that significantly transform [political and social] structures."[42] Defined this way, revolutions are archetypal events: a revolutionary process comprises countless events in which structural changes occur. Events make structural changes in many different ways. They can reconfigure power dynamics directly, or they can transform "the very cultural categories that shape and constrain human action" and in so doing open new political possibilities.[43] For Alain Badiou, an event occurs when a formerly excluded part, unthinkable and unnamable within the existing categories of thought and language, suddenly appears to challenge the dominant structure. Such an event is naturally exhilarating: it allows a glimpse into new political possibilities previously truncated and obscured by the dominant order, and for this reason, Badiou believes that an event is hugely affective and can inspire participants to take up revolutionary actions "in fidelity" to the event's emancipatory potentials. Yet events are also evanescent: the radical possibilities of an event only take on concrete form and direction when there is concerted effort to grasp, elaborate, and inscribe—that is, to mediate—them into the world.[44]

Documentary and Political Relationality

The documentaries discussed in this book didn't only represent events. They intervened into them, shaped how they were interpreted and inscribed, and, occasionally, even created events entirely for the camera. Studies of documentary film have long paid attention to the filmmaker's relationship to the filmed subject. This relationship has been investigated in the organization of the film text (modes of documentary) and in the composition of individual frames (types of gaze). Documentary production, however, often involves a great many institutions and social actors, summoned by the filmmaking event to interact with one another. To think about documentary as event is to broaden our consideration of the kinds of relationships that come into being around the camera during the filmmaking process.

As mentioned earlier, gaining the access to film required significant maneuvering, which then fostered and materialized new affiliations and solidarities, as well as new power dynamics on the ground. While on-site, filmmakers worked with, or competed against, other participants and power-holders in influencing the event's unfolding. Sometimes filmmakers brought props and organized action on-site to intensify the event and inscribe symbolic meaning into the mise-en-scene. Other times filmmakers scripted and directed large-scale political performances, mobilizing a large number of people to act themselves in front of the camera. Reenactments were also practiced. The Sino-Soviet coproduction *Victory of the Chinese People* (1950), filmed upon the founding of the PRC, reenacted, with real ammunition and the participation of the People's Liberation Army (PLA), four major military victories on the Communist Party's path to taking state power. During the Great Leap Forward in the late 1950s, a new practice of "artistic documentaries" employed actors and nonactors to (re)enact events that supposedly had happened in real life.

This book does not dismiss dramatization or reenactments simply as fabrication, nor does it automatically accept actuality footage shot on location as faithful representation. Instead, by thinking about documentary as "eventful" undertakings, I ask what problems these productions attempted to solve; whose visions, scripts, and directions were followed; what inclusions and exclusions were involved in the production process; and what were the event's implications for revolution's further directions. As many of the documentaries discussed in this book can be considered propaganda films, the eventful reading suggested here also helps us move beyond a simplistic Cold War era understanding of propaganda as state-orchestrated manipulation, falsification, or brainwashing, while at the same time retaining our evaluative capacity to assess the political, ethical, and epistemological implications of propaganda production.

I show in the book that propaganda documentaries frequently mediated specific relationships and attempted to address concrete and localized problems. Documentary's ideological content, rhetorical strategy, and aesthetic choices were inseparable from their material, infrastructural, and communal work on the ground, and from the specific political relationalities underlying their production. A single propaganda documentary could incorporate a variety of political visions; which visions were featured more prominently, and which were obscured, depended on the power dynamics on the ground. Zheng Junli's wartime propaganda documentary, *Long Live the Nation(s)* (1941), for example, brokered crucial strategic relationships between the Nationalist party-state and non-Han regional power-holders and incorporated—with difficulty—competing political visions, including the filmmakers' own. Filmed around the same time as *Long Live the Nation(s)*, Wu Yinxian and Qian Xiaozhang's *Nanniwan* (1943) was the CCP's first "campaign film" showcasing the Communist army's production campaign to alleviate food and material shortages in the base area of Yan'an.[45] The film was meant to mediate the important relationships between the Communist army and the local population, whose support was crucial for Communist survival in face of Nationalist embargo. Shot on expired film and printed by hand frame-by-frame, the film's handicraft production showcased the self-reliant ingenuity of Yan'an's cottage industry. Shown only locally to troops and villagers in the Yan'an area, the film also adopted an egalitarian aesthetic, not singling out any soldier in close-up, even though the filmmakers, as experienced practitioners from Shanghai's best film studios, often used them in the past. Documentary aesthetics, in this case, must be considered as "situated" within the documentary event, shaped by the specific mediation work the film was meant to perform.[46]

Thinking about propaganda documentary eventfully, I suggest, also applies to a specific kind of propaganda film that film scholar Thomas Waugh has named the *solidarity film*.[47] A staple in documentary history in China and around the world, solidarity films are transnational film productions that aim to build solidary relationships across revolutionary movements. Umeya's documentary of the 1911 revolution could be considered an early solidarity film. Joris Ivens, the quintessential solidarity filmmaker, made numerous solidarity films in China during the wartime and after 1949, and his acts of solidarity included donating his camera to Yan'an. Soviet filmmakers also made China a locus of solidarity filmmaking. Early examples include *Shanghai Document* (1928) and a series of short films made by Roman Karman in Yan'an at the end of the 1930s. Two films made in 1949–1950, *Victory of the Chinese People* (1950) and *Liberated China* (1951), were nominally Sino-Soviet coproductions but dominated by Soviet scripting and direction. They became documentary "blockbusters," with their exhibitions among the largest film events in the first years of the PRC.

As mentioned earlier, *Victory of the Chinese People* (1950) reenacted four major battles during the Civl War leading to the Communist victory in 1949. These reenactments, directed by Soviet filmmakers, were spectacular and costly events mobilizing massive numbers of PLA solders and using real ammunition to re-create battle scenes on color film. I will discuss this reenactment in chapter 3. Here it suffices to note that the question is not whether the reenactment was "fabrication," or whether documentary should involve reenactments or not, but who deemed which images valuable, on what grounds, and for what purpose. CCP filmmakers had in fact filmed all the major battles on actual battlefronts with considerable risk (at least three died filming on the battlefront). They fought closely with the PLA soldiers, filming them during the day and searching for and burying those who died in battle at night. Filmmaking in this case became an act of anticipatory commemoration: when filming their comrades before they charged into battle, the filmmakers often framed the soldiers from eye-level, panning across them frontally in a medium shot, thus registering the soldiers' images for possibly one last time. Using 16mm black-and-white film stock, and filming on the actual battlefront, the CCP filmmakers could not produce moving images as spectacular as the Soviet reenactment in color and 35mm. And the replacement of the former with the latter should not be evaluated simply as an adoption of Soviet socialist realism or an upgrade in terms of color technology. Rather, questions must be asked about what kinds of documentary events, based on what kinds of political relationality and power structure, gave rise to these different images and their underlying political and ethical implications for revolutionary processes.

Documentary and Knowledge Formation

Aimed at large-scale political and social transformation, revolutions are by nature contingent, experimental, and risky. New problems and contradictions emerge at every step, and new knowledge must be formed to grasp, analyze, and respond to new situations and navigate the directions of change.

Knowledge formation in revolutionary processes, however, has inherent difficulties. "Knowledge does not know of the event," writes Alain Badiou, because, "captivated by the desire for decision," knowledge dismisses the indiscernible.[48] Knowledge formation, for Badiou, is often a process of ossification: it consolidates the already articulated and institutionalized gains of a past revolution, at the expense of the emergence of new movements with its still unnamed proposals for further emancipation. This is not only a matter of an established structure of knowledge fending off challenges from "events" whose proposals the structure does not recognize; it is also a matter of hegemonic power. Revolutionary parties, or revolutionary state apparatuses, are engaged in producing hegemonic ideologies to set new norms for political and social life. There is a tendency for power holders and revolutionaries alike to defend the hegemonic norms they create. Yet such a tendency is fundamentally anti-event, prone to rigidity and exclusivity, and may result in epistemological failures where the revolution no longer understands itself.

Various Marxist theorists have discussed the idea that a revolutionary class must be especially *reflexive* with regard to the nature of the hegemony it seeks. Making a distinction between a "leading class" and a "dominant" or "corporate" class, Antonio Gramsci coined the phrase *revolutionary hegemony* to refer to a noncoercive and nonoppressive hegemony led by a "leading class" capable of incorporating into its interests those of other classes.[49] On the establishment of such a hegemony, Raymond Williams observes that "any hegemonic process must be especially alert and responsive to the alternatives and opposition which question or threaten its dominance. The reality of cultural process must then always include the efforts and contributions of those who are in one way or another outside, or at the edge of the terms of the specific hegemony."[50] For a revolutionary movement to remain revolutionary, it must be inclusive, and its epistemology must be open to assessment and contestation and reflexive of the problems, exclusions, and oppressions that inadvertently emerge in the revolutionary process. In other words, political relationality and knowledge formation are interrelated: political relationality determines whose knowledge, and what kinds of knowledge, should be valued and which others will be excluded; the formation of knowledge, particularly political knowledge, articulates what kinds of contradictions exist in the society, how to go about solving them, and, in the process, transform political relationalities as well.

Documentary has long had affinities with what Bill Nichols calls "discourses of sobriety," the discursive and practical arenas of the sciences, economics, politics, and education that are responsible for knowledge production in society.[51] Through the twentieth century, documentary served as an epistemological media forming and imparting various kinds of knowledge in revolutionary processes. Documentary forms frequently employed in historical industrial and educational films, such as process films, cinematic mapping, diagramming, and forensics, were apt at creating stable categories and procedures for decision-making. At the same time, documentary was also a media particularly attuned to emergent, open-ended, and contingent developments that may be too new to have a name, particularly in revolutionary processes where everything was changing rapidly in an unprecedented fashion. Therefore documentary as an epistemological media became where the dialectics between structure and contingency, causality and indeterminacy, and between differently situated knowledges from different points of view, were played out.

The process film, for example, has been used widely in industrial and educational contexts to illustrate multistep productive tasks. The typical process film assumes a certain "transparency" of the documentary image and depicts streamlined production processes with self-evident successful results. Tom Gunning has argued that early process films enacted a "basic narrative of industrial capitalism" by showcasing successful industrial production processes culminating in "delighted consumption."[52] Salomé Aguilera Skvirsky discusses the process film (she calls it "the process genre") in terms of its attention to, and celebration of, laboring acts, particularly in the context of anticapitalist political projects. My attention to the process film in this book foregrounds its management of temporality, visibility, and contingency, understanding these as having epistemological significance and consequences for revolutionary *processes*.

As mentioned earlier, Chinese viewers have been familiar with process films since the early twentieth century through American and Chinese industrial and educational films. Left-wing filmmakers in the 1930s had subverted the capitalist process film in their work while creating what they considered progressive alternatives. Cheng Bugao and Xia Yan's *Spring Silkworm* (1933), discussed in chapter 2, was organized as a process film very different from the capitalist counterpart. Instead of portraying commodity production as a set of streamlined and mechanical operations, the film embedded the laboring process of traditional silkworm farming in the rituals and rhythms of communal life worlds; instead of offering the conventional happy ending, the film ended with a harvest that nevertheless brought out destitution due to plummeting global silk prices. The process film, in this subversive retelling, revealed what the seeming "transparency" of the capitalist process film had obscured: the destruction of life worlds by the "invisible hand" of the global market.

Socialist documentaries made in the Communist base area of Yan'an and in the PRC frequently depicted processes of transformation. *Nanniwan* (1943), on Yan'an's production campaign mentioned earlier, could be considered a socialist process film: with an egalitarian aesthetic, it followed agricultural and handicraft productions in Yan'an from the production campaign's onset to its successful completion. Process films were also made in the early 1950s depicting the processes of land reform and other socialist transformations, such as the reform of lumpen proletariat trampers and sex workers.[53] Such films served many functions. They provided visualizations for new social norms, created stable expectations, and managed uncertainty during times of upheaval. During the Great Leap Forward campaign, documentaries depicting labor processes provided sensorial training for new industrial workers, inculcated a socialist industrial temporality, and disseminated work routines and experimental technologies, such as how to build reservoirs and construct backyard furnaces for iron and steel production. The practice of "documenting tomorrow" pushed the logic of the process film to its limit by bringing a magical and abundant communist future into palpable view, and the docu-fiction hybrid of "artistic documentaries" inculcated beliefs in the production campaign's inevitable success despite its highly experimental nature. As socialist industrial films reacquired some of the "transparency" of their capitalist counterparts, and as the Great Leap Forward resulted in devastating consequences, the urgent questions become: What may have become obscured in socialist process films? And what forms should "reflexivity" in revolutionary cinema take?

If process films, by showcasing sequential action and outcome, managed contingencies and stabilized expectations temporally, documentaries also created maps and diagrams for the spatial navigation of tumultuous (geo)political relationships. The early 1950s saw documentary mappings of class relationships and geopolitical affinities, as China embarked on socialist transformations at home and positioned itself in the international arena at the onset of the Cold War. These mappings, however, became obsolete quickly. With land reform and the nationalization of industries, domestic class composition went through rapid change. Meanwhile, growing ideological differences following de-Stalinization destabilized relationships within the Socialist Bloc. Newly independent states, having invested great efforts and hope in the non-alignment movement, found their processes of decolonization increasingly entangled with Cold War politics, making alliances between them unstable and vulnerable to power shifts.

These new situations gave rise to new questions. Internationally, there were the questions of how to build solidarity within the Socialist Bloc when there were ideological divergences, and how to manage relationships with nonrevolutionary states, such as Indonesia, while supporting revolutionary activities in them. Domestically, everything about socialist construction must be worked out. How to envision a socialist economy and distribution of power within that economy, how to envision a socialist modernization process, and at what speed to launch it? What about the class politics in the country: Would the "enemy classes" such as the capitalists continue to exist when the economic foundations for them were no longer present? Would new class antagonisms form, and what would be their nature?

In the mid-1950s young filmmakers at Xinying, under the guidance of film critic Zhong Dianfei, began to experiment with documentary forms to suit the new times. A number of critical documentaries exposing problems from wasteful production to low-quality products were released in 1956 during the Hundred Flowers Campaign (1956–1957). Other documentaries moved away from the omniscience of maps and diagrams and the depiction of predetermined production processes and instead foregrounded open-ended journeys of exploration and playful experimentation. Indeed, this phenomenological approach—of withholding judgment for the time being and allowing the lens to encounter the world in its rich concreteness—has been a persistent undercurrent in twentieth-century Chinese documentary. In this book, I discuss it in relation to Liu Na'ou's amateur documentary (home movie and travelogue) made in the 1930s, Zheng Junli's propaganda documentary *Long Live the Nation(s)* in the 1940s (mentioned earlier), and documentaries made around the Hundred Flowers Campaign in the mid-1950s. Disrupted by the Anti-Rightist Campaign of 1957 and the Great Leap Forward, this tendency returned in early 1960s, when, after the Great Leap Forward, China again found itself at a cross-roads in the wake of the Sino-Soviet split. In line with the experimental policy of "wife diplomacy" promoted by the party to build closer relationships with nonrevolutionary states, Wang Guangmei accompanied Liu Shaoqi, president of the PRC, on a state visit to Indonesia. Documenting this diplomatic visit was a color documentary, *Chairman Liu Shaoqi Visits Indonesia* (1963), which mapped little but wandered plenty and featured Wang Guangmei in a traditional qipao dress serving the role of a "diplomatic wife."

For those who were rightly anxious about the revolution's future, wandering seemed a "bourgeois" luxury unsuited to the high stakes of the revolutionary project. The young Xinying filmmakers were criticized as treading a "bourgeois line" during the Anti-Rightist Campaign in 1957–1958. In 1967, at the height of the Cultural Revolution, Liu Shaoqi was condemned as a traitor and capitalist roader, and *Chairman Liu Shaoqi Visits Indonesia* went through a denunciatory rerun. The film was scrutinized, forensically, for Wang's and Liu's capitalist proclivities, and Wang was forced to dress as how she had dressed in the film and be ridiculed in mass struggle sessions.[54]

The political future of the revolution was indeed at stake at that time, causing profound anxieties among young revolutionaries who participated in the Cultural Revolution. Yet if we understand revolutions as fundamentally experimental acts, an essential aspect of revolutionary epistemology must address how to navigate uncertainty, how to discern, interpret, and account for failure, which is inherent to experimental processes. It is beyond the scope of this book to tackle the complex question of how uncertainty and failure were managed in Maoist China. What I observe in this book is that some people absorbed the risk of failure more than others. "Wife diplomacy," for example, was meant to create a division of labor where women, occupying a lower position of power in diplomatic exchanges, served as more flexible mediators between China and its ideologically heterogenous allies, thereby absorbing more risks of Cold War geopolitics than their husbands. "Class enemies" absorbed the biggest portion of revolution's inherent risks, as old class categories and class struggle were revived in the wake of the Great Leap Famine and the Sino-Soviet split, even though comprehensive socialist transformations had radically altered the economic foundations for class politics, and the party leaders had affirmed the near obsolescence of old class categories by the mid-1950s.

In the years leading to and during the Cultural Revolution, documentary became crisis-ridden. Film scholar Jason McGrath observes a "formalist drift" in fiction films at this time, where "Chinese revolutionary cinema increasingly claimed a privileged relationship between the text and an external truth rather than a lived reality."[55] Although documentary was arguably the mode of cinema that relied most heavily on filming lived realities, it also underwent a "formalist drift," having to create images with clear predetermined meanings and visualize archetypical class categories that had little correspondence to actual contradictions found in lived realities. Indeed, historically an eventful medium, documentary in this period had an anti-event tendency, not responding to emergent contradictions in the society, but rather, repetitively asserting existing categories even when the camera couldn't find the manifestation of those categories in real life, and must remediate other media such as sculptures, paintings and class education exhibitions to propagate the class stereotype.

Documentary had been long tasked with mediating the relationship between the party and the people since CCP's Yan'an days. A crisis in documentary, then, indicated broader crises in how the party–people relationship was mediated and how political knowledge was formed. Earlier I borrowed Alain Badiou's concept of the "event" to discuss documentary's "eventful" attention to emergent revolutionary proposals from the excluded. Documentary's anti-event turn in the years leading to the Cultural Revolution allows us to critique Badiou's appraisal of the Cultural Revolution on his own terms. Badiou has positioned the Cultural Revolution as an anti-establishment revolutionary event. While this book is not an assessment of the Cultural Revolution, my discussion on documentary's anti-event tendencies raises question on whether the Cultural Revolution was an event, or an anti-event, or both. In other words, if the Cultural Revolution encouraged the "masses" to challenge the "party," it's important to note that the masses and the party were not fixed entities but had been in continuous transformative relationships with each other. By then both had become exclusionary and crisis-ridden entities, entwined with the crises of mediation that underlay their mutual constitution.[56]

The politics of documentary, writes Nico Baumbach in discussing Jacques Rancière's views on the medium, "should not be about its explanatory power, its efficacy as a delivery machine for facts and information, but rather *the forms of community* that are implied by the regimes of identification through which art, facts and politics are perceived and recognized."[57] As eventful media, documentary operates at the nexus where the formation of political relationality (forms of community) and the formation of knowledge (what counts as art, facts, and politics) come together, which makes documentary a privileged site to investigate how mediation of these relationships shaped revolution's energies and entropies, successes and failures. In the immediate decade after the Cultural Revolution, documentary was indeed one of the most important media for the party's rehabilitation efforts to "correct past wrongs." When the party wished to close the books quickly, documentary revisited the revolution's archives and mobilized historical documentary footage (including those from films discussed in the earlier chapters of this book), in order to release revolutionary history from its teleological hold and ask the urgent questions of what went wrong and how to learn lessons from the past. Patricia Zimmerman has used "reverse engineering" to describe documentary as a conceptual practice. "Reverse engineering is a process whereby something is disassembled in order to understand how it works, and then rebuilt into something new and better," writes Zimmerman.[58] Documentary's "rehabilitation" in the post-Mao decade resonated with what Zimmerman describes as the impulse to "reverse engineer." Yet if in the 1980s documentary still attempted to learn lessons from the past and mend the party-people relationship with the interactive and democratizing potential of television, independent documentary, arising in the aftermath of the Tian'anmen protests of 1989, had no other recourse but to sever its ties with the party and reimagine other sites of emancipatory politics as the Chinese revolutionary century drew to a close.

Chapter Outlines

Chapter 1 presents China's defeats in colonial wars of the nineteenth century as the condition for its disadvantageous integration into the international media circuit. These conflicts were central to the emergence of radical politics and documentary media at the turn of the twentieth century. It discusses Chinese photography and filming activities in Japan in the wake of the Russo-Japanese War, Japanese filmmaker Umeya Shōkichi's participation in Sun Yat-sen's revolutionary activities, and partisan and educational filmmaking after the founding of the Republic of China in 1912. Engaging with debates on early Chinese film history, I foreground early documentary's imbrications in global capitalism and transnational politics with Japanese, American, and Soviet influences and argue for its importance in revolutionary agitation, partisan politics, and modernization.

Chapter 2 discusses documentary filmmaking from the mid-1920s to the mid-1930s, a turbulent period of intensified political struggle that saw the rise of Marxist-inflected, leftist politics and the increasing threat of Japanese invasion. While extant historiography has largely concluded that documentary cinema was not as significant in the emergence of progressive cinema in China as it was in Japan and the Soviet Union, I show that documentary did in fact contribute substantially to filmmaking in both Hard (Marxist) and Soft (modernist) cinema camps. Building on the first chapter's emphasis on transnational media circulations, chapter 2 shows how Chinese filmmakers distinguished their filmmaking from American commercial newsreel and Soviet avant-garde filmmaking and negotiated between liberal premises of objective journalism, Marxist attention to class consciousness, and a modernist emphasis on open-ended subjective experience.

Chapter 3 takes up the development of documentary filmmaking during the Sino-Japanese War (1937–1945) and the Civil War (1946–1949), a period in which propaganda films came to maturity. Yet instead of reading propaganda documentary as a purely ideological construct, I propose to understand it as processes of negotiation and collaboration among different segments of society, with filmmakers serving as mediators between conflicting interests in power hierarchies. Documentary dramaturgy is thus central to the chapter's investigations: Who performs, who directs, and who writes the script? I pay attention to developments in both the wartime capital of Chongqing and the Communist stronghold of Yan'an, and to the transnational practice of "solidarity film."

Chapter 4 focuses on documentary practices during the Great Leap Forward and argues that cinema became further entangled in material production nationwide, thanks to the expanding infrastructure of film production and exhibition. During this period documentary was the mode of filmmaking that experienced the greatest growth. New forms of documentary came into being, such as "artistic documentaries," a hybrid genre combining documentary with other fictional genres such as musical, historical drama, and even sci-fi in the practice of "documenting tomorrow." Rapidly made and delivered by mobile projectionists to sites of mass labor all over the country, documentary instilled in new workers the rhythm and speed of industrial time through sensory training, taught experimental vernacular technology, and projected palpable images of an abundant future to energize sleepless labor.

Chapter 5 explores documentary as providing cognitive mapping and forensic examination, on the one hand, and inducing boundary-defying immersive experiences, on the other. At stake at this time was the question of how to imagine proletariat subjectivities and communities in the new socialist society. As the cinema closest to the party, and with production centralized in Beijing, documentary enjoyed the status of the "cinematic vanguard" and was deeply implicated in the creation and dissemination of political knowledge (and doctrine). I show how documentary served cartographic functions to orient viewers to new international and domestic terrains during the Korean War and created stable images of socialist unity when tension grew in the Socialist Bloc in the wake of de-Stalinization. Through the 1960s and early 1970s, as China confronted the intersecting crises of international relations, domestic politics, and revolutionary epistemology, documentary also came into a crisis. The chapter reflects on the difficulty of taming the documentary image into unequivocal signifiers to reified categories of analysis.

Chapter 6 examines documentary's participation in the party-led "rehabilitation" campaign to correct past wrongs, as well as documentary's own "rehabilitation" into a more democratic, reflexive, and interactive political medium in the post-Mao decade. This period saw affirmation of documentary's evidential value at the Gang of Four trials and renewed interests in on-location shooting and media reflexivity. Challenging the extent of rehabilitation sanctioned by the state, documentary stubbornly brought the past into view by reorganizing archival footage into montages that subverted teleology for a historiographic reorientation. Television, the new media of the day, brought further impetus to innovations in documentary form. Television documentaries of the 1980s built much-needed connectivity between the people, the party and the state bureaucracy, and explored Chinese waterways as sites of historical and cultural sedimentation as well as infrastructure of circulation and connection. The chapter ends with a discussion on landscape documentaries including the controversial landmark documentary series *River Elegy*, and the epilogue briefly discusses how this book's findings inform our understanding of contemporary independent documentary and its political strivings.

CHAPTER 1

EMERGENCE

Colonial War, Nationalist Revolution, and Documentary's Beginnings

Film histories typically designate 1895, when the Lumière brothers had their screening in Paris, as the year cinema was invented. In Asia, however, this year marked a crucial turn in the region's power dynamics. The First Sino-Japanese War (1894–1895) between China, the region's traditional hegemon, and Japan, the rising powerhouse, for control of Korea concluded with China's defeat. Perceiving the Qing government as incapable of modernizing the country, Chinese political elites intensified their agitation for radical reform. In 1911 a revolution erupted to topple the imperial rule of the Qing, and usher in the Republic of China.

This chapter discusses the emergence of documentary along with reformist and revolutionary agitation at the end of the nineteenth and the beginning decades of the twentieth century, covering a period of about thirty years, from the prerevolutionary stirrings, to the revolutionary uprising, to the contestation for power in the postrevolutionary years. A challenge of working on "documentary's emergence" in this early period is the question of how to trace an emergent and amorphous media form that was still in the earliest process of formation. As discussed in the introduction, John Grierson coined the English term *documentary film* in the 1920s. The present-day Chinese term, *jilu dianying*, emerged in the mid-1930s, as an imported term from the Japanese *kiroku eiga*, one of the several literal translations of *documentary* in Japan, though this usage did not become stabilized until the 1940s.[1] In the time period covered by this chapter (1895–1928), not only was documentary film a nascent practice, cinema itself was an emergent media form too, with its names, meanings, and affiliations in flux.

The question of how to locate an object of study when it has barely come into view is certainly not unique to the study of early documentary; it is relevant to historical writing in general, as even the most well-defined and seemingly stable entities harbor change. In *The Archaeology of Knowledge*, Michel Foucault argues for an abandonment of preconceptions about historical unity, continuity, and stability and proposes that instead we understand historical processes as frequently disrupted and always ripe for new emergences.[2] For Foucault, who through his scholarship has gifted us a particular attunement to how power shapes our social lives, emergences are best understood as "the entry of forces . . . their eruption, the leap from the wings to center stage."[3] In other words, something emerges because there are forces that compel it into being, and continue to construct its distinction from other practices.

Foucault's understanding of emergence as confluences and confrontations of historical forces offers a fruitful direction for this chapter's inquiry. Etymologically, the Chinese word *jilu*, or documentary, has richly sedimented meanings referring to acts of collecting, sorting, tying up, unclogging, transcribing, and record-keeping.[4] What were the stakes of *jilu* in China in the late nineteenth and early twentieth centuries, when modern media technologies arrived with intensifying colonialism and warfare? How should we describe the force fields in which the practice of *jilu* received new urgency and energy and became forces of their own? Who was insisting on documenting, in which media, for what purposes, with what kinds of impact? And how might these early practices shape subsequent understandings of documentary cinema as an emergent medium? It is by attending to the act of *jilu*, and the various force fields in which it participated, that this chapter starts to trace the emergence of documentary along with that of revolutionary action.

This chapter foregrounds colonial wars and the nationalist revolution as the intense force fields from which documentary emerged as a high-stakes medium. It begins with the First Sino-Japanese War (1894–1895), a war that radically reconfigured the power dynamics in East Asia with Japan's victory and the Qing Empire's defeat. I argue that China's repeated defeats in colonial wars and its disadvantageous integration into the international media circuit raised the stakes of media and prompted Chinese political elites to seize new media technologies—print, photography, and film—for reformist and revolutionary agitation. I then follow Chinese photography and filmmaking activities in Japan in the wake of the Russo-Japanese War (1904–1905) and trace Japanese filmmaker Umeya Shōkichi's long-term engagement with Sun Yat-sen's revolutionary activities. I argue that early practitioners of photographic and film documentations understood mediation as deeply connected to political interests and power struggles and consciously used the camera to assert one's own political interests and intervene in the power dynamics on the ground. I also show that as global trotters, revolutionaries and filmmakers shared transnational networks, enabling financial, organizational, and symbolic resources to flow between the mass art of cinema and the mass art of politics. After 1911, as warlords and political parties competed for dominance in a politically fragmented China, power-holders such as Sun Yat-sen and Feng Yuxiang resorted to cinema to perform their distinct visions of political leadership and gain popular support. Meanwhile, as international discourses on cinema as an educational tool drew increasing attention from China's modernizing elites, and as American industrial and educational films sought to modernize China's traditional industries, the Commercial Press's effort at creating an educational cinema for China also enabled the making of the country's first long-format feature drama films and heralded the flourishing of a domestic film industry. By highlighting Japanese influence before and during the 1911 revolution via Chinese students and visitors to Japan, and American and Soviet influences in the 1910s and 1920s via film imports and political alliance, I foreground cinema's deep imbrication in global capitalism and transnational politics. As the period in this chapter has been extensively studied in the framework of Chinese modernities, by revisiting media technologies' imbrications in colonial wars and imperialist rivalries, I argue that modernity can't be extracted from the geopolitics of imperialism and colonialism, which must be investigated in order to understand the stake of Chinese media cultures that grew around modern media technologies.[5]

By locating cinema in social lives beyond the entertainment quarters, this chapter also aims to enrich our understanding of early cinema in China. Existing scholarship on early Chinese cinema has been heavily focused on fiction films. This focus has to do with an established genealogy that strongly associates early cinema with theater, first proposed in the 1980s by China-based scholars Zhong Dafeng and Chen Xihe. Zhong and Chen drew from writings on cinema in the early twentieth century, particularly from the filmmaker Hou Yao's *Methods of Writing Film Scripts* (*Yingxi juben zuofa*, 1926), to argue that cinema, upon arrival in China, was conceived as a form of drama.[6] This conception was manifested in the name cinema was given in its earliest years—*yingxi* (shadow play)—and in cinema's entry into gardens, teahouses, and other entertainment venues where theater performances had been traditionally held.[7] Centered on cinema as shadow play, this genealogy has productively drawn our attention to the synergy and rivalry between cinema and theater, and to formations of early film genres, particularly melodrama and martial arts films.[8] At the same time, it has also oriented early cinema research strongly toward the entertainment sector and fiction film, leading scholars to conclude that in the 1910s and 1920s, cinema was primarily a form of commercial mass entertainment with scarce participation from intellectuals. Zhong Dafeng observes that intellectuals interested in making films for serious purposes could not compete with commercial studios in the market.[9] Yingjin Zhang notes that cinema in the 1920s was seen "as a lowly trade by Chinese cultural elites," and intellectuals not only didn't pay attention to it but saw filmmaking with contempt at this time, evidenced by negative comments received by Hong Shen, a dramatist who accepted an invitation to write screenplays for a commercial film studio.[10]

Recently, scholars have begun to dispute the drama-centered genealogy of cinema. The most sustained challenge comes from Emilie Yueh-yu Yeh, who has shown, with meticulous historical research on early film exhibition, that in Hong Kong and Guangzhou, cinema was more often called *yinghua*, which Yeh translates as "photo pictures," rather than *yingxi*, or shadow play, thereby reestablishing cinema's close connection to projected images such as lantern slides, which had been used widely in public lectures and other institutional settings prior to cinema's arrival. Yeh also shows that in Hong Kong between 1900 and 1924, films in the documentary category, such as actualities, newsreels, travelogues, and science films, were more frequently exhibited than drama-based fiction films. Far from being confined to entertainment quarters, cinema was used by various government, charitable, educational, and civic organizations for a multitude of purposes.[11]

Indeed, as I will show in this chapter, as soon as we begin to pay attention to the large variety of films in the broadly defined documentary category, we encounter a variety of organizations, communities, and individuals—political and cultural elites—who had been engaged with cinema in the medium's earliest days in the country. Contrary to the established idea that Chinese elites were oblivious to cinema until the 1930s, documentary as an emergent medium was brought into being by Chinese elites and welcomed into many arenas of political, economic, and social life. A process of co-becoming, cinema helped Chinese elites to reinvent themselves and consolidate their authority, while also shaping new political subjectivities as the Qing gave way to the Chinese republic.

1895: The Media Event of the First Sino-Japanese War

In his now classic *War and Cinema*, Paul Virilio calls the Russo-Japanese War the first "war of light" and observes that the searchlight, used by the Japanese Army in that war to illuminate the terrain and detect enemy movements, foretold "a future where observation and destruction would develop at the same pace."[12] Whether actually deployed in battle or not, the searchlight had in fact been featured in Japanese woodblock prints made in the First Sino-Japanese

1.1. Kobayashi Toshimitsu, *Our Army's Great Victory at the Night Battle of Pyongyang* (*Heijō yasen wagahei daishōri*), 1894. Woodblock print. Courtesy of Museum of Fine Arts, Boston.

War. In *Our Army's Great Victory at the Night Battle of Pyongyang* by Kobayashi Toshimitsu (fig. 1.1), an intense beam emitted by a searchlight on the hills demarcates an enflamed killing field. The Qing soldiers scatter in chaos and are annihilated as they are seen. The Japanese troops, in contrast, safely hide in the darkness of the night, in orderly formation, appearing as steely as the cannons they operate.

Modern media technologies' close connections to warfare and their complicity in colonial conquests have been well documented in existing scholarship. Modern visual technologies of reconnaissance, detection, and targeting have been crucial to military operations. Camera technologies, from the optics that allowed accurate telescopic vision to the mechanical shutter that ensured smooth release of film, were developed in tandem with "target-acquisition techniques" that made long-distance targeting, gunfire, and bombing possible.[13] As modern weaponry's power of destruction grew strong enough to rapidly and drastically change any terrain, photography and cinema's capacity for accurate and instant mapping has also been crucial for surveying war zones in constant upheaval.

Certainly, what Kobayashi's woodblock print depicts is an idealized and imagined scenario, illustrating perfectly what Antoine Bousquet in his study on military perception calls an "enduring martial dream: to see without being seen, to instantly apply deadly force at a remove, to conjugate vision with annihilation."[14] Yet if the searchlight helped annihilate the Qing troops on the battleground, the woodblock print, produced en masse and entering a global circulation of news and images, subjected the Qing to a second death, alerting us to media technologies' other imbrication with war: they make war into media events.

The Qing defeat in the war was a watershed moment for the Chinese Empire: it lost a major portion of its modern navy, was forced to cede Taiwan, and had to pay indemnities that significantly reduced the state's resources for modernization. The biggest setback for the Qing, however, according to the historian Benjamin Elman, was the loss of confidence among its political elites, who became bitterly disappointed in the imperial state and agitated for more radical reforms that ultimately brought the dynasty down with a revolution in 1911. This disappointment, Elman observes, had to do with the politics of media at the time.

The Japanese state, supported by Japan's commercial mass media industries, launched a successful media campaign, boosting the morale of the Japanese Army and citizenry and creating a narrative of Japan's destined rise and the Qing's inevitable fall. Kobayashi's woodblock print was one among many that were cheaply reproduced and circulated en masse at the time, portraying the Japanese Army as disciplined, modern, and equipped with advanced technology, and the Qing troops as incompetent, antiquated, and fighting with primitive weaponry.[15] Elman points out that this depiction was in fact inaccurate. Qing naval power was arguably superior to Japan's in tonnage and armament. Before the war, international observers had overwhelmingly predicted that the Qing would win. Elman believes that the Qing defeat was attributable to contingent factors such as military strategy and coordination among various navy troops, and he calls the narrative of the inevitability of Japan's win and the Qing's doom as an "optical illusion."[16]

I agree with Elman on the success of Japanese propaganda, yet I believe Chinese elites were by then too media savvy to take Japanese propaganda at face value. They were certainly disappointed with the Qing's military defeat, but equally important was their keen awareness of China's disadvantaged incorporation into an international media circuit dominated by imperialist and mercantile interests, and of the Qing's inability to create healthy mediations between the state and the public in terms of shared political knowledge.

Cinema, with its first screenings taking place just as the First Sino-Japanese War drew to a close, was too new as a media technology to be used in this war. Many other modern media, however, such as the daily newspaper, the illustrated magazine, mass-produced prints, and photography, had by then formed a global network of publicity, to which China had been forcefully incorporated. Colonial warfare had aided the arrival of these media technologies in China. The first known instance of photography in China was an act of military reconnaissance during the First Opium War (1839–1842), when two colonial officers traveling with the British Army set up a daguerreotype camera on the banks of the Yangtze before the British assault on Zhenjiang in July 1842.[17] The forced opening of "treaty ports" for foreign settlement after the Opium Wars also gave rise to China's earliest newspapers. By the time of the First Sino-Japanese War, most of China's newspapers were owned by foreign missionaries and merchants based in treaty ports, where legal provisions of extraterritoriality helped weaken the Qing state's monopoly on information and censorship.[18]

Scholarship on early Chinese media cultures has paid substantial attention to the flourishing popular media culture in the late Qing, where newspapers gave rise to new styles of Chinese prose writing, and pictorials, relying on technologies of lithography and photography, offered mimetic depictions of novel objects and events to satisfy what Laikwan Pang calls a "realist desire" among China's urban reading public.[19] This desire, as Pang argues, was driven by anxiety as much as curiosity, as China confronted an expanding world increasingly hard to comprehend or control. Yet while the Chinese-language newspapers and pictorials offered vivid depictions of world affairs, their foreign ownership, service to mercantile interests, and profit motive brought limitation and bias to their reporting, as the Chinese journalist Ge Gongzhen observed.[20] The news reports and illustrations of the First Sino-Japanese War certainly quenched the readers' "realist desire" by providing riveting and often fictionalized details of the battles. For example, a report in the *Xinwenbao* gave gory details of a Chinese Army officer's death by the enemy's bullet, his blood and brains splattering on the soldiers beside him. Yet gory details aside, the public had little reliable information on the war. This partly had to do with the difficulty of transmitting accurate information from the battlefronts safely— historians confirm now that the Qing government reports were in fact ridden with misinformation, which resulted in unsound judgment as the war erupted and progressed. The Qing state censorship also meant that newspapers had no choice but to scout unofficial sources of (unverifiable) information, from foreign news media to rumors and street talk. Finally, driven by profit motives, Chinese-language newspapers selectively delivered positive news (for China) for better sales, while dismissing negative news as Japanese propaganda.[21]

The eventual defeat of the Qing shocked the public and greatly damaged the Qing state's legitimacy. A fresh round of political agitation by the political and cultural elites ensued, and taking control of the media became one of the elites' most urgent political actions. Chinese-owned political newspapers mushroomed after the war. Among the newly founded was *Shiwu bao* (Contemporary affairs), soon to become a leading forum for reform politics. For its inaugural issue in 1896, the reformist Liang Qichao penned an editorial entitled "On the Benefits of the Press to State Affairs." Comparing the circulation of information in a country to that of blood and the pulse in the body, Liang argued that "whether a country is strong or weak depends on whether it has circulation or blockage. . . . One gets sick when the blood and the pulse do not circulate."

China was weak, he wrote, due to various blockages of communication, between the rulers, the ministers, and the people, and between China and the outside world. "Not knowing the conditions of our neighboring [countries], it's as though we had no ears and eyes. Not being able to inform people of state policies, or transmit people's sufferings to the rulers, it's as though we had no throats and tongues." Here Liang envisioned the press as mediating political relationships between the state and the people, and between China and the world. It could supplement one's natural perceptive faculties, so that one could understand the world and one's position in it beyond one's immediate surroundings. Liang criticized the Qing state for its monopoly on information, which implied a failure—or blockage—of healthy political relationality. In contrast, he wrote, the governments in the West "protect the press as a mother bird protects her young," such that their journalists could record (*ji*) and transcribe (*lu*) all things: parliamentary debates, state budgets, developments in population, economy, military, science, and affairs in neighboring countries.[22]

While Liang praised the freedom of the press in Euro-America, he was clear-eyed about Euro-American domination internationally and understood that Western media representations of China often provided ammunition and legitimacy for conquest. Writing again in *Shiwu bao* in 1897, he lamented, "I read Western newspapers and they report on . . . the disorder in the Chinese polity . . . how wild and uncivilized the Chinese are, how ignorant and dishonest, how empty Chinese Confucianism is. The meaning is clear: they will eliminate China at once."[23] Perceiving the Qing as failing to support healthy mediation between the state and the people and unable to counter Western domination and mediate China's relationship to the world, Chinese elites saw their engagements with modern media technology as political intervention.

1906: Documentation as Intervention

In 1906 Cheng Yu, founding editor of Shanxi's first newspaper, *Jin bao*, arrived in Japan. Like many other Chinese who came to Japan on study tours, Cheng filled his days inspecting modern industries and educational institutions. Besides studying, however, he had another mission: to photograph the trophies that Japan had captured from the Qing in the 1894–1895 war, now on display in Japan.

Cheng came to Japan in the wake of the Russo-Japanese War, which had ended in a stunning Japanese victory. The Qing, with its regional hegemony crushed during the First Sino-Japanese War a decade before, was forced to stay neutral while Russian and Japanese troops fought bloody battles on the Qing territory of Manchuria. Japan's victories in both wars consolidated the country's dominant position in the region and drew many visitors and students from other parts of Asia to witness and learn from its successful modernization. By 1905 the number of Chinese studying in Tokyo had surged to at least between eight and nine thousand, with some estimates suggesting as many as twenty thousand.[24] Other than students, increasing numbers of Chinese visitors—many of them government officials, journalists, and other reformist intellectuals—traveled to Japan to learn about the country's modern institutions and industries.

Another Kind of Travel Image: Cheng Yu and Photographic Remediation

Scholars have long established that in Euro-America, early photography and film had deep connections to travel, exploration, and imperialist expansion.[25] "Images become our way of possessing the world," writes Tom Gunning when discussing travel images in relation to early cinema, the industries of postcards and travel souvenirs, and the institution of world fair exhibitions. Gunning also observes that the routes of early travel films marketed by Edison and Biography directly followed the colonial wars of the period. China was an important subject of travel image-making by Western and Japanese filmmakers. Earlier I mentioned that the first known instance of photography in China was an act of military reconnaissance by British Army officers during the First Opium War. The Boxer Rebellion and the occupation of Beijing by the allied forces in 1900 were also amply represented in photography and early film.[26] According to Markus Nornes, Japanese filmmakers traveled with Japanese troops to Beijing during the Boxer Rebellion, and the resulting footage became the first *jiji eiga* (current events film) in Japan.[27]

If travel images, as early film companies in Euro-America advertised, could bring "the whole world within reach," what kinds of images would a traveler from China make overseas?[28] Cheng Yu devoted the first pages of his book *Traveling in Japan in 1906* (*Bingwu riben youji*) to photography. The book opened with fifteen copperplate photographs of war trophies, each labeled with a brief description (fig. 1.2).[29] They featured objects captured by the Japanese Army from Chinese naval ships, such as canons, guns, fragments of motors, and apparatuses for ventilation. They also featured cultural objects that the Japanese took as trophies when winning battles on land in the Chinese territory, such as plaques etched with imperial Qing calligraphy and stone lions captured from Chinese government office buildings. Cheng meticulously recorded, in text, all the inscriptions on these objects and described the locations where he found them: in public parks, in museums, and at the Yasukuni shrine. Following these photos of war trophies were a number of photos documenting "ethnographic" exhibitions at the Japanese Imperial Museum related to "backward" Chinese

1.2. Photo from Cheng Yu's travelogue. Cheng's caption for the image indicates that these thirteen cannons were placed behind the Yushukan, a war museum at the Yasukuni Shrine in Tokyo, with a sign that reads, "War Trophy from the 27th year of the Meiji period." Cheng Yu, *Bingwu riben youji* (Traveling in Japan in 1906) (China: n.p., 1907).

customs such as foot-binding and opium-smoking. Only after confronting his readers with these images did Cheng include photos from his visits to a school, a silk manufacturing plant, and the industrial and commercial expo in Tokyo and Osaka. His written travelogue came after the photographs, offering his observations and reflections on Japan's modernization program.

What Cheng Yu presented in the opening photographs was not an exciting and exotic world within the viewers' reach, but rather a world that had extended its forceful reach through warfare, and whose vistas of modernity were founded on narratives of conquest and displays of power. "In the midst of busy cities and markets, on quiet hilltops and by the riverside, [the Japanese] have placed [these trophies] to show off their military achievements," he wrote in the book's preface. "Most of our compatriots who travel here, from officials to literati, from merchants to students, avoid passing by these objects of national shame. If they see them, they quickly walk away, too embarrassed to confront them."[30] Cheng and many other Chinese who found themselves in Japan at the time experienced Japanese modernity with deep ambivalence. They encountered exciting new knowledge on their journeys, but also stumbling blocks such as these war trophy displays that ambushed their pride and reminded them of the relations of subjugation that underpinned their overseas stay. While other travelers tried to avoid these sites, however, Cheng sought them out, had them photographed, and foregrounded their images in his printed travelogue.

Technologies of image reproduction, such as photography and film, diminish the aura, or the cult value, of objects, moving these objects from ritual spaces where they command reverence into spaces of mass politics where they can be exhibited, debated about, and remediated further, writes Walter Benjamin in his well-known essay "The Work of Art in the Age of Its Technological Reproducibility."[31] Objects such as a plaque with Qing imperial calligraphy or weaponry produced at China's new arsenals bearing Qing imperial seals were once auratic: they served ritual functions to authenticate Qing modernization efforts. Their capture by the Japanese Army removed them from the Qing ritual context, and their exhibition in Japan's museums, public parks, and Shinto shrines co-opted their auratic energy to consecrate Japan's new ritual spaces of modernity/coloniality. If the exhibitions were the first round of appropriation of these objects, Cheng's photography ushered in a second round of remediation, which, as Jay David Bolter and Richard Grusin write, could ushering in "a process of reforming reality."[32] Cheng observed that Chinese travelers to Japan avoided these war trophies because they were emplaced in a Japanese ritual context to enshrine a relationship of subjugation. His photographs snatched these objects out of Japanese ritual spaces and state narratives and changed their materiality from iron, steel, and stone into photogravure on paper, light enough to carry in one's hand, so that the Chinese viewers' relationship with them could be reconfigured.

Referring to photography as *sheying* in his 1906 travelogue, Cheng was among the earliest users of this term. In the first three decades since its arrival in China (1840s–1870s), photography had been referred to mostly as *zhaoxiang*, or a means to produce portraits, according to art historian Yi Gu. By the late nineteenth and early twentieth centuries, however, the use of the photographic technology spread into other arenas, prompting changes in how it was referred to. In military and industrial modernization, government officials commissioned photographic albums on the four major arsenals and other state-sponsored projects of modern industry and railroads for inclusion in memorials to the throne, and photography became seen as an expedient and improved way to produce technical illustrations (*tu*).[33] Increasingly incorporated into news reporting and popular media, photo albums such as *Photographic Illustrations That Transcribe the Truth About the Russo-Japanese War* (*Ri'e zhanzheng xiezhen zhaoxiang tu*, 1904) were understood as offering eyewitness accounts to momentous contemporary events.[34] It was through its use as *tu*, a traditional Chinese term for technical illustrations, and as *xiezhen*, a term borrowed from Japanese with the meaning of "transcribing truth," that photography became increasingly understood as a modern medium privileged with the epistemic virtues of accuracy and objectivity, and the Chinese term for photography changed into *sheying* (seizing shadow).[35] Capturing light reflected from existing material objects, photography, or *sheying*, was conceived to be bound to physical reality in the process.

As an act of remediation, Cheng Yu's photos engaged with, but went beyond, both expectations of photography as technical picture and as eyewitness.[36] Reminiscent of the photo albums of China's major arsenals, Cheng's images resembled technical illustrations of industrial and military objects, except that these objects were now placed in Japanese contexts for the display of the victor's power. Made on his journey in Japan, these photos documented what he witnessed in person. Yet Cheng's narrative of the process of photographing these objects, presented in the preface of the book, emphasized photography as an intervention more active than eyewitnessing. With no pretense of technical proficiency—most likely Cheng did not know how to operate a camera—Cheng told readers that he had hired a Japanese photographer to do the job. The difficulties he encountered had to do not with technicality but with access: photography was forbidden in these places of public display, and it was only after a great deal of persistent maneuvering that Cheng managed to have the photos made. Some photos had to be shot from faraway, with the object of interest behind a wooden fence.[37] Beyond *tu* and *xiezhen*, Cheng's photography was an act of struggle that defied ground rules and aimed not at recording reality but transforming it.

In 1906, when Cheng Yu was touring Japan, a young Chinese student by the name of Zhou Shuren had left his medical studies in Sendai and moved to Tokyo to start writing. Years later, writing under the penname Lu Xun, he attributed his conversion from medicine to literature to a fateful encounter with a lantern slide from the Russo-Japanese War in his medical classroom in 1905—a story that has become a foundational narrative of modern Chinese literary history.[38] Primarily used to teach medical science, such as exhibiting microscopic images of microbes, lantern slides in Lu Xun's classroom also featured news items. This particular lantern slide depicted a public execution of a Chinese prisoner by the Japanese military for allegedly spying for Russia, and the scene included a mainly Chinese crowd who came to watch the spectacle. Shocked by the complete apathy on the Chinese onlookers' faces, the young student decided that "the people of a weak and backward country, however strong and healthy they may be, can only serve to be made materials or onlookers of such meaningless public exposures."[39] Quitting his medical studies, Lu Xun took up writing to heal the spirit of the nation.

Not unlike the Chinese travelers in Cheng Yu's account who, in their journeys in Japan, stumbled on the public displays of war trophies from the Qing,

Lu Xun was also reminded of the coloniality intrinsic to modernity in his medical classroom. The turn-of-the-century medical science, Ari Heinrich observes, "was deeply infused with (if not fundamentally derived from) the phenomenological values of war and colonialism at the linguistic, conceptual, and technological levels," and "the language of bacteriology . . . was none other than the language of war."[40] The technology of the lantern slide, a predecessor to film projection, also shared origins with the technology of the searchlight and the microscope, as Frederich Kittler has shown.[41] Classroom behavior was disciplined, as Chenshu Zhou reminds us, such that students responded to pedagogical materials with studious absorption and propaganda materials with unanimous cheer.[42] In other words, Lu Xun's classroom could be understood as a power-charged assemblage of imperial ideologies, technologies and disciplines, such that on his journey to learn, like Cheng Yu and other Chinese visitors, the medical student kept on being confronted by objects that brought these underlying relationships to the fore.

The impulse, for both Cheng Yu and Lu Xun, was to reach for a medium of their choice to respond to these relationships of subjugation on their own terms. Lu Xun turned to writing, a traditional medium now reconceived and refashioned by reformers such as Liang Qichao for the modern press. Cheng Yu turned to photography, a new medium of technological reproduction that could bring matters close to hand and recontextualize their reception. While it wasn't acceptable to either of them to be passive onlookers, their understanding of what needed to be done was somewhat different. Lu Xun saw the onlookers' apparent indifference as manifesting a deficiency in spirit, which literature could help change.[43] Cheng Yu, on the other hand, understood the importance of the context of viewing as always disciplined by the dominant power and sought to reconfigure it through photographic remediation.

Rebuilding the Navy with Film

In the same year that Cheng Yu was producing his travelogue and Lu Xun was beginning to write, another group of Qing subjects in Japan tried their hand at filmmaking. In June 1906 Yuan Xiluo, studying education in Japan, joined his fellow students Zhu Shuyuan, Wang Zengxian, and others to found the Society for Aiding and Reinvigorating the Navy (Buzhu haijun xingfushe) in Tokyo. The aid society's first activity was to make a film about the Imperial Chinese Navy. The plan was to screen the film to both domestic audiences in China and overseas Chinese communities, to educate the public and generate donations for the Qing's rebuilding of its naval forces.

The Qing had built a sizable modern navy in its modernization drive in the late nineteenth century, but the First Sino-Japanese War annihilated the entire

Beiyang Fleet, composed of the dynasty's most powerful warships. Burdened with indemnity payments and hindered by a lack of technical expertise and political consensus, the Qing waited until the early years of the twentieth century to start rebuilding its navy.[44] Unable to build its own warships, the Qing relied on Japanese expertise, even though Japan was the enemy that had destroyed the Qing fleets in the first place. Between 1903 and 1911 the Qing sent more than three hundred students to Japan to study naval technology and commissioned warships from Japanese shipyards.[45] Scholars have shown that popular efforts in support of the navy's rebuilding had heightened nationalism both inside China and among overseas Chinese communities. Organizations to support the rebuilding of the navy were founded in Indonesia, Japan, Hong Kong, and the United States as well as other diaspora communities.[46] The aid society established in Japan by Yuan Xiluo and his fellow Chinese students was the earliest of these overseas organizations.

By 1906 Japan had already seen the flourishing of an early cinema culture.[47] If woodblock prints were the mass visual media during the First Sino-Japanese War, cinema was the new media for the Russo-Japanese War. Western and Japanese film companies rushed to make war films—both reenactments made in studios and actualities shot on location—and marketed them around the world.[48] In Japan these war films were exhibited widely by both commercial companies and the Japanese state in its first attempt to harness cinema for propaganda. They joined other media to energize Japanese nationalism, which Chinese students, from Lu Xun to Yuan Xiluo, experienced palpably in their classrooms. The nationalistic sentiment was so strong that when Japan signed the Treaty of Portsmouth, riots broke out in the streets of Japan, protesting the premature ending of the war.[49] These films also generated huge box office revenues, helping Japanese exhibitors move from itinerant exhibitions to permanent theaters, and to invest further funds in film production.[50] Given what they would have witnessed in Japan, it wasn't surprising that Yuan Xiluo and his friends would choose cinema as a medium to inspire patriotism and generate donations for the Qing's navy building.

The film made by Yuan and his fellow students is no longer extant, yet we can learn about the filmmaking process from Yuan's three-part essay published in *Shen bao* in July 1906.[51] Similar to Cheng Yu, these students also had the urge to remediate. From Japanese distributors, they purchased films on the Boxer Rebellion and the Russo-Japanese War, not to exhibit them directly to a Chinese audience, but to re-edit the footage into films that expressed their subject positions. Soon, however, these students discovered that ready-made moving images of the Chinese Navy were unavailable. "We wanted to use the moving image (*huodong xiezhen*) to encourage our compatriots to revitalize the navy, yet there weren't any images of Chinese warships in sight. Isn't that a pity?" Yuan wrote.[52]

Just as the students sought Qing Navy images in vain, a Japanese newspaper article alerted them to the completion of a Qing-commissioned warship at Kobe's Kawasaki Dockyard. Overjoyed to find that a ceremony for a trial sail of the new ship would take place at the dockyard, three students—Yuan Xiluo, Zhu Shuyuan, and another whose surname was Zhong—traveled to Kobe to film the event so that they could use the footage in the aid society's film. A network of Chinese merchants in Japan warmly supported the students' film venture. Chen Pingqi, a Kobe-based merchant, put up the three students from Tokyo for the night. Zhang Xuchu, a merchant based in Osaka, hired a local Japanese cinematographer to come to Kobe on the day of the ceremony. Yuan explained in his essay that as racism intensified during Japan's rise in the early twentieth century, the Chinese community in Japan longed for a stronger home nation to withstand discrimination. Chen commented to Yuan, "Looking at the harbor, we saw warships passing by one after another, powered by motor engines, and sporting national emblems. Besides Japanese ones, there were British, French, German, American, and Italian ships. But it's been a long time since we saw the shadow of our nation's sails and heard the sound of our motors. How our hearts have ached for this! . . . Our merchants and people have been humiliated, but we have nowhere to appeal to."[53]

The Chinese students and merchants certainly hoped that the film would eventually contribute to the rebuilding of the Qing Navy, which in turn could mean a stronger China to better support overseas Chinese communities. What became apparent during the filmmaking process, however, was that the act of filmmaking was already a substantial intervention to change the power dynamics on the ground and gain respect for the Chinese. Upon his arrival at the shipyard, Yuan was disappointed at first to find only five other Chinese present: the Chinese consul and his translator, a Chinese naval officer, and two students who barely spoke Mandarin. If the young Lu Xun was disappointed by the Chinese onlookers' indifference toward Japanese violence, Yuan was disappointed by the lack of enthusiasm among the Chinese in Japan toward the Qing's rebuilding efforts. Wang, the translator from the Chinese consulate, felt the same way. He told Yuan that a few days before, the president of the Kawasaki Dockyard Company, Matsukata Kojiro, had inquired about the size of the Chinese attendance at the ceremony. Knowing that the number would be small, Wang was too ashamed to answer Matsukata's question.[54]

With the help of the film camera, Yuan and his colleagues began to take command of the situation, turning indifferent bystanding into energetic participation. The filmmakers had brought fifty Qing yellow-dragon national flags and distributed them among the Chinese and Japanese attendees of the ceremony. These colorful props enlivened the scene and maximized the visibility of the Chinese presence. "The yellow-dragon flags blew in the wind. Each lifted the flag, and shouted 'Long Live!' The Japanese and the Europeans congratulated us, also shouting, 'Long Live!' Human voices and applause erupted like thunder." The hired Japanese cinematographer filmed the ship as it entered the harbor, as well as the people cheering under the Qing banner. Wang was overjoyed by this lively scene and felt he could finally stand up to Matsukata: "Even though few Chinese were present today, the three of you traveled from Tokyo to make a film about our country's navy development. This is unprecedented. You are true patriots. Now I can reply to the president of the shipyard."

The film camera's intervention in the event did not go unopposed. One source of opposition came from none other than Matsukata, the president of the shipyard company. Upon being introduced to the Chinese students from Tokyo, Matsukata was suspicious of their intentions. After learning that the students were making a film for the Society for Aiding and Reinvigorating the Navy, he asked to read the aid society's statement and expressed disagreement over the document's emphasis on the "Chinese nation," which he criticized as "being too biased." The Qing and Japan must be "united as a single yellow race to oppose the white race," Matsukata insisted. During the filmmaking, Matsukata competed with the Chinese students, inserting himself into the process as the ritual master and objecting to the camera's emphasis on the Chinese presence at the ceremony. When the cinematographer asked the Chinese consul and navy officer to stand closer to the camera, Matsukata intervened and argued that the Chinese shouldn't stand apart from the Japanese, but rather everyone should stand together in an undifferentiated group to demonstrate undivided friendship.[55]

Scholars of Japanese early cinema debate whether the fiction versus nonfiction divide emerged in Japan during the Russo-Japanese War period. Coining the term *homogenous cinema* to describe the lack of differentiation between fiction and nonfiction films at the time, Komatsu Hiroshi argues that viewers did not seem to mind whether films were shot on location or reenacted in a studio. Realism was not understood to require documentary images' indexical relationship with the historical and physical world. As long as what appeared on the screen conformed to known facts, the viewers accepted constructed scenes as true accounts.[56] Disagreeing with Komatsu, Markus Nornes argues that film reviews during the Russo-Japanese War already put significant value on films shot on location, understanding them as more likely to convey the real situation (*jikkyō*) than constructed films. He writes about a film entitled *Scene of His Imperial Highness the Prince of Korea and Ito Hirobumi Entering the Imperial Palace* (1907), made in Japan and shown all around Korea to combat rumors there that the prince had been assassinated by the Japanese on his visit to Japan.[57] This, Nornes suggests, demonstrates a clear understanding of cinema's documentary qualities.

It is significant that Nornes's example concerns a film on colonial relationships between Japan and Korea, and that viewers in Korea who feared for the prince's safety particularly appreciated the film as evidence for the prince's well-being. I do not intend to join the debate on whether cinema was "homogenous" in Japan in the early twentieth century, but cinema has certainly never had a homogenous audience or practice. For viewers in China, Korea, and other places that were subjugated to various degrees in global media circuits, the stakes surrounding media truth were high. As I have argued so far in this chapter, Chinese elites understood media representations as deeply imbricated in power struggles, and this awareness not only produced a savviness in media consumption, as they did not take "known facts" for granted, but also produced a contestive stance in media production when they had a chance to engage in it. While Lu Xun in writing and Cheng Yu via photography remediated the existing mediation of lantern slides and war trophy displays, Yuan and his friends directly intervened in unfolding events on the ground through on-location shooting. Their amateur and diasporic filmmaking is marginal to both Chinese and Japanese film histories, yet it prompts us to think about on-location shooting not simply as enabling the filmed image's "indexical" relationship to reality, but as a contested process where the presence of the camera and the filmmakers facilitated the unfolding of events and the becoming of realities in specific directions.

The Chinese elite's media practices, such as the filmmaking at the dockyard in Kobe, were meant to usher in the "becoming" of China as a stronger nation, but it was also an activity that helped these political elites to undergo an ardent process of "becoming" as well. The imperial exam, the traditional route to officialdom, was terminated in 1905. Chinese elites had to find other ways to maintain their status, and many sought to associate themselves with modernization, industry, and technology. Yuan Xiluo came from an elite Jiangsu family. His elder brother Yuan Xitao was a literati-turned-reformist, who later served as the education minister of the Republic of China. Yuan Xitao had already been promoting new learning since the late nineteenth century. In 1904 he had gone on a study tour to Japan, where he had observed the use of films in propaganda and education. With the elder Yuan's help, Yuan Xiluo and his colleagues began to screen their completed film on the navy, along with other films they purchased in Japan, in Jiangsu in the summer of 1906, using a projector they brought back from Japan, and donating all ticket sales to navy rebuilding efforts.[58] *Shen bao* reported film exhibitions at city-god temples and schools. Originally planned for just one night, the screening ran fully booked for three nights at the Lou County city-god temple. The film stirred up great passion: *Shen bao* reported that one could hear endless curses and reproaches from angry viewers when the image of Ding Ruchang, the admiral who had surrendered the Beiyang Fleet to the Japanese, appeared on the screen. Even though Ding had already committed suicide by then, the audience couldn't forgive his capitulation to Japan.[59]

For the young people at the Society for Aiding and Reinvigorating the Navy, these initial activities of filmmaking and screening proved the effectiveness of cinema in influencing public opinion and soliciting donations. The bylaws of the aid society, published in *Shen bao* on August 31, 1906, listed filmmaking and distribution as the group's most prioritized activity: "purchase motion pictures and camera equipment, make films on Chinese and foreign military education and customs, and have projectionists tour with the films to lecture on world affairs and the importance of the navy."[60]

The elder Yuan brother became so enthusiastic that he began to bring cinema into the new popular education associations, which had mushroomed in local communities at the beginning of the twentieth century. By the late Qing the discussion about China adopting constitutionalism had become heated. Since a well-educated and responsible citizenry was considered essential to local self-government within a constitutional framework, reformist elites had already begun to look to citizen education as foundational for political reform.[61] Local elites had always been involved in the management of local education, and they again came to the fore to promote new learning. Popular education associations, encouraged by the Qing government and led by local notables, had emerged in the last years of the Qing to organize education for the public at local temples, schools, and meeting halls.[62] Initially focusing on public speeches and lectures, these local educational initiatives soon began to make use of visual aids—lantern slides and cinema—as they helped attract the public and held the attention of audiences. In 1907 Yuan Xitao founded the Popular Education Association (Tongsu jiaoyushe) in his hometown of Baoshan County, Jiangsu. Under his leadership, the association reportedly got hold of a film projector (likely the one his younger brother had brought back from Japan) and screened educational films on sanitation, elementary education, and the Russo-Japanese War, with each screening narrated by a lecturer to "enlighten and open minds of the lower class," much like the Japanese film narrator (*benshi*).[63]

1911: The Transnational Making of a National Revolution

On October 10, 1911, revolutionaries aiming to overthrow the Qing state led a successful rebellion in the city of Wuchang (present-day Wuhan). Thus began the Xinhai Revolution that eventually ended more than 250 years of Qing rule and ushered in the first Chinese republic.

I began the introduction of this book with the premiere of *The Chinese Revolution*, shot on-site in China and documenting the early development of the 1911 revolution that would eventually topple the Qing dynasty. Taking place on the evening of November 26, 1911, at the Michitaza Theater in Nagasaki, Japan, the screening attracted more than a thousand viewers. Among them, more than two hundred were Chinese, and some of them were passing through Nagasaki en route to China to join the revolution. Many brought with them revolutionary army flags in celebration. Accompanied by *benshi* narration, the film aroused wild hoorays and applauses and ended with a Chinese student giving a rousing impromptu speech stirring the audience into ecstatic cheers.[64]

The Chinese Revolution was produced by M. Pathé, Japan's leading early film production company, founded and headed by Umeya Shōkichi, a Japanese member of Sun Yat-sen's Revolutionary Alliance and a long-term financial supporter of Sun's revolutionary endeavors. The friendship between Umeya, a pioneer of Japanese film exhibition and production, and Sun, the energetic leader of the Xinhai Revolution (1911–1912), allows a glimpse into the role of early cinema in the intense national and revolutionary becomings of the early twentieth century.[65] These two figures shared journeys, creative energy, and various strands of transnational connections—commercial, financial, political, and personal—which concurrently enabled the revolution in film and in reality (fig. 1.3).

M. Pathé and the Production of a Revolution

Umeya was born in 1868 to a merchant family in Nagasaki, a bustling port city that for a long time was one of the few places in Japan open to international trade. With a sizable Chinese trading community in the city, and with the

1.3 Umeya Shōkichi (*left*), Sun Yat-sen (*middle*), and Umeya's wife Toku (*right*), courtesy of Ms. Ayano Kosaka, great-granddaughter of Umeya Shōkichi.

family business regularly sending and receiving cargo to and from Shanghai, Umeya grew up with Chinese friends and had a familiarity with China. His first trip abroad in 1882, at the age of fourteen, was to Shanghai. He was impressed by the city's Euro-American grandeur but also witnessed racism and inequality in the semicolonial city, which sowed the seeds for his sympathies for China and for his pan-Asian political outlook. Having spent his early twenties working for his family business in international trade, selling rice to Korea and speculating on gold mining in China in an increasingly globalized economy, Umeya left Japan in 1891 after suffering financial losses in the boom-and-bust cycle typical of transnational capitalism. He relocated first to Amoy and then to Singapore, where he opened a photography studio.[66] In an era of intensifying global capitalism and imperial expansion, adventures such as Umeya's were one of the avenues open to aspiring young men from nonelite families who sought economic and social advancement into the elite class. Umeya's experience in Southeast Asia helped him gain access to Japan's political center. Already a Pan-Asianist and eager to aid Japan's movement to the South (*nanshin*), he collaborated with the Japanese politician Oi Kentaro on a scheme to facilitate Japanese settlement in Malaya to work on rubber plantations, though the plan was abandoned as the First Sino-Japanese War broke out, again orienting Japan toward Northeast Asia.[67]

Umeya and Sun Yat-sen met in Hong Kong in 1895, on the cusp of the First Sino-Japanese War. Umeya had by then relocated with his family and his photo studio to the colonial city. Convinced of Sun's revolutionary vision and wanting to be part of it, he began to channel income from his photography business to fund Sun's activities, even helping secure weapons for the (aborted) Canton Uprising in 1895. Facing arrest in Hong Kong due to his continued involvement in Sun's efforts, Umeya fled to Singapore in 1903 and, with help from Sun's revolutionary circles, took up film exhibition, a perfect business for revolutionaries to generate fast cash. Working as a traveling exhibitor in Singapore and Southeast Asia, Umeya built a fortune from exhibiting newsreels during the Russo-Japanese War, which brought in a large number of excited viewers cheering for the victory of an Asian power. This windfall helped Umeya continue to fund Sun's revolutionary activities, even finding money to support the Chinese-language newspaper *Minbao*, published in Tokyo, which became an important overseas vehicle for Sun's revolutionary organizing.[68] It also endowed Umeya with substantial capital to launch his own film distribution and production company, M. Pathé, named after the French firm Pathé Frères, in 1906, upon his return to Japan.[69]

Earlier in the chapter I discussed the impact of the Russo-Japanese War on Japanese cinema. The popularity of war newsreels generated significant income for film exhibitioners, allowing them to expand distribution and go into production. Meanwhile, as a form of war reporting, cinema grew in status, from a novel kind of entertainment to a powerful tool to influence public opinion. Umeya's M. Pathé exemplified and contributed to this shift in film culture in Japan; not only did Umeya accumulate his initial capital by exhibiting Russo-Japanese War newsreels, but he was one of the most important film promoters who sought to raise the status of cinema from entertainment to enlightenment. Sun Yat-sen and Umeya had discussed in depth the idea of cinema as a vehicle for social intervention. Sun allegedly suggested that Umeya engage in cinema for the benefit of the public.[70] The best way to raise the status of cinema and serve the public, in Umeya's judgment, was to connect motion pictures to science, industry, and education. In 1906 M. Pathé imported more than 120 scientific and educational films from Europe.[71] These films proved impactful: films on bacteria, imported from Germany, taught sanitation to the public during a cholera outbreak in Yamagata.[72]

By 1911 M. Pathé had grown into an ambitious production and distribution company, importing and producing newsreel, educational, and scientific films. Tom Gunning has observed in early nonfiction cinema both a global consciousness and an encyclopedic desire, exemplified by Albert Kahn's color-photography project "The Archives of the Planet" in the 1910s and 1920s, and by the ever-expanding film catalogs of the world and its peoples and sights, such as those offered by Pathé Frères.[73] Calling his company M. Pathé, and with Pathé Frères as his long-term supplier, Umeya certainly shared this worldly and encyclopedic impulse, taking pride in cataloging scientific and educational films that his company could make available to Japanese audiences. He published *A Treasured Encyclopedia of Moving Pictures* (Katsudō shashin hyakka hōten) in 1911, with synopses of about four hundred scientific and educational films, selected from more than ten thousand in the film catalogs he had amassed.[74] In the same year, besides *The Chinese Revolution*, the company also put out a popular feature-length documentary on the Japanese explorer Nobu Shirase's expedition to Antarctica, a nationalistic undertaking to beat European and American teams in claiming the first arrival to the icy continent.[75] Between Antarctica and the Xinhai Revolution, one can gauge the ambition and capacity of Umeya's enterprise, all the more impressive as he not only had both undertakings filmed but also had contributed to them financially.

In October 1911, when the Xinhai Revolution broke out in China, Umeya immediately dispatched a production team composed of cameraman Hagiya Kenzo, six crew members, and a journalist from the Nagasaki-based daily newspaper *Toyo hinode shinbun* (East ocean sunrise news). They spent the next few months following the revolution's development, filming at least three successive installments of a multipart actuality film until Sun was appointed president of the Republic of China in the final days of December 1911.[76] The resulting film, *The Chinese Revolution*, premiered in Nagasaki, Umeya's hometown, where his engagement with China began and a large Chinese population resided. As I related at the beginning of this section, it received an enthusiastic response. Markus Nornes has described Russo-Japanese War film screenings in Japan as a media mix of the benshi's story-telling, the audience's banner-waving, and the political agitators' impromptu public speeches.[77] Now this was the Chinese moment to celebrate victory. The reporter for *East Ocean Sunrise News* even noticed the presence of Chinese conservatives in the audience—the families of the Qing ministers of Hubei now in exile in Japan—timidly applauding with everyone else.[78]

Conventionally, revolutions are imagined to arise from political and social processes quite separate from cinema, though revolutionaries could seize the power of motion pictures to propagate their messages to the masses. The career of Umeya and his making of the Xinhai Revolution on screen and funding of it in reality demonstrate a deeper and multifaceted entanglement between cinema and revolution. Cinema as a business could absorb quick capital from mass spectatorship and channel the funds into political and social movements that create further occasions for filmmaking (and world-making). As a globalized media form, cinema's involvement also foregrounds the transnational dimension of nationalist revolutions: in this case, both the filmmaker and the revolutionary were adventurers and globetrotters, with overlapping identities, transnational itineraries, and networked resources that allowed them to move fluidly between the mass art of cinema and the mass politics of revolution.

Cinema for a Modern Republic

The Xinhai Revolution toppled the Qing and ushered in a republic. The next two decades saw tremendous transformations in the country. Fierce struggles among the country's old and new political elites continued as political power became fragmented, with powerful warlords controlling various regions of China, and the most dominant among them sharing control over a weak Beiyang central government in Beijing. The warlords' contestations for power lasted a decade and a half, until the Nationalist Party subjugated rival military powers through the military campaign of the Northern Expedition in 1927, two years after Sun Yat-sen's passing. Meanwhile, intellectuals, students and the working class began to organize and empower themselves with the May Fourth Movement in 1919 and the founding of the Chinese Communist Party in 1921. The Nationalist Party's consolidation of power in 1927 was coupled with ruthless suppressions of workers' uprisings led by the Communists in the same year, and the forced exodus of the Communist Party from the cities into the countryside.

Accompanying the ongoing political contestations were transformations in the economic, social, and cultural spheres. Filmmaking in this period underwent significant development. Chinese-made short films of melodrama and comedy had begun to emerge by 1913. By the 1920s, domestic film production had grown considerably, even as imported films, mostly from the United States, continued to dominate the market. Film magazines began to cultivate fandom, film schools opened to train actors and other film professionals, and film companies mushroomed. Film scholars studying this cinema culture have focused on the vibrant melodrama, comedy, and martial arts film productions, which creatively adapted American "low" film genres such as westerns, adventure serials, and detective films.[79] What has not received adequate attention are non-drama-based films that could be retrospectively categorized as documentaries: educational, industrial, and current affairs films meant for educational and propaganda purposes and exhibited in connection with a variety of political, military, and educational institutions. This second cinema culture also bore international influences—it responded to the proliferation of American educational and industrial films in China in the 1910s and developed with an awareness of international, and particularly Soviet, political cinema in the 1920s. In addition, these non-drama-based film productions had close connection to drama films: the Commercial Press, a producer of educational films between 1917 and 1925, enabled the first feature-length drama film production in 1921; Lai Manwai, a Hong Kong filmmaker who produced current affair films in the 1920s in relation to the Nationalists' Northern Expedition, also produced melodramas and became a significant player in the popular film industry. The rest of the chapter engages with this overlooked cinema culture as the continuation of documentary emergence in this early period.

Cinema with a Higher Purpose

In 1918 Cheng Yu, who appeared earlier in this chapter photographing war trophies in Japan, applied to the Ministry of Education for approval to build a factory in Shanghai to produce and distribute educational films. With fifty thousand yuan as his registered capital, Cheng in the application recalled the vibrant cinema culture he had witnessed in Tokyo years before and argued that cinema as visual communication was particularly effective in public education, as it could allow the uneducated and illiterate to learn with their own eyes. Yet even though popular education associations had mushroomed after the revolution, there had been a shortage of China-made films for educational purposes. Most imported films were made "without any higher purpose," and some even taught people to commit crimes, Cheng complained. Even when imported films were of educational value, their English intertitles were illegible to the Chinese viewer, reducing the films' educational effect to as indirect as "scratching one's foot from outside the boot." In the application, Cheng elaborated on his aspiration to make educational films for the Chinese public, on subject matter from astronomy, geology, and agriculture to mining, civil engineering, and medicine.[80]

Cheng was certainly not alone in thinking about cinema in relation to public education. As discussed earlier, China's reform and revolutionary elites such as the Yuan brothers and Sun Yat-sen himself had understood cinema's educational value, and the Yuan brothers brought it into popular education as early as 1906. As the 1911 revolution brought the imperative of nation-building and modernization of the society to the fore, cinema's efficacy in public education and its value for the new Chinese republic became further acknowledged and explored. The German-educated Cai Yuanpei, upon becoming the education minister in 1912, noted in the government's directive that moving pictures should be developed to support public education.[81] Chinese newspapers and magazines widely reported on cinema's pedagogical and productive use: in teaching biology, history, geography, and sanitation in America, France, and Germany, in voter education in Italy, and in measuring and optimizing workers' productivity in American and German scientific management.[82] The civil engineer Liao Weici, who would go on to design some of China's major railroads, penned numerous essays on cinema and photography for the newly founded magazine *Science* when studying for his doctorate at Cornell between 1915 and 1917. Having translated excerpts from Leonard Donaldson's book *The Cinematograph and Natural Science* (1912), Liao wrote, in the translator's preface, about cinema's marvelous capacity to take viewers on a virtual journey of learning: "Now there is a thing that can in one small room, next to the kitchen fire, take young people on journeys all over the world. It can teach medicine, biology, psychology, and can control and manage customs and education. It goes so deep into the human being, moves us so far, and its use can be so great."[83]

Supported by extensive citations from international practices, this interest in cinema's educational use certainly drew from developments elsewhere. Cinema's pedagogical use in Euro-America was informed by a variety of ideas about what cinematic vision was. In scientific research, the epistemic virtue of objectivity emerged in the nineteenth century, around the same time when the technology of photography mechanized vision.[84] Cinema, with its photographic nature and its ease to be connected to lenses with various scales of magnification, was not only a popular cultural institution but also part of the enterprise of modern science, a "cultural technology" linked to "laboratory instruments of graphic inscription and measurement."[85] Meanwhile, informed by the modern discipline of psychology, the progressive education movement in Europe and America emphasized the benefits of learning through direct experience.

Cinema, with its seeming immediacy to the object of its depiction, was thought to proximate direct experience, and hence be an effective teaching aid.[86] Besides being used to teach scientific disciplines, cinema was also used to teach civic virtues and inculcate national and imperial subjects. Its visual communication was understood as an additional value, as it could bypass linguistic differences. The rise of educational cinema in the United States in the 1910s, for example, was driven by the need to teach patriotism and "world citizenship" at a time of massive immigration and global expansion of American imperialist interests.[87]

In the 1910s the eruption of the World War I led to a decline in imported films from Europe and a drastic increase in American film imports.[88] American industrial and educational films also circulated widely in China. These films supported American industrialists' efforts to standardize and integrate global production and sought to educate Chinese producers to adopt new production practices for the global market. As World War I disrupted raw silk imports from Europe while generating a high demand for silk cartridge bags in military use, American manufacturers turned to China and Japan for raw silk imports, and concerted efforts were made to teach Chinese farmers new methods to produce raw silk suited for the fast spinning wheels in American factories.[89] The YMCA in Shanghai and the American Embassy in Beijing screened films at public lectures and lent industrial films to schools.[90] The University of Nanking, an American missionary college, also began to use films to teach modern production techniques for silk and cotton around this time.[91]

American industrial films were employed to reconfigure long-standing practices of silk production and the corresponding ways of life. In chapter 2 I will return to the topic of silk production when discussing Cheng Bugao's film *The Spring Silkworm* (*Chun chan*, 1932) as left-wing docu-fiction. Here it suffices to say that it was a growing awareness of cinema's efficacy in education from international practices and institutional exhibitions of imported, mostly American, industrial films that prompted aspiring Chinese producers such as Cheng Yu to seize the technology for their own purposes. Cheng's application was approved, but for reasons unknown to us, his plan didn't materialize. Around the time of his application, however, a much larger and stronger player, the Commercial Press, had entered the fray.

Filmmaking at the Commercial Press

Founded in Shanghai in 1897, the Commercial Press was China's leading publisher of textbooks, dictionaries, and technical manuals. Between 1903 and 1914 it operated as a joint venture with Kinkōdō, one of the largest Japanese textbook publishers, and through this collaboration, the Commercial Press acquired the latest printing technology and was introduced to new visual education technologies, such as lantern slides, which it had begun producing by 1914, and cinema.[92] In 1917 the company acquired film cameras and studio equipment cheaply from an American businessman whose plan for a film production company in Nanjing had failed.

On filmmaking, the Commercial Press was explicit about its import-substitution aims. Its petition to the government in 1919 requesting a tax exemption for its filmmaking described imported films as "flippant and mendacious, very harmful to the maintenance of customs and popular sentiment. They frequently satirize inferior conditions in our society, thus providing material for derision." The petition called for China to make its own films to replace the imported films in both domestic and overseas markets, to "mitigate foreigners' spiteful feelings, and mobilize affections of overseas Chinese toward their homeland."[93]

The Commercial Press's filmmaking centered on documentary categories. Between 1917 and 1924 its film division produced forty-eight short films. While these films were lost to Japanese air raids in 1932, written records of the titles remain and show that 65 percent of these films were in documentary categories, including scenery films, educational films, and current affairs films (*shishi pian*).[94] Scenery films sought to inspire nationalistic feelings about the beauty of the Chinese landscape and centered on sites with strong symbolic meanings, such as scenic spots along the Yangtze River, on the Tai and Lu Mountains, and at the West Lake in Hangzhou. Current affairs films included shorts on specialized schools for blind children, women's sports, military training routines, and early childhood education. News films focused on contemporary political and social activities in Shanghai, such as the burning of confiscated opium by the municipal government in January 1919 and a parade celebrating the end of World War I.[95] Included in the current affairs film category was also a short called *Workers Leaving the Commercial Press*, clearly inspired by the Lumière brothers' *Workers Leaving the Lumière Factory in Lyon*, demonstrating pride in the Commercial Press's leadership in China's nascent film industry. These films were often screened in institutional contexts, along with lantern slides.[96] The company also made films on sporting events such as the Far Eastern Championship Games, which took place in Shanghai in 1921, and marketed them overseas.[97]

While the majority of its productions were not dramatic, the Commercial Press did make drama films, alerting us to the close connection between documentary and drama, education and entertainment. Its catalogs listed drama-based films as new drama (*xinju*) and old drama (*guju*), altogether amounting to 35 percent of its total productions. "Old dramas" featuring Mei Lanfang's stage performances were successfully exported to Chinese communities in Southeast Asia. "New dramas" were moral tales dealing with contemporary topics. In 1921 the Commercial Press enabled the making of the earliest Chinese-made feature-length film, *Yan Ruisheng*, lending its filmmakers, equipment, and studio space to the short-lived China Film Drama Study Association (Zhongguo yingxi yanjiushe) for the film's production. A dramatic reenactment of a well-publicized murder case in Shanghai in the previous year, in which a man named Yan Ruisheng killed a prostitute for her jewelry, the film was in effect a docudrama and put the Commercial Press's expertise in on-location shooting to excellent use. Many scenes were shot in Shanghai's fashionable hangouts, which the protagonists of the actual murder case had frequented, intensifying the film's ghastly realism. The financial success of the film led to a surge of domestic incorporation of film companies and a flurry of urban crime drama. In the same year, the Commercial Press again lent its personnel and studio for the making of *Red Beauty and Skeleton* (*Hongfen kulou*), an adaptation of a French detective novel about a criminal gang employing beautiful women to seduce and murder young men and claim their life-insurance payments.

Yan Ruisheng and *Red Beauty and Skeleton*, made in 1921, were two of the three earliest long feature films made in China. The fact that the Commercial Press, a publisher of textbooks and a maker of educational lantern slides and film, enabled these films' production demonstrates the importance of educational cinema in the development of Chinese cinema as a whole. It is worth noting, however, that although the Commercial Press lent its know-how and technology to the making of these films, it did not produce them itself; nor did it pursue its own production of similarly lowbrow films, most likely because it wanted to maintain its identity as a maker of educational materials. Indeed, recent scholarship has attributed the end of the Commercial Press's film venture to its identity as an educational publisher and its inability to compete with other film studios solely focused on making sensational drama films for profit.[98] The company's film unit became an independent production company in 1926 and went on to make six more films that never achieved popularity, before closing its doors in 1927.

The year 1927 was when Lai Manwai released his compilation film on the Nationalist Party's Northern Expedition, a film that drew resources from both Lai's commercially successful film studio and the Nationalist Party as party-sponsored propaganda. I now turn to party filmmaking in this period to discuss how cinema contributed to the making of political leadership in the postrevolutionary years of political fragmentation and consolidation.

Rivalries of Political Leadership on Film

The 1911 revolution left China politically fragmented between 1911 and 1927, and political and military power holders eagerly used modern media to influence public opinion and compete for power. Much like present-day social media, the circular telegram, when sent to news outlets to be printed in the papers on the same or the following day, became the quickest way for warlords to expound on their political views, attack their rivals, and issue ultimatums. A "war by telegram" often preceded actual military conflict between rival warlords.[99] Photography and film further allowed power-holders to reach a wider public in a society with a large illiterate population. In the wake of the 1911 revolution, Sun Yat-sen's photographic portraits were among the most reproduced images, gracing posters, newspapers, photography albums, stamps, postcards, and bank notes.[100] Moving images of Sun Yat-sen were also numerous, filmed by both domestic and foreign filmmakers. Warlords such as Wu Peifu, Li Zongren, Bai Chongxi, Sun Chuanfang, and Feng Yuxiang all had their stints on the silver screen in the 1920s.[101]

As a large number of Chinese early films have been lost to war, this chapter has so far relied almost entirely on written materials. The two films that I will discuss in this section, however, have been preserved in some form. Both are portrayals of political and military leadership: *A Record of the National Revolutionary Army's War on Sea, Land, and Air* (*Guominjun hailukong dazhan ji*, 1927, hereafter *War on Sea, Land, and Air*), by Lai Manwai, and *A Record of Feng Yuxiang's Northern Expedition Work* (*Feng Yuxiang beifa gongzuo ji*, 1929, hereafter *Feng Yuxiang's Northern Expedition*), made by Feng's talented subordinate Zhao Yiyun, under the guidance of Feng himself. Even though what remains is incomplete—in the case of *War on Sea, Land, and Air* we have only fragments from later versions of the film, re-edited by Lai Manwai in 1940 and again in 1950—these preserved moving images allow us to take a close look at the filmmakers' deployment of cinema to articulate ideas about political leadership. Lai's portrayal of the Nationalist Party, relying on long shots, train journeys, and aerial perspectives, highlighted the political elites' command of modern technologies and the territorializing capacities of their disciplined troops. Zhao's cinematic portrait of Feng, on the other hand, heavily used close-ups and medium shots to communicate corporeal intimacies between the commander and his troops, grounding leadership in acts of pastoral care.

Lai Manwai's Party Film

On November 28, 1927, the nine-reel, eighty-minute compilation documentary *War on Sea, Land, and Air* premiered at Shanghai's Palace Cinema.[102] Released in the same year as the Soviet filmmaker Esfir Shub's *The Fall of the Romanov Dynasty*, this film by Lai Manwai aspired to provide a "systematic military and political history" of the revolution.[103] Newspaper advertisements lauded the film's territorial coverage over more than ten provinces and all combat zones and its spectacular display of modern military technologies in action: "Military weapons such as mortars, field guns, torpedoes, submarines, warships, and fighter aircrafts, whatever should be there is there."[104] The film's lively images of Nationalist Party dignitaries, especially those no longer alive, promised another attraction. "If you want to pay respect to Sun Yat-sen, Liao Zhongkai, and other martyrs of our party and great men of recent history, seeing them in person and in movement, please watch this film."[105]

Like Umeya Shōkichi, Lai Manwai had been a long-time member of Sun Yat-sen's Revolutionary Alliance. Born in Yokohama, Japan, to Chinese parents in 1893 and growing up in Hong Kong, Lai's earliest encounter with cinema was none other than watching a Russo-Japanese War newsreel when he was fourteen years old. Passionate about photography, theater, and film, Lai founded a spoken drama troupe in Hong Kong in 1913. After an initial foray into cinema in 1914, when he collaborated with the Ukraine-American film exhibitor and producer Benjamin Brodsky on two fiction shorts in Hong Kong, Lai started a business in film exhibition in 1921 and founded the production company Minxin (New people) the year after.[106] Believing cinema would serve the revolution and modernize the nation, Lai focused on producing films in the documentary category in Minxin's early years: the company produced one dramatic feature and more than thirty scenery, educational, current affairs, and Peking opera films before relocating from Hong Kong to Shanghai in 1925.[107] While its early repertoire shared similar themes with those of the Commercial Press, Minxin distinguished itself with its persistent filmmaking on Sun Yat-sen and his Nationalist Party's activities, thanks to Lai's party affiliation.[108]

Lai began filming Sun's activities in 1923. His camera rolled at the First National Congress of the Nationalist Party in 1924 and recorded Sun's public speech in the same year launching the Northern Expedition, a military campaign against the northern warlords and to reunite the country. After Sun's untimely death in 1925 and Chiang Kai-shek's rise to Nationalist Party leadership, Lai continued to film the Northern Expedition under Chiang's command.[109] Edited footage from these events was first released as part of Minxin's short film offerings. After Chiang Kai-shek consolidated hegemony in the country, Lai selectively compiled his accumulated footage into a nine-reel, eighty-minute film.[110] Approved by the Nationalist Party branch office in Shanghai as the "only long-format film for party propaganda,"[111] the film was one of the earliest "party" films in China, a fact that Minxin acknowledged openly in the film's publicity materials: "We at Minxin are all loyal followers and believers [of Sun Yat-sen]. We have long hoped to depict and propagate the revolution's achievements via the silver screen and contribute to the revolution's speedy completion."[112]

Covering military actions on sea, land, and air, Lai's film heavily featured modern technologies of mobility and combat, using them to construct the political leadership of the party. Lai began his cinematic chronicle of the Northern Expedition with train travel by Sun Yat-sen and Chiang Kai-shek to Shaoguan, where Sun was to preside over a military parade to mark the beginning of the campaign. Similar to city symphony films such as *Berlin: Symphony of a Metropolis*, which was released in the same year, Lai filmed railway travel with visual attraction and dynamism, creating dancing geometric patterns on screen with moving rail tracks and the beams and lattices of a railway bridge. Yet different from that of *Berlin*, the camera in Lai's film was placed at the front of a rapidly advancing train, allowing the viewer to experience the train's forward movement from the active position of the driver rather than the passenger, while constructing the Northern Expedition as an unstoppable force of modernization and unification. Besides train travel, the film's fighting sequences also featured an aerial shot, likely the first such sequence achieved by a Chinese filmmaker. To reconstruct a battle in air between Chiang Kai-shek's troops and those of the warlord Sun Chuanfang, Lai took great risks to tie himself and the camera to a fixture on a small airplane and filmed the aerial view from an opening in the bottom of the plane. As the plane smoothly glided over residential areas, farmland, and a river, the absolute verticality of the camera's bird's-eye perspective flattens the moving landscape, enabling an abstraction of space.[113]

Both the train and the aerial views had been part of cinema since the medium's very beginning. The arrival of a train was among the very first film offerings by the Lumière brothers, who also made a short film from a captive balloon in 1898. Lynne Kirby observes that railroad and cinema were analogous machines of vision and movement. "As a machine of vision and an instrument for conquering space and time, the train is a mechanical double for the cinema and for the transport for the spectator into fiction, fantasy, and dream," Kirby writes.[114] In the 1920s, when Dziga Vertov wrote his essays on the kino-eye, the ability to "ascend with an airplane" and "plunge and soar together with plunging and soaring bodies" was already understood as an essential quality of the cinematic.[115] The train and the airplane in Lai's film, however, offered different ways of seeing and traveling through time-space: the train foregrounded rhythm, speed, and momentum, while the aerial view flattened and abstracted space. Both rearticulated the national space into a territory that could be conquered and surveyed from the highly technologized vantage points under the political and military elites' command.

Besides being mounted on a train and an airplane to create mediated visions of the territory under command, Lai's camera also sought to create portraitures of party elders and panoramic views of military formations, creating a visual hierarchy to support the Nationalist Party's elitist leadership. Party dignitaries, from the deceased Sun Yat-sen and Liao Zhongkai to Chiang Kai-shek and others, are presented together at the onset of the film in a long montage sequence. Introduced to the audience one by one, framed mostly in medium shots and occasionally in close-ups and long-shots, these figures pose for the camera as though in portrait photographs, with only slight body movements to enliven the image. The use of the portrait format here was not an instance of "regression" to still photography but a deliberate transmedial practice that sought to endow the figures with qualities of personal worth, dignity, and decorum, associated with still portrait photography since the late nineteenth century.[116] Meanwhile, movement within the images created a pleasurable illusion that the person in the photo was coming back to life. Dressed in a Western-style suit, Sun Yat-sen, who was no longer alive at the time of the film's release, looks straight into the camera from a frame that dims his surroundings and foregrounds him as the center of the viewers' attention. After holding still for five seconds, Sun then takes off his hat and bows slightly to the audience.

The masses, in contrast, are filmed in long shots and presented as an anonymous but united, energetic, and disciplined force that does the footwork of territorialization. A high-angle view of people gathering to welcome Sun Yat-sen's arrival overwhelms the screen with the crowd's swelling volume and energy; an eye-level shot of marching troops showcases the army's purposeful and orderly movement. Following the troops as they travel on foot, Lai uses the moving figures of soldiers to animate cinematic landscapes of mountains and rivers, playing with the troop's quivering reflections in water to highlight their emplacement in a national landscape as the generative force that enables its territorialization. In one scene, the troops were filmed walking along a riverbank in single file, with those at the head of the column turning onto a small wooden footbridge to cross the river. With the soldiers' rectilinear movement in the foreground, their reflection in the river as they cross the bridge a bit further on, and the faint outline of mountains in the far background, the layered image creates an aesthetics of the modern military and its territorialization by combining the geometric with the picturesque. In the film, the leaders and their troops occupy different formal spaces and seldom interact. Even when they do, such as in military parades where the leaders inspect troops, they are spatially separated, with the soldiers marching underneath the podium and the leaders watching from a commanding height.

Lai Manwai and his Minxin company had claimed, with great pride, their close connections to the Nationalist Party. The film was unabashedly a party film, made to consolidate the party's prestige and articulate the party's leadership. Not only the film text but the film's exhibition context were governed by order and hierarchy. In an attempt to distinguish the film from other lowbrow commercial productions, its advertisement encouraged the audience to be reverent and orderly when attending the film. Viewers who wore Sun Yat-sen–style jackets, school uniforms, or military uniforms to the film would enjoy half-price tickets. Those who came to see the film in a group of more than ten people could also get a half-price discount, if they had a letter of certification from a recognized social institution.[117]

Feng Yuxiang and a Different Model of a Leader

Also making use of film, the warlord Feng Yuxiang chose to perform his leadership very differently. Born in a poor family and not well-educated, Feng rose through the ranks in the army and by the 1920s was among the most powerful warlords in the country. The Soviet Union, in its bid to influence the Chinese revolution, backed Sun Yat-sen's Nationalist Party from early 1920s and then in 1925 began to back Feng's military establishments as well, urging Feng to work with Chiang Kai-shek to form a pro-Soviet political force in China. Made between 1927 and 1928 and premiered in Shanghai in 1929, *Feng Yuxiang's Northern Expedition* bore significant Soviet influence, as it was made shortly after Feng's return from a study trip to the Soviet Union in 1926. The filmmaker was Zhao Yiyun, Feng's talented subordinate, who had briefly studied filmmaking in Moscow during Feng's time there.[118]

As mentioned earlier, Lai Manwai emphasized the elite status and decorum of the Nationalist Party with the format of the bourgeois photographic portrait. Feng Yuxiang, in contrast, introduces himself in Zhao's film with mischievous mugshots. Framed in close medium shots resembling a police mugshot, which had been in use in China since the early twentieth century, Feng stands naked from the waist up, directly facing the camera. With a slight smile, he turns squarely to his left and then to his right for the camera to capture profile views, in the process exhibiting his broad shoulders, bulky torso, and perfect posture as a military man. As mugshots, this sequence is self-deprecating: Feng strips himself of any marker distinguishing him as an army general and stands naked under the scrutiny of the camera and, by extension, of the viewer. Yet in exposing his muscular and well-trained body, the sequence is also proudly exhibitionist. The film as a whole featured no modern military technology, no train journeys or aerial shots, no territory ripe for conquest; instead, it was shot almost entirely in Feng's military compound. It foregrounded Feng's powerful corporeal presence and the bodily care and discipline he as a leader imparted on his soldiers (fig. 1.4).

1.4 Feng Yuxiang's "mugshots" in *Feng Yuxiang's Northern Expedition Chronicle* (1929).

Lai's film featured able-bodied party leaders and soldiers and included no scene of death or injury caused by war. Feng Yuxiang, on the other hand, is seen scrubbing a wounded soldier's back and helping him put on socks. Such scenes of care abound in the film: Feng shaving a soldier's head; Feng squatting, serving soldiers food and eating with them; Feng inspecting and cutting soldiers' fingernails and toenails. Framed frequently in close-ups, these intimate scenes of corporeal contact between the army general and the soldiers endowed the film with an intense tactility. Clearly influenced by Soviet montage theory, Zhao films a single process from multiple angles and with multiple framing, to create a fast-paced montage that turns these mundane activities into thrilling cinematic experiences. The bodies are not only cared for with hygiene and nourished with food, but also trained to perform spectacular gymnastic feats. In a long take, a stationary camera records a half-naked Feng dancing with a sword in a martial arts routine, his bulky body moving across the frame and filling it with energetic presence. The soldiers also showcase their creative formations on the horizontal bar in a sports game. In contrast to the solemn marching of the troops in Lai's film, these improvisational performances staged on the training ground add a sense of joyful free play to the film.

As Zhao was a subordinate of Feng in his army, Feng undoubtedly had control over the film and most likely shaped the film as its de facto director. While it did screen briefly in a cinema in Shanghai, the film was more likely an internal production, meant to be shown to Feng's soldiers and recruits as a training or publicity film. Soldiers observe Feng performing his sword routine and learn to copy his movements. Prisoners of war, after receiving pocket money from Feng and being given the option of being sent home by train, talk among themselves about staying to serve in Feng's army because, as the intertitle suggests, "you see how nice he is!" These pedantic moments in the film reveal the expectation that the film would help to build and expand Feng's army. Another potential audience might be Feng's Soviet financiers. His short visit to the Soviet Union in 1926 was a transformative experience for him, bringing more ideological coherence to his thinking about China's future and his role in it. The film's down-to-earth aesthetics drew resources from the proletarian political culture of the Soviet Union, as well as traditional Chinese and Christian ideas of pastoral care (Feng had converted to Christianity). The film might have served to showcase his adherence to populist principles and thus his suitability for Soviet support.

At the beginning of this chapter, I discussed the stakes of *jilu*. Both films discussed here have titles that end with the character *ji*, a "record," and both records served partisan purposes. *Feng Yuxiang's Northern Expedition* was most likely produced for purposes of recruitment and fundraising to enhance Feng Yuxiang's political influence and military power. *War in Sea, Land and Air* was a highly selective compilation of footage accumulated over a politically turbulent period, a partisan historiographic act that illuminated as much as obscured actual historical processes. Projecting a unified nation under the Nationalist Party, it erased any reference to the supporting roles played by the Soviet Union and the Chinese Communist Party in the Northern Expedition. Nor did it include any reference to Chiang Kai-shek's brutal suppression of the workers' uprising in Shanghai and the massacre of Communists and trade unionists around the country just a few months before the film's release.

A diligent filmmaker, Lai Manwai had in fact documented many of these events that he didn't include in the film. He filmed the Nationalist Party's First National Congress in Guangzhou in 1924, which officially inaugurated the Nationalist-Communist alliance. In February 1927, with the progressive dramatist Ouyang Yuqian, Lai filmed the general strike in Shanghai that led to the workers seizing control of the city and prompted Chiang to take repressive measures after he took control. While Lai's diaries prior to Chiang's anti-Communist purge indicate his friendly relationships with people from across the political spectrum, including the anti-Communist Zou Haibin and the Communist Li Dazhao, and Lai would continue to work with both the left and right over the course of his long film career, the Nationalist dignitaries Lai included in the film were almost all from the conservative wing of the party, who stood by Chiang Kai-shek's bloody repression of Communists and trade unionists.[119] Featuring Sun and Chiang prominently and giving them the most screen time, the film effectively established Chiang's status as Sun's successor.

This chapter has shown that photographic and film documentations (*jilu*) were deeply imbricated in colonialism, transnational politics, and revolutionary agitation and consolidation. Cinematic texts carried with them nationalist ideologies, visions of political leadership, and new technologies for agricultural and industrial production. Meanwhile, film production and exhibition not only provided opportunities for filmmakers to remediate/reframe existing narratives and intervene into power dynamics at the site of filmmaking; they also financed revolutionary activities with fast cash and addressed spectators who could be the next revolutionary recruits. The political and cultural elites' interest in cinema's political and pedagogical use prompted the Commercial Press's foray into filmmaking, supporting the rise of a domestic film industry. It's to this domestic film industry's engagement with documentary and the concurrent rise of amateur filmmaking in Shanghai that I turn in the next chapter.

CHAPTER 2

BOMBS AND SEAFARINGS

Documentaries Hard and Soft

On May 30, 1925, gunshots erupted on the busy Nanking Road in Shanghai's international settlement. At the gate of the Laoza Police Station, the police force under British command fired into a ten-thousand-strong crowd of angry Chinese who had gathered there to protest the previous killing of Chinese workers in a Japanese factory, and to demand the release of student activists. In all, twelve were killed and seventeen were wounded.[1] Upon hearing the news, Chen Jianran, who had just founded the United (Youlian) Film Company earlier that year, rushed to the scene by car with his colleagues. From the car window, the cinematographer Liu Liangchan filmed police washing away traces of blood on the ground and recorded damage from gunfire on the streets. The filmmakers sped away in their car, arousing suspicion, and were chased by police on horseback. By the time the police caught up, the camera had been safely hidden under the actress Xu Qinfang's fashionable wide-leg pants. The police found nothing and let the film crew go.[2]

The footage shot on that day was edited into a three-reel film entitled *The May Thirtieth Shanghai Movement* (*Wusa Huchao*). The film is no longer extant, but some accounts remain of how it was made and how it circulated. Shot with the newest Eyemo portable camera, the film presented mass actions and police repression in parallel action: Tongji University students parading by the coffin of their slaughtered classmate, British reinforcement troops arriving by sea at the Bund, the colonial police's occupation of universities in the concession areas, and scenes of public speeches, mass rallies, and the general strike that brought the city to a halt.³ It showed the dead and the injured, traces of blood on the street, and, in close-up, a bullet surgically removed from a wound, followed by an intertitle, "Alas, a gift bestowed by imperialism."

The screenwriter Xu Bibo, who penned the intertitles, recalled how difficult it was to gain access to hospitals and morgues where the injured and the dead were sent. Helped by sympathetic doctors, filmmakers disguised themselves as medical workers to infiltrate heavily guarded hospitals in the international concession so they could film injured protestors getting medical treatment. The Helen Road Morgue, also in the international concession, was off-limits, but the Joint Committee of Workers, Merchants, and Students (Gongshangxue lianhehui) helped locate five corpses of protestors at the Tongren Fuyuan Hall, Shanghai's largest indigenous charity, located in the Chinese area of the city (Huajie). The charity's helpful staff even constructed a temporary skylight in the roof to ensure sufficient light for filming. The Chinese area of the city also served as a refuge for film exhibition. Prohibited from exhibition in the foreign concessions, the film premiered on June 27, 1925, at the Republican Cinema (Gonghe daxiyuan) near the Old South Gate, and all revenue from a total of seven days of screenings was donated to assist workers on strike. The film studio also donated a free copy to the Shanghai Federation of Students, which was screened at fundraising activities.⁴ Activist networks also brought the film to neighboring cities, such as Hangzhou and Suzhou.⁵

The May Thirtieth Movement in 1925 was the first instance of large-scale working class militancy across the country, in which the Communist Party, founded in 1921 in Shanghai, played an important organizing role. The fact that filmmakers had captured the movement as it happened and managed to film and exhibit these moving images by exploiting crevices in Shanghai's foreign and Chinese jurisdictions, demonstrate substantial development in filming capacity and an intimate awareness of the semicolonial urban space for subversive filmmaking. Giving attention to blood stains, bullets, and corpses, and to workers and students in collective formation on the streets, cinema restored traces to events, objects, and bodies against acts of erasure and obscuration.

The May Thirtieth Movement heralded a period of radicalization and militancy among China's growing numbers of industrial workers, progressive intellectuals, and students. This period of activism was met with violent suppression, imprisonment, and massacre of Communists and unionists by the Nationalist Party in 1927, soon after it scored decisive gains in the Northern Expedition and consolidated control of the industrial powerhouse of Shanghai and other crucial lower Yangtze regions. Suffering huge losses, the Communists had to leave the cities for the countryside, where they established various small bases from which they could withstand the Nationalists' continuous onslaught. Meanwhile, political polarization intensified ideological struggles in social and cultural arenas through the 1930s, a decade that began with

Japanese occupation of Manchuria and ended with full-scale Japanese invasion, mass destruction, and displacement.

How to find one's foothold and orientation in such a turbulent period of political struggles, mobilization, and displacement? As I mentioned in the last chapter, Chinese intellectuals such as Liang Qichao had long realized that our immediate perceptual capacities no longer sufficed, and that mediated perception of the world beyond one's immediate surroundings was necessary to grasp the complex reality of our existence in a world of imperial expansion, global capitalism, and changing technology. What role could cinema play in such mediations? How could different modes of actuality-based filmmaking turn the sensory and empirical unfoldings before the camera into experience and knowledge, to help with social analysis, political mobilization, and personal healing?

This chapter centers its discussion on the developments of documentary modes of filmmaking, particularly news films, docu-fiction, and amateur home movies and travelogues from the late 1920s to the mid-1930s. Existing historiography of this golden age of Shanghai filmmaking and of the fierce ideological debates on cinema waged in 1932–1936 between filmmakers from the Marxist Left-wing camp and the non-Marxist modernist camp (the hard versus soft cinema debate) has not given much consideration to documentary modes of filmmaking. The scholarly consensus has been that unlike in the Soviet Union or in Japan, where documentary and small-scale cinema energized proletarian filmmaking, Chinese filmmaking in the 1920s and 1930s had been largely confined to film studios. The failure to make use of small-scale camera technology and develop a militant documentary movement, for film scholar Laikwan Pang, was a missed opportunity for China's left-wing filmmaking of this period.[6]

I agree with Pang that there was indeed a missed opportunity, and Chinese progressive filmmaking would have been very different if more of it had involved 9.5mm and 16mm small-scale filmmaking outside the commercial film studios. However, I argue in this chapter that documentary modes of filmmaking contributed much more substantially to China's left-wing film culture than has been previous recognized. In addition, our understanding of the hard versus soft cinema debate also must take into account documentary practices in both camps. Left-wing filmmakers such as Cheng Bugao moved between documentary and fiction filmmaking. In fact, Cheng's leftward turn happened when he became keenly aware of the incommensurability between the infotainment of the American newsreel and Chinese wartime filmmaking, when covering the Battle of Shanghai in 1932 as a news filmmaker during the Japanese bombing of the city. Noticing Cheng's extensive experience in documentary filmmaking allows us to understand his earliest left-wing films—*Torrent* (*Kuangliu*) and *Spring Silkworm* (*Chuncan*), both made in 1933—as docu-fiction. Both experimented in different ways with documentary modes of filmmaking to connect the phenomenal world of immediate experience to the larger dynamics of class struggle, capitalism, and imperialism.

On the other side of the debate, I show that a serious reconsideration of the soft cinema proponent Liu Na'ou's film theories must take into account his amateur filmmaking in 1932–1934, just when the hard versus soft debates were being waged. Amateur filmmaking in Shanghai, particularly among the Euro-American and Japanese-speaking diasporic communities, was certainly not a "revolutionary" practice. Yet I show, through a close reading of Liu's film within the context of his life's journeys, how his attention to relationality, whether at home or on the road, and his aesthetics of improvisation and intersubjectivity entailed emancipatory potentials as well. While the left-wing filmmakers tried to connect immediate experience to broader structures of power to awaken the consciousness of the oppressed, Liu sought to illuminate the protective tactics and equities already practiced by existing communities themselves and used cinema not as a technique of awakening but as an apparatus of attunement.

Following the first chapter's emphasis on transnational media circulations, this chapter attends to Chinese filmmakers' interactions with American commercial newsreels and Soviet avant-garde filmmaking such as that of Dziga Vertov, and how they negotiated between liberal premises of objective journalism, Marxist attention to class consciousness, and modernist emphasis on open-ended intersubjective experience. Yet while transnational circulations of ideas and practices were important, Chinese filmmakers remained loyal to the realities they faced on the ground, creating distinct film forms to advance their political and ethical visions.

Newsreels: A Global Industrial Media

In 1925, when Chen Jianran and his film crew filmed the May Thirtieth Movement in Shanghai, the term *documentary* had not been in circulation in China. What had become familiar to Chinese filmgoers by then were news films (*xinwen pian*), referring to regularly released newsreels and stand-alone actualities. Chinese film studios occasionally produced stand-alone actualities, but they were far from having the capacity to release newsreels regularly until much later, when the state became involved in newsreel production in the mid-1930s and during the war.[7] Before then, newsreels were imported, with American productions dominating the Chinese market after World War I.

Following Pathé's release of the first newsreels in France in 1907 and in the United States in 1911, newsreels had been established in Euro-America as a staple of film production by the 1920s. Newsreels, however, rarely appear in studies of documentary cinema. Indeed, John Grierson defined documentary cinema in opposition to newsreel. "The peacetime newsreel is just a speedy snip-snap of some utterly unimportant ceremony," wrote Grierson in his *First Principles of Documentary*. With their "tit-bits" manner of observation, these money-making newsreels were superficial, he decried. "The newsreel had gone dithering on, mistaking the phenomenon for the thing in itself, and ignoring everything that gave it the trouble of conscience and penetration and thought." Only when going beyond the sorry state of the newsreel could one enter the realm of "the documentary proper," where filmmaking achieves the status of an art, and where "we pass from the plain (or fancy) descriptions of natural material, to arrangements, rearrangements, and creative shapings of it."[8]

Grierson's critique pitting the creative art of the documentary against the money-making and mindless "infotainment" of newsreel was strategic: he hoped to find a niche for British documentary to counter American newsreels' dominance of the international film market. By the 1920s, newsreel production had concentrated in a small number of large film corporations, mostly American, such as Paramount, Metro-Goldwyn-Mayer, and Fox.[9] As newsreel production and distribution relied on extensive networks of correspondents with privileged access to filming locations, as well as the infrastructure to swiftly process and transport films to cinemas, and as operation costs became even higher with the adoption of sound recording technology in 1927, only the biggest film companies that had benefited from vertical integration could afford to make and market newsreels.

While imported American newsreels had long been part of Chinese film culture—often they were viewers' first encounters with actuality-based filmmaking—Chinese films companies in the 1920s and 1930s had no capacity to sustain regular newsreel production of their own. One reason was that Shanghai filmmakers had limited accessibility to filming locations. Chen Jianran's documentation of the May Thirtieth Movement illustrated the difficulty of on-location shooting in Shanghai's heavily policed semicolonial urban space. In addition, Shanghai film studios had difficulty expanding their capacities through vertical integration. While Chinese capital had largely fueled film production, foreign capital dominated distribution and exhibition. Upscale theaters had exclusive contracts with Hollywood and thus were legally bound to exclusively show Hollywood films, which occupied 90 percent of all China's screen time in the second half of the 1920s.[10] Starting from the mid-1920s on, some Chinese companies attempted to build their own distribution and theater networks, yet these limited expansions of studio capacity were quickly disrupted by war. The Star Company (Mingxing) began to grow exhibition networks in late 1920. The United China Film Company (Lianhua), formed in 1930 and having absorbed Lai Manwai's Mingxin, built distribution networks extending to northern China, while its rival, the Heaven Company (Tianyi), took the lead in distributing to South China and Southeast Asia. Unsurprisingly, these big three—Star, United China, and Heaven—were most actively engaged in news film production in late 1920s and 1930s. Yet United China's theater chains in Manchuria were lost to the Japanese invasion in 1931.[11] Japanese bombing and burning of Shanghai in 1932 destroyed film studios as well as film theaters, disproportionally affecting those screening domestic films located in the Chinese part of the city. In short, Chinese film studios at the time never reached the capacity threshold to attempt regular newsreel production.

Chinese filmmakers in the 1920s appreciated the newsreel for its lively presentation of worldly affairs. In 1925, the filmmaker Cheng Bugao praised the newsreel in 1925 for providing more accurate and accessible news than the newspaper due to its nature as a visual record. Newspapers were often controlled by partisan interests, journalists often recorded unreliable hearsay, and the illiterate had to have the news read to them, Cheng wrote. In contrast, newsreels could offer "eyewitness" accounts, allowing "the viewers to feel as if they were on-site themselves."[12] Eyewitnessing an event across the globe was no small feat, and Cheng admiringly described the formidable capacities of four leading American newsreel producers and recounted the chain of operations, from acquisition of footage to transporting the completed film, that enabled a newsreel on the sinking of the Japanese ocean liner *Raifuku maru* in the Atlantic to reach a New York cinema just seventy-six hours after the accident.[13]

At the time he penned this essay, Cheng was just twenty-seven years old and had begun his film career with the Continental Film Company (Dalu) only a year before. His earliest films were one dramatic feature and two short documentaries: a film portrait of the powerful warlord Wu Peifu, and a scenery film called *Luoyang Scenes*. By 1928 Cheng had joined the Mingxing Company. A much larger company, Mingxing was expanding; it was among the first film companies to adopt sound technology and began to develop news films along with vertical integration. At Mingxing, Cheng directed both fiction and news films. From *Battle of Shanghai* (1932) to *Torrent* and *Spring Silkworm*, Cheng's films allow us to understand how Chinese news films developed as a response to the eruption of war in Shanghai and the further fragmentation of the city. The hybrid form of docu-fiction that he developed demonstrates a fluid understanding of documentary and fiction as mutually supportive means to capture emplaced experience within one's milieu of survival and struggle. It also sheds light on documentary's involvement in the rise of left-wing filmmaking.

The Bombing of Shanghai as International News

Joseph Clark's book-length study of American newsreel begins with the Lindbergh parade on June 13, 1927. This ticker-tape parade, where millions on the streets of Manhattan celebrated Charles Lindbergh's historic transatlantic flight as the quintessential "American achievement," was a "watershed moment for the American newsreel." Not only was the Lindbergh flight and parade the most significant newsreel event since World War I, creating an outstanding box office success, the ticker-tape parade could be understood as "a fitting metaphor for the newsreel system itself." Entitled *News Parade*, Clark's book posits "the parade" as the central logic of newsreel's spectacularization of world affairs that invited the audience to "watch the world as a passing pageant."[14]

Contrary to the United States, the "watershed movement" for news films in China was far from celebrative. In fact, it was a deadly Japanese air raid on the city of Shanghai on January 28, 1932, that brought news films to the forefront of film production and exhibition. Lasting from January to March, and with the official truce signed in May, Japan's "undeclared war" on Shanghai resulted in tremendous loss of life and destruction of the city. The Lindbergh parade was a mass celebration of spatial integration, whether it was the integration of the transatlantic space connected through aviation technology or the integration of New York's urban space by the parade. The air raid over colonial Shanghai, in contrast, laid open the dark secret of aviation development and tore urban spaces apart vertically and horizontally. Vertically, Japan's dominance of the air space rendered the city underneath defenseless. Horizontally, only the Chinese part of Shanghai's segmented urban space was targeted for destruction, with homes and businesses burning, streets reduced to rubble, and refugees fleeing to the foreign concessions for protection. The bombing resulted in severe damage to the Chinese film industry, and a large portion of early films were burned. Almost all early Commercial Press films were lost in the bombing. Lai Manwai's film company lost its warehouse and along with it, *War on Sea, Land, and Air*.[15] Chen Jianran's film on the May Thirtieth Movement was also lost to the bombing. Yet the air raid also spurred a flurry of news film production by international and Chinese filmmakers, though filmmakers from different backgrounds commanded very different spatial coordinates.

On the day after the air raid, *Shen bao* reported that three American film companies—Fox, Hearst, and Paramount—had applied for permits from both Chinese and colonial authorities to carry out filmmaking. Their cameras had already been rolling on the day of the bombing, the article said, and the Chinese government welcomed their efforts. W. W. Yen, the Chinese representative to the League of Nations in Geneva, had been unsuccessfully seeking the organization's sanctions on Japan for its occupation of Manchuria. Upon receiving the news of the Shanghai air raid, Yen reportedly tried to coordinate a radio transmission of the sound of the bombing to the League of Nations delegates, yet authorities in Geneva blocked this effort.[16] The writer for *Shen bao* praised American filmmakers for offering invaluable help in bringing the sensory evidence of Shanghai's destruction into the space of international politics.

The excitement over American newsreels from the war zone of Shanghai was shared by the American film historian Terry Ramsaye, writing for the film industry trade paper *Motion Picture Herald* on March 5, 1932. By then newsreels on the Shanghai bombing and the subsequent battle had already been exhibited in American cinemas for a few weeks, and Ramsaye celebrated these films for revitalizing the American newsreel. Newsreel films had been in the "doldrums of late," considered "a mere commercial entertainment item," he wrote. Yet the coverage of the Battle of Shanghai heralded a new era of newsreel, where "real reporting and real showmanship is about to dawn."[17]

At the time of Ramsaye's writing, the newsreel in the United States had been attracting criticism. The regularity of newsreel production and its requirement for studio-perfect images had pressed editors and filmmakers to favor predictable and easy-to-shoot scenes such as parades, ceremonies, and sporting events, which had become the mainstay. In the unrelenting words of the critic Robert Littell, newsreels had become "trivial, lazy, and misleading," feeding the audience with "a diet that is mostly marbles champions, prepared statements, parades, puns, and young men who can play piano with mittens on their hands."[18] The eruption of war in East Asia created an opportunity for the American newsreel to reinvent itself, as a serious and heroic endeavor that exposed unfolding world politics otherwise hidden from view. "The thunder of the guns and detonations of bombs, the black menace of death and destruction, in this undeclared war are made real despite the evasions of diplomats and the polite words of Geneva," wrote Ramsaye, adding that the camera—now with a microphone—would not lie.[19]

Ramsaye's claim of camera truth was premised on a simple affirmation of photographic realism: that the camera showed what was there. This camera truth, based on unhindered access granted by American power and proclaimed neutrality, was personified by the newsreel cameraman. Ramsaye's account of newsreel production in the Battle of Shanghai emphasized American filmmakers' full access to the warring parties: the eight American filmmakers filmed on both Chinese and Japanese sides and trailed the American fleet rushing from Manila to Shanghai. The only person who might not have had full access was the only Asian American among the eight: H. S. "Newsreel" Wong, who was caught in the "thick of the attack" in Shanghai. According to Clark, the predominantly white and male newsreel cameraman had by the early 1930s risen to the status of American cultural hero. Adventure-explorers who brushed shoulders with grave danger but always managed to extract themselves safely from every messy situation, the newsreel cameraman became a role model for young men and allowed American audiences to "implicitly negotiat[e] a neutral yet heroic role for the United States" in international conflicts.[20] This combination of heroism and neutrality was self-serving. Examining American newsreel reports on the Sino-Japanese War which began in full force in 1937, Clark observes a prevailing Orientalist condescension that attributed war not to the logic of imperialism but to an "Oriental madness" and reduced the

68 Bombs and Seafarings

2.1 Advertisement spread for Hearst Metrotone newsreels on the Battle of Shanghai, *Motion Picture Herald*, March 5, 1932.

destruction of war to visual thrills for Americans to consume at a safe distance.[21] This condescension had certainly been there in 1932 too: an advertisement for Hearst Metrotone newsreels on the bombing of Shanghai read, "No matter which sides wins—they leave it to Leo's Hearst Metrotone News to rush you the hot news of the scrap!" And the voice-over of the "globetrotter" was said to tell the story so well that "it happened in China!—but you know more about it than the Chinese!" (fig. 2.1).[22]

The Battle of Shanghai: A Chinese News Film

While the American newsreel filmmakers kept themselves busy in Shanghai, moving between warring camps with ease thanks to American neutrality and their journalist badges, Chinese filmmakers also plunged themselves into filmmaking, though their productions faced much graver challenges. They certainly couldn't move around as easily as the Americans; in fact, almost all Chinese filmmakers stayed in the Chinese part of the city, with some gaining access to the trenches of the Chinese soldiers engaged in intense ground fighting with Japanese troops. Chinese filmmakers had no access to the Japanese side, nor did they have access to the operations of non-Japanese colonial troops in Shanghai. In terms of production time, Chinese films took much longer to be completed and exhibited than their American counterparts. The latter had been exhibited in the United States and around the world as early as February and March, and exhibition toward the end of March was already considered late.[23] Chinese news films began to hit the cinemas in Shanghai in May, two months after the battle ended, and shortly after the official truce was signed on May 5. The slow production was likely due to the significant damage experienced by film studios and the lack of exhibition space, as screenings of patriotic anti-Japanese films were banned in the "neutral" foreign settlements, while in the Chinese part of the city, film theaters suffered severe damages.

In other words, while the Battle of Shanghai created an opportunity for the American newsreel to reinvent itself and strengthen the cult of the omnipresent newsreel cameraman, to the Chinese filmmakers, it highlighted the incommensurability of the newsreel format with Chinese realities, an incommensurability that could be understood in both spatial and temporal terms. Even though both were shot on location, American newsreels transcended spatial limitations and were quick in the making. Chinese ones, on the contrary, were fully emplaced in the part of the city suffering the heaviest destruction. Their production was slowed considerably, and they faced an audience directly affected by the war.

Filmmakers, critics, and audiences grasped this incommensurability not instantly but gradually, during the processes of production, exhibition, and criticism. Forced to compete with Hollywood newsreels, Chinese film companies had long internalized Hollywood's evaluative criteria. Advertisements in *Shen bao* for the earliest released Chinese productions promised stimulating and authentic war spectacles filmed on location by risk-taking filmmakers, similar to how Hollywood newsreels would be promoted. The publicity for Lianhua's *History of Shanghai Battles* (*Shanghai zhanshi*), the first film to meet the audience, claimed the film would display "blood splashes in Shanghai, infinitely stimulating, heavy and dynamic," even though critics found that the film consisted mostly of scenes of refugees and Red Cross operations, with few actual battle scenes. To hunt for authentic battle scenes, some Chinese film companies sought footage from non-Chinese filmmakers. Others created fake battle scenes either with reenactments or by perusing imported newsreels of other wars.[24] When advertising their production *The Glorious History of the Nineteenth Route Army* (*Shijiulujun guangrongshi*), the Huimin Studio went as far as to give its "word of honor" that the film consisted of nothing but "all real action," with no recycled battle image from other wars cut into the film. "Down with fake battle films claiming to be shot on site!" they proclaimed. "Though war films are many, only ours is real."[25]

This scramble for authenticity, however, soon led to the question of what authenticity meant in these circumstances. Did it simply mean getting the most sensational battle images on camera? American companies could celebrate the newsreel cameramen's achievements of rendering remote sufferings visible across the world, facing no quibbles about profiting off such images. Chinese companies, filming on the wreckage of war, faced greater public scrutiny. In film criticism, what became gradually foregrounded was the ethics of representation. Shanghai critics were vigilant toward film companies' opportunistic behavior. One critic wrote, "Since the eruption of the Sino-Japanese War in Shanghai, there have been countless victims, but the film world has gained huge opportunities, and they all put capital together to make war films."[26] Beyond the issue of making a profit from their compatriots' sufferings, there was also a general sense that war images could be easily turned into pleasurable spectacle, rather than arousing empathy and indignation for the victims. The emotional distance of American neutrality was undesirable for Chinese filmmakers and audiences.

As ethics and empathy were increasingly seen as foundational to an authentic news film of the Battle of Shanghai, fictionalization emerged as a possible solution proposed by critics. Criticizing the "lack of vision" of the Chinese film studios, one commentator wrote, "If the film companies had vision, they'd try to make ingenious use of the material from the unprecedented Battle of Shanghai, to create films with a plotline. By doing so, the films would not only provide the audience with stimulation and excitement, but also imprint the enemy's brutality onto people's brains and arouse their patriotic feelings. The power of [plot-driven films] is much stronger than war films in the news style."[27] Other commentators echoed this sentiment. Reviewing six domestic news films on the Battle of Shanghai, one critic wrote, "Each film has strengths and shortcomings, but, in a manner of speaking, all are just news films." The critic suggested adding plot to news films for the purpose of creating emotional resonance with the audience.[28]

One wonders whether these critics advocating for fictionalization might have been anticipating Cheng Bugao's *Battle of Shanghai*, which, at the time of their writing, was in production at the Mingxing Company. Released fairly late, in July–August 1932, the film was said to combine the best of news and drama films. The only domestically produced sound film on the subject, its actuality footage was said to have been shot on location with great risk to the filmmakers (though Cheng's memoir decades later admitted that there had also been reenactments).[29] Meanwhile, the filmmakers "resorted to the art of film and drama" by including a fictional part centered on a few protagonists played by Mingxing's star actors: a grocery store owner and his daughter (a school teacher) and son (a high school student), both working as volunteers to help war victims in the Chinese part of the city.[30]

Combining battle footage and fiction cinema was not a new idea for filmmakers in China. As it was costly to re-create battle scenes, Shanghai filmmakers had frequently used actuality footage, shot by themselves or from stock films, to save on costs when making fiction films. Lai Manwai, for example, had reused his own actuality films in fiction films. His filmmaking of the Northern Expedition, discussed in chapter 1, resulted not only in the documentary *War on Sea, Land, and Air* but also in a fiction film entitled *Romance on the Battlefield* (*Zhandi qingtian*), released in 1928, which was a love story set during the Northern Expedition and liberally used actuality footage to create a grand and realistic backdrop.[31] During the Battle of Shanghai, the Tianyi Company reportedly purchased actuality footage from the American newsreel cameraman Charles Hugo for the making of the fiction film *Two Orphan Girls on Battlefield* (*Zhandi ergunü*).[32]

While these earlier cases used actuality footage as a backdrop to support dramatic development, the priority in Cheng's film was placed squarely on actuality, with the fictional part serving to frame the news footage and create further emotional depth and orientation. Advertised as a news film, the film's publicity material differentiated it from conventional newsreels. There were no "opportunistic" motives, the advertisement claimed, citing the film's belated release as a virtue, as longer production time meant higher production costs and more serious investments in the film. Not your typical newsreel that was swiftly made and then quickly forgotten, this film was made to last, for the purpose of "producing a great and timeless memento" of the tragic event.[33]

A war film destroyed by subsequent wars, *Battle of Shanghai* is no longer extant. What we know from contemporary film reviews is that it looked different from news films or drama films, leading to puzzlement among critics over how to read it. The fictional characters were not well-developed, but perhaps the real protagonists of the film were the soldiers, crowds, and the city itself, wrote one critic, who offered "trigger warnings" to viewers on how overwhelming their emotions might be when the Northern Railway Station and the Commercial Press were bombed into ruins and intense fighting appeared on the screen.[34] *Battle of Shanghai* was a box office hit. It ran from late July through late December 1932, attracting such a large audience that additional screenings had to be arranged.[35] Following this success, Cheng continued with his experiments between documentary and fiction. In the year after the release of *Battle of Shanghai*, he made two films, *Torrent* and *Spring Silkworm*, in collaboration with the leftist dramatist Xia Yan. Both were among the earliest left-wing films emerging from Shanghai, and both were, to varying degrees, docu-fiction hybrids.

Scholars have long observed documentary's absence from left-wing cinema of the 1930s. As Laikwan Pang writes, "There was hardly any voice heard in 1930s' Chinese left-wing cinema circles advocating the use of documentaries, which were produced and watched in China since the 1900s." Instead, she argues that the realist project of leftist cinema was "closely conjoined with, or constantly contaminated by, its sentimentalism and fictional aspects." Pang suggests that left-wing filmmakers' choice of fiction, and particularly melodrama, over documentary had to do with leftist cinema's embedment in Shanghai's commercial film industry: the profit imperative meant that filmmakers had to entertain a broad viewership, whose preferences had been shaped by China's historical narrative traditions that favored sentimental morality tales and sagas.[36]

Cheng Bugao's engagement with and innovations in news films bring further understanding to Chinese filmmakers' choices between documentary and fiction in this period. Certainly, box office considerations played a role in Cheng's adoption of a fictional framing in *Battle of Shanghai*: after all, Mingxing's popular stars played the fictional characters. Yet the fictional elements of *Battle of Shanghai* did not imbue the film with melodramatic excess. Instead, in a manner more related to reportage literature than to melodrama, the film's fictional framing pieced together fragmentary footage due to constrained access and anchored war footage in empathetical subject positions to offer an indigenous alternative to the infotainment of the American newsreel.

Originally a French word referring to journalistic work in general, *reportage* in the 1920s had developed into an important mode of agitational investigative writing in left-wing literary movements around the world. In China, reportage literature had emerged after the May Fourth Movement in 1919 and grown along with leftist politics in the mid- to late-1920s, before becoming the endorsed mode of writing by the League of Leftwing Writers upon its founding in 1930. In his book-length study of Chinese reportage literature, Charles Laughlin observes that from its early days, reportage had served as a critical alternative to mainstream journalism. I began the chapter with the May 30 massacre in 1925, documented by Chen Jianran's film. May 30 and the subsequent workers' and students' movement also brought a flourishing of reportage literature: critiquing the procapital and noncommittal reporting by Shanghai's mainstream newspapers, such as *Shen bao*, left-wing intellectuals resorted to reportage to offer impassioned eyewitness accounts of police killing and founded *Truth Daily* (*Gongli ribao*) to report on the workers' movement. Having eschewed the liberal notion of journalistic objectivism, reportage as a mode of nonfiction writing drew from the Chinese tradition of personal essay and travel literature to ground empirical investigation and personal, subjective experience. As Laughlin writes, "Reportage authors attempt to make actual historical experience meaningful, to rescue the truth of actual events from the hollowing, reifying effects of journalistic objectivity." Furthermore, Laughlin notes that this subjective experience was not located in the psychological depth of a bounded individual. Instead, it was to unfold in emplacement, as the writer visited places, encountered events and people, and responded to the dynamics of the political and social ecology in which the writer found him or herself.[37]

In other words, if the lone, conflicted hero of realist fiction was too much of a product of capitalist modernity to capture the interconnectedness of historical experience, reportage shifted attention from interiority to environment, subjectivity to intersubjectivity.

Reportage literature rarely featured fictionalized characters; the personal voice tended to be that of the reportage writer, who traveled on location and described what they saw. The fictional characters in *Battle of Shanghai* served similar narrative functions. Not engaging in melodrama, the fictional characters stood in for the filmmaker and served as eyewitnesses to the devastation of their home city. In Cheng's other films, such as *Torrent* and *Spring Silkworm*, fictional characters did support some melodrama, but their roles in interrogating representations of historical events and in witnessing and anchoring historical experiences never diminished.

Torrent: From News Film to Left-wing Cinema

> *"September 18" "January 28"—machine guns, airplanes, bombs, canons. . . . All kinds of intense sounds, a big stimulation of the spirit—reactions—changes—finding a way out—transformation of the thoughts—social transformation—the film world has also transformed.*
>
> —Cheng Bugao

In his essay on the making of *Torrent* in 1933, Cheng Bugao wrote about the Japanese invasion of Manchuria on September 18, 1931, and the bombing of Shanghai on January 28, 1932, as what prompted transformations in his mind and in filmmaking.[38] Having intimately experienced the Shanghai bombing of 1932 when making *Battle of Shanghai*, Cheng brought this transformative experience into his later films.

One of the harbingers of the left-wing film movement, *Torrent*, like *Battle of Shanghai*, was a hybrid film combining fiction and documentary. Set in Fu village, about fifty kilometers upstream from the city of Hankow, and in Hankow itself, the film tells the story of poor villagers struggling to defend their homes from a flood while the corrupt landlord has stolen funds for disaster relief, escaped to the city, and refused to help the villagers fight for their lives. There is a subplot of a love story between Fu's daughter Xiujuan and the schoolteacher Tiesheng, who leads the villagers in their struggles against the flood and the landlord. Played by Mingxing's most popular stars, the young lovers and their story of separation and misunderstanding were clearly meant to satisfy fans of the stars and audiences attracted to melodrama. Yet the film's main message was left-wing: it drew attention to class struggles intensified by a disaster that displaced and killed the poor, while further enriching the powerful.

Cheng had conceived the idea for the film when making a news film for the Mingxing Company in the Hankow region during a devastating flood of the Yangtze River in 1931. The news film was commissioned by an organization in Hankow for the purpose of raising funds for disaster relief. In his memoir, Cheng wrote about the massive loss of human and animal lives he witnessed in the region during a monthlong stay to shoot the film. In contrast to the Shanghai bombing a year later, the devastation wrought by the flood was not as visible. "A large lake, calm as a mirror, looked very poetic. Some told me that it had been a slum, with several hundred homes, countless parents and children, sisters and brothers, couples and friends. With no money to defend themselves against the flood, and no support to help them evacuate, all were drowned."[39] The only traces of this massive loss of life that could be seen were household objects, dead animals, and children floating past; refugees, stranded on roofs of submerged houses, wasting away from hunger and waiting in vain for rescue.

The submerged devastation in the countryside formed a stark contrast to urban Hankow's unperturbed sights and sounds. Upon arriving in Hankow, Cheng found a city well-fortressed and bustling with entertainment. The streets were flooded, but instead of presenting a threat, the flooding created a special atmosphere of fun and romance. The upper floors of Western-style mansions kept the wealthy dry and allowed occupants to leisurely drink wine and watch the flood from the safety of their balconies. Fashionable upper-class young men and women eyed each other from their small boats on their way to entertainment venues open for music and dance.[40] Around the same body of water, Cheng observed great differences between the city and the countryside, and between the classes.

In 1933, when Cheng met with Xia Yan, the left-wing dramatist and reportage writer newly hired by Mingxing, to discuss their collaboration, Cheng suggested repurposing the news film he shot during the 1931 flood within the framework of a fiction film. The fictional element in *Battle of Shanghai* aligned the news film's subject position with the residents of the Chinese area of the city. The fictional film of *Torrent* had further ambitions. Instead of emplacement and empathy, it sought connection and analysis by probing into larger hidden power structures that allowed the devastation to happen, and in the process, it also reflected on cinema's mediating roles.

The film made a remarkable spatial intervention: it shortened the distance between the city and countryside, allowing the viewer to understand the two spaces as connected, with the former in an exploitative relationship with the latter. The underlying structure of exploitation was manifested in the melodramatic plot of the struggle between the landlord who has relocated to a safer urban dwelling with stolen government funding, and the villagers who are left to fend for themselves without aid. Also exploitative was the spectatorial relationship in which the rich are equipped with technologies of vision and mobility, and the poor are rendered into objects of ridicule and spectacularization. Binoculars allow the landlord Mr. Fu and his family to entertain themselves by watching people perish in the flood from their balcony. A motor boat enables the Fu family to tour the flooded sites. *Torrent* presented the news footage of the flood from Mr. Fu's and his family's points of view, either framed within a binocular shot or shot from a moving motor boat, which Cheng had indeed hired (much like Mr. Fu) when making the news film.

Weihong Bao has offered a masterful reading of *Torrent*, particularly the scenes in which Mr. Fu and his family consume the spectacles of the flood through a mobilized virtual gaze.[41] I argue further here that this mobilized virtual gaze, available to the rich, in fact shares the same privileges as that of a news cameraman, and we can understand this scene as offering a reflexive critique of the news film and of Cheng's own role as a news filmmaker. Indeed, in 1931, when he shot the news film of the flood, the Mingxing Company had heavily invested in sound technology and aspired to vertically integrate like its Hollywood counterparts. To produce its own news films was part of Mingxing's ambitions. Like the American newsreel cameramen, Cheng moved freely between the countryside and the city, between hapless flood victims and wealthy urban dwellers, and his film was meant to arouse the charitable sentiments of the latter. In terms of making distant suffering into an image, the news filmmaker's camera was not unlike Mr. Fu's binoculars, and his travels were "in the same boat" with the Fu family. Fiction here served to creatively treat the actuality footage, illustrating how easily images of distant suffering could lapse into spectacle, while creating a hidden mise-en-abyme that explored the reflexive potential of cinema.

Spring Silkworm: Between Layers of Realities

After the success of *Torrent*, Cheng Bugao and Xia Yan collaborated on their second film, *Spring Silkworm*. Released later in 1933, it was an adaptation of a novella of the same title by Mao Dun (Shen Yanbing), a leading writer in the New Literature movement. Set in a village in Zhejiang with a long tradition of silkworm cultivation, the film tells the story of silkworm farmer Old Tongbao, who works with his family and neighbors to ensure a good silk cocoon harvest, only to descend even deeper into debt as Japanese dumping of cheap artificial silk in the Chinese market causes the price of silk cocoons to plummet.

The story explored a crucial question that Cheng and Xia had already begun to ask with *Torrent*, namely, how could one grasp one's real conditions of existence, when the experiential world one lived in no longer sufficed to offer this knowledge? A good harvest traditionally meant a secure livelihood. Old Tongbao had every reason to expect it to happen again. Yet with China's economic integration into the global capitalist economy, commodity prices were no longer determined by local demand and supply, and local products faced competition from imported goods. While *Torrent* juxtaposed class difference and dramatized class struggle to reveal rural devastation as resulting from systemic oppression rather than an isolated natural disaster, *Spring Silkworm* adopted a different strategy. Set mostly in the village, *Spring Silkworm* does not engage in melodrama of any sort: no heartbreaking love stories, no struggles between good peasants and evil landlords. Instead, the production was intimately tied to the life cycle of silkworms as it documented silkworm farming as work, ritual, and a communal way of life for villagers. Along with this concrete reality of silkworm farming, however, lurks another reality of world markets and capital, which stays invisible and abstract most of the time in the film, surfacing only here and there, in gossip about silk prices, in small shipments of imported goods into the village, and when Old Tongbao borrows money at a high interest from the local wealthy residents. In other words, Cheng and Xia did not create a drama of two visible and concrete class opponents struggling with each other, as they had in *Torrent*. Instead, here the drama occurs between two layers of realities: the phenomenological realities of agricultural work and harvesting in the village, and the more abstract but no less real world of commodity prices and global capitalism. The film reaches its climax when these two realities clash with each other, plunging Old Tongbao and his family into debt and despair.

The "documentary" aesthetic of *Spring Silkworm* was unmistakable. The process of silkworm cultivation was depicted so true-to-life that when screened at Pordenone Silent Film Festival in 1995, the film was described in the catalog as "an almost semi-documentary drama about a family of silkworm-growers in a village outside Shanghai. Every stage of the process is meticulously charted, giving the film at times a Flaherty-like flavor, despite being shot in a studio."[42] In his memoir, Cheng Bugao describes the filmmaking process: "The film's main character were the silkworms. In order to do a good job, the company hired three expert [silkworm cultivators] from Suzhou to help raise silkworms at the studio and bought six pieces of silkworm seed-paper for use." The production of the film, like in documentary filmmaking, was attuned to the actual life processes of the filmed subject, allowing the contingencies of these processes to shape the filmmaking process. "How much the silkworms grew, that was how much we filmed." Despite the high opportunity cost, Mingxing vacated one of the company's two studios and devoted it entirely to silkworm rearing and the making of this film. Filming the silkworms' life cycle in a studio turned out to be a challenging task. Intense lights killed a batch of baby silkworms just hatched from the eggs, and another batch during the silkworm's shedding of its old skin, or molt. The rest survived the filming and grew to maturity. When they began to spin silk cocoons, Cheng and his colleagues slept in the studio and filmed every three hours for one day and two nights to document the cocooning process with time-lapse cinematography (fig. 2.2).[43]

Besides the silkworms' life stages, the film also took pains to document the rich material and ritualistic processes of traditional silkworm cultivation, enacted by actors following expert cultivators' instructions. When writing about early industrial films, Tom Gunning observes that these films tended to depict

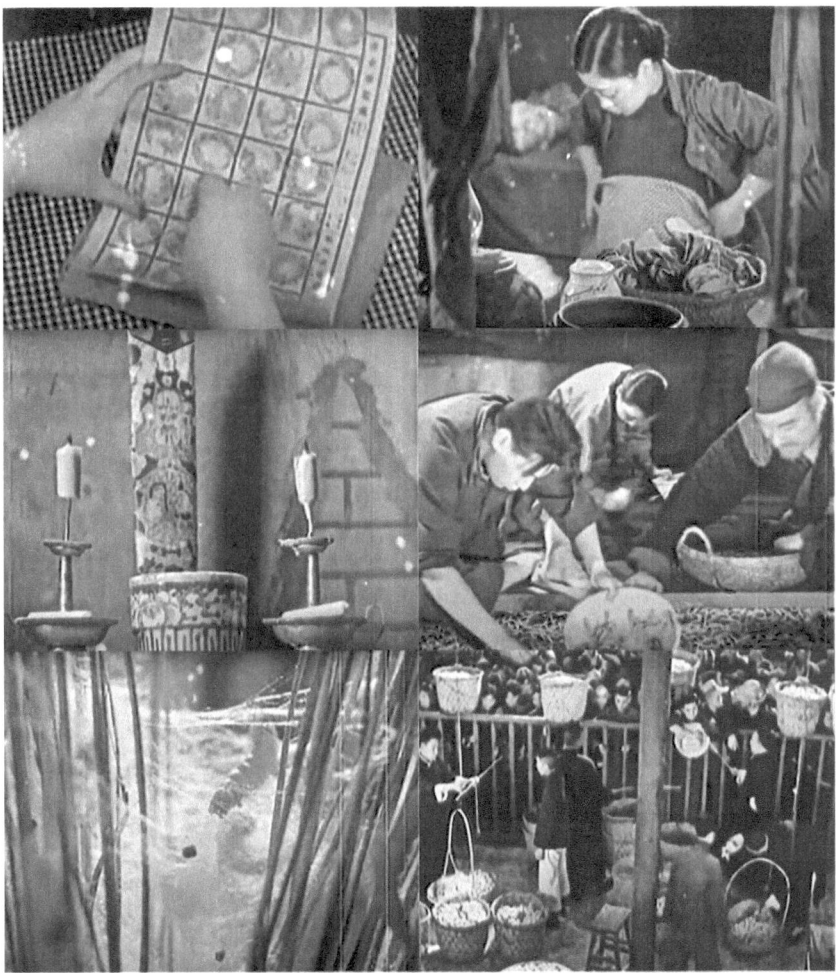

2.2 The process of raising silkworms in *Spring Silkworm*.

processes of industrial production, which transformed raw material into consumer goods. Culminating in "scenes of pleasurable consumption of the manufactured good within a comfortable or even glamorous bourgeois interior," these films, for Gunning, enacted a "basic narrative of industrial capitalism."[44] In chapter 1 I discussed how American industrial films had been used as early as the 1910s to modernize Chinese silk farming. In the 1920s the University of Nanking (Jinling daxue), founded by American missionaries, also used and made educational films to teach Chinese farmers how to select and grow cotton breeds more suited for industrial processing.[45] Cheng Bugao would have been familiar with these process films. Indeed, he had often depicted production processes in his films, including the process of filmmaking itself: his *Amorous History of the Silver Screen* (1931) offered an on-screen tour of a film studio, guided by protagonists who worked in the studio and could explain the filmmaking process to the audience. Yet by attending to the precarity of those whose labor sustained such production processes, Cheng's "process films" deviated from the "basic capitalist narrative" and disrupted simple, happy endings. In *The Amorous History of the Silver Screen*, an actress worried about her own obsolescence, as she could no longer catch up with the increasing technologization at the studio. *Spring Silkworm* was an elegy for preindustrial silkworm farming, whose laboring process was deeply embedded in the rituals and rhythms of communal lives. The bountiful harvest at the end of the production process led not to satisfaction and fulfillment, but to bewilderment, despair, and the shattering of the farmers' life worlds, as they found themselves deeper in debt than if they had produced nothing at all.

Upon its release, *Spring Silkworm* attracted polarized reviews. Many praised its realism. The film was "undoubtedly a miracle that happened in the film sector in 1933," wrote the critic Yao Sufeng: "Without slogans, fantasy, or exaggerated drama to unleash brute and empty emotional release, it captured reality and depicted, with great precision and texture, the destinies of Chinese peasants and Chinese silk production under imperial encroachment. It gave us deep thoughts, resonance and experience."[46] The critic Ling He wrote, "Unlike many Chinese films that arbitrarily transplant foreign life and sensibilities into Chinese cinema," *Spring Silkworm* offered a realistic depiction of the Chinese countryside.[47] Others, however, criticized the film as flat, boring, and uncinematic. The harshest criticism came from the critics Huang Jiamo and Liu Na'ou, who would soon engage in a hard versus soft cinema debate with left-wing critics and filmmakers. Their criticism of *Spring Silkworm* foreshadowed the arguments they would put forth in support of a "soft cinema." Huang's main criticism of *Spring Silkworm* was its lack of visual pleasure: "The biggest problem is the lack of interesting favor (*quwei*). Even though life in China's countryside is dull, with skillful direction one could still make a few fresh and lively scenes to suit the appetite of urban viewers. Yet this film is set against a boring background, with a very scattered narrative structure, and particularly uneconomical editing."⁴⁸ For Liu Na'ou, the film was neither a documentary nor a drama. Some might say it was a documentary (*jishi dianying*), but the film did not consistently employ realism and visualize all growth stages of silkworms, Liu complained. As a drama, its structure was too scattered, and its climax, hinging on the low price of silk cocoons, was too abstract to create dramatic intensity. In short, Liu wrote, "The film *Spring Silkworm* could be said to trouble audiences' viewing habits with unrecognizable images."⁴⁹

Cheng Bugao and Xia Yan responded to some of these criticisms in a panel discussion organized by the Shanghai *Morning Post* (*Chenbao*). "Many felt the film 'had too little drama,' the tempo [original English] was too slow. There are reasons for that," Xia explained. "This is not a melodrama [original English], but a sketch (*sumiao*) in the extreme, and to adopt it for film involved substantial risk." After expressing gratitude to the Mingxing company for tolerating this unconventional choice, Xia continued, "We chose this subject because we felt the issue of silk production was worth paying attention to (and since I raised silkworms in childhood, I was very interested), and the novella *Spring Silkworm* not only provided a realistic sketch of the problem of silk, but also attempted a serious answer to the rural problem by connecting it to the entire social economic structure. So when writing the screenplay, I paid a lot of attention to the point of 'education.' And the filming of *Spring Silkworm* also adopted the method of 'documentary cinema' (*jilu dianying*) for this reason." Cheng described how he attempted to retain the "tune" (*diaozi*) of the novella in the film, saying that the work "is a sketch [original in English], quiet, delicate. Every paragraph and sentence has real emotions and flavors to it. I tried to transmit these real emotions and flavors through every scene, every shot."⁵⁰

Both Cheng's and Xia's discussions used the word "sketch," both in English and in Chinese as *sumiao*. In this time period, "sketch" was also found written in Chinese as *suxie*, *texie*, and even in transliteration as *sugaiji*, referring to quick and brief documentation of observation and impression. When used in fine arts, the term most often meant quick life drawings on site, which became common practice only in the 1920s and 1930s, as Western fine arts and photography changed the way painting was done in China.⁵¹ In literature, it was mostly used in association with reportage literature to designate short explorative and impressionistic writing.

As mentioned earlier, reportage literature was a flourishing new mode of writing in the late 1920s and 1930s in China. While *Spring Silkworm* was a novella, Mao Dun was a veteran in reportage writing. He had penned the reportage "The Afternoon of May Thirtieth" (*Wuyue sanshiri de xiawu*) in 1925, addressing the police massacre of workers which culminated in the May Thirtieth Movement that began this chapter. In 1936 he launched an ambitious project called "One Day in China," soliciting writings from people of all walks of life across the country, on events that happened to them on May 21, 1936. The resulting anthology depicted life in China in a broad cross-section.[52] With Xia Yan—himself also a reportage writer—adapting Mao Dun's "sketch" of the Chinese countryside into cinema, *Spring Silkworm* could be seen as a cinematic experiment at the onset of left-wing filmmaking to move away from the default mode of cinema at the time (namely, melodrama) with the help of the documentary aesthetics of reportage. And this experiment could not have materialized without Cheng Bugao's long engagement with and innovations in the news film and docu-fiction, from *Battle of Shanghai* to *Torrent*.

Besides reportage, the experiment of *Spring Silkworm* also drew from other media, such as print journalism, news films, and educational cinema. While the life cycles of the silkworms and the work of silkworm cultivation determined the film's texture, tempo, and attention to everyday material practices, *Spring Silkworm* did include one sequence set outside the village. The film begins with a teacher giving a lecture on China's traditional silkworm cultivation in an urban school classroom. It then cuts to the Shanghai harbor where artificial silk from Japan is being unloaded to be sold to the Chinese market. An intertitle gives a table of statistics on the volume of imported Japanese artificial silk. Newspaper clippings on Japanese silk monopolizing the Euro-American market appear on the screen, stacking on top of each other and progressively magnifying in an animation sequence. Cheng Bugao attributed the inclusion of the statistics table to the screenwriter Xia Yan: "The screenwriter added a lot of statistical materials, which the novel didn't have, but in my personal opinion, they had great effects. It was an innovative method for cinema."[53]

Despite being submerged in fiction films, persistent engagements with documentary modes of filmmaking were at the very onset of left-wing filmmaking, counteracting the melodramatic tendency, supporting formal innovations, and asking fundamental questions about how to use cinema's capacities in photographic realism and temporal-spatial manipulation to discern the layers of realities in which one lived.

Small-Scale Films

When writing on China's left-wing film movement, Laikwan Pang observes a missed opportunity to develop a "real extensive proletarian film movement" in China using the 16mm film technology.[54] Strong interest existed among Chinese left-wing filmmakers in using small-scale cinema (*xiaoxing dianying*) to launch a proletarian film movement. In an essay published in June 1930, the filmmaker Shen Xiling praised small-scale cinema, and 16mm film in particular, for its low cost, portability, and running time, and suggested using this technology to make and screen films in factories and villages to counteract the commercial film industry. In September 1931 a directive issued by the Leftwing Dramatists Association also included small-scale cinema in its recommendation: "Besides writing film scripts for and sending our members to different film companies, we should also prepare funding to produce our own films . . . using 'small-scale cinema' to record the situations of factory workers and the peasantry."[55]

What would have happened if these plans had materialized? Pang conjectures:

> Documentaries might have been developed on a much larger scale, and Chinese audiences might have been able to accept a wide range of styles in narrative films. Aesthetically, it might have freed up the stability of many cinematic techniques designed for narrative films and allowed more experimentation. Politically, this film movement might have been more intimately controlled by the Party and able to present a strong revolutionary ideology more forcefully. In fact, a real extensive proletarian film movement might have been realized for the first time anywhere in history. But none of these events happened, and the left-wing cinema movement continued its own historical trajectory.[56]

Pang is right that this was indeed a missed opportunity. As she argues in her book, left-wing filmmakers worked at the commercial film studios and had to rely on popular genres such as melodrama to maintain films' entertainment value. I demonstrated in the previous section that space for formal experimentation did exist in the film studios, and documentary played an important role in such experimentation. Overall, however, such space was indeed limited. The 16mm film technology could have allowed filmmakers more independence from the commercial film studios and more room for innovation. It was unclear why leftist filmmakers did not manage to harness the new small-scale film technology in the early 1930s. Pang suggests that the cost, though much lower than that of 35mm filmmaking, was still prohibitive. The lack of technical expertise could be another reason. No matter what the reason was, as far as we know, small-scale cinema became a reality for left-wing filmmaking only in 1938, when the Communist Party arranged for filmmaker Yuan Muzhi to acquire a 16mm camera and film stock in Hong Kong. Yuan then traveled to Yan'an with one 16mm camera and one 35mm Kinamo, a gift from Joris Ivens, to start filmmaking in the CCP base areas.

Despite not being in the hands of left-wing filmmakers until much later, and absent in film historiography so far, small-scale filmmaking did exist in China. When Shen Xiling wrote about the technology in 1930, small-scale films in 16mm and 9.5mm had already been made in homes and institutions, as amateur and educational film. Institutional production of educational films in the 16mm was to develop rapidly in the 1930s with the support of the Nationalist state.[57] For lack of space, I will focus in this chapter on amateur small-scale filmmaking, tracing its aesthetic and political contributions to the evolving practices of documentary cinema in China.

Small-Scale Amateur Film in Shanghai

Many of the amateur filmmakers in Shanghai's late 1920s and early 1930s were foreign settlers, and their numbers grew steadily. Shanghai saw the founding of its first "Amateur Film League" in November 1929. The league had fifty members to start with, but the membership doubled in size by January the following year.[58] Between December 1929 and July 1930, the league hosted at least seven monthly film contests at the Japanese Club and the YMCA, among other venues. Each contest had set themes, such as "winter" for the first and "rain in Shanghai" for the seventh. The Kodak service station in Shanghai, the league's corporate supporter, sent experts to serve on the jury and supplied prizes—Kodak cameras and film stock—for the contest winners. Though the league was open to all nationalities, most members belonged to Shanghai's Japanese-speaking community, including those hailing from colonial Taiwan. Japanese-speaking contestants received the majority of all contest prizes. The top two winners in the second contest in January 1930, for example, were both employees at the Taiwan Bank.

The inaugural issue of the Amateur Cinema League's Japanese-language bulletin, published in January 1930, has survived, allowing us a glimpse into how Japanese-speaking practitioners in Shanghai conceived this cinema. "Never bending for a second, time flows. The momentum of time changes the appearance of everything. Our human existence is merely a brief moment in the expansive universe," a man named Masaru wrote in the inaugural essay. Life was an unbearable burden, and humans shared the agonizing destiny of having to leave their younger generation behind and disappear from existence, he lamented. Cinema could serve as a means to remedy this passage of time. "To tell this short history of survival as it is, cinema has immense value," Masaru said. "From theater to family! From streets to residence! Ah, time flows, and therefore cinema came to be taken seriously within the family."[59]

While Masaru saw cinema as a means of preserving personal memories for the family, another contributor, Masuo, in his essay "16mm Films Set Against the Backdrop of the Great Shanghai," wrote about the promotional activities of camera suppliers and the enthusiastic response this new technology received from the Japanese-speaking community. Masuo's first encounter with 16mm and 9.5mm amateur films was at screenings cohosted by the American Eastman Kodak company and the Japanese company Chiyo Yoko Photo Supplies in July 1930. Not many Japanese in Shanghai had seen these home movies then,

Masuo wrote, yet by December that year, when the newly founded Amateur Film League organized its first contest at the Japanese Club, more than four hundred people showed up despite the rain, including filmmakers and their family members, to see the twelve participating films. Masuo observed that camera sales increased exponentially thereafter.[60]

The popularity of amateur filmmaking among the Japanese-speaking diaspora in Shanghai certainly begs further research. What can be gleaned from the single surviving issue of the league pamphlet is, first, an interest in using cinema to strengthen the family. When traditional family ties had been severed by migration, cinema was seen as a means to aid the reproduction of family relations in the diaspora. Meanwhile, there was also an excitement about exploring the city space of cosmopolitan Shanghai, where the amateur filmmakers hoped to build new homes and communities. Finally, similar to most amateur filmmakers around the world, league members were fascinated by film technology and the creative opportunities it afforded. Claiming to be a complete amateur with no previous experience with filmmaking, a contributor, Ginma, shared with the readers some technical tips he had learned from his own experiments with lighting and aperture, concluding, "Since the beginning, cinema as a business has been too viewer-oriented. 16mm film offers a different world of a pure and free spirit. . . . As they say, 'Pay no attention to the muscles of experts, no tricks, tastes, or conventions, this is a field of pure art. In front of us, amateur explorers of 16mm film extend a new, infinite, virginal land that should be opened up.'"[61]

Amateur filmmaking was also practiced among European and American settlers in Shanghai, as well as among the Chinese population. As early as 1926, English-language newspapers reported exhibitions of amateur films made by foreign residents of Shanghai on events in the city, such as horse races. In 1934 the *Shanghai Times* interviewed a man named G. C. Large involved in the organization of another amateur film group in Shanghai. By then, the mainly Japanese Amateur Film League had stopped its activities. Large estimated there were "hundreds of amateur cinematographers in Shanghai, some of them were experts," and expressed his wish to build a society according to the model of amateur film clubs in Euro-America. The society could organize film contests and pool resources to produce films based on stories from local authors. "The possibilities for work in the outlying districts are almost unlimited and Shanghai contains a wealth of material for plays unequalled by any other city in the world."[62]

Meanwhile, from September to November 1934, a serialized essay with forty installments entitled "On Small-Scale Cinema" (*Xiaoxing dianying lun*) was published in the *Min bao*, a daily newspaper affiliated with the Nationalist Party. Praising small-scale cinema for "liberating film from the cinemas," the author, Liang Cheng, explained that professional filmmaking, due to its high technical requirements, needed trained actors, set designers, and other professional talent. Small-scale cinema, on the other hand, "belongs entirely to the amateur: it's mobile, requires no professional actors, and opposes indoor filming. With a grounded realism (*xieshi zhuyi*), it makes everything real (*xianshihua*). This is the specificity of small-scale cinema."[63] In daily installments, Liang wrote about small-scale cinema's independence from the capitalist film industry, which enabled cinema to be "liberated" from commodity status and allowed it to be employed by families and organizations to fulfill artistic and social aspirations.[64] He also discussed the diverse forms that small-scale cinema could take. "Small-scale cinema can have the flavor of novels, but also the flavor of essays [or] sketches.... [It] can create poetry as well as academic papers. It can be used as a sketch to describe everything." Liang's vision for small-scale cinema was aligned with documentary modes of filmmaking, listing "scenery film (*fengjing dianying*), actuality (*shixie dianying*), news film (*xinwen dianying*), and documentary film (*jilu dianying*)" as its main categories.[65] Filmmakers could film their own family life, especially children, who could act uninhibited before a camera. They could film on their way to work, creating an impression of city life "from the moving wheels of buses, trams, bicycles, and amid them, the handsome modern girls, the innocent children, men, women, the old and the young."[66] Beyond the urban scenes, life in the countryside could be made into small-scale films, too. Inspiration for small-scale films could come from all sources, including prose poetry, folk songs, nursery rhymes, even children's elementary school textbooks. Liang created sample shooting scripts to show how one could turn the talented music composer Nie Er's *Song of the Harbor Workers* (*Matou gongren ge*), Zhong Jingwen's folk poetry, and texts from school textbooks into small-scale films.[67]

Up to this point, my discussion of amateur cinema has been largely confined to written sources. Few personal films from the 1920s and 1930s survive to allow for textual analysis. An exception to this is Liu Na'ou's *Man Who Holds a Movie Camera*, filmed in 1933 on a 9.5mm Pathé Baby camera and discovered in the late 1990s, in the attic of the Liu family house in southern Taiwan. With its title paying tribute to Dziga Vertov, whom Liu had introduced to Chinese readers in his numerous theoretical writings, this film is a home movie and travelogue covering four locations: Liu's hometown of Tainan, Tokyo, Fengtian (present-day Shenyang) in Manchuria, and Guangzhou in the south of China.[68]

A Man Who Holds a Movie Camera: Liu Na'ou's Amateur Filmmaking

Liu Na'ou has already been mentioned as a critic of *Spring Silkworm*. Born to a prominent family in southern Taiwan in 1905, he attended high school and university in Tokyo before moving to Shanghai in 1928 to establish himself as a prominent member of the modernist literature and film circle.[69] Credited with introducing "New Sensationism" to the Chinese literary scene in the late 1920s, and among the leading voices advocating for a "soft cinema" in the early 1930s, Liu promoted avant-garde theories and represented an important strand of cinema thinking in the 1930s in Shanghai. As a producer and screenwriter, he also worked in the commercial film industry, writing, directing, and producing numerous films at the Yilian film company and other film studios, such as Mingxing and Yihua.

Little known during Liu's lifetime was the fact that he also made amateur films. It is unclear whether Liu Na'ou was connected to the Amateur Cinema League in Taiwan or Shanghai.[70] He was not listed in the inaugural bulletin of the Shanghai Amateur Cinema League, which included names, telephone numbers, and street addresses of its fifty-two earliest members. The league was mostly composed of amateurs shooting in 16mm.[71] Liu, who filmed on the cheaper 9.5mm, may not have qualified. Yet given his close connection to Japan, it is also possible that he might have engaged with the league quietly. Masaru, who wrote the inaugural essay for the league's bulletin, signed his name in the very unconventional kanji characters as 魔沙留 (Mosa Liu in the Chinese pronunciation). As Mosa could refer to Formosa, the Portuguese name for Taiwan, and Liu shares the same pronunciation with Liu Na'ou's surname, I am inclined to wonder if Masaru could be Liu writing under a tongue-in-cheek penname.

Liu's status in the literary and film world by 1930, as well as his connection to Japan, would certainly have made him an appropriate choice to inaugurate the bulletin. Yet this unproven, possibly far-fetched speculation only demonstrates the difficulty of researching an activity that was disavowed by the person engaging in it. Never in his writing did Liu mention his amateur filmmaking, nor is there any record of public screenings of his films. There could be many reasons for this disavowal. Patricia Zimmermann has described, in the context of American avant-garde filmmaking in the 1920s, how avant-garde filmmakers had disavowed amateurism to defend their own professional identity, which, she argues, obscured the close alignment between amateur cinema and the avant-garde in film history. Liu had been attempting to establish himself as a professional filmmaker and critic and may not have wished to publicize his amateur activities for a similar reason. Meanwhile, as anti-Japanese sentiments increased in China in the late 1920s and early 1930s, Liu tried to obscure the fact that he hailed from southern Taiwan, a Japanese colony, and was a Japanese colonial subject. He often referred to himself as from Fujian instead. Liu had reasons not to be seen as too close to Japanese establishments in Shanghai, such as the Amateur Cinema League. His film, documenting his hometown in Taiwan and his travels in Tokyo and colonial Manchuria, would have to be kept under wraps, too.

The fortunate survival of Liu Na'ou's amateur film offers us an opportunity to examine how his small-scale filmmaking and his theoretical work mutually informed each other. If the left-wing filmmakers, such as Cheng Bugao and Xia Yan, connected experiential realities to structural global realities by exploring the operations of capital and class, Liu's amateur filmmaking was aimed at reclaiming, to some extent, the autonomy of the experiential. By exploring aspects of life not entirely determined by the logic of capital or empire, his camera attended to familial relationships, friendships, and experiential relationships with land, water, clouds, and other aspects of the environment.

These explorations, carried out with a small-scale camera, not only restored, for Liu, dimensions of his personal life that had been disavowed but also affected his understanding of cinema. Scholars who have worked on Liu's theoretical writing on film know that he was not the most coherent writer. Seen as a dandy in his personal life, Liu's theoretical sampling was also broad and eclectic, drawing from European, American, Japanese, and Soviet sources.[72] His amateur film, however, offers insights into his shifting theoretical interests not as an eclectic sampling, but as arising from a process of hands-on experimentation and learning, which one can trace in these reels. Liu had prioritized montage as the "soul" of film, yet he became over time more and more interested in the film camera rather than the editing table as the interface between filmmakers and their immediate milieu. He had also harbored a modernist interest in visual abstraction, yet working with a small-scale camera, his efforts to create abstract patterns from his immediate surroundings were at most half-hearted. Instead, he reveled in pans, tracking shots, long takes, and other gestural camera movements that built relations between things and people and preserved shared experiences of a particular, concrete time and space. For Liu, it was through cinema—both the camera movements and the editing—that subject and object could come together as one, and the world could be made whole again in a cinematic reality, transcending existing categories or any effort at categorization.

On Home Ground: A Kino-Eye for Relationships

Commenting on Vertov's *Man with a Movie Camera* (1929) in 1932, Liu Na'ou wrote:

> Here there is no lead actor, or far-fetched plot. [The film's] aspiration is to represent a whole "life," a unified gathering of life (*jutuan shenghuo*) of the metropolis. At dawn, the man with a movie camera starts his walk around the city. He shows to the people, who are still asleep, the existence of these silent fragments. Then the city wakes up.... Families preparing for work, the crowds in the streets, all of this is depicted so smoothly and perfectly, with such

intimate emotion, and in an all-encompassing rhythm. . . . Thus, the film has two basic elements, the unified gathering of life of things and people on the streets, and the "man with a movie camera" who directs this gathering. The former is the object, the latter is the "Kinoglaz." The film's content is but the relationship between the two.[73]

In 1933, when Liu made his own amateur film, he didn't give the film a title, nor did he use his actual name as the filmmaker in the credits. Instead, at the beginning of the first reel, Liu simply credited the film in Japanese as "a work by the man who holds a camera" (*Kamera motsu otoko sakuhin*) and in English as "Film by the Man who has camera [*sic*]." Not signing with his actual name might have to do with the disavowal I discussed earlier, but Liu certainly had Vertov in mind and intended this amateur film to be a tribute.

Much like what he wrote about Vertov, in his own film Liu Na'ou also attempted to gather fragments and make a whole, although the two films exhibited very different aesthetics and had different points of departure. The word "hold" (*motsu*) in the Japanese title of Liu's film was significant, for Liu's handheld 9.5mm camera endowed the film with a flexibility and embodied expressiveness absent in Vertov's work. Vertov filmed in 35mm and on a tripod. Very rarely did the camera approximate human vision in a pan or a tilt or handheld motion. Instead, camera movements were almost always achieved by mounting the camera on a moving vehicle. Even though the filmmaker transported, directed, and manipulated the camera, the camera vision was largely disembodied and impersonal (except for a sequence in which the filmmaker performed a narrow escape from an approaching train, discussed later). This was desirably so, for the kino-eye was valued for its mechanical capacities that exceeded those of the human eye. In contrast, Liu filmed with a 9.5mm Pathé Baby camera, and almost all his footage was handheld. This allowed an embodied vision, and a much closer and more interactive relationship between the filmmaker and his subject, as he could approach and follow the latter's movement much more easily.

Earlier in this chapter I observed an emphasis on the family in amateur film discourse in Shanghai, exemplified by the Japanese-language bulletin published by the Amateur Cinema League, and by a Chinese-language serialized article by Liang Cheng. Both recommended that filmmakers document family life, particularly children. It seems that Liu's amateur filmmaking also began at home. The first reel of the film, entitled "The Light of the Human" (*Ningen no hikari*), was set in Liu's ancestral home in southern Taiwan. Even though one cannot precisely pin down the time of the filming, this reel's cinematography was by far the most rudimentary of the film's four reels and thus almost certainly shot the earliest among the four. The reel opens with a medium close-up of Liu's wife Suzhen holding their baby son and smiling at a handheld camera.

The next shot shows the little boy timidly walking, at his mother's coaxing, toward his father's camera, which is handheld at a low angle below the boy's eye-level. A close-up of the little boy's face, sweaty and immersed in sunlight, follows. The intimacy between the toddler and the handheld camera grows with each shot.

A prominent family in southern Taiwan, the Lius owned a large family home and estate. Liu Na'ou spent his childhood and adolescence there before leaving for Tokyo for higher education and, after graduation, relocating to Shanghai to start his career. With his long sojourns in Tokyo and Shanghai, it might seem that Liu had moved away from his home base, but in fact, Taiwan remained the force field that propelled and conditioned Liu's "cosmopolitan" wandering. The Taiwan-based historian Lin Zhengfang believes that Taiwan's colonial policy, especially its quota system at universities to limit educational opportunities for native youth, propelled Liu's departure from the colony. As universities in the metropoles of Japan did not adopt a quota system for colonial subjects, they became common destinations for young people, especially young men, from elite Taiwanese families. Taiwan was also a central factor in Liu's relocation to Shanghai. Liu had planned to go to France to study literature, but Shanghai was the Europeanized alternative "closer to home," which satisfied his mother's wish for her son to stay nearby. In addition, by then many of Liu's Taiwanese acquaintances from Tokyo had moved to Shanghai, as Japanese businesses sought to employ Taiwanese colonial subjects in their expansions into China.[74] Even though, as mentioned earlier, Liu obscured his origins in Shanghai where anti-Japanese sentiments were strong, his life trajectories—his departures, relocations, disavowals, and eventual assassination—were all deeply connected to his home in Taiwan as a colonial space in the expanding Japanese Empire.

The first reel of Liu's film is a love letter to his ancestral home in southern Taiwan, whose lush garden offered a paradise for children's play and a gathering place for a close-knit, local community of family members and friends. Liu had three young children of his own, but a large number of children from the extended family appear in the film. Liu's handheld close-ups capture children's curious glances into the camera, and his tracking shots watch over toddlers' wobbly steps as they learn to walk and navigate their environment. The camera often stays at the children's height when documenting them. The small children's proximity to the ground and the soil, and their sweaty faces bathed in the sunlight, intensify the sensuality of the silent film footage, allowing it to convey extravisual senses of touch, smell, and temperature. The camera is also attentive to generational relationships within the extended family. Adults, men and women, old and young, appear almost always together with children and thus become anchored in a lineage. In a tracking shot, Liu films the arrival of an older woman, a matriarch of the family, by rickshaw. With bound feet, she shares the same unstable and tentative rhythm of movement as the youngest toddler, as they walk to the house in each other's company. Foregrounding life cycles, lineages, and a close-knit community grounded on the soil that supported flourishing fruit trees and endless newborn babies, Liu depicted his Taiwan home as a place where life thrived in the safe haven built by familial relationships (fig. 2.3).

In the film that clearly influenced Liu, Dziga Vertov's *Man with a Movie Camera*, the cameraman is introduced in the opening shot, a special-effect-generated image where a miniature cameraman stands on top of a giant camera. Soon afterward, the cameraman is shown leaving an apartment building in early morning, carrying the tripod on his shoulder to film the city. The

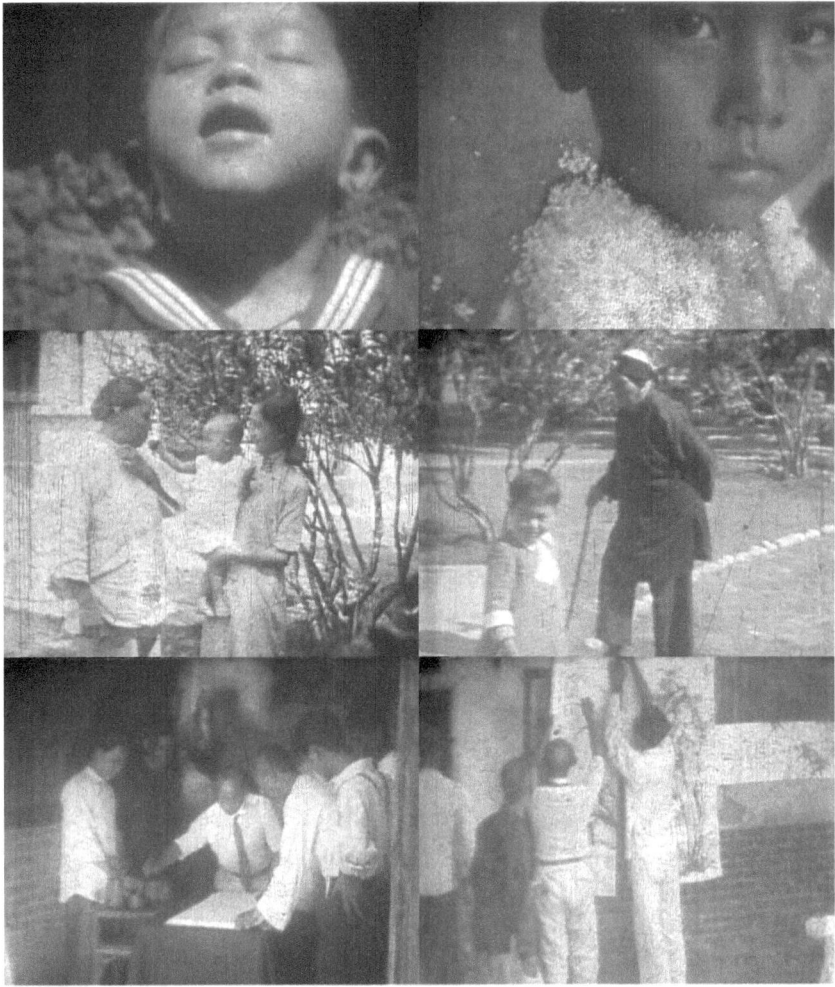

2.3 The multigenerational family in *A Man Who Holds a Movie Camera*.

filmmaker's first act of filming on screen is ridden with risk: placing the camera on the railway tracks, the filmmaker cranks the camera as a train approached. The next few shots are among the very few handheld moments in Vertov's film, showing the train arriving at threatening speed, with the filmmaker dangerously close to, and his foot caught by, the railway track.

In contrast, the first shot of Liu's film features his wife and son; the filmmaker is implied in the shot as the mother and son smile toward him, behind the camera. Liu's first direct appearance happens soon after. Wearing a casual white tank top as he sits with his baby son, Liu looks up and smiles to the camera while peeling a potato. The next sequence shows him leaving home in a rickshaw for the train station, with someone else behind the camera filming his departure. At the station, the train arrives without drama. With someone behind the camera continuing to film him, Liu comfortably sits at the train window and waves to the camera.

There is no explanation as to where Liu is going. Most likely it was a short local trip, as he does not carry much luggage. Yet this self-portrait was significant. Unlike Vertov's cameraman, who seems a lone hero going about filming the new Soviet world as his object, Liu's film anchored the filmmaker and the act of filmmaking in the midst of relationships, whether posing in front of the camera as father and son, or across the camera as the filmmaker encouraging smiles from his subjects (fig. 2.4).

Liu was, of course, prone to departures, hence his introduction of himself as the one leaving. This local train station probably saw Liu making countless departures, sitting by the train window and waving goodbye to his extended family. While Vertov's cameraman is visibly in danger when filming the advancing train on the railway tracks, Liu's departure looks comfortable and congenial. Inherent danger, however, underlay his travels across geopolitical lines as a colonial subject in an aggressively expanding empire. Perhaps it was in light of these risky crossings, that the home ground—with its protective familial ties and local networks—became for Liu and his family members a haven of mutual protection, despite, and because of, the larger processes of imperialism engulfing Taiwan.

I do not intend to suggest here that Liu or his extended family could set themselves apart from colonialism. Like all other families, the Lius were deeply imbricated in Taiwan's coloniality. As mentioned, Liu's departures and relocations had much to do with his origin in Taiwan and the opportunities that were opened, and closed, to him due to his colonial subjecthood. While families often outlive political regimes, and the Liu family's wealth and prestige had predated Japanese colonialism, to sustain this wealth and prestige required careful maneuvers within the political environment. Art-making, then, aided the family in the larger power game of social survival and reproduction.

2.4 The filmmaker's self-portrait in relationship in *A Man Who Holds a Movie Camera*.

The only person who appeared in the reel "The Light of the Human" and was identified by name was the painter Ye Hanqin. Liu filmed Ye painting two pictures of orchids, a favorite subject for Chinese literati painting that symbolized moral purity and reclusion from the world. It is not entirely clear from the film where Ye painted, though most likely it was at the Liu family house, as Ye was accompanied by members of Liu's extended family. What is clear is that the Liu family network encompassed Taiwanese cultural elites, and art circulated within this network, in the same way that literati art had circulated to strengthen horizontal, personal bonds among the gentry class in past dynasties. Painting, in the film, was not an individualistic, but rather a collective, endeavor. One person grinds the ink stone to make ink. Another person holds the edges of the rice paper to keep it flat. Many others surround the painter, witnessing his painting in action. The completed paintings are hung on the wall for everyone to examine. A mise-en-abyme moment, this filmed scene of artmaking comments on the family, and the personal connections it fosters, as the space where art and cultural memories circulate, further strengthening these personal ties and supporting them with ethical foundations. Similarly, picturing the family as a garden of sunlight, fruit trees, children, and community gatherings, Liu's "Light of the Human" as home movie and collective art making also reasserted the importance of family as a seat of memory, growth, and mutual protection, and its preindustrial local rootedness as a form of indigeneity.

Be Like Water: An Aesthetics of Improvisation

> When you arrive at a place with a body of water, you should have a drink. . . . The advantage of water lies in changing tones of light, in natural reflections, which can enrich composition and offer a sense of peace.

If the film's first reel is rooted in family, the next three reels—set in Tokyo, Shenyang, and Guangzhou, respectively—are travelogues documenting Liu's multiple explorations: of the larger world, himself, the camera, and the relationships between them all.[75]

My reading of these three reels centers on water. At a time when a great deal of long-distance travel was done by the sea, and for a man from Taiwan, a Pacific island, water was an integral part of journeying. Amorphous, shifting, unstoppable, and connected, water was also a popular subject for modernist cinema as expressive of the liquidity and uncertainty of modern ways of life. Walter Ruttmann's *Berlin: Symphony of a Great City* (1927) and Joris Ivens' *Rain* (1929) both begin with bodies of water. Liu's three reels of travel all involved water too: the "Tokyo" and "Guangzhou" reels begin with a lake and the ocean, respectively, and the "Scenery" reel ends with a seafaring journey. As the film went on, Liu explored water in increasingly all-encompassing ways, first as a narrow technical problem with aperture and composition, then as an evocative metaphor to negotiate attachment and mobility, and finally, as a welcomed moment of contingency to let go of control and improvise on his relationships with the camera and with the pro-filmic world around him.

The second reel of Liu's film, the "Tokyo" reel, begins with a lake in a park, with small rowboats scattered across its surface. Filming from a distance, Liu experiments with different ways of rendering the lake on camera. A half-tracking, half-panning shot slowly follows a boat as it glides over the water. Another pan, filmed from behind a wooded area, uses the silhouette of trees in the foreground to add a layer of abstract patterns to the shot, creating additional visual interest. Finally, a direct shot into the water catches glittering, reflected light.

Full of such experiments to record the same subject in different ways, Liu's film could be considered a "scrapbook" where numerous studies, sketches, and "takes" were deposited, with the filmmaker having no qualms about displaying his process of learning. As mentioned, amateur filmmakers shared an interest in the technicality of cinema. One can find this interest in achieving technical proficiency among amateur filmmakers in the Japanese-language trade journal in Shanghai discussed earlier. Flying over the Japanese countryside in a small plane, Liu experimented with aerial filming in a highly unstable aircraft. Filming from a moving vehicle, he chased luminous clouds behind the hills on the horizon. In Toyko's city center, he tried to produce his city symphony moments by exploiting the geometry of modern architecture with a skewed camera angle. Liu's experiments, however, went much further than the technicality of filmmaking. He was ultimately interested in cinema as a means to express personal feelings and thoughts, and to mediate his relations with the world in which he found himself.

Documenting travels in Fengtian, the capital city of the de facto Japanese colony of Manchuria, the "scenery" reel ends with a seafaring journey that would take Liu back to Taiwan. Filming from the side of the steamship shortly before departure, Liu's camera slowly pans over the large crowd on the shore waving their goodbyes and lingers, at the end of the pan, on a woman holding a baby in her arms and wiping tears with a handkerchief. Countless long streamers of ticker tape flutter in the wind, tying the ship to the shore. As the ship departs, Liu films the widening expanse of water as it slowly fills the frame, with a single strand of ticker tape hanging over the expanding body of water, the last manifestation of attachment to the shore. The following shot depicts a splendid sunset over a sparkling ocean. Even though the sunset was a technically difficult shot to accomplish, what was most striking was not Liu's successful management of light, but his decision to frame the sunset with the silhouette of a ship rigging in the foreground. Composed of metal fixtures and a heavy rope, the rigging creates a ready resonance with the fragile ticker tape above the water in the last shot. The two shots form a poetic pair that comment on the changed conditions of anchoring and attachment, entwining the nostalgia of leaving the continent with the splendor of ocean journeys, rooting oneself to the rootless steamship, the media of distance and its overcoming.

If the lake in Tokyo aroused technical interest, and the journey by sea leaving Manchuria evoked contemplation on mobility and attachment, it was in the "Guangzhou" reel that water ceased to be a technical or poetic *object* for the camera. Instead, the "Guangzhou" reel was thoroughly inundated: from shot length and rhythm to framing and performance, water shaped how the reel was filmed in all ways. The "Guangzhou" reel begins with a powerful splash of waves, shot aboard a cruise ship, which Liu and his six friends have taken to tour the harbor. The strong wind tosses the women's permed hair, while the men hold on to their hats. Knocked about by the wind and waves, no one can hold a pose for more than a few seconds, and neither could the filmmaker hold the camera still enough to attempt any long takes. Framing had to respond to the wind and waves as well. The instability of the cruise ship required that the filmmaker come close to the subject and frame them in medium shots or close-ups, as a long shot would most likely lose focus in such a situation. With the filmmaker and camera in close proximity, and recognizing the futility of posing to the camera, everyone is freed from their pretense of control. They burst into laughter, making faces at and flirting with the camera.

Emblematic of the larger conditions of mobility, contingency, and displacement on which chance encounters and friendships came into being, water brought to the filmmaking process the necessity and fun of improvisation. This forms a contrast with the first reel, "The Light of the Human," in which Liu filmed his family within the ordered intimacy of a lineage structure. His close-ups of children expressed paternal care. His medium and long shots of adults, often picturing them with children, emphasized their roles in the intergenerational family. Having no such assured structure, interactions across the camera in the "Guangzhou" reel became more equalized, spontaneous, and responsive to one another. Liu's friends were familiar with the camera: in fact, one of them had a still camera and was taking photos with it on the same journey. As equal partners in image-making, their reactions to Liu's camera were playful, flirtatious, performative. Keeping his foothold on a ship responding to the wind above it and ocean currents beneath it, and courting subjects that were his equals in defining the moment of image creation, the filmmaker gave up his control of the image readily, replacing it with the joy of improvisation.

Even though only the first third of the eleven-minute "Guangzhou" reel was filmed on water—first on the cruise ship and then on small rowboats at the harbor—the liberating energy of improvisation, nudged on by the wind and waves, is sustained in the rest of the reel, making it the most boisterous reel of the entire film. Liu films the feet of his friends, graced by high heels and the lower hem of a silky cheongsam, walking up and down staircases, an act of dynamic balance that requires the body to rapidly change its center of gravity. Like musical notes on sheet music, the unrehearsed rhythm of rambling up and down disrupts the structural monotony of the staircase with an incidental dance, creating a musical—indeed jazzy—aesthetic of contingency (fig. 2.5). This is then put in contrast with a military parade at the end of the reel. The rigidity of the military march and the freedom of the staircase ramble form a dialogical pair to explore two sides of modernity: increasing regimentation and the possibility of its disruption.

As explored previously, left-wing filmmakers connected bodies of water to the liquidity of capital and commodity exchange (*Spring Silkworm*) and expressed class contradictions and struggles around a wild body of swelling water (*Torrent*). There is no question that Liu's friends came from reasonably wealthy strata of the society, and that capital was among the underlying structures that sustained Liu's journeys with a film camera. It is also true, however,

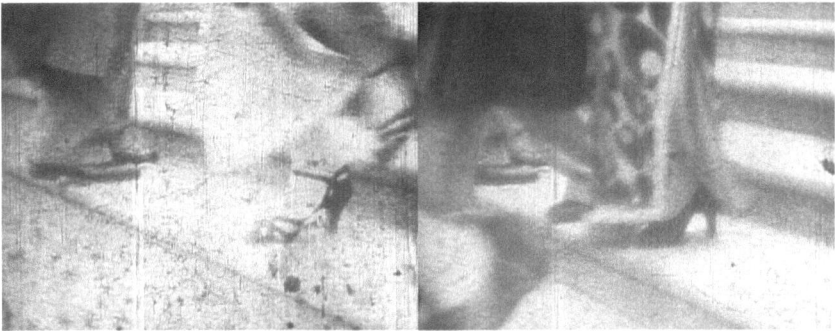

2.5 Walking the steps in *A Man Who Holds a Movie Camera*.

that something else also came into being amid the brutal movement of capital and commodity exchange, and amid the forced mobility of people, in response to the larger underlying structures of capitalism and imperialism. Marx long understood the dialectics of capitalism, calling it a system that sowed the seeds of its own destruction. As a modernist, Liu was attracted to this "something else" and responded to it with his camera. Filming like water, Liu understood travel as a loosening of traditional ties, a forging of new ones through shared mobility and chance encounter, and an aesthetics of contingency that could disrupt existing structures of control and replace them with improvisation, which by nature required collective participation and mutual modulation. Therein he saw a utopic potential.

The Softness of Intersubjectivity

In "On Cinema Art," serialized in *Film Weekly* between July 1 and October 8, 1932, Liu Na'ou made a distinction between "cinematic reality" (*yingxi de shizai*) and "actual reality" (*zhen de shizai*). He argued that cinema's photographic realism was insufficient to create a lively cinematic reality. "What's captured on film is only the "photographic," the raw material," he wrote. Only through the mechanical superiority of the kino-eye and the creative intervention of the montage, with the capacity to "deconstruct, analyze and interpret all phenomena, re-organizing them into thematic work," could cinema transform the profilmic reality into a cinematic reality. Liu concurred with European proponents of "pure cinema" that everyday life as it is would not be attractive on the screen. In the same article, when introducing ideas of "pure cinema," he wrote: "The appearance and state of everyday life do not attract us. We must use new form and employ all mathematical and abstract bodies and shapes to create new symbols."[76] Even though Liu did voice his disagreement with pure cinema proponents over the issue of plot—he was against abandoning it altogether—overall, in 1932 he was very much interested in cinema's capacity to impose its own structure onto the profilmic reality, organizing it into energetic, rhythmic, and abstract forms of cinematic realities distinct from everyday life.

Liu's theoretical writing on film shifted focus after 1933. He became more interested in the creative capacities of the camera, rather than the editing table, and saw the camera as representing subjective engagements with the world, rather than projecting a mechanical and impersonal organizing force onto the pro-filmic reality. "The camera position represents a perspective, and this perspective is changing incessantly. This is a revolution. . . . In film, the viewer can jump into the position of the person in the film and see and experience all that he sees. This is a jump from objectivity to subjectivity," Liu wrote in "Camera Apparatus: On the Functions of Position and Angle," published in 1934. In the same article, he also discussed camera movements such as panning and tracking, which he used frequently himself in amateur filmmaking. "[A pan's] function includes abandoning, following and manifesting the object, and observing space. . . . A pan's manifesting quality is particularly useful for revealing new existence, new facts or unintentional developments." Writing about tracking shots, he lauded the camera's flexibility to perform much more than what the word "tracking" entails: "The word 'tracking' doesn't do it justice anymore. Rather it's tracking, pushing, zooming out, bringing along, lifting up, descending, swirling, flying, or a mixture or hybrid of all of them."[77]

Liu's film theoretical work drew from many sources, including European and Soviet and Japanese avant-gardes as well as Hollywood. While I do draw attention to the shifts in Liu's theoretical thinking, I certainly do not intend to attribute this shift to the singular influence of his amateur filmmaking. Indeed, Liu's film reviews responded to the evolving film culture in Shanghai as a whole, including imported and domestic films on exhibit and film technologies available to filmmakers both inside and outside of the studios. However, Liu's experiments with small-scale amateur filmmaking in the documentary mode were a significant contributor to his theoretical writing, particularly between 1932 and 1934, which has so far gone unacknowledged. Central to Liu's shifting theoretical discussion was a reconsideration of the nature of the pro-filmic reality, understanding it not as passive material to be disassembled and reorganized by a mechanical kino-eye and on an editing table, but as an active participant to which the filmmaker's subjective camera responds.

As Liu's amateur film was a "scrapbook" of experiments, one can find many traces where the filmmaker experimented with camera perspectives and movements. Besides water, Liu was attracted to the built environment. Inspired by the city symphony mode of filmmaking, he relied on modern architecture's streamlined appearance and the camera's tilted angles to create geometrical compositions of Tokyo's city center. This way of filmmaking might suit city centers where modern architecture such as government buildings and department stores abound, but would it also suit residential neighborhoods where the architecture is not streamlined but richly textured, with each house different from its neighbors and window decors revealing the everyday habits of the individual households? In one scene, Liu trains his geometrical composition on a Tokyo neighborhood, tilting the camera such that the main street runs diagonally through the screen. Typically, a city symphony film of the 1920s shot in 35mm would stay with this diagonal composition with a fixed camera on tripod. Yet filming with a handheld camera, Liu starts panning while continuing to keep the diagonal composition. Like an unfolding scroll, his pan brings more and more houses into the shot, and soon enough, his camera is attracted to the different architectural details on the houses' balconies and windows. The point of the shot is no longer the diagonal geometric form imposed on the street, but the necessity of responding to rich details of the residential architecture itself. In the midst of panning, Liu simply adjusts the camera position and abandons the diagonal composition, so that his camera lingers on the intricate details of the houses before the shot ends. It was not the filmmaker, but the street along with the filmmaker, that decided how this shot should be filmed (fig. 2.6).

During his travels, Liu filmed many more residential areas than city centers, used more panning, tracking, and long takes than montage to capture the rich tapestry of life in these habitats, showing them a similar level of interest he showed to his home in Taiwan. Upon returning to Taiwan at the end of the "Scenery" reel, however, Liu took it upon himself to film the outside of his home, a colonial-style, multistory villa, in the city-symphonic mode, panning over its surface to search for geometrical patterns, and tilting upward from the bottom of the house to admire its height. This study of the external appearance of the house never appeared in the film's first reel, which was grounded in the children's wobbly steps in the family garden. Having just returned from a journey of exploration and experimentation, the filmmaker now uses the camera with more agility and expressivity, approaching his home region with fresh eyes. In a playful sequence of tropical flora and fauna in silhouette and close-up, agricultural fields in long shot, and his home villa in the countryside rendered modernist urban, Liu created a countryside symphony that asserted, for better or for worse, rural southern Taiwan as a part of Taiwan's colonial modernity.

The period 1932–1934 was exactly the moment when the hard versus soft cinema debate was raging between the left-wing filmmakers and the opposing camp led by critics like Huang Jiamo and Liu Na'ou. Liu's "On the Attitude of the Author," composed in October 1933, was targeted at the left-wing

2.6 "City Symphony" sequence in central Tokyo (*above*) and finding the best camera position in Tokyo's residential areas, in *A Man Who Holds a Movie Camera*.

filmmakers, whom Liu perceived to have imposed too strong an ideological structure on the observable world. An author-filmmaker should assume an attitude of aesthetic observation-reflection that allows the author and the object of observation to become one. "This attitude doesn't bring with it any 'side thoughts,' and is pure and naked," Liu wrote. When the film author did not have this attitude, the film would suffer in quality: "Its characters will be clichéd, without personality. Its ideas will be trite, with no creativity. . . . Even if the author has passion and a sense of justice, the integrity of the work will still be broken." The attitude of observation-reflection was against such "pedantry." It adhered to the principle of empathy, in which the subject and the object became one.[78]

How should we understand this merging of subject and object? Here I suggest that the prerequisite of such merging was equity. In other words, there should be no structural difference in power between the filmmaker and those in front of his camera. The filmmaker must not impose a predetermined categorization or argument; instead, an improvisation, which means a mutual transformation in collaboration, must occur, just as wind and water enter a film's rhythm, how architectural details refuse diagonal framing, and how rambling up down staircases produces incidental music and then dances to it.

The last reel of Liu's amateur film is short, little more than three minutes, documenting a carnival in Taiwan. The island's colonial hybridity can be seen plainly in the various costumes worn in the parade. There are lion dances, umbrella dances, local operas with actors walking on stilts, fan dances in Japanese kimono, and performance of clowns dressed like Chaplin. Liu had been against the use of intertitles, deeming them an imposition of a "formulaic process of appreciation" on the viewers.[79] Here, there is no intertitle to explain what the parade is, but that might precisely be the point. Careful viewers can make out from what is written on a float in the parade that this is a celebration of the Greater East Asia Co-prosperity Sphere, a Japanese imperialist concept. Dancing for the Co-prosperity Sphere? Anyone aware of the atrocities committed by Japanese imperialism would find this an utterly unacceptable act. Yet were all these participants criminals or collaborators? Or were some of them, at least, joining the crowd to participate in something different from what the parade nominally was for? What did it mean to survive and dance in a colony? Was that a compromise, or a struggle, or both? Liu filmed amid the crowd, and apart from it from a height, perhaps on a second-floor rooftop. Like a child, he stares at the dancers' inexplicable movements and immerses himself and us in rituals that have much longer histories than Taiwan's history as a colony. Different from the news parade—the American newsreel's pretension that facts of the world were totally legible and could be paraded in front of the viewer's eyes to produce knowledge of the world—Liu's unnamed carnival in colonial Taiwan was a mystery. It was certainly colonial, yet the unhindered and joyful kinetics of the communal celebration also exceeded the logics of subjectification. It called for empathetic understanding.

This chapter brings documentary into the hard versus soft film debate. I've shown that working in a semicolonial city under bombardment, Shanghai filmmakers were acutely aware of the spatial inequalities along lines of class, nationality and race. This awareness prompted the leftwing filmmakers such as Cheng Bugao and Xia Yan to use docu-fiction to expose structural oppressions and to problematize the politics and ethics of visibility with a heightened reflexivity.

Compared to Chen Jianran's and Cheng Bugao's limited access to filming in their own city due to policing and warfare, Liu Na'ou's extensive travels and sojourns in the Japanese Empire and the treaty ports of China were clearly privileged acts. Yet Liu's obscuration of his Taiwanese origin and disavowal of his own amateur filmmaking remind us that, for a colonial subject such as Liu, privilege and precarity were entwined and hard to separate. Despite the family wealth, Liu's lineage in Taiwan must navigate complex colonial politics for its survival. Benefiting from his colonial subjecthood to live a cosmopolitan life, Liu nevertheless fit oddly in the categories that motivated nationalist and leftist politics at the time. His amateur filmmaking was autobiographical, depicting the various protective spaces and communal networks that sustained and socialized himself: families, neighborhoods, friendships, and carnivals. These were places where one's multifarious and shifting subject positions became apparent, and one's communion with others could be achieved despite the differences in status and power. Of course, this was only a utopic—and delusional—longing. Liu ultimately did not survive his precarious border-crossings: he was assassinated in 1940, most likely in retribution for his employment by the Japanese occupational force in Shanghai.

What is to be gained by including Liu, who was clearly not a revolutionary, in a book on revolutionary becomings? PRC film scholarship had long dismissed soft film theories as simply a petite bourgeois take on cinema as entertainment. In recent decades, however, film scholars such as Zhang Zhen, Weihong Bao, and Victor Fan have challenged this dismissal.[80] Fan argues that soft film proponents in fact shared with their Marxist counterparts a vision of film as an educational tool, though for soft film theorists, cinema educates by offering an aesthetic experience of immersion that returns immanence to life.[81]

My engagement with Liu Na'ou in this chapter demonstrates the importance of his amateur filmmaking to the formation of his film theories. This book's exploration of a "soft" documentary aesthetics of attunement, intersubjectivity, and improvisation, however, will not end with this chapter. Having repeatedly surfaced through the twentieth century, such a soft aesthetic was important for the political, ethical, and epistemological health of revolutionary movements. Certainly, revolutions must expose underlying structures of exploitation and mobilize their demolition. Left-wing filmmakers such as Cheng Bugao, Xia Yan, and many others took up this challenge. Meanwhile, media in revolutionary processes must also stay empathetic to survival tactics, attuned to shifting power dynamics, and open to emergent developments and potentialities that do not yet have names. In the end, perhaps the revolution should be hard as well as soft.

CHAPTER 3

WINNING REALITIES

Wartime Propaganda and Solidarity

> *Get out of the studio! Get out of the studio, to the frontlines, to the rear areas. Wherever you go, the dynamism of the masses in the War of Resistance will supply infinite raw materials for your art. No need to sensationalize, no need to insert romance, you only need to represent the real lives of the masses as raw material, as reportage, as documentary. Even if the film is only a few hundred inches long, it's a precious piece of art. This is the value of documentary.*
>
> —Xu Suling, 1941

In July 1937 the Japanese military launched an all-out assault on China, heralding the start of a brutal war that lasted for eight years. In August 1937 heavy air raids halted film production in Shanghai. After three months of intense fighting, Shanghai fell under Japanese occupation in November. With film studios blasted asunder and film production temporarily suspended, a large number of filmmakers left Shanghai to join the War of Resistance. Many went to the Nationalist-controlled hinterland (*dahoufang*) and joined the two state film studios, the Central Motion Picture Studio (Zhongdian) in Chongqing and the China Motion Picture Studio (Zhongzhi), based first in Hankou and later in Chongqing after Hankou fell in October 1938. A small number moved to Yan'an to bring filmmaking to the

Communist base areas. Still others moved to Hong Kong to continue their work there.[1] Wartime was a crucible from which new film aesthetics and media practices emerged, and documentary, with its fast speed of production and proximity to the struggles on the ground, became prioritized in both Chongqing and Yan'an as the most important mode of filmmaking for wartime propaganda. In 1945, upon Japan's surrender, the Yan'an-based Communist film unit took over the Japanese film establishment in Manchuria (Man-ei) to found the first Communist film production powerhouse, the Northeastern Film Studio (Dongbei dianying zhipian chang). Under the leadership of Yan'an filmmakers and supported by filmmakers from Man-ei, the Northeastern Film Studio trained the first generation of Communist documentary filmmakers who documented the CCP's military campaigns against the Nationalists on its path to state power.

This chapter begins by considering the development of documentary filmmaking during the Sino-Japanese War (1937–1945), in both the Nationalist-controlled hinterland and Communist Yan'an. It then discusses Communist battlefront filmmaking during the subsequent Civil War between Nationalists and Communists (1946–1949), and the Sino-Soviet documentary coproduction upon the PRC's founding that reenacted the People's Liberation Army's major victorious battles from the Civil War. Central to this chapter are questions of how to engage with and evaluate the politics, aesthetics, and ethics of propaganda documentaries.

The English term *propaganda* has acquired pejorative connotations since the Cold War, when it was considered a specialty of totalitarian regimes intended to brainwash their subjects.[2] In reality, as a form of communication for mass persuasion, propaganda has been widely practiced throughout human history by various parties, from religious and civil organizations to revolutionary movements and national states.[3] *Xuanchuan*, the Chinese word for propaganda, has a long history. Weihong Bao provides a useful genealogy in her discussion of propaganda cinema in wartime Chongqing. Bao shows that while in premodern times *xuanchuan* meant dissemination of ideas and information by the state's ruling elites, by the early twentieth century, as modern media technology enabled a variety of social actors to disseminate information to a wider audience, the word came to refer to any propagation of information and knowledge, be it for educational, commercial, political, military, or other purposes. In her work on cinema in wartime Chongqing, Bao observes that intensified wartime propaganda needs vastly expanded media networks and brought many social actors into pluralistic "propaganda spheres." Drawing from Oskar Negt and Alexander Kluge's understanding of the public sphere as inclusive and dialectic, Bao contends that the "historical formation of the propaganda sphere" should not be excluded from our discussions on the public sphere. Far from an "anomaly," propaganda is in fact "an essential chapter in modern mass-mediated society."[4]

I agree with Bao that we must consider propaganda seriously as an essential aspect of mass media. The history of documentary, in particular, has been intimately related to propaganda. We've already met many instances of propaganda in the first two chapters of this book, from the Japanese propaganda of the First Sino-Japanese War, to Lai Manwai's party film to bolster the Nationalists' leadership, to Chen Jianran's documentation of workers' protests and Cheng Bugao's docu-fiction to raise class consciousness. Bao has emphasized in her work how propaganda prompted developments in media infrastructure and technology, and a re-conceptualization of cinema as an "affective medium." In this book I foreground the eventfulness of propaganda documentary production and propose a way of studying propaganda that would take the specific relationships built across and around the camera, and the inscriptions from these relationships, as the foundation on which to think about the political and ethical stakes of propaganda.

As I will discuss, wartime propaganda documentaries were tasked with the making and dissemination of "winning realities" that would propel an advantageous unfolding of the war. Yet such "winning realities" often hadn't sufficiently emerged to be part of the observable world, and therefore, creating these emergent realities in documentary often relied on dramatization and (re)enactments. In this book's introduction and chapter 2, I have discussed at length the fallacy of photographic realism, that is, the idea that actuality footage shot on location is faithful representation, due to the indexicality of the photographic image. I have argued that each step in documentary production, from rallying support to gain access, to negotiating the power dynamics on the ground, to organizing the various inscriptions from different participants, does substantial mediation work. We cannot categorically dismiss dramatization or (re)enactments as fabrication, just as we cannot treat actuality footage as automatically truthful. Instead, the specific relationships underlying these dramatizations and (re)enactments matter. Far from a top-down transmission of messages, propaganda documentary was made with input from many participants who occupied different positions in society, and who came to the project with different visions and interests. One can find these power-charged interactions inscribed in the film text and form itself, and in the documentation of the filmmaking event.

My emphasis here—on contact, interaction, and relationality as underlying the politics, ethics, and aesthetics of propaganda production—is certainly informed by the specific nature of documentary filmmaking, where relationships across and around the camera are rarely contractual and therefore much more varied, uncertain, and dependent on broader power structures in society. Bill Nichols, in thinking about the camera's gaze in relational terms ranging from empathetic to indifferent to interventionist, has offered a catalog of documentary aesthetics and corresponding ethical stances in his proposal to evaluate documentaries via an "ethical accounting."[5] Nichols's seminal work provides great insight into how to conduct a textual analysis of documentary with a concern for its ethics. Here I further argue for the importance of supplementing textual analysis with research into the production process. Evaluation of a propaganda documentary's ideological, political, and ethical implications must take into account the material, infrastructural, and communal work it does on the ground, and the specific political relationality underlying its production. What concrete problems did it try to solve? Whose visions and directions did the production follow? What was included and excluded? Reading a propaganda documentary "eventfully" in this way can help us move beyond the Cold War notion of propaganda as complete falsification and brainwashing, while regaining our critical capacity to evaluate the specific political and ethical implications of a propaganda work. This approach to propaganda will be developed in this chapter and the remaining chapters of the book.

Thinking about propaganda production in relational terms is especially pertinent here because one prominent type of wartime documentary that this chapter engages with is the "solidarity film," which aimed to create a particular political and ethical relationality in revolutionary struggles. The film scholar Thomas Waugh coined the phrase *solidarity film* to refer to works made by progressive filmmakers who turned to cinema "to champion each new front of revolutionary struggle."[6] Waugh primarily uses the term to discuss the Dutch left-wing filmmaker Joris Ivens's documentary productions during wartime, including *The Spanish Earth* (1937) on the Spanish Civil War, and *400 Million* (1938) on the Chinese War of Resistance. Writing on Soviet cinema, Rossen Djagalov expands the solidarity film to cover broader left-wing cross-cultural filmmaking, including Soviet propaganda films about the non-Russian Far North, the Caucasus, and Central Asia, though he acknowledges that calling these Soviet films "solidarity films" can be problematic, as "the increasingly Stalinized version of international solidarity they had to reproduce—namely, loyalty to the USSR, the only proletarian state—rendered these films unwatchable in the post-Stalin era."[7]

Solidarity, as Sally J. Scholtz defines it, is "a moral relation that marks a social movement wherein individuals have committed to positive duties in response to a perceived injustice."[8] Solidarity films are typically cross-cultural, bridging different sites of struggle and allowing distinct social groups to enter allyship. Taking clear sides, they help amplify the struggle to gain support and in this sense can be understood as propaganda films. Yet if "propaganda film" as a designation emphasizes the film's aim to persuade with the "messages" it carries, "solidarity film" puts the emphasis on the relationships that underlie the film, and that the film attempts to forge. In fact, having emerged in the 1930s, in the context of heightened propaganda efforts by hegemonic forces such as state governments, solidarity films were meant as a progressive alternative, an expression of internationalist solidarity amid the global propaganda war waged by warring states. It was the people-to-people collaborations on the ground and a shared sense of justice that were supposed to drive solidarity filmmaking, rather than the interests of nation-states. Even though Djagalov doesn't elaborate on the reason why he finds it jarring to call Soviet propaganda films "solidarity films," my conjecture is that these films created relationships that fell short of the equality, mutuality, and reflexivity of a solidary relationship.[9]

Films discussed in this chapter all aimed to build solidary relationships, though they differed in terms of among whom, under what conditions, and how successfully. This chapter begins with a study of Zheng Junli's *Long Live the Nation(s)* (1941), China's first propaganda film to foster solidarity among the various ethnic groups who lived in China's border regions. Though the film was made under the Nationalist Party's supervision at the state-controlled China Motion Picture Studio in Chongqing, Zheng, as a left-wing filmmaker, brought his own understanding of ethnic relations and internationalist solidarity to the filmmaking. In addition, a variety of people holding different positions of power in society and belonging to different ethnic groups participated in the film's production. Paying attention to the specific forms of their participation, I argue, helps us understand this propaganda documentary, and the terms of solidarity it manifests, as arising from laborious and power-charged processes of negotiation, rehearsal, performance, and inscription.

Moving from Chongqing to Yan'an, I discuss Yan'an cinema—the beginning of filmmaking directly under CCP control—in the context of solidarity filmmaking. Not only was Yan'an cinema supported by solidarity filmmakers (Ivens donated his camera), but the Communist base area of Yan'an was where different constituencies, from peasants and soldiers to intellectuals, came to build solidarity with one another in revolutionary transformation. I discuss Mao Zedong's Yan'an Talks as a foundational but also paradoxical text articulating the desired political relationalities between different social segments finding themselves in Yan'an, and between these segments and the party. I then analyze Wu Yinxian and Qian Xiaozhang's film *Nanniwan* (1942), handmade in Yan'an, as manifesting formal qualities of a solidarity film suited to the specific local conditions of Yan'an at the time. With Yan'an filmmakers moving to northeastern China at the end of the Sino-Japanese War to take over the Japanese colonial film establishment in Manchuria, I discuss the resulting Northeastern Film Studio's battlefront filmmaking as arising from the deeply ethical and solidary relationships between the filmmakers and the soldiers whom they filmed during the day and buried at night.

The final segment of the chapter discusses Soviet solidarity filmmaking in China, specifically *The Victory of the Chinese People* (1950), a Sino-Soviet documentary coproduction led by Soviet filmmakers upon the founding of the People's Republic of China. The massive reenactments of battle scenes in the film, shot spectacularly in color, followed top-down directions of Soviet filmmakers to create the teleological certainty and grandiosity of what I call a "victory aesthetic." Replacing the black-and-white battlefront actuality filmed by Chinese filmmakers in intimate and equal relationships to the soldiers during the actual battles, these extremely costly reenactments manifested serious contradictions underlying solidarity filmmaking. Along with translations of Soviet theories of documentary dramaturgy into Chinese, they consolidated a socialist realist approach to documentary production in the first years of the PRC.

Propaganda as Winning Realities

In 1938, less than a year into the war, Zheng Yongzhi, the director of the state-owned China Motion Picture Studio, wrote proudly about the studio's capacity for speedy production and distribution of news and documentary films from China's war front. Previously a film education unit in the military, the studio was well positioned for battlefront filmmaking. Zheng reported that filmmaking units had been dispatched to all the active battlefronts to "record our Nationalist army's heroic resistance on-location."[10] Footage taken on the battlefront was then swiftly compiled and edited into newsreels and special reports. By late 1938 the studio had already made five installments of the War of Resistance newsreel (*Kangzhan teji*). Besides the regularly released newsreels, one-off special reports (*haowai*) documented notable events, such as the successes of Chinese air forces in battle, or the Japanese bombing of Guangzhou. Zheng wrote glowingly about the expanding distribution networks that enabled timely exhibitions of these films to domestic audiences in both urban and rural areas, as well as to viewers in Hong Kong, Southeast Asia, Europe, and the United States. The special reports could reach cinemas in Wuhan and Hong Kong the day after the filmed event happened, with "record-breaking" efficiency, as Zheng proudly put it.[11]

As part of the allied powers, China participated in an expanding, international network of wartime documentary circulation. British, American, and Soviet documentaries were regularly exhibited in Chongqing and its surrounding areas. International filmmakers such as Joris Ivens and Roman Karmen traveled and filmed in China. For its timely production and international reach, Zheng saw documentary as the most important component of the "cinema of resistance and construction" (*kangjian dianying*), a new kind of cinema suited to the wartime that he hoped to build. In his "Guidelines for Making a Cinema of Resistance and Construction," published in 1941, Zheng specified that newsreels and documentaries should take up 45 percent of wartime film production, with fiction films (40 percent), cartoons and resistance-song films (10 percent), and others (5 percent) making up the balance.[12]

Having left their Shanghai studios behind, filmmakers who traveled inland saw documentary as a catalyst for a new cinema. Xu Suling, whose call for filmmakers to leave the studio is quoted at the beginning of the chapter, observed that wartime cinema catered to a very different audience. Glamorous film stars and fantastical plots might have attracted urban viewers prior to the war, yet now cinema must be brought to rural areas and serve a much broader mass audience, who were unfamiliar with the film medium and wouldn't recognize Shanghai film stars or resonate with stories set in urban China. Xu criticized some of his colleagues for being too attached to the studio. "Holding on to the traditional way of filmmaking they knew in Shanghai, they continue to hide in the studio, invent stories of resistance in terms of heroes and beauties, and attempt to fit these stories into old film forms." Documentary, on the other hand, could help filmmakers transition into a new way of filmmaking. "Chinese masses in resistance very passionately need cinema," Xu wrote. "They need authentic documentations of their lives, of their struggles.... They need to find their own faces, own lives, own consciousness, own struggle, in film and on screen."[13] By leaving the studio and immersing themselves in the lived realities of a society fighting a war of resistance, filmmakers could help those in struggle gain affirmation for their courageous efforts and heighten the awareness of the work yet to be done. Through timely documentary representation, viewers could grasp and reflect upon the tumultuous changes as they happened in their lives.

While Xu encouraged filmmakers to leave the studio behind and immerse themselves in resistance work, Zheng Yongzhi saw documentary as a means to craft winning realities. The wartime need for propaganda, Zheng observed, demanded a reconsideration of what reality was, and how documentary filmmaking should relate to it. A propaganda documentary should not just record what was before the camera (the pro-filmic reality) but should directly affect "how [reality] undergoes development."[14] By capturing positive developments on the side of the resistance and negative events for the enemy, a film could encourage one's own people in resistance and demoralize the enemy, thus propelling realities to unfold in a winning direction. In his guidelines for wartime filmmaking, Zheng provided templates for twenty ways to create a "positive" portrayal of Chinese resistance, twenty ways to create a "negative" portrayal of the enemy, and fourteen ways to depict national construction, including exposing the Japanese imperialists' oppression of their own people, demonstrating heroic Chinese resistance at the front lines and in the rear areas, and showcasing China's agricultural and industrial production to support resistance efforts. Japan had invested heavily in cinematic propaganda since the beginning of war, which had put China at a disadvantage, Zheng warned. Japan's propaganda "has slandered China as a barbarian nation deserving 'punishment,' praised their imperial army as securing peace and preventing Communist developments in

East Asia, and aimed to deceive all the people in Japan and around the world."[15] Zheng called on filmmakers to use the "weaponized cinema" (*wuqi dianying*) to refute Japanese slander, gain support from the international community, and arouse the nation to fight the enemy.[16]

If Xu saw documentary filmmaking as attuned to the unfolding lived realities of war on the ground, in direct contrast to studio filmmaking, which followed preexisting, well-tested storylines in isolation, Zheng emphasized the strategic use of documentary to create "winning realities" and designated templates for them. Since many of these winning realities may not have manifested themselves yet, the filmmaker had to bring them into existence by rallying help from various participants and relying on dramatization and enactment in the filmmaking process. Filmmakers had left the studio, but they carried with them some of the essential aspects of studio filmmaking, from scripting, to dramatization, to the direction of acting, as they moved to a much larger arena to organize stories that could help China survive and win the war.

In 1939, the filmmaker Zheng Junli set out with a small crew to China's northwestern borderlands. Having been a leading actor in Shanghai's film world, Zheng transitioned into directing in late 1930s, as he moved inland to join the resistance. Like Cheng Bugao, Zheng began his directing career first with news films and documentaries. With a background in studio filmmaking, Zheng worked laboriously to rally power-holders' support and direct mass enactments, masterfully realizing on screen a unified China that hadn't been realized in actual life.

Zheng Junli as a Progressive Propagandist

Long Live the Nation(s) (*Minzu wansui*, 1941), directed by Zheng Junli and produced at the China Motion Picture Studio (under the leadership of Zheng Yongzhi), was among China's earliest propaganda documentaries portraying national unity between Han Chinese and the non-Sinic peoples living in China's hinterland and border regions. I render the title as *Long Live the Nation(s)* because the Chinese title harbors an ambiguity: nation (*minzu*) here could be understood as singular or plural. A loan word from Japanese, *minzu* has a complex genealogy. Sun Yat-sen's official ideology saw China as a republic that united five *minzu* (nations, or ethnic groups): the Han, the Mongolians, the Tibetans, the Muslims, and the Manchus. During the Sino-Japanese War, the Nationalist Party's ideology shifted to considering China's various ethnic groups as a single nation, a *Zhonghua minzu* sharing common ancestry in the mystic figure of the Yellow Emperor.[17] Whether this film celebrated the nation in the plural or in the singular is a question of political significance to which I will return.

Conceived as a symphony, with a prelude and a finale, the film was composed of five segments, on Tibetans, Mongolians, Muslims, the Miao and Yao, and the Luoluo, respectively. Only an incomplete copy of forty minutes of the film is still extant. The segment on the Muslims is lost. Besides the incomplete film copy, Zheng's diaries documenting his filmmaking journey to northwestern China between 1939 and 1940 have been preserved, along with his editing script for the film. Both documents allow us to partially reconstruct the filmmaking process.

Long Live the Nation(s) was meant to portray a unified China of different peoples standing together in resistance against the Japanese invasion. A unified China, however, was not to be found in reality at the time. Historians agree that during its rule in China, the Nationalist government wielded fairly limited authority in the border regions. The Qing Empire (1644–1912) had drastically expanded its territory, bringing non-Sinic peoples under a loose imperial rule. The fall of the Qing saw political fragmentation along ethnic lines, which continued through the Republican period, with vast expenses of inland and border regions being controlled by various military leaders who were "theoretically [Nationalist]-aligned but functionally autonomous."[18] By the time of the Sino-Japanese War, Lhasa had long declared independence after the fall of the Qing, Xinjiang was in the hands of the pro-Soviet warlord Sheng Shicai, and the Muslim Ma family ruled Qinghai. The forced relocation of the capital from Nanjing to Chongqing during the war helped extend the Nationalists' influence into the frontiers to some extent, but with their military tied up with the war against Japan, their domination in the hinterland could not be supported by military might. Instead, the Nationalists had to rely on the tireless labor of intellectuals and cultural practitioners, who wrote and published, organized touring drama troupes and mobile film projector teams, and staffed government-sponsored Chinese schools in Mongolian- or Tibetan-speaking regions.[19] In other words, if the construction of a unified nation was always a belabored process, here the labor was disproportionally shouldered by cultural workers such as Zheng Junli, who had to coordinate between local and national authorities to create the desired emergent realities through their work.

Before exploring the film text and its production process, a brief introduction of the filmmaker is due. Like Lai Manwai, Cheng Bugao, and Xia Yan—who have made appearances earlier in this book—Zheng Junli is recognized today as among the leading filmmakers of twentieth-century China. Born in 1911 in Shanghai to a poor Cantonese fruit-seller's family, Zheng began his artistic career in 1928, when he entered the drama school of the South China Society (Nanguo she) to study with Tian Han and Ouyang Yuqian, both progressive dramatists leading China's modern drama movement.[20] A handsome young man and a talented actor, Zheng soon rose to fame in both the theatre and film worlds; by the mid-1930s, he had become among the brightest stars in

Shanghai's film industry. Zheng's talent was not limited to acting. He was a daring revolutionary, and a prolific writer and translator capable of both theoretical and historical work. Radicalized in Shanghai's progressive milieu, Zheng read voraciously on European avant-garde theater and the Soviet proletkult movement, risked arrest in rallies led by underground Communists, and served on the executive committee of the Chinese Leftwing Dramatists Association upon its founding in 1930, when he was only nineteen.[21] By 1934 he had published a well-researched *History of Modern Chinese Cinema*, in which he adopted a Marxist and anti-imperialist perspective to critique Hollywood domination in China, and discussed difficulties facing China's "indigenous film industry" (*tuzhu dianying*) as it competed with imported cinema for audiences.[22] His interest in theories of acting, particularly the Stanislavski method, led him to translate Richard Boleslavsky's *Acting: First Six Lessons*, published in Shanghai in 1937, on the eve of the city's fall to Japanese occupation.

Zheng Junli's coming of age in Shanghai of the 1920s and 1930s, his long engagement with Shanghai's progressive politics, and experiences in the city's semicolonial realities and cosmopolitan culture had endowed him with an internationalist outlook as well as a nationalist urgency. China's borderlands played an important role in Zheng's imaginations for both the nation and the world. In an essay in 1941 recounting the making of *Long Live the Nation(s)*, Zheng wrote, "I'm a man of the South but I have since childhood longed for the North. Compared to the South, the North feels more like a magnificent China."[23] With Beijing serving as the imperial capital for the Yuan, Ming, and Qing dynasties, northern China had indeed been the seat of China's imperial power for a long time. By the early twentieth century, the country's border areas, especially the northeastern and northwestern border regions, had become the places where British, Russian, and Japanese imperial powers competed for influence. After the Mukden Incident and the Japanese occupation of Manchuria in 1931, and with Japan's repeated attempts to seek alliances with the Mongolians and Chinese Muslims, border regions became increasingly understood as areas of great strategic importance for China's national survival.[24]

No doubt exposed to nationalist discourses of border security, Zheng Junli's attraction to the "North" had another salient underpinning: his interest in socialism and the Soviet Union. Mongolia had adopted a socialist system since the mid-1920s. By the late 1930s, progressive journalists such as Du Zhongyuan had traveled to Xinjiang and painted a picture of the region as a slice of the Soviet Union in China, thanks to the pro-Soviet policies of the warlord Sheng Shicai, who controlled Xinjiang, and the proximity of Xinjiang to Soviet Central Asia.[25] Under Sheng's pro-Communist policies, Xinjiang was de facto independent from the Nationalist central government and had collaborations with the Communist stronghold of Yan'an, whence cadres, including Mao Zedong's brother Mao Zemin, were sent to Xinjiang. In other words, frontier regions were charged with many different meanings in wartime China. They were certainly taken as strategically important for national interests, yet they were also imagined as liminal, transnational places where progressive alternatives existed. The film star Zhao Dan, a close friend of Zheng Junli, was so taken by Du Zhongyuan's written account of Xinjiang that he and a number of colleagues organized a drama troupe and traveled to Xinjiang in 1939.[26] While shooting *Long Live the Nation(s)* in Gansu and Qinghai, Zheng wrote to Zhao Dan, asking for a chance to travel to Xinjiang to film part of the work, though that wish did not materialize due to a lack of funding and film stock.

After the fall of Shanghai, Zheng was among the first filmmakers to organize into traveling drama troupes, performing resistance plays along the way before relocating to the wartime capital of Chongqing. While in the hinterland, Zheng worked mainly in spoken drama, but documentary filmmaking offered the progressive star a chance to transition into filmmaking from acting. The initial commission from the state film studio was not a feature documentary but a series of "National Defense" newsreels showcasing war efforts in China's northwestern region. This was a challenging project involving precarious travels to Gansu, Ningxia, and Qinghai via rudimentary modes of transportation, and the itinerary was further expanded to the Southwest to include Sichuan and Yunnan in 1940, after Zheng successfully completed filming in the Northwest. Zheng not only finished the project but went far beyond making short newsreels. While on the journey and in the editing room, he began to envision a feature-length documentary that would not only bring together China's disparate border regions on screen to create a "winning reality" of national unity, but also express his internationalism and understandings of documentary art.

Land and Clouds Without Bombs

What did the winning reality look like for Zheng Junli, and what kinds of work did he undertake to capture it on cinema? Take a cursory look at *Long Live the Nation(s)*, and one notices that while the film was made at the height of the war, it included few images of war, destruction, and displacement. Such images had been prominently featured in other contemporaneous documentaries on the Sino-Japanese War. Lai Manwai, immediately after the Japanese air raid on Shanghai in 1937, went out to film the city's devastation and edited the haunting images into *A True Record of Shanghai's Battle of Defense Against Japan* (*Songhu Kangzhan jishi*, 1937). Joris Ivens's *400 Million* (1939), a solidarity film, and Frank Capra's *The Battle of China* (1944), a U.S. military production, both reporting on the Sino-Japanese War, begin with Japanese bombing from the air and horrendous images of destruction and death. "City of Shanghai, 20,000 killed. Nanking in ruins, 10,000 dead. Hankow, 15,000. Canton, 20,000. All civilians, not a single soldier, 150,000 dead. The sky becomes your enemy. The walls of your own home become a death trap," intones the voice-over in *400 Million*. Both films depicted the panicked and massive exodus of people from occupied territories and the refugees' tenacious journeys inland.

In contrast, *Long Live the Nation* begins with a sequence in the midst of the boundless desert of China's Northwest. There is no bombing, death, or destruction. A fixed camera is placed at slightly higher than human height. In comparison to the flattening effect of aerial shots that opened *The Battle of China*, this framing preserves the depth of field and grounds the viewer in the enormity of the land. A traveler leading a train of camels on a journey; a queue of laborers walking to work on a dry salt field. The human and animal figures are small compared to the environment, but they journey on, assuredly, on solid ground, traversing a land undivided in its depth and breadth, a space of free movement and potentiality.

Zheng's choice to begin the film with no figurative depictions of war was closely connected to his engagement in war mobilization on the ground: he had observed audience reactions up-close and understood what kinds of films could serve as good wartime propaganda. During the making of *Long Live the Nation(s)*, Zheng's crew traveled with a film projection team for part of their journey. During their travels, they not only filmed but also staged screenings, organized drama performances, and exhibited paintings and posters to mobilize the masses for the War of Resistance.[27] Zheng frequently noted in his diary how audience responded to these propaganda efforts. A newsreel screening in the county of Guyuan (in present-day Ningxia) brought a crowd of three thousand, almost 70–80 percent of the town's population, which Zheng found encouraging. Yet the newsreels shown were unsuitable for use as propaganda. As Zheng observed, "the explosions [in the films] were too big and too numerous. They spread an air of terror."[28]

Working between production and exhibition, the filmmaker as propagandist drew from his observations on audience reception to reconsider the film form. In *Long Live the Nation(s)*, images of destruction, burning, and deaths appear in only one sequence. With two layers of superimposition—a map of China and lengthy intertitles condemning Japan's war acts—the images are sufficiently obscured and distanced for the "air of terror" to be dampened.

Meanwhile, music, lacking figuration but profoundly corporeal and affective, became a vital supplement to the moving image, creating what Weihong Bao describes in her discussion on propaganda as the "vibration in the air."[29] Throughout the film, the sound track repeatedly forms dialogical relationships with the images, creating complex layers of affect and meaning. In the aforementioned first sequence of the film, set in the desert, what discloses the danger of the moment is not the image but the accompanying music, an original score composed by the talented musician Sheng Jialun. The oboe begins and sustains a penetrating E note, as alarming as a siren. After a number of ominous short and low-pitched rhythmic phrases that sound out the threat of war, the winds and strings make their ascent and play, in the tenacious walking speed of the *moderato*, variations on the leitmotif inspired by Mongolian and Tibetan folk melodies. This sequence ends with a long shot of a Tibetan stupa and a man dressed in Tibetan clothes standing on its elevated platform and blowing into a Tibetan horn. Instead of registering the diegetic sound of the horn, the nondiegetic music in the soundtrack emulates its sounds of alarm with symphonic orchestration, with flutes and violins soaring to reach a high note of both alert and hope, highlighting the polyphonic nature of cinematic art and its calls for action.

If the film's first sequence features vast expanses of the land, the common denominator for its second sequence is the sky and its atmospheric clouds and mists. Composed of iconic images of national landmarks such as the Temple of Heaven in Beijing, the Great Wall, and the Big Goose Pagoda in Xi'an, this montage sequence brings these sites into a unified national space, despite the fact that some of them were already under Japanese occupation. The Great Wall, for example, was filmed with a model in the film studio. What lent this sequence a unifying luminosity was the sky and clouds, against which most of these images were framed.

When the sky became an active arena of warfare and the land lay in ruins in the war zones, Zheng reclaimed the sky and the land as restorative spaces in the hinterland. Filming the sky and the clouds was among Zheng's persistent interests throughout the trip. His diaries frequently mentioned the color of the sky and whether clouds were present. Gray rain clouds were avoided. A great deal of time was spent waiting for the sky to clear, and for the luminous, white clouds to appear. Long waits in vain were a common occurrence, as the crew experienced one day at Bronze Valley (Qingtongxia, in present-day Ningxia): "As there were no clouds at the edge of the sky, the image looked dull, so we waited, waited . . . waited, until four o'clock in the afternoon, the wind arose and gray clouds closed in, the sky looked like a gray curtain. Disappointed, we had to leave."[30] When the clouds did appear, they were met with ecstasy. Zheng wrote about his encounter with clouds on Mount Hua in beautiful classical Chinese prose:

> At the beginning of its formation, the cloud is like fungi from a moist stream. Then it grows into silk, and the silk is woven into threads, threads into fabric, and fabric into ribbons. They float and envelop the mountains, and then again transform into thread, and scatter into silk. Soaring toward the sky, the silk congeals into white jades, into crystals. Waves of jade and crystal arose from underneath my feet. If yesterday I was driven by a strong wind, then today I'm

buried by the white clouds. The clouds strike my eyes, permeate my heart as I breathe. I become a cloud, turning white.³¹

Waiting for the clouds, which Zheng Junli and his crew did throughout their journey, was an act of both immersion and intention. Filmmakers experienced an intensely immersive, and at times ecstatic, relationship with the contingent environment in which they found themselves. Yet they never let go of their directorial designs and role as propagandists and insisted on the best images suitable for an uplifting propaganda film. The dialogical relationships between image and sound, and between immersion and intention—so plentifully manifested in the film's prelude—underlay Zheng's aesthetic experiments to capture the elusive "winning realities" and create a film of propaganda and solidarity.

Documentary Dramaturgy as Political Performance

Writing on Ivens's solidarity filmmaking, Thomas Waugh describes how Ivens and his cinematographer John Ferno frequently staged scenes during their shooting. "Using their heavy tripod-based Debrie camera, Ivens and Ferno developed a kind of documentary 'mise-en-scene,' a collaborative shooting style 'staging' 'real' actors in 'real' settings that eventually made up about two-fifths of the finished film."³²

Even though staging and reenactments had been practiced throughout film history, by the 1930s, their use had become more intensified, even when portable film technology allowed easier on-the-spot documentation. According to Waugh, Ivens regularly used studio vocabulary such as "retake" and "covering shot" on location, and this practice of enacting the "mise-en-scene" was shared among most major documentarists of the period. Scripting became widely practiced. "Writers became standard crew members, not only for commentaries, but to provide plots, continuity, and dialogue."³³ With propaganda needs mounting during the war, scripting and staging allowed filmmakers more control in the production process to create documentary with stronger affective impact and persuasive power.

Zheng Junli relied heavily on staging when making *Long Live the Nation(s)*. In an essay published in 1943, soon after the film's release, he acknowledged that 90 percent of the film was scripted and staged, a much larger percentage than for Ivens. In his essay, Zheng claimed not to have been aware of the prevailing practices in international documentary when he set out to make the film. Instead, he "had undertaken dramatization (*xijuhua*) intuitively."³⁴ By the time he penned the essay, however, Zheng had read more on documentary theory and become familiar with the writings by the British filmmaker Paul Rotha and the Soviet filmmaker Roman Karman. Making a contrast between Karman, who opposed staging and encouraged cinematographers to document spontaneous happenings, and Rotha, who gave more space to the filmmaker's "creative treatment," Zheng justified his own use of dramatization by quoting from Rotha's book *Documentary Film* (1936) that the "essence of the documentary method lies in its dramatization of actual material."[35] Rotha's use of "dramatization" in this context did not refer specifically to the practice of scripting and staging, yet Zheng was astute to sense Rotha's emphasis on documentary direction as a substantial intervention to clarify and execute the production's aims, and to offer versions of realities crafted by the filmmaker and others involved in the production. For Rotha, an objective depiction of an external reality is impossible because "there can be no such thing as truth while the changing developments in society continue to contradict each other." Instead, as Zheng further quotes Rotha, documentary "determines the approach to a subject ... [and] this approach is defined by the aims behind production, by the director's intentions and by the forces making production a possibility."[36]

Zheng Junli's use of dramatization were both pragmatic and visionary. Practically, the extreme wartime shortage of film stock pressured him to make every shot count by extensive scripting. The territorial coverage of the film and the lack of an adequate transportation system also meant that the filmmakers had to undertake long and arduous travels and could spend only a short time in each location. This meant that they had to rely on staging instead of waiting for actions to happen spontaneously.[37] Yet, more important, many of the actions Zheng staged for the camera were not "reenactments" but "enactments": they came into existence for the express purpose of filmmaking. Zheng wrote candidly about how filmmaking proceeded on the grasslands of Suiyuan (present-day Inner Mongolia):

> The population density at the border is low. Few families live in one square *li*. But my work required that I film massive scenes of more than a thousand people, dozens of tents or yurts, four to five thousand heads of cattle. Each time, thanks to a call by local authorities, we troubled people who were within one to two hundred *li* away to move with their tents, family, and food, and abandon their daily life to come to our designated location to work.[38]

Zheng recounted how families arrived with all their household belongings on the backs of oxen, camels, and horses, and how long-distance travel exhausted the cattle. "It was as though whole tribes were moving." Pregnant sheep miscarried. More than a hundred baby lambs younger than a month old died on the way. The pasture at the filming location could not provide enough food for the cattle, and the animals became frightened and restless. People wanted to leave. A huge amount of hay, water, and dry firewood had to be organized immediately to feed the animals and placate their owners. "I really felt [what we were doing] was a crime," Zheng wrote.[39]

In Xu Suling's call for filmmakers to get out of the studio, Xu assumes that "the masses" were simply out there, ready to be filmed. Zheng's account demonstrates that considerable work was involved in staging the masses for the screen. Performances of such a massive scale could be organized only with the support of local political elites, and indeed they were the political forces that facilitated the film's making. The film's opening credits included Nationalist officials such as Fu Zuoyi and Zhu Shaoliang, the Qinghai Muslim warlord Ma Bufang, and the Uyghur nationalist Isa Yusuf Alptekin. Zheng's diaries give details on how local authority figures such as Ma Bufang, Arjia Rinpoche, and the Mongolian ruler Khanddorj, who ruled Suiyuan, helped create mass performances for the camera.[40] Some of them provided their own performances for the film, such as Arjia Rinpoche, who presided over a prayer ceremony at Kumbum Monastery. Others organized the performances of those under their authority. Officers under Khanddorj, for example, mobilized Buddhist lamas, soldiers, and civilians to participate in acting.[41] The gathering of Mongolian nomads and their cattle, which Zheng described in the earlier quote, was organized by Khanddorj and his subordinates.

Although these local power holders had de facto control of the border regions, as small political entities seeking to survive in and benefit from a regional war, they had to be careful to choose the right allies and modulate their relationships with any external power. There may have been many motivations for them to support this film. Some might have wanted to showcase the military might of their forces and their leadership among the local people. Some might have benefited from publicly displaying their support for the War of Resistance, especially if they were under suspicion for colluding with Japan. This may have been at least part of Khanddorj's motivation, as he was being closely monitored by the Nationalist government.[42] Others might see helping with filmmaking as an easy form of compliance with the state's demands in exchange for future benefits. In other words, diverse political and material interests existed in an ostensibly nationalistic film conveying the simple message of national unity in resistance. Filmmaking must be understood here as a mediating event in which various power holders sent political signals, exchanged favors, and managed the broader power dynamics among them.

Local political elites aside, the filmmakers were also important players in this mediating event. They not only served as the mediator that made the event happen but also represented the state and served as a direct link between the people and the central government. One could see the propagandists in action in the film, putting up posters and telling stories about Japan's atrocities at Kumbum Monastery, or giving lessons to the Luoluo people on Sun Yat-sen's

"Three Principles of People." Moving among the state, the local elites, and the people, the filmmakers were treated by the local elites with both courtesy and suspicion. Zheng's diaries repeatedly mentioned how he and his film crew were either being courted by various local elites, as though they were "imperial envoys" (*qinchai dachen*), or being investigated, as though they were spies.[43]

Finally, lamas, soldiers, students, and nomads who performed in front of the camera hailed from specific social networks of religious, political, and economic patronage. Some shared nationalist sentiments toward China. Many, though, had no particular nationalist leanings, as the nation-state had not reached far into the border areas.[44] Lowest in the power hierarchy of the mediating event, these people were mobilized by their local authority figures by way of various benefits and received doses of nationalistic training "on set" from the filmmakers, while lending their images to the cause of anti-Japanese resistance.

Even though the people in Zheng's finished film look reasonably relaxed, the work of dramatization in a cross-cultural context was far from easy. The filmmaker did not understand the language of the people he filmed and had to rely on translation to give directions, which resulted in further misunderstanding. "I showed them by acting it out myself, but the more they mimicked, the stiffer they became. In Xikang, I wanted to film a Luoluo smiling and waving his hand. It took three hours, with more than a hundred people waiting on the side. I stamped my feet with frustration, and that friend was petrified, not knowing where to put his hands. I had to stop work and let him go and destress."[45] Zheng's candid description of how filming was carried out offers a glimpse into the difficulty of soliciting performances from nonactors on camera and allows us to imagine what kinds of directorial work have gone into seemingly transparent propaganda documentaries. Later on, the PRC propaganda filmmakers relied on political performances that gradually became inculcated in the general population. In comparison, Zheng had a harder time, as he filmed among populations that had not yet been integrated into the nation and were not accustomed to political performance. It can be argued that propaganda films such as the one Zheng was making were precisely the media that helped rehearse and inculcate such performances (fig. 3.1).

The Aesthetics of Solidarity for Nations in the Plural

As mentioned earlier, the film's Chinese title, *Minzu wansui*, harbored an ambiguity: it was unclear if the nation was intended to be singular or plural. Zheng's editing script for the film would suggest that he envisioned "nations" in the plural. The script specified that the prelude of the film would include figures of traditional authority for every *minzu* depicted in the film. Besides the tablet of the Yellow Emperor (for the Han), the script included scenes of Mongolians

3.1 Images from around the Kumbum Monastry in Qinghai. Stills from *Long Live the Nation(s)*.

paying respect to the tomb of Genghis Khan, Muslims praying at a mosque under an Islamic flag of a crescent moon and star, and Tibetans prostrating before an image of the Dalai Lama.[46] All these images, however, are missing in the actual film that has survived. Instead, after a sequence featuring the Yellow Emperor tablet and the iconic sights of the national landscape (as described earlier in the section on land and clouds), a panning shot across the sky transitions seamlessly to a vertical tilting shot down to the Generalissimo Chiang Kai-shek, who stands on a podium to oversee a military rally, connecting the sky to the state authority embodied in Chiang. A montage sequence follows this shot, illustrating what the intertitle calls a "total war mobilization": street rallies holding Chiang's portraits and energetic factory productions of textiles and weaponry for military use.

This is probably the most didactic scene in the entire film. Entirely missing from Zheng's editing script, it can be reasonably treated as a later insertion. During the editing process, Zheng came into conflict with his supervisors at the China Motion Picture Studio.[47] As a progressive filmmaker, Zheng had opposed Chiang's regime ever since its suppression of the Shanghai workers' uprising in 1927. While the war forged a temporary alliance between the

Nationalists and the Communists, and many progressives worked for the Nationalist party state in resistance, such collaborations were half-hearted at best and were ridden with disagreements and conflicts. Waugh, in his study of Ivens's *The 400 Million*, discusses Ivens's compromises and frustrations during the filmmaking process. A progressive filmmaker, Ivens had wanted to feature the Communists in the anti-imperialist struggle. The Nationalist state studios, however, created insurmountable hurdles to prevent Ivens from getting to Yan'an to report on the Communist stronghold. Under pressure to foreground Chiang and the Nationalist government and minimize the visibility of the Communists in the film, Ivens in the end managed to insert only brief shots of Zhu De and Zhou Enlai, the leaders of the Communist Eighth Route Army.[48] Likewise, Zheng Junli resisted legitimizing Chiang's party state in his film, and this conflict with the studio led to the termination of his employment.[49]

The insertion of Chiang Kai-shek's image as the sole leader of the nation and the erasure of other sources of authority in the film's prelude marked significant differences in the way the state-run film studio and the filmmaker conceived of the nation. However, even though the film's prelude had been considerably modified under the studio's pressure to express the Nationalist party ideology, one can still discern the filmmaker's pursuit of an aesthetics of solidarity in the film. As mentioned earlier, having come of age in Shanghai's semi-colonial realities, Zheng was keenly conscious and critical of colonial racial and developmental hierarchies and the Orientalism of Hollywood's representations of other peoples. His *History of Modern Chinese Cinema* issued a Marxist critique of Hollywood domination in China and advocated for China's "indigenous film industry" as it struggled to represent China's situated realities on the ground. While Zheng was aware of the border regions' significance for China's security, as these areas had long been areas of contestation among the British, French, Japanese, and Russian imperial powers, he did not share the Nationalist party state's reimperializing effort to extend stronger state power into these regions and exercise a tighter control. The Soviet Union's nationalities policy, especially the granting of national sovereignty and the right of self-determination, was widely known in China. Chinese progressive intellectuals saw parallels between the national question in the Soviet Union and in China—both were problems left behind by previous imperial expansions of tsarist Russia and the Qing—and drew inspiration from Soviet discourses to reconsider nationality issues in China.[50]

Zheng Junli's film, diary, and editing script testify to the filmmaker's respect for the societies and peoples in front of his camera. Against developmentalist hierarchies, the film stressed the contemporaneity of the societies it portrayed. Whether it was Tibetan religious ritual and dance at Kumbum Monastery in Qinghai or the Luoluo's construction of the Burma Road in Yunnan, Zheng built mise-en-scene layered with interconnected action and evoked senses—visual, auditory, aromatic—to immerse viewers in the contemporaneous dynamism of the societies being depicted.

Take the segment on the Tibetans as an example. It begins with an extreme low-angle shot of prayer flags fluttering against a sky with luminous clouds. Instead of a high-angle shot to "look down" on the traditional habitat of Tibetans, the camera stays low to the ground and slowly turns, emulating the spatial experience of admiring the prayer flags from below. In the following shot, Tibetan lamas, dressed in ceremonial robes, play seashell horns and Tibetan long horns on the gilded roof of Kumbum Monastery. Now the camera angle moves higher, as the camera films from the roof of the monastery, but it is important to note that this is not a disembodied high-angle shot emphasizing mastery of the terrain, but an intimate point of view shot that shares with the viewer what the lama sees from the monastery roof: a vast expanse of grassland on which the sound of the horns, emanating from the ritual center of the monastery, serves as a cohesive presence.

The next sequence begins with the household fire-offering ritual, typically performed in open air in the mornings. "We burn pine and cypress branches as offerings to the heavens. We sprinkle milk on the ground, hoping green grasses will sprout from the earth, so our cattle and sheep may eat their fill each day." The male voice-over explains in the first person, making the ritual understandable and relatable for viewers of other cultures. As three men and women circle the fire and sprinkle milk in the foreground, a number of women, richly adorned with fur hat and ornaments, come out of the tent in the background one by one, their linear procession adding geometric contrast to the circular motions around the fire in the foreground. The camera then follows the women as they milk the cows and get the cattle ready for a day's roaming and feeding. Certainly choreographed—most likely the Tibetan women have put on their festive clothing not meant for their daily chores—this sequence nevertheless captures, without mystification but with respect, sophisticated symbolic and material productions undertaken simultaneously and in close relationships to each other as integral aspects of daily communal lives.

Besides the camera's incorporation of situated and embodied points of view and the richly layered mise-en-scene attending to symbolic and material productions, the film also employs dynamic montage sequences to depict production processes, whether material or cultural. One sequence depicts Miao men transporting felled logs down a mountain. Each log requires sixteen people, who carry it on shoulder poles down the mountainside via a narrow passage. This is not unlike tightrope walking with a heavy load, and one could easily slip and fall off the cliff. To celebrate this incredible feat of strength and coordination, Zheng uses thirteen shots, from multiple angles (high and low) and with different framing (long, medium, close-up, panning), to construct a montage

3.2 Montage sequence studying the process of logging in the mountains. Stills from *Long Live the Nation(s)*.

sequence accompanied by the single-note rhythmic music of the Miao mouth-harps (*kouxian*) (fig. 3.2). Another sequence uses twenty-seven shots to depict a Miao communal ritual where men play free-reed mouth organs (*lusheng*) in chorus and women dance a circle dance. The ecstatic swaying of the musicians' bodies and the long reeds of the *lusheng* fill each frame with tremendous dynamism. The circle dance brings further contrapuntal vectors of movement to the musicians' sway. Like a symphonic movement, this sequence gathers momentum and ends in a crescendo, as the montage between frames becomes ever more rapid, drawing the viewer into an overwhelming, almost trance-like experience (fig. 3.3).

These meticulously constructed, multishot montage sequences in the film were achieved with the most rudimentary means. Zheng and his crew were equipped with only one Eyemo camera on the trip and had to do multiple takes from a variety of angles and distances. This made the filmmakers' own work comparable to the work of the people in front of the camera. The montage sequence of log transportation, for example, showcased not only the loggers' amazing balancing act under their heavy load but also the filmmakers' hard labor scaling the nearby mountain ranges to film the repeated activity from

3.3 Montage sequence of a Miao communal ritual with music and dance. Stills from *Long Live the Nation(s)*.

different distances and angles. Such sequences would have been shot by multiple cameras in more capital- and technology-intensive production contexts, such as those provided by well-funded Euro-American and Japanese studios. Zheng and his crew's painstaking act of creating these stunning montage sequences with a single camera suggests a desire on the part of the filmmakers to substitute labor for capital and skill for technology—just as the Luoluo loggers did—in order to create an indigenous cinema equal to, or even better than, the much better equipped cinemas at the metropole.

While the filmmakers' labor-intensive production was comparable to the daily work performed by the people in front of the camera lens, the filmmakers also welcomed opportunities to co-inhabit ritual spaces conducive to building connections with those they were filming. The camera could not have created a trance-like experience with the Miao mouth-organ music and dance had the cinematographer not brought the camera into its midst. The ethnographic filmmaker Jean Rouch observes that the camera can induce a "film-trance" when the filmmaker becomes an active participant in a ritual and, like other participants, is also "possessed" by it.[51] *Long Live the Nation(s)* is full of immersive moments when the camera joins rituals, dances, and the daily work of those in front of it and around it, creating ecstatic feelings of becoming-one, not unlike how Zheng Junli felt when he wrote that he "became" the clouds.

Zheng Junli's *Long Live the Nation(s)* is a remarkable wartime documentary. The fortunate fact that the film and the diary of the filmmaker both survived the war offers us a rare opportunity to understand how a propaganda documentary was made on the ground, through the participation of people positioned differently in terms of power, ideological commitment, and social embedding. Propaganda documentaries appear deceptively transparent and straightforward, but these texts are in fact layered with inscriptions by historically situated actors brought into interaction through the filmmaking. With this newly gained understanding of propaganda production, I now move from Chongqing to Yan'an, the Communist stronghold, to discuss emergent documentary filmmaking there.

Joris Ivens Meets Yuan Muzhi

> *Documentary never existed in China. In capitalist societies, confronting social realities with a camera is not permitted, as such confrontation can expose the darkness of the society and create difficulties for the ruler. Documentary was born in the October Revolution of the Soviet Union.*
>
> —Yuan Muzhi, 1941

In the summer of 1938, Yuan Muzhi met Joris Ivens in Hankou. Renowned leftist documentary filmmaker, Ivens came to the war-torn country to make *The 400 Million* (1939), a solidarity film documenting China's war of resistance. Yuan Muzhi, leading left-wing filmmaker from Shanghai, was on his way to Yan'an, the Communist base area, to found the Yan'an Film Troupe (Yan'an dianying tuan), the Chinese Communist Party's first filmmaking entity.

Yuan Muzhi's meeting with Ivens was a fruitful one. At the meeting Ivens promised to donate a 35mm Kinamo film camera and film stock to Yan'an's new film unit, which he promptly fulfilled a few days later, passing the camera discreetly to Yuan's collaborator Wu Yinxian. Also at the meeting, Yuan learned from Ivens new ways to think about documentary and its significance for progressive filmmaking. After the meeting, and before leaving for Yan'an, Yuan wrote a short essay, "On Documentary," based on his conversation with Ivens. This essay was incorporated into an interview with Yuan a few years later and published in the Chongqing-based *Chinese Cinema (Zhongguo dianying)*.[52]

As quoted at the beginning of this section, in the essay, Yuan traced documentary's origins to the October Revolution. Yuan explained that before the October Revolution, cinema in Russia was controlled by the capitalists and only imitated Euro-American productions. After the revolution, the Red Army gained control of the cinema technology and began making news films in great numbers. It was by compiling and editing these news films that the Soviet filmmaker Dziga Vertov created the documentary form. While documentary as a mode of filmmaking was particularly suited to wartime material conditions and could well serve wartime propaganda needs, Yuan's vision for documentary went beyond wartime contingencies. For its attunement to people's lived experiences and struggles on the ground, documentary could serve as "the preparatory stage for the creation of a new film art." It was from documentary, Yuan wrote, that the magnificent Soviet feature films, such as the beloved biopic *Chapayev* (1934), were developed, and he called on filmmakers around China to launch a documentary movement to "create the foundation for a great new film art."[53]

Certainly, it was an exaggeration for Yuan to say that "documentary never existed in China." The first two chapters in this book would argue otherwise. Yuan was among Shanghai's leading leftwing filmmakers, and, as I demonstrated in the previous chapter, even though fiction was the predominant mode for Shanghai left-wing cinema, documentary figured importantly as well. Yuan had his own "documentary moment": he included in his fictional feature films *City Scenes* (*Dushi fengguang*, 1935) and *Street Angel* (*Malu tianshi*, 1937) a three-minute-long montage sequence depicting the semicolonial city of Shanghai in the "city symphony" mode.

Yuan's Soviet-centered historiography for documentary's origin was most likely Ivens's input. By 1938, when Ivens came to China, he had been involved in international left-wing filmmaking for a number of years. The Workers' International Relief (WIR), the Berlin-based socialist organization founded in 1921 by the Comintern, had endeavored to build a worldwide proletarian cinema. Even though the rise of Nazism in the 1930s severely curtailed WIR's activities in Germany and the Comintern disbanded the organization in 1935, WIR had supported and connected left-wing filmmaking around the world, from the Proletarian Film League (Prokino) in Japan to the Workers' Film and Photo League in the United States. Among the most active filmmakers traversing this network of activist filmmaking, Ivens had traveled to the Soviet Union with WIR support to make *Song of Heroes* (1932) and had worked closely with Nykino and Frontier Films, offshoot organizations of the Workers' Film and Photo League in the United States, on his solidarity documentaries such as *The Spanish Earth* (1937) on the Spanish Civil War and *The 400 Million* on China.[54]

Ivens and Yuan had both pursued progressive filmmaking and understood its difficulty in societies where authorities had long suppressed left-wing organizing. Ivens had witnessed the challenges his comrades in Europe and America faced. In China, he experienced constant surveillance by the Nationalists, who thwarted his plan to travel to Yan'an and film the Communist base areas there.⁵⁵ As I discussed in chapter 2, documentary filmmaking in semicolonial Shanghai also faced obstacles on all fronts, from difficulties in gaining access to film location, to infrastructural and financial shortage, to war destruction. For this reason, both Yuan and Ivens looked on Soviet cinema with deep admiration, considering it as a cinema made without capitulation to the capitalist mode of production and fully supported by a revolutionary regime representing the interests of the working people. Of course, these were imaginations that did not align with Soviet realities—the 1930s already saw the rise of Stalinism that placed heavy disciplinary pressure on filmmaking activities, which I will discuss later in the chapter. Yet what motivated Yuan Muzhi, heading to Yan'an to found the Chinese Communist Party's first filmmaking entity, was a deeply held ambition, to build an emancipatory cinema for China. This new cinema would begin with filming China's Red Army in Yan'an.

Making a Yan'an Cinema

By the late 1930s Yan'an had attracted international attention as the bastion of Chinese communism. Even though the Nationalist party state had made every effort to obstruct journalistic access to it—they successfully prevented Joris Ivens from going there—some still managed to make their way to Yan'an. The American journalist Edgar Snow visited in 1936, took photographs, and recorded 16mm film footage of the base area. He exhibited these in February 1937 at the Yenching University in Beijing, where he taught journalism and wrote his *Red Star Over China*. It was Snow's writing and film, along with other contributions by American progressives to China's communist movement, such as the dispatches from Agnes Smedley, that brought increasing attention to China in leftwing circles internationally and paved the way for Ivens' filmmaking mission in China in 1938.⁵⁶ Edgar Snow's reporting also influenced Yuan Muzhi's decision to film in Yan'an. The actress Chen Bo'er, who would later join Yuan in Yan'an and in time became his partner, attended Snow's talk and exhibition at Yenching University when she passed through Beijing with a touring drama troupe. Snow's footage of Yan'an's revolutionary culture made a deep impression on Chen, and her excited recounting of this event to Yuan inspired the latter to plan a filmmaking trip to Yan'an himself.⁵⁷ In addition to Snow, the Soviet documentarist Roman Karmen, who, like Ivens, had filmed the Spanish Civil War before arriving in China, made it to Yan'an, met with Mao Zedong and other leaders, and filmed there in May and June 1939.

The founding of CCP's own film unit in Yan'an would certainly improve international visibility of the Communist base area and cultivate solidarity with it among the international left. Meanwhile, Yan'an filmmaking must also answer pressing existential needs associated with the extraordinary project of constructing a revolutionary polity in the loess hills of poor, rural northern Shaanxi, under economic blockades by the Nationalists and military attacks by the Japanese. Yan'an's immediate survival depended on whether it could build solidarity among its different constituents locally: the growing Communist army and its cadres, the progressive intellectuals and students arriving from all parts of China, and the peasants in the region who benefited from CCP-led land reform but now shouldered the burden of supporting the army with provisions, most importantly grain. Finally, besides seeking international solidarity and securing its immediate survival, the Communist base area also faced a fundamental challenge: the proletariat—the politicized industrial working class that was the classical revolutionary subject anticipated by Marxist theories—did not exist in Yan'an. The idea that Communist revolutions could happen in agrarian societies without a substantial working class was, indeed, Mao's key invention after the Nationalists had pushed the Communist Party to rural outposts such as Yan'an. Therefore, while Zheng Yongzhi, the Nationalist cultural bureaucrat, could lay out simple templates for "winning realities" that propaganda films made in Chongqing should endeavor to depict, propaganda in Yan'an had to serve more complex needs, from building international and local solidarities to transforming the masses into emergent revolutionary subjects.

Mao Zedong's Yan'an talks on literature and art formed a foundational text for Maoist revolutionary culture. Delivered in May 1942, they were meant to lay out the guidelines for Yan'an cultural production. Some of the ideas in these talks weren't new. Like Zheng Yongzhi, Mao also argued for the importance of depicting one's allies and enemies with clear attitudes and called on writers and artists to expose the enemy's cruelty and the "inevitability of their defeat" and extoll "the masses of the people, their toil and their struggle, their army and their Party." What was radically new, however, was Mao's emphasis on cultural work as the transformative experience that would usher in mutually constitutive relationships among the cultural workers, the masses, and the party and give rise to new revolutionary subjects. While Zheng Yongzhi, with the resources and territorial reach of the Nationalist government, focused on building the infrastructure of film production and circulation, Mao, in the resource-poor outpost of Yan'an, saw the creation of new political relationalities as the most important task at hand. He called on the intellectuals to interrogate their own socialization associated with their class positions, and "gradually move their feet over to the side of the workers, peasants, and soldiers, to the side of the proletariat, through the process of going into their very midst and into the thick of practical struggles and through the process of studying Marxism and society."[58]

This process was meant to be dialogical and transformative. The intellectuals and the masses would serve as both teacher and pupil for each other, and both would shed their nonrevolutionary socializations in the process to forge new, class-based political subjectivities. While Mao's Yan'an talks discussed how intellectuals and the masses must interact with each other to produce a transformative revolutionary culture, the Communist Party, as the vanguard of the revolution, was the third participant to the desired political relationality laid out by Mao. The party, as Mao stated, was composed of "political specialists who know the science or art of revolutionary politics." Its task was to collect opinions from the masses, "sift and refine them, and return them to the masses, who then take them and put them into practice." In other words, the party's leadership role in the revolution could be understood in terms of mediation: as revolutionary specialists, the party mediated between Marxist-Leninist principles and Chinese historical realities, and, so doing, it held supervisory and disciplinary authorities over both the intellectuals and the masses. Cultural work, indispensable to the revolution, must be "subordinated to the revolutionary tasks set by the party in a given period." In the flux of revolutionary becomings, the party was, supposedly, the designated kernel of stability, the vanguard who could tell what was "proletarian" from what was "bourgeois," serving as a corrective force to safeguard revolutionary transformations.[59]

Mao's Yan'an talks alert us to importance of cultural productions in Yan'an and the complex needs placed on them. In light of Mao's conception of revolutionary culture, it is not surprising that documentary film, involving direct contact and collaboration between filmmakers and the masses, and under the direct supervision of the party, would be considered the foundation for a revolutionary cinema. Yuan Muzhi had already harbored this ambition when he arrived in Yan'an in the fall of 1938, having learned about progressive documentary filmmaking from Ivens. Equipped with two cameras—the 16mm camera that Zhou Enlai had arranged for him to purchase in Hong Kong, and the 35mm Kinamo gifted by Ivens—Yuan and his collaborator Wu Yinxian set out to make a feature-length documentary, *Yan'an and the Eighth Route Army* (*Yan'an yu balujun*). Yuan and Wu filmed the guerrilla warfare waged by the Eighth Route Army against the Japanese troops. They captured on camera the Canadian Communist doctor Henry Norman Bethune performing surgeries on injured soldiers close to the frontlines, and documented Yan'an's flourishing cultural productions energized by progressive youth arriving from across China. As the footage accumulated, the filmmakers guarded the reels against any possible damage. Yuan kept the film reels within his reach when he slept.[60]

With Yuan's talent, manifested so brilliantly in the films he had made in Shanghai, and with his ambition to build foundations for a new cinema through documentary, this film would have been a landmark production. Unfortunately, the film was lost before it could be completed. Due to the embargo imposed by the Japanese and the Nationalists, provisions for postproduction were almost nonexistent in Yan'an. After filming concluded in 1940, Yuan and the music composer Xian Xinghai traveled to Moscow to work on the film's postproduction at Mosfilm. During the German invasion and the hectic evacuations to Central Asia in 1941, the film footage was irrevocably lost by the studio. Yuan and Xian ended up stranded in Soviet Central Asia, unable to gain safe passage to return to China. Xian tragically died of illness in Moscow in 1945. Yuan finally made it back to China after the war in 1946, just in time to help the CCP take over the Japanese colonial film establishment in Manchuria.[61]

Intended to be the most important documentary out of Yan'an, *Yan'an and the Eighth Route Army* was never actualized. What was actualized in Yan'an were a number of shorter films and, perhaps more important, a growing film unit that in time became the foundational institution for CCP filmmaking during the Civil War and into the People's Republic. While Yuan was stranded in the Soviet Union, filmmaking in Yan'an continued under the direction of the experienced cinematographer Wu Yinxian, who had worked closely with Yuan in Shanghai prior to the war. Between 1940 and 1945, working with an extreme shortage of film stock and postproduction capacity, Wu and the rest of the Yan'an Film Unit finished a number of short films, such as *The Soviet Red Army Is Invincible* (*Sulian hongjun shi buke zhanshengde*), made in 1941 by re-editing Soviet newsreel footage on the German invasion and the Soviet war of self-defense, for which Wu created animated maps and intertitles; *Uniting Production and Battle* (*Shengchan yu zhandou jiehe qilai*, also known as *Nanniwan*), a thirteen-minute documentary filmed by Wu Yinxian and edited by Qian Xiaozhang between 1942 and 1943, on the CCP army's cultivation of Nanniwan near Yan'an to alleviate food and material shortages; and a number of other short actuality films documenting sports events, celebrations, and other important meetings.[62]

Nanniwan was the earliest film completed and widely screened in Yan'an, and the first film made after Mao Zedong's Yan'an talks. Unlike *Yan'an and the Eighth Route Army*, meant for international distribution, this film, with its image quality compromised by the use of expired positive film stock and by the rudimentary postproduction conditions, was made to answer the challenges faced by the Communists in Yan'an and exhibited only locally.

By the time of *Nanniwan*'s production in the summer of 1942, Yan'an had been in a severe economic crisis for more than a year. Founded in 1934, the Communist base areas of Shaan-Gan-Ning, of which Yan'an was a part, had always been in a precarious economic situation, as the local peasant economy could hardly support a growing Communist army, and the Nationalist blockade made it hard to secure provisions from outside. While the second United Front between the Nationalists and the Communists, formed in late 1937, temporally lessened the blockade, a military conflict between the two sides in early 1941 again led to a breakdown of relationships and intensified the Nationalist blockade of the Communist base area. This, compounded by Japan's military assault on the region and poor harvests, resulted in a severe economic crisis in the base area in 1941 and 1942. This period saw hyperinflation, grain shortages, and the worsening of army-peasant relations, as the army had no choice but to extract further grain from peasants in lean years. The situation was so bad that party leadership raised the question of whether to abandon the Shaan-Gan-Ning area for a new base elsewhere.[63] Mao insisted on staying and developed a mass-line strategy to tackle the economic crisis, which Mark Selden calls the "Yenan Way," and which the Yan'an production campaign, including the cultivation of Nanniwan, exemplified.[64]

Nanniwan begins with Mao Zedong sitting at a desk in front of his cave dwelling and writing, in calligraphy, the slogan he had coined for the Yan'an production campaign: "With our own hands, make food and clothing aplenty" (*ziji dongshou, fengyi zushi*). This is followed by reenacted scenes of soldiers arriving in the Nanniwan area on foot and on horseback. Having no ready shelter and no food supplies, the soldiers make use of what is readily available on-site, building sheds from tree branches and hay and gathering wild greens for food. As the soldiers settle in the area, they clear the fields, sow seeds, build bridges and cave dwellings, and engage in cottage industry productions of paper, textile, and agricultural appliances. A three-minute sequence concludes the production campaign with a celebration of harvest. Dinner tables are set with dishes of rich food. Harvested vegetables and grains pile up and fill the frames. Farm animals such as chickens, ducks, oxen, and horses roam freely in a lush countryside dotted with ponds and streams, looking no different from the typical scenery of the fertile and water-rich regions of the south of the Yangtze. As the problem of food and supply scarcity is solved, the last third of the film showcases reinvigorated military training, where soldiers perform military drills such as marching, climbing, and horse-riding.[65]

As the film began production shortly after Mao Zedong's Yan'an talk, both Wu and Qian endeavored to make the film according to their interpretations of Mao's teachings. Understanding documentary as a mode of filmmaking closest to the masses, Wu spent considerable time at Nanniwan living with the soldiers stationed there. Qian edited the film in a straightforward manner to ensure legibility to viewers unfamiliar with cinema.[66] One notable feature of the film is a lack of interest in personification. Unlike Joris Ivens, who manufactured specific personal stories such as that told by Sergeant Wang in *The 400 Million*, Wu and Qian made no attempt to tell personal stories. Soldiers are always filmed in collective formation. This is a film made predominantly with long shots and extreme long shots. Medium shots and close-ups are rare, and when they are used, medium shots tend to frame a group of people working with their heads down, with their faces not fully visible to the camera, and close-ups frame hands and feet busy at work. A possible explanation is that while international solidarity films such as Ivens's need personification to communicate distant experiences to home audiences, this film was not meant to travel far afield. As mentioned before, while Yuan Muzhi's film, under postproduction in the Soviet Union, was meant for international circulation, *Nanniwan*, shot on expired film, was a product of Yan'an's cottage film industry and meant to serve the local community. As a large portion of the population was involved in a production campaign, personification would not be necessary for the viewers to identify with the activities in the film. In fact, it is conceivable that showcasing specific soldiers and laborers might even hinder identification, by fostering competition on who gets to be in the movies.

Foregrounded in the film instead is the overall kinetic energy of bodies in collective labor and the skillful work accomplished by everyone's deft hands, making this film a good example of what Salomé Aguilera Skvirsky calls the "process genre." Films of the process genre represent processes of production with clear steps of sequential labor, from the work's beginning, through its middle phases, to its successful completion. By showing the step-by-step success of people making and doing things, these films make "palpable the awesome transformative potential of human labor" and impart in viewers a deep sense of wonder and satisfaction as they witness the realization of this potential.[67] Even though the production campaign in Nanniwan had begun in March 1941 and Wu Yinxian began filming only in the summer of 1942, he made sure that the soldiers reenacted their arrival and the beginning of their work in the area so that the film could depict Nanniwan's transformation sequentially, from clearing the fields and sowing the seeds to the successful harvest and positive transformation of the environment. The film was exhibited widely in Yan'an and its surroundings to soldiers, students, and peasants alike. The film was silent, but during screenings a phonograph would play Beethoven's *Pastorale* Symphony, and a narrator would be present to explain the film to the audience.[68] From grain to nuts, from ducks to oxen and horses, the products of labor were shown on screen in great quantities at the end of the successful production campaign. One can imagine the satisfaction and hope such a film could inspire on its Yan'an viewers, who faced severe economic scarcity and the uncertainty of the base area's future.

Nanniwan's presentation of step-by-step production recalls *Spring Silkworm* (1932), one of the earliest left-wing films produced in Shanghai, discussed in chapter 2. *Spring Silkworm* could be understood as a process film, too, as it follows the process of silkworm farming and depicts a successful harvest, though the film's ending frustrates the satisfaction: due to Japanese dumping of artificial silk in the Chinese market, the market price for silkworm cocoons drastically falls, leading to the silk farmers' bankruptcy. The drama of *Spring Silkworm* lies exactly in this tragic ending that subverts a successful process. It snatches from the viewer the pleasure of seeing things work out after hard and skillful work and demonstrates the counterintuitive and brutal workings of global capitalism and the price mechanism that can turn a harvest into a trap through the devaluation of the product. The restoration of the process genre in Yan'an, then, offered even more than a boost of confidence in the viability of the production campaign and the Yan'an economy. It restored the hope that in this revolutionary outpost, and in the communist future it prefigured, things would again be what they appeared to be, and labor, as long as it was earnestly and diligently applied, would lead to a sure harvest.

Film the Living, Bury the Dead: War Filmmaking as Solidarity

Due to the extreme shortage of supplies, film production was not substantial in Yan'an. The editor Qian Xiaozhang wrote, in retrospect, that it was "a miracle" that the film *Nanniwan* was ever completed.[69] Just as the soldiers in the film made paper, textiles, and agricultural tools by hand, the Yan'an filmmakers also made films with artisanal methods: Qian handprinted the film frame by frame. Under such conditions, it was also nothing short of a miracle that the Yan'an Film Troupe managed to train around forty to fifty photographers and cinematographers in two educational programs that took place in Yan'an in 1945, substantially contributing to the CCP's filmmaking capacity during the Civil War that broke out a year later.

After Japan's unconditional surrender in August 1945, the Soviet Red Army took control of former colonial Manchuria and facilitated the CCP's takeover of the Japanese colonial film establishment, the Manchurian Motion Picture Corporation (Man-ei), in Changchun. Man-ei was a treasure trove of up-to-date film technology and supplies for film production. Acquiring Man-ei meant that the CCP now had its first full-capacity film studio. Racing with the CCP to gain control of Japanese colonial industrial establishments in the Northeast, the Nationalists took Changchun in 1946, but the precious studio had been safely relocated to the CCP-controlled area of Hegang, and on the basis of the studio, the Northeastern Film Studio was founded there in the same year. Having just returned from the Soviet Union, Yuan Muzhi served as the studio's director, and his partner Chen Bo'er, who had been an indispensable creative force in Yan'an's spoken drama productions, served as the party secretary. Yan'an filmmakers took up leadership positions in the studio.[70] Former Man-ei filmmakers and staff, including more than seventy Japanese and Korean members, had relocated with the studio to Hegang and now offered their technical expertise to the CCP's first film studio.[71]

On the foundation of the Yan'an film unit and Man-ei, the Northeastern Film Studio under Yuan Muzhi's leadership began production in early 1947, at the height of the Civil War. It placed a priority on making news and documentary films, while also experimenting with fiction films, educational films for children, and animation. On May 1, 1947, the studio released the first two installments of its newsreel series, *Democratic Northeast* (*Minzhu dongbei*). An international version was made and screened at the Prague International Youth Festival in the same year. The studio's filmmaking capacity grew exponentially between 1947 and 1949. While only three teams of cinematographers filmed on the front lines of the Civil War in 1947, by 1949 the number had risen to thirty. Between 1947 and 1949 filmmakers from the Northeastern Film Studio shot 300,000 feet of actuality footage and enabled the studio to complete seventeen installments of *Democratic Northeast* and many other wartime actualities covering the crucial battles during the Civil War.[72]

The studio was able to make such rapid expansions of filmmaking capacity thanks to the training programs it had organized. Altogether more than seven hundred filmmakers were trained by the Northeastern Film Studio between 1947 and 1949, and news and documentary filmmaking were the most important aspect of the training.[73] Most of these newly trained filmmakers were immediately dispatched to the battlefront to film the military advances of the People's Liberation Army (PLA). To aid these newly trained filmmakers working on their own in battle, Qian Xiaozhang edited six issues of an internally circulated pamphlet, *News Cinematography Circular* (*Xinwen sheying tongxun*), between October 1948 and March 1949 to serve as a reference guide. These pamphlets can no longer be located, yet we do know the titles of some essays included in them. There were some translated writings from Soviet filmmakers, such as excerpts from Roman Karman's essay "The Cultivation of a Documentary Cinematographer" in the first issue, and Yuri Raizman's essay on the making of *The Battle for Berlin* (1945) in the fourth issue.[74] The majority of essays were written by Chinese filmmakers sharing their practical experiences on how to shoot on location in battle: how to organize multiple filmmakers to cover an unrepeatable battle scene; how to film mass formations while paying attention to individuals within that formation; and how to protect the camera from the vicissitudes of war filmmaking, from freezing weather to gunfire.

Filmmakers' memoirs published years after the event describe battleground filmmaking as risky but rewarding experiences. Not just observers with a camera, filmmakers worked with the soldiers before the battle, filmed them in military action, and buried some of them after the battle. The cinematographer Han Kechao recalls that he dug trenches and helped transport injured and deceased soldiers at night, while filming the battles during the day.[75] Shi Yimin wrote about entering Tianjin with the PLA troops and discovering, by chance, the hiding place of Chen Changjie, commander-in-chief of the Nationalist troops, whose capture he participated in and filmed. Filmmakers were also themselves killed in action. The second issue of the *News Cinematography*

Circular was devoted to commemorating three cinematographers who were killed in battle.[76] For the soldiers, being filmed on the battlefront held significant meaning. The cinematographer Lei Ke recalls that just before the PLA's crossing of the Yangtze River en route to Shanghai, he had filmed a squad of soldiers signing their names on a public letter stating their determination to fight the enemy. After he finished filming, he overheard a soldier saying to his friends, "We'll go into battle soon. I'm so happy we were filmed just now."[77] Like the soldiers' signatures on the public letter, cinema could preserve indexical traces of the lives that might be lost during the battle. While military cultures typically discouraged expressions of fear, the soldiers found consolation in being filmed prior to their battles. In Yan'an, recording the soldiers' faces was avoided, possibly due to the competitive impact that would have on the community. At the battlefront, however, filmmakers frequently used close-ups and medium shots to record the soldiers' faces as a service of anticipatory remembrance to them, as they went into battle.

Crossing the Same River Twice: Spectacular Reenactment and the Soviet Solidarity Film

The Civil War between the Communists and the Nationalists ended in 1949 with Communist victory. Filmmakers trained in Yan'an and at the Northeastern Film Studio had documented all the major battles leading to the Communist Party's capturing of state power, edited them into newsreels or stand-alone documentaries, and screened them in cities coming newly under Communist control as the PLA advanced. Soon after the founding of the PRC, however, these black-and-white films shot in battle became quickly obsolete, replaced by a Sino-Soviet coproduced documentary that reenacted the Communist victory in color.

In October 1949, just after the grand ceremony of the founding of the People's Republic of China in Beijing, soldiers of the PLA's Fourth Field Army, who had just recently arrived and settled in their new station near Tianjin, were ordered to set out to the Northeast, where their battalions had fought deadly but victorious battles against the Nationalist army a year before. Cannons, tanks, and tens of thousands of soldiers were loaded onto trains. Soon the open plains near Jinzhou, where the dust of war had barely settled, were shaken again by cannons and gunfire. In the eight-month period between autumn 1949 and summer 1950, four battles marking the PLA's most important steps to victory during its war against the Nationalists were reenacted by the same army units who had fought them.[78] Also reenacted were numerous celebratory scenes of the PLA soldiers marching into liberated cities such as Tianjin, Beijing,

Nanjing, and Shanghai. The result was the CCP's first-ever documentary in color, *Victory of the Chinese People* (*Zhongguo renmin de shengli*, 1950), directed by Leonid Varlamov, the prize-winning Soviet war cinema specialist.

Victory of the Chinese People was one of two Sino-Soviet coproduced color documentaries made upon the PRC's founding. Unlike the other film, *Liberated China* (*Jiefangle de Zhongguo*), directed by Sergei Gerasimov, which focused on contemporary developments in China, such as the land reform and reorganization of the industry, *Victory of the Chinese People* showcased major battles won by the PLA in 1948–1949. The film was a high-profile undertaking. The Communist leader Liu Shaoqi was put in charge of the film's overall planning, and Mao Zedong was involved as well: he personally wrote to General Lin Biao, asking Lin and his troops to offer every assistance to the Soviet filmmakers. The army also generously permitted the Soviet filmmakers to use real ammunition, which had cost lives to acquire from the retreating Nationalist army and was precious for the resource-limited People's Republic. Wu Benli, a Yan'an filmmaker who assisted in the making of *Victory of the Chinese People*, confessed that he had shed tears watching ammunition being wasted just for cinematic effect.[79]

It is puzzling why such costly reenactments were considered necessary. All four battles depicted in *Victory of the Chinese People* had been filmed by Chinese filmmakers in real time and on the actual battlegrounds less than a year before. The Battle of Liaoshen, decisive for the CCP's control of the Northeast, had been covered by more than thirty Yan'an and Northeastern-trained filmmakers, including Wu Benli himself. Three among them were killed while documenting the battle. The Battle of Crossing the Yangtze, in which the PLA crossed the Yangtze River in thousands of small ferryboats en route to take over Nanjing and Shanghai, was covered by a team of ten cameramen led by Wu Benli. Footage from these battles had been edited into documentary films, and, according to Wu Benli, the Soviet filmmakers had watched these films when preparing to film their reenactments.[80]

Wu Benli professed to cry over the wasteful use of ammunition for cinema, but there were other reasons for sadness. Wu's fellow filmmakers had fallen when filming on the battlefields. The precious footage from the battles also included moving images of soldiers who were killed soon after being filmed. Even though these images were black-and-white and not masterfully done, they cost lives to make and recorded lives that were lost. Their replacement by a spectacular dramatic rendition must not have gone down well for the Yan'an filmmaker.

So far, this book has touched on many instances where filmmakers staged scenes and directed actions when making a film about real historical events.

Cheng Bugao created a fictional family to anchor actuality footage from the Battle of Shanghai in 1932, making up for Chinese filmmakers' limited access to battlefronts. Zheng Junli enacted scenes that did not pre-exist to create a winning reality. Wu Yinxian reenacted the soldiers' arrival in Nanniwan to cultivate the land there, in order to present a complete and satisfying production process to the viewer. Joris Ivens used dramatization to draw the audience emotionally closer to the distant people whose struggles were depicted on the screen. In other words, dramatization has always been a part of documentary filmmaking. What need to be asked are concrete questions about the politics, ethics, and aesthetics of dramatization in specific cases: What kinds of dramatization, for what aims, who directs and is directed, and what is gained and lost?

The making of *Victory of the Chinese People* was an important event in the development of Chinese documentary. This film, and the subsequent translations of Soviet writings on documentary, helped establish a particular practice of socialist realism in documentary.

Aesthetics of Victory

How is *Victory of the Chinese People* aesthetically different from the documentaries made by Chinese filmmakers during the war in 1948–1949, such as *The Last Battles to Liberate the Northeast* (*Jiefang dongbei de zhuihou zhanyi*, 1948) and *Million Heroes Crossing the Yangtze* (*Baiwan xiongshi xia jiangnan*, 1949)?

Most obviously, *Victory of the Chinese People* is in color. Even though China had already had its first color film, *Eternal Regret* (*Shengsi hen*, dir. Fei Mu, 1948), color technology was still new and exciting, and the film's chromatic vibrancy undoubtedly delighted the audience at the time. Besides being in color, the film was spectacularly filmed. The filmmakers' skillful deployment of large army units and civilian populations for reenactment, carefully choreographed mise-en-scene featuring multiple layers of action, and frequent use of unobstructed and panoramic shots made the scale of military action look considerably larger than in the Chinese films shot in actual battles.

When filming the actual battles, the Chinese filmmakers took up the typical positions of combatants: they shot in trenches, from bunkers, and over the shoulders of their fellow combatants. In open spaces, their cameras were often placed close to the ground, as the filmmakers repeatedly had to drop down to the ground to avoid incoming bullets. When shooting cannon fire, they tended to crouch behind a cannon and film its operation by fellow soldiers from that vantage point. Rarely could they shoot multiple cannons in one frame. *Victory of the Chinese People* was filmed differently. The camera did not assume the position of a combatant. Few shots were from the trenches, or from the ground level. Panoramic shots allowed military actions to be viewed in large splendid formations, for example, with snipers on the roofs closest to the camera, soldiers charging on horseback in midrange, more soldiers charging on foot across midrange and into the depth of the field, creating multiple layers of simultaneous action in the terrain. In another unobstructed long shot, dozens of cannons were all lined up and fired one after another, creating a series of timed explosions in a single frame.

Besides panoramic and long shots, *Victory of the Chinese People* also made use of uninterrupted long takes, which would be much harder to do when filming in actual battle. The reenactment of the PLA's occupation of the Presidential Palace in Nanjing was filmed with a long take that followed the soldiers as they ran through the palace's long corridor to get to the office abandoned by Chiang Kai-shek. Lasting for twenty seconds and accompanied by triumphant music with a tempo of more than 180 beats per minute, this shot breathtakingly brings the viewer into the depth of the image itself, creating an exhilarating sensation of the last sprint to victory.

Differences also existed between the Chinese films made on the battlefronts and the Sino-Soviet coproduction in terms of how some relationships were depicted. *Victory of the Chinese People* endeavored to depict relationships between the leader and the soldiers, the army and the people, and the victor and the vanquished. The film included boisterous scenes where rural people fed the army food and water and where city residents lined the streets to welcome the army into liberated cities, such that the victory was understood to belong to all, rather than just to the army. The most illustrious Nationalist generals, now prisoners of war, participated in the reenactment of their capture, such that their subjugation could be performed publicly on screen. When depicting the relationships between the soldiers and their top officers, *Victory of the Chinese People* adopted a clearer visual hierarchy. When filming rallies and ceremonies, the camera filmed soldiers from a high angle, presenting them as an undivided collective acting in unison. The officers, in contrast, stood on elevated platforms, physically separate from the soldiers, and the camera filmed them reverently from a low angle. Such differences in camera angle existed but were rarer in the Chinese films made in battle. As mentioned earlier, filmmaking at the front allowed soldiers to leave images of themselves before they went into battle, and they were filmed, more often than not, at eye-level or lower, in long or medium shots, resembling portraiture (fig. 3.4).

The unobstructed panoramic and long shots, the uninterrupted long takes, the large scale of action, and the reenactments mobilizing a massive number of military and civilian participants—none of this could be achieved without an assured control over the society and the territory. Indeed, compared to the battlefront films produced by Chinese filmmakers, *Victory of the Chinese People* exuded a sense of confident control as its aesthetics of victory (fig. 3.5).

3.4 Stills from *Million Heroes Crossing the Yangtze*.

3.5 Stills from *Victory of the Chinese People*.

Learning from the Soviet Union: Documentary Dramaturgy for Socialist Realism

For Soviet filmmakers, restaging revolution was not a new practice. In the immediate years after the October Revolution, mass reenactments of revolutionary action in street theater were seen as a good way to bring still unorganized masses into simulated revolutionary action and in the process transform them into revolutionaries.[81] The largest reenactments of "storming of the Winter Palace" mobilized eight thousand amateur actors and one hundred thousand spectators in 1920, even though the original attack on the Winter Palace involved only about a hundred people.[82] In time, these spectacular reenactments entered photography and cinema and became how the October Revolution was remembered. Soviet publications later used photos from the reenactment in 1920 as documentary images from the actual event.[83] Sergei Eisenstein and Grigori Aleksandrov's historical film *October*, made in 1927 to celebrate the tenth anniversary of the revolution, was also a large-scale reenactment deemed so superb that "it was for many years passed off by the Soviet leadership as the authentic newsreel footage of this historical event."[84]

Besides the established practice of reenacting landmark actions in revolutionary history, documentary dramaturgy more generally had also been adopted during the Stalinization of the Soviet Union as a dominant practice in adherence to socialist realism. In the 1920s Dziga Vertov had been an outspoken critic of dramatization. Calling theatrical performances and film dramas "surrogates for life," Vertov had believed that footage from unrehearsed everyday life could better serve as "a thermometer or aerometer of our reality, and its significance was unquestionably higher than the inventions of individual authors, individual writers, or directors."[85] Vertov's well-known idea of Kinopravda, or film-truth, was premised on the idea that "*Kinopravda* doesn't order life to proceed according to a writer's scenario, but observes and records life *as it is*, and only then draws conclusions from these observations."[86] On this ground Vertov criticized Eisenstein and Aleksandrov's *October* as a "complete flop," despite the immense government funding behind it, "because the method of the theatrical fiction cannot sustain any significant theme, and this theme is squandered for fictional, toy-shop trivia."[87]

By the time of *Victory of the Chinese People*'s making, however, the tide had long turned in the Soviet Union. Between 1928 and 1932, as Stalin consolidated his power and purged dissenting voices, and as the Soviet Union underwent a "cultural revolution" to establish socialist realism as the guiding principle for the arts, Vertov was criticized for the "naturalism" of his work and accordingly sidelined.[88] By 1932 the use of dramatization in nonfiction films became a common practice, and seamless staging had become a point of pride among filmmakers. A participant at a conference of Soviet filmmakers in 1932 reported that one of his film studio's reconstructions was so successful that "there is not a single shot that has not been staged. Everything, right down to the most distant long shot, was staged yet at numerous screenings no one noticed.... Since we organized the facts ourselves, we were able to impart a certain dynamism, we could choose what to include, and so the work acquired a dramatic spine."[89]

The Sino-Soviet coproduction of *Victory of the Chinese People* introduced Chinese filmmakers to Stalinist practices of documentary dramaturgy. Numerous translated essays of Soviet film theory and criticism, published in China between 1952 and 1953, further asserted its value. In an article entitled "Authenticity in Documentary" (1953), the critic I. Nazarov characterizes Vertov's "kino-eye" as a long discredited documentary practice, because "it films reality with a cold naturalism, superficially gliding over the appearance of reality, and does not manifest the profound essence of reality. It doesn't comprehend reality politically." Even though the intention of such filmmaking is to be "objective," Nazarov writes, the result is exactly the opposite. It would be "a distortion of reality... no less toxic than fabrication." Why would this alleged "naturalism" be so detrimental? Nazarov gives a few examples. Criticizing one scene in Yakuv Bliokh's documentary *Fishermen of the Caspian* (1949), in which one fishing team is awarded a red flag for winning a productivity competition, Nazarov observes: "The scene was shot with low light, as if it had been something very common, meaningless, and ordinary. The narration was vague and hurried... without showing the profound essence of this event, and the great meaning of socialist competition, which, as we know, is the basis of labor relations in the Soviet society." In another example, a leader of a collective farm makes an arrogant appearance in a documentary, behaving in a boastful manner. Nazarov reasons that even if this cadre might indeed have been a bit arrogant, this would not represent his "essential" character, but rather an "accidental and secondary one that only became manifest because of the particular environment created by the act of filming." In both cases, the actual appearance of things captured by the camera was considered inadequate to reveal the essential nature of things and people. This inadequacy was due to various contingencies during the filmmaking, such as inadequate lighting or people's "accidental" behavior in front of the camera. Naturalism, which Nazarov defined as the indiscriminate recording of the visible world, would inevitably distort "reality," because the visible world—or visuality itself—could not be fully trusted. Facing a world where the "essence" and the "accidental" coexisted and were hard to tell apart, filmmakers could not be detached record-keepers but must be "artists and propagators" to reorder the visual world with political awareness: to discern the important from the trivial, grasp the essential as distinct from the contingent, and understand the hierarchies of meaning and temporality, so that they could "go deep into the essence of phenomena, reveal the total meaning of a fact, call people to rush toward the future, and manifest the future in the activities of today."[90]

The fact that documentary must reorder the visible world indicated a need for scripting. As the film critic R. Grigoriev argued in "On the Documentary Screenplay," translated and published in China in June 1952, a documentary script prepared before shooting "would subject our work to a unified intellectual and artistic vision." A good script would allow filmmakers to stage scenes with a unified aesthetics and help filmmakers think through elements such as sound, rhythm, composition, and color arrangement before the event. Grigoriev identified Leonid Varlamov, director of *Victory*, as one of Soviet Union's most skillful documentary script writers.[91] Indeed, during the filming of *Victory*, Varlamov put his skills to full use, exerting much influence on the Chinese filmmakers with whom he worked.

All the Chinese filmmakers who collaborated with Varlamov and Gerasimov had been trained either in Yan'an or at Northeastern Film Studio. By the time of the coproduction, they had joined the new Beijing Film Studio, founded by incorporating filmmakers from Yan'an, Northeastern, other PLA film units, and the former Nationalists' filmmaking establishments in Beijing. According to Beiying's annual report of 1950, the filmmakers' experiences working on the Sino-Soviet coproductions "improved production quality in the studio as a whole."[92] Recalling his experience working on the film with the Soviet filmmakers, the filmmaker Chen Bo wrote, "I was deeply in awe of Comrade Varlamov's talent and creativity in the artistic creation of documentary films." Varlamov impressed Chen not only with his written script, which for Chen showed great knowledge about the Chinese revolution, but also his "sharp political vision" which endowed the film with "rich powers of visual expression." Chen recounted how, when staging the grand entry of PLA troops into liberated Beijing, Varlamov chose to film the closed gate of the American Embassy at the moment when PLA soldiers passed by, so that the rifles on the shoulders of the soldiers pointed right at the American national crest on top of the gate. In Shanghai, inspired by the red flag flying on top of colonial-style buildings, Varlamov staged a scene in which the old Nationalist flag was torn down by PLA soldiers and thrown from the top of a government building. The camera followed the discarded flag's dramatic descent from the rooftop, following its twists and turns, until it landed on the pavement below, to be swept into the dustbin of history. Chen wrote, "Comrade Varlamov's sensitive political vision and his ingenuous artistic imagination combined to create a documentary. These great, moving, and truthful scenes excited countless hearts of Chinese and foreign audiences and left me—a beginner in filmmaking—with indelible impressions. If I could claim to have some ideas about documentary-making later, it all came from experiences with this teacher.... From his creative work, I began to understand the creative strategies of socialist realism in film art."[93]

The Sino-Soviet documentary coproductions, *Victory of the Chinese People* and *Liberated China*, were extremely influential in China. The former premiered in China on October 1, 1950, simultaneously in China's fifteen largest cities, to celebrate the first anniversary of the founding of the PRC.[94] The latter premiered on December 30, 1950. Both films enjoyed unprecedented publicity campaigns in China. Tens of thousands of flyers and posters were printed in each city, delivered to factories, posted on public bulletins, and scattered from the sky by the air force. The films were publicized by parades, banners hung on buildings, and paper archways constructed in workers' quarters. Those who attended the films received as keepsakes free commemorative badges, minted according to designs solicited from the public. Within the first two weeks of its opening, 2.24 million people attended *Victory of the Chinese People*. Between 1951 and 1953 the two films continued their rounds of exhibitions in small cities and screened widely in the countryside, including ethnic minority regions in Inner Mongolia, Tibet, and Yunnan, by mobile film projection teams that had been rapidly trained to perform the task. The Soviet Union had, since the end of the World War II, been engaged in numerous documentary coproductions with other allied socialist countries, including Hungary, Poland, Albania, Czechoslovakia, East Germany, and Bulgaria. Coproductions with China further forged common horizons of experience within the Socialist Bloc and showcased socialist victories and achievements to the rest of the world. Both films won the Stalin Prize for Literature and Art and were exhibited widely in the Soviet Union and the Socialist Bloc. Their exhibitions in India, the United States, and Western Europe were facilitated by Chinese diaspora communities and progressive networks.[95]

Much more can be said about these coproductions and their impact on international socialist culture. Here, however, I wish to call attention to the political relationality underlying their production, not to dismiss these films as intended acts of solidarity, but to acknowledge, and reflect on, the extraordinary demands solidary relationships place on us. By staging expensive reenactments, *Victory of the Chinese People* replaced actual battle scenes shot by Chinese filmmakers who risked their lives and had close relationships to the soldiers, many of whom were subsequently killed in battle, leaving their last images on film. The massive dramaturgy employed by the Soviet filmmakers, along with the color film technology, might have produced spectacular images, but they also brought new hierarchies to the process of filmmaking and created new norms for documentary dramaturgy. According to Chinese filmmaker Shen Rong, who participated in the making of *Victory of the Chinese People*, Varlamov was authoritarian in his direction of the Chinese people who served as "actors" for the documentary, yelling at them when they failed to perform according to his instructions in front of the camera, which brought clashes between him and Chinese filmmakers such as Shen himself.[96]

In this chapter I have studied a number of propaganda documentaries, made in both Chongqing and Yan'an during the Sino-Japanese War, shot by Chinese filmmakers on the battlefront of the Civil War, and reenacted under the direction of Soviet filmmakers after the founding of the PRC. Taking an eventful approach to these propaganda films, I've shown that their political messages and aesthetic forms had a great deal to do with the political relationalities that underlay the films' production. Probing these power relations helps us better understand the specific mediating work these films did on the ground. I have also argued that while dramatization and (re)enactment abounded in propaganda documentaries, attending to the specifics of who directed, who performed, and according to whose visions and scripts can help us better evaluate these films' politics, ethics, and aesthetics.

This eventful approach is, I believe, valuable for engaging with solidarity films, as these aim explicitly to achieve solidary relationships between peoples in struggle. This chapter has discussed Zheng Junli's filmmaking in China's borderlands as a painstaking and compromised creation of interethnic solidarity on screen. By examining the filmmakers' negotiations with various political forces and authorities, dramatization of mass performance, and the aesthetic interventions he brought to the film through cinematography, editing, and sound, I have shown that the filmmaking process brought a variety of actors together to rehearse and inscribe multiple political visions. By contrasting early CCP filmmakers' more equalizing mediation in Yan'an and on the battlefront in the Civil War with the hierarchy of values underlying the reenactments of *Victory of the Chinese People*, I've shown how propaganda films served varied mediation roles at different historical conjunctures, creating different political relationalities in their production and circulation.

With the discussion of *Victory of the Chinese People*, I also hope to reconsider Soviet solidarity filmmaking in China. And here I temporarily depart from the chronological organization of the book to briefly comment on early Soviet solidarity filmmaking in China. The Soviet Union and China had loomed large in each other's revolutionary politics, and China had figured importantly in Soviet solidarity films through most of the twentieth century. Edward Tyerman has shown that Soviet documentaries made in China in the 1920s, such as *The Great Flight* (*Velikii perelet*, 1926) directed by Vladimir Shneiderov, and *Shanghai Document* (*Shankhaiskii dokument*, 1928), directed by Yakov Bliokh, were among Soviet filmmakers' first experiments with an "internationalist aesthetic." Tyerman observes that while these early Soviet films articulated "a new spatial and temporal relationship between China and revolutionary Russia," underlying these films was "an abiding tension between recognition and mastery, community and hierarchy." *The Great Flight*, for example, showcased "the dual power of Soviet avion and Soviet cinema to traverse, perceive, and give meaning to Eurasian space." And *Shanghai Document*, with its masterly parallel montage intercutting between the Chinese part of the city and Shanghai's foreign settlement, also "claim[ed] a unique authority to traverse the disparate spaces of the city and reveal the meaning of their juxtaposition, a capacity it denies to its Chinse subjects."[97]

Confidently asserting the power of Soviet political analysis, *Shanghai Document* was in fact made between 1927 and 1928, when a failure in political analysis of Chinese revolutionary situations had resulted in severe setbacks for both Chinese and Soviet revolutionary movements. In China, the alliance between the Communists and the Nationalists, brokered by the Soviet Union, ended violently with the Nationalist Party's bloody suppressions of Communist organizations. Gravely weakened, the CCP had to retreat from urban centers into the countryside. Meanwhile, as the CCP in its early years readily received directives from the Soviet-led Comintern, this setback was understood as a Soviet policy failure. Seeking responsibility for this failure intensified Soviet intraparty struggles, resulting in the forced exile of Leon Trotsky, the fiercest critic of Stalin's China policy, in 1928 and the subsequent consolidation of Joseph Stalin's hegemony.[98]

The setbacks in Soviet and Chinese revolutions in the 1920s alert us to the inherent epistemic challenges of revolutionary unfoldings, whose immense complexities on the ground far exceed top-down political analysis. Political relationality and revolutionary epistemology become conjoined in this context. Whose visions and experiences are valued and given authority, and whose get overlooked and erased in social (re)productive processes, matter not just ethically but also epistemically. Mao's Yan'an talks, and the subsequent development of the Maoist mass line, can be understood as attempts to address issues of political relationality and revolutionary epistemology, though unquestioned authorities remained in these conceptions, particularly in relation to the place of the party. With *Victory of the Chinese People*, the era of postrevolutionary construction began for the young PRC, and with it, further epistemic challenges on how to actualize revolution's promises, and how fast to do that.

CHAPTER 4

WHEN TAYLORISM MET REVOLUTIONARY ROMANTICISM

Great Leap Temporalities

In 1959, at the height of the Great Leap Forward campaign, the Central Newsreel and Documentary Film Studio (Zhongyang xinwen jilu dianying zhipianchang, hereafter Xinying) in Beijing released the short documentary *An Inch of Time Is Worth an Inch of Gold* (*Yicun guangyin yicun jin*, hereafter *Inch of Time*), directed by Chen Guangzhong. Taking as its title an old saying about the value of time, the film itself is an exemplary piece of time management, packing its ten-minute length with a potent audiovisual rhetoric to emphasize the importance of time to the ten-year-young PRC. The film begins with a black screen and a persistent tick-tock of a clock in the soundtrack. Tick-tock, tick-tock, the invisible clock worked tirelessly, compelling the audience to experience the unstoppable lapse of time.

Time was of crucial importance to the new PRC, for the Communist revolution that had brought it into existence had also thrown it into a temporal conundrum. While classical Marxist theory had outlined a relatively clear temporal progression for stages of social transformation and predicted the realization of socialism through a worldwide proletarian revolution initiated in the most advanced economies, such a revolution had failed to occur. Instead, capitalism broke at its weakest link in Russia and China, leaving these countries in an unprecedented situation. Politically they adopted what they considered to be socialist policies and regarded themselves as the vanguard societies to lead the world to communism. Yet economically, they lagged far behind advanced capitalist countries. This temporal schism—between political aspiration and developmental stage—meant vulnerability for the PRC in a Cold War environment. The Great Leap Forward was a bold experiment intended to defy the determinism of conventional developmental time; through it New China was meant to rapidly industrialize and close the rift between its development stage and political aspiration.

A time-based industrial art, cinema became the leading means of inculcating a complex temporal aesthetic during this period. Documentary, as the mode of cinema that experienced the greatest growth, was particularly important to the construction of this aesthetic. Rapidly made and delivered by mobile projectionists to labor sites all over the country, documentary in the Great Leap Forward did tremendous mediating work to address the temporal difficulties that underlay the production campaign. Tracing cinematic presentations of "unit time productivity" to American Taylorist motion study films and Soviet use of cinema in industrialization, I argue that industrial documentaries during the Great Leap Forward inculcated time discipline and trained newly urbanized workers to heed and transcend clock time with revolutionary will and technical innovation. Meanwhile, I examine the compression of temporal distinctions between the present and the future, achieved by the "artistic documentary," a new form of docu-fiction that had emerged during the Great Leap Forward, which made "documenting tomorrow" a possibility. Situating "artistic documentary" in the mass campaigns to construct reservoirs and other water works in rural China, I show that by bringing the anticipated (though far from certain) benefits of these construction projects into palpable visibility, artistic documentaries boosted confidence in these projects and energized the construction, even when it required the masses to put in extremely hard physical labor around the clock. Serving as do-it-yourself manuals, documentary also facilitated the excavation of historical technology for contemporary use, and propagated vernacular technologies, such as those for the building of "backyard furnaces" for mass production of "indigenous" iron and steel. Finally, documentary consolidated the normativity of the Great Leap temporality by associating dissenting experiences of time exclusively with the alleged political conservatism of the intellectual as the bourgeois class, while requiring the working class to live up to a work schedule of 24/7.

Tracing documentary's profound entanglements with material productions in industry, agriculture, and infrastructure, this chapter argues that cinema was among the most important media that propelled the Great Leap Forward: it was so prevalent in the production cultures of the time that it would be impossible to imagine the Great Leap Forward without it. Investigating documentary's complex temporal operations in the production campaign, therefore, allows us to better understand media's contribution to the massive and tragic failures of the Great Leap Forward, which ended in early 1961 amid economic collapse and widespread famine. A powerful medium offering step-by-step instructions on how to accelerate the arrival of Communism, documentary nevertheless failed miserably at acknowledging and managing the mounting risks inherent to the radical experiment that was the Great Leap Forward, with devastating consequences.

Time, Revolution, and the Great Leap Forward

In the fall of 1949, after witnessing the founding of the People's Republic of China in Tiananmen Square, the writer Hu Feng expressed his exhilaration in a poem published in the *People's Daily*, entitled "Time Has Begun." Hu described the PRC's founding as a radical reconfiguration of temporality, where time "leapt to its feet" to answer Mao Zedong's command, "March forward!"[1]

This sense of a new era dawning had often accompanied revolutions in modern times. Hannah Arendt in her study of the French and American revolutions described the modern conception of revolution as both a historical and a historiographical act, bound up, "with the notion that the course of history suddenly begins anew, that an entirely new story, a story never known or told before, is about to unfold."[2]

In the case of the Chinese Communist Revolution, a radical transformation of time was not only an aspiration but also a perceived necessity; rapid industrialization seemed to be the only path to survival in a Cold War environment. Yet could time truly leap to its feet and begin a bold forward march, when severe material limitations threatened to bind the country's pace of progress to the conventional time of sequential development, that tick-tock of clock time one hears at the beginning of *Inch of Time*?

With the tick-tock continuing its rhythmic assault on the audience, *Inch of Time*'s first sequence appears on the screen: a montage of different kinds of clocks, including a wooden pendulum clock, a metal wall clock, an alarm clock and a young woman looking at a wristwatch (fig. 4.1). A female voice-over speaks, "Time always moves at sixty minutes an hour, and twenty-four hours a day." Time seems to a large degree ungovernable by political visions. It has an autonomous logic and pace of its own.

The tension between the revolutionary aspiration to remake time and the rationality and autonomy of modern time underlaid China's Great Leap Forward, a mass campaign to speed up industrialization. After prolonged warfare China had been one of the poorest countries in the world when the Chinese Communist Party assumed power in 1949. Its GDP per capita in 1950 was only one fourth of that of the United Kingdom in the 1820s. On the eve of rural collectivization, in 1952, its grain output was 630 pounds per capita, less than 60 percent of that in the Soviet Union in 1928.[3] Despite this, Mao Zedong announced in November 1957 that it would take China only fifteen years to catch up with Great Britain in steel production.[4] Mao's optimistic prediction

148 When Taylorism Met Revolutionary Romanticism

4.1 A collage of clocks and wristwatch in the beginning sequence of *An Inch of Time Is Worth an Inch of Gold* (1959).

was based partly on good economic performance during China's first five-year plan (1953–1957). Both agricultural and industrial production grew at double-digit rates, and the production goals of the first five-year plan were fulfilled ahead of the scheduled time in 1957.[5] More important, Mao's forecast came from his belief in the power of mind over matter and in the organizational advantages gained through China's socialist transformation, which had been consolidated by then.[6]

Initiated in the fall of 1957, the Great Leap Forward plunged the nation into a production spree, with news of extraordinary productivity gains in agriculture and industry reported across the country. To support industrialization, rural China went through radical collectivization, with all agricultural production and much of everyday life organized by the new institution of the people's commune, which swiftly spread nationwide. As agricultural yields were hyperbolically reported, the state increased the procurement of agricultural products and, meanwhile, moved productive labor out of agriculture and into industry. The excessive agricultural procurement and the use of agricultural labor for industry resulted in widespread famine in rural China and loss of life on the scale of tens of millions.[7]

A Great Leap in Cinema

In chapter 3 I discussed the founding of the Northeastern Film Studio in 1946, and its training programs for filmmakers, particularly battlefront filmmakers to document the unfolding military campaigns on CCP's path to state power. After the People's Liberation Army took control of Changchun in October 1948, the Northern Film Studio moved back to Changchun from Hegang and became one of PRC's powerhouses of film production (its name changed to Changchun Film Studio in 1955). Meanwhile, in 1949, Yuan Muzhi, Qian Xiaozhang, and more than forty other filmmakers and technicians from the Northeastern Film Studio moved to Beijing to join the new Beijing Film Studio. Filmmakers at the latter came from a number of previous establishments. The majority were veteran filmmakers who had been filming on the battlefront for the Communist Party. This included more than thirty teams of film correspondents associated with the Northeastern Film Studio, and another thirty-plus associated with the Huabei Film Group, a film unit of CCP's Jin-cha-ji military district. Other filmmakers and staff came from the previously Nationalist-controlled Central Film Studio (Zhongyang dianying sheying chang) and other private film companies in Beijing. Between 1949 and 1953, the Beijing Film Studio became PRC's center for newsreel and documentary filmmaking. In 1953, upon the founding of Xinying, the whole news and documentary film operation at the Beijing Film Studio, along with filmmakers, technicians, and teams of local correspondents, were transferred to Xinying.[8]

In 1949 and 1950 the PRC's basic infrastructure of newsreel production was laid down. News offices were set up in the provinces. Film correspondents, based at the news offices, filmed local newsworthy events and sent the footage to the headquarters in Beijing (the Beijing Film Studio before 1953 and Xinying after that) for postproduction. This was an efficient and centralized system, allowing footage from all over the country to be edited together into newsreels, film magazines, and other regular film programs, such as *Short News Report* (*Xinwen jianbao*), created in 1950, *New Countryside* (*Xin Nongcun*), created in 1955, and the English-language *China Today*, created in 1954. As mentioned in chapter 3, Yuan Muzhi had envisioned documentary as the foundation for a new cinema. Indeed, in the first years of the PRC, newsreel and documentary production were taken most seriously. The party saw them as, and granted them the title of, the "vanguard of people's cinema."[9]

Even though infrastructure for newsreel and documentary production had developed in the early 1950s, before the Great Leap Forward, China's expansion of its filmmaking capacities was kept slow and measured. The Great Leap Forward brought urgency to the expansion of film production. On March 8, 1958, the *People's Daily* published a commentary that encouraged filmmakers and artists to make great leaps forward in cultural and art productions. A day later, the Ministry of Culture held a meeting to usher in the Great Leap Forward in cinema, with about two thousand artists and cadres in attendance. A meeting convened by the Film Bureau in May of the same year made more concrete production goals: in ten years, the conference proposed, the number of films produced in China and the scale of the Chinese film industry should rival those of the United States.[10]

The Great Leap Forward in cinema resulted in a large expansion of the film industry within a short time. In 1957, at the onset of the Great Leap Forward, in order to expand motion-picture production, the Shanghai Film Studio was divided into three studios: Haiyan, Tianma, and Jiangnan. The Shanghai Animation Film Studio and the Shanghai Translation Film Studio were set up at the same time. New studios were being built in Beijing, Xi'an, and Guangzhou. Between 1958 and 1960 all the provinces, with the exception of Tibet, established provincial-level film studios, and another Science and Education Film Studio was founded in Beijing. Between 1957 and 1960 the total number of film studios in China rose to thirty-four, in comparison to six before the Great Leap Forward began.[11]

Exhibition spaces increased tremendously as well. The total number of film-screening venues and mobile units increased from 648 in 1949 to 9,965 in 1957, and then to more than 15,000 by the end of 1959.[12] Cinemas proliferated in urban areas, and mobile projection units traveled extensively, screening films regularly in factories, barracks, schools, workers' clubs, and open-air village squares. "In order to educate the laboring masses with film, we prioritized the development of screening units in factories, mines, rural areas, . . . and gave special beneficial policies to economically backward areas and ethnic-minority areas," wrote Chen Huangmei, the head of the Film Bureau in the Ministry of Culture in the late 1950s. This policy priority meant that cinema had a nationwide reach beyond the urban centers and into the rural areas and work units: in fact, by 1959, more than three-quarters of the exhibition venues were located in factories, mines, army bases, and the countryside.[13]

Documentary cinema was the mode of film that experienced the greatest growth during the Great Leap Forward. In the two years of 1958 and 1959, the total quantity of documentary and newsreel films produced was 1,717 reels, exceeding the entire volume of 1,306 reels made in the nine years between 1949 and 1957. 1,228 reels were made in the single year of 1960.[14] There were many reasons for the increase. First, newly established provincial-level studios often lacked capacity to make fiction films—well-equipped studio spaces were often unavailable; it was hard to find trained screenwriters, directors, actors, and set designers to make feature films. Out of the thirty-four film studios in operation in 1960, only twelve had the capacity to make fiction films.[15] Documentaries were much easier to make. Shot on location, they didn't require elaborate studios. Documentary filmmakers were also readily available in the provinces, thanks to the infrastructure for newsreel and documentary production that had been put in place in the early 1950s. Film correspondents sent by Xinying had been stationed in the provinces and regularly provided newsreel footage to Beijing. This network of filmmakers merged into newly established provincial studios to help with production, leading to a flourishing of documentary filmmaking.[16] Second, political campaigns such as the Anti-Rightist Campaign in 1957 and the Pull Out the White Flags, Put Up the Red Flags Campaign in 1958 made it challenging to write politically safe scripts for feature films.[17] Documentary, involving the participation of the masses who represented themselves on the screen, became a safer option. More important, as I will elaborate in the rest of the chapter, documentary responded most speedily and effectively to production needs of the time; it became a productive force driving the production campaigns in industry, agriculture, and infrastructure.

Faster Than the Clock: Inculcating a Socialist Modern Time

Cinema, as a time-based medium, has been crucial in shaping the modern sense of time, writes Mary Ann Doane. By studying early cinema's participation in the structuring of time and contingency in capitalist modernity, Doane argues that the moving image as a technology was central to the formation of modern ideas about continuity versus discontinuity, contingency versus determinism, and temporal irreversibility versus archivability. It was through cinema and other kinetic experiences of urban modernity that time gained modern representability and became palpable to the human senses.[18]

Inch of Time offers a good point of departure to investigate how cinema inculcated a socialist modern temporality on screen during the Great Leap Forward. The socialist modern time is both old and new, a primordial longing reaching its contemporary realization. "It has been people's perennial desire to record and master time," says the voice-over in a sequence about five minutes into the film. Historical timekeeping apparatuses—such as the sundial, the water clock, and the hourglass—are shown one after another on the screen, each framed in quiet and static long shots. The next sequence places these traditional and indigenous means of recording time in contrast with the luxurious clocks from the West: the camera pans over a long row of ornate European clocks on display at the Palace Museum in Beijing. Initially brought to China by Jesuit missionaries and later made in small numbers in China by Chinese craftsmen who had learned the skills from Western clockmakers, these clocks were marvels of automata, with figurines automatically appearing and ringing bells at the strike of the hour. "Time became a private plaything in the hands of the ruling class," the voice-over comments. Instead of letting the technology of automation grow into an industry that could relieve the toiling masses from harsh labor, the ruling class kept technology for its own petty enjoyments. "These Western clocks had been ticking for more than 200 years, but China stagnated and didn't move forward," the voice-over reflects. Meanwhile, images of historical objects that symbolize China's stagnation and backwardness appear on the screen in succession: the marble boat at the Summer Palace that sails nowhere, heavy carts on ancient wooden wheels pushed by manpower, and wooden plows pulled by exhausted peasants to till muddy fields.

When explicating the concept of "aura" in Walter Benjamin's writings, Miriam Hansen writes about aura as emanating from traces of a bygone time, traces that lure the present viewer into a compulsive search for the future nestled in the past. In other words, traces from the past are powerful not only because they are historical evidence of sorts, but, more important, because they embody futurity: they are missed premonitions, unheeded prophecies, and lost opportunities, whose meanings cannot be grasped until the present time and all too late. "The futurity that has seared the photographic image in the chance moment of exposure does not simply derive from circumstantial knowledge of its posthistory, or that of its subject; it emerges in the field of the beholder's compulsive searching gaze. The spark that leaps across time is a profoundly unsettling and disjunctive one," writes Hansen.[19] The aura of these historical objects is unsettling, not because it points at a possible reinterpretation of the past, but because it unleashes imagination and creates urgency for grasping the present and making the future.

Indeed, this unsettling and disjunctive spark ignites the next sequence in *Inch of Time*. The stagnation represented by the marble boat, carts, and plows is disrupted by the dynamic next shot: a train rushes toward the camera at full speed. Reminiscent of the Lumière brothers' *The Arrival of a Train* (1895), this shot associates the arrival of communism in China with a radically new tempo, kinetic energy, and cinematic shock. In the next sequence, the camera is placed in a moving vehicle, surveying street scenes in Beijing, reminiscent of the "phantom train ride" films that immerse the viewers in the experience of motor mobility. "In the past, a couple of hundred years were like one day; today, one day equals twenty years," announces the voice-over. From the car window, one sees a modern Beijing ready to take off with well-built streets and a clock tower looming over its railway square. Marching music replaces the tick-tock sound of the clock in the sound track, embellishing this new regime of accelerated time with movement and passion.

The new time ushered in by the arrival of a socialist state has not only a new tempo and space, but also a new system of production. "Everyone knows the old saying, 'An inch of time is worth an inch of gold,' but do we really understand the value of each minute and second?" the voice-over asks rhetorically. A fast-paced montage sequence follows: a postal worker rapidly stamping postmarks (fig. 4.2) and sorting letters, a typist working on a typewriter, a chef

4.2 A postal worker featured in Frank Gilbreth's film clip (circa 1912) that studies how to optimize stamping motions for postal workers (*left*), and a Chinese postal worker at work in *An Inch of Time Is Worth an Inch of Gold* (1959) (*right*).

making dumplings. The shots alternate between the adroit hands in close-up and the worker framed in a frontal medium shot. The voice-over calculates aloud: "The letter-sorter can sort two letters per second, more than a hundred letters per minute, and more than seven thousand letters per hour."

Such images of rationalized production share common features with Taylorist images from 1910s and 1920s America, particularly Frank Gilbreth's motion studies of brick-laying and postmark stamping. Developed in the 1880s and 1890s by Frederick Winslow Taylor in the United States, scientific management was a practice to rationalize industrial production by breaking down a specific task into separate modules and analyzing, standardizing, and propagating the best practices in each module. An important figure in the scientific management movement, Gilbreth began to use motion-picture technology in 1912 to record the sequential actions of workers for the purpose of motion optimization. By replaying the motion-picture footage of work routines, Gilbreth and his associates claimed that they could detect superfluous movements and propose ways to streamline workers' motion and optimize unit time productivity. In his films, the worker and the workstation were often placed against a white background with a grid pattern, next to a special clock with a second hand that moves twenty times a minute (fig. 4.2).[20] Both the clock and the grid were meant to help measure the worker's movements when the film was examined in slow motion, under the magnifying glass.[21] In *Inch of Time*, the grid was absent, yet the frontal, exhibitionist shot of a person at work and the camera's attention to the worker's productive body movements were similar. Occasionally, a clock was placed in the mise-en-scène; in other cases, the ticking of a clock could be heard in the soundtrack.

As mentioned in chapter 1, the role of film in Taylorist management had been known in China as early as 1914, when a newspaper article discussed cinema's use in the United States and Germany to measure and optimize workers' productivity.[22] By then, reformers and educators had already become very interested in the use of educational, scientific, and news films in industrialization and public education. This interest, as I elaborated in chapter 1, had led to China's earliest concerted effort to produce educational films by Shanghai's Commercial Press between 1917 and 1926.[23]

In the 1950s China's state-led industrialization was heavily influenced by the Soviet Union, whose industrialization process in the 1920s had also been much influenced by the theory of scientific management and the technique of motion study. Following the October Revolution, the Soviet Union was confronted with the difficult tasks of fighting a civil war, rebuilding a war-torn economy, and developing industrial production. In search of organizational and technical solutions to these problems, Lenin proposed to adopt principles of scientific management in the country, arguing that even though scientific management was a capitalist methodology, in the hands of the working class it could be a powerful tool to develop the national economy. As motion study films showcased optimal movements a worker could learn to emulate quickly, Lenin found them particularly useful for rapid industrialization in which a large number of new workers, mostly from a peasant background and undereducated, must be trained.[24]

Chinese readers learned about the efficacy of Taylorist motion study films from *The Party on Cinema*, a collection of Lenin's and Stalin's writings and speeches, initially published in Moscow in 1938 and translated and published in China in 1951. The volume collected Lenin's numerous writings and his conversations with other party cadres on cinema's use in industry. Lenin explained how corporations in Western Europe and the United States had been using films to motivate workers to adopt new technologies, and how the training of new workers could be effectively done by sitting the workers down in the "film-screening hall at the factory." *The Party on Cinema* reported that besides setting up mobile screening units around the country and "film-screening halls" in factories, Lenin also ordered screenings of short educational films on trains and steamships, and set aside foreign exchange to import industrial and educational films from overseas for labor training. One episode reported at length in *The Party on Cinema* is particularly telling on cinema's importance for the adoption of new technologies in industry. In 1920 a Russian engineer had developed a new hydraulic-mining method, yet many engineers didn't believe that it would work. Two short films showcasing both new and old technologies were made and widely screened to mining engineers and, in the end, to Lenin himself. The films convinced Lenin that the new technology was superior to the old, and he subsequently issued orders to promote it in all suitable mines in the country. Lenin also requested that twelve short films on mining technologies be made and screened to miners and other workers all over the country, including the Urals, Ukraine, Byelorussia (present-day Belarus), and Siberia. "Two films reorganized the whole mining industry," Nikolai Lebenov, the editor of *Party on Cinema*, wrote excitedly, arguing that cinema was the most important medium for spreading new industrial technology.[25]

A predominantly agricultural society at its founding, the PRC faced similar tasks of labor retraining in the 1950s as the Soviet Union did in Lenin's time. During the Great Leap, the state moved massive labor forces from agriculture into expanding industries: in 1958, 16.4 million peasants, about twice the size of the total industrial labor force in 1957, were relocated to cities to support the expansion of industry and construction. The government also mobilized over one hundred million peasants to undertake large irrigation and land-reclamation projects and to build and operate "backyard iron furnaces."[26] An industrial temporality wasn't easy to inculcate in an agricultural population. According to E. P. Thompson, workers in England took several generations to fully adapt to clock time during the Industrial Revolution.[27] Chinese state newspapers in the early 1950s frequently reported a lack of time discipline in industries.[28] Cinema became a convenient means to train time discipline and inculcate modern senses of time among new industrial workers.[29]

A Taylorist, rationalized temporality, however, was insufficient for building socialist modernity. Gilbreth's time-motion study films may have been valuable at identifying the optimal solution for a work routine, yet they were nevertheless management tools to discipline work, create upward pressure on unit productivity with punitive consequences for workers who failed to optimize and meet the production targets. It's worth noting that workers and trade unions had bitterly resisted Taylorism in the United States, Europe, and even the Soviet Union.[30] A socialist modernity must rely on a complete reconceptualization of labor as an inherently creative and humanizing activity, where workers are no longer alienated from their labor and can control the production process. Elsewhere I've written on the Communist Party's reentry into China's industrial cities upon victories in the civil war and on the grassroots aspirations for labor self-governance that eventually became subjugated to production demands.[31] Facing the task of rapidly building national industries, and having chosen to adopt a Soviet-style centralized economic planning system, in which workers continued to have insufficient control over the production process, how could the party solve the contradiction in its labor politics, disciplining workers according to a rational, industrial time to maximize production for the state, yet still attempting to achieve a "socialist modernity" with unalienated labor?

Marx observes that in a capitalist system, workers are estranged from their labor. They cannot decide on their own productive activities, nor can they use or own the value of what they produce. Instead, they become machine-like instruments performing tasks dictated to them by the owners of capital and by the management: "Labour is *external* to the worker, . . . not voluntary, but coerced; it is *forced labour*."³² Contemplating the ideal scenario of unalienated labor, Marx writes:

> Let us suppose that we had carried out production as human beings.... In my *production* I would have objectified my *individuality*, its *specific character*, and therefore enjoyed not only an individual *manifestation of my life* during the activity, but also when looking at the object I would have the individual pleasure of knowing my personality to *be objective, visible to the senses* and hence a power *beyond all doubt*.... Our products would be so many mirrors in which we saw reflected our essential nature.³³

From Marx's discussion of labor alienation and his stress on visuality, we may gain insight into one of cinema's roles in PRC's striving for rapid industrialization. Besides serving as a medium for labor training, cinema—in particular, documentary films of labor—can provide the many "mirrors" in which workers can see themselves, hence alleviating the contradiction between the PRC's labor policies and the workers' expectations of nonalienation and autonomy at work. In *Inch of Time*, workers were portrayed as self-actualizing and joyful at work, surpassing production quotas with will, skill, and command of technology. The film showcases a food-factory worker, whose adroit hands could wrap biscuits at four seconds per package with machine-like precision. While the calendar year is still 1959, she had already completed the production quota up to June 1961. Another worker at a machine-parts factory creatively retooled her machines, which allowed her to complete the production quota of fifty-seven months in merely sixteen months. A worker's fast-moving hands and machines become her time-travel vehicle; the future is in her hands and can be summoned ahead of time. As Taylorist images of work routines give way to workers' innovations and voluntarism, orchestral music begins to enrich the sound track with an ever-faster tempo and musical flourish. The film ends with a lively montage sequence where close-ups of clocks and images of workers and machines are intercut into a dance with one another, accompanied by a soundtrack where the ticking of a clock can still be heard but is overwhelmed by a musical fanfare in the allegro. Faster than the clock time, workers are the true vanguards whose productivity and voluntarism move the society into the future.

Documenting Tomorrow:
The Docu-Fiction of Artistic Documentary

In April 1958 the Central Film Bureau invited a group of filmmakers and writers to watch the latest crop of documentary films made at the height of the Great Leap Forward. After the screenings, the poet He Jingzhi reportedly criticized those films for depicting the fruits of labor too modestly. *Spring in the Mountains* (*Shanqu de chuntian*, 1958) and *Split Mountains to Bring Water* (*Pishan yinshui*, 1958) had moved the poet with their monumental scenes of collective labor, but their endings—"just a few small trees and a small patch of irrigated rice paddies"—left him unsatisfied. Could documentary filmmakers "give us more splendid scenes of the spring and bigger waves of water?" asked He. Perhaps the films could end with the lush spring scenery taken from the water-abundant Yangtze region, to indicate that this was what tomorrow would look like in the arid northern regions too? After all, the poet asked, "Why can't documentary document tomorrow?"[34]

Writing a few months later, Ding Jiao, vice director of Xinying, recounted He Jingzhi's observations before expressing his agreement. Yes, documentary could "document tomorrow," Ding wrote, because the future was already embodied in the present: "Our people are bold in thinking and courageous in action. Their unceasing energy for perpetual revolution and progress has placed new demands on the art of today." People's aspirations for the future were a crucial part of the present that must be represented.

These ponderings on whether documentaries could "document tomorrow" was part of a larger discussion concerning the new official aesthetic of "combining revolutionary realism with revolutionary romanticism" and how it could be applied to documentary.[35] First coined by Mao Zedong in March 1958 when discussing the future of Chinese poetry, this new formula was subsequently publicized by writers such as Guo Moruo and Zhou Yang and became widely adopted in literature and the visual arts.[36] It emphasized the dialectical relationship between realist thinking and revolutionary aspiration and encouraged artists to use bold imagination in their work.

The foregrounding of aspirations was not entirely new: wartime documentary had created "winning realities." Yet Ding Jiao observed that some filmmakers were reluctant to embrace it. These comrades must understand that dreams were also part of reality, he argued, because in a society progressing in such big strides, it would take only a short time for dreams to become reality. "Many seedlings of Communism have emerged, and many fairytale-like miracles, full of revolutionary romanticism, have already occurred in the great tidal waves of life. Literature and art must fully reflect and passionately celebrate them," wrote Ding, who went on to identify "exaggeration and imagination" (*kuazhang he xiangxiang*) as the most important artistic strategies for revolutionary romanticism.[37]

The drive to combine revolutionary realism with revolutionary romanticism led to the development of a hybrid mode of cinema called artistic documentary (*yishuxing jilupian*). Initially suggested by Zhou Enlai as a means to increase film production and represent the Great Leap Forward in a timely manner, artistic documentary was supposed to be based on real events but could employ professional actors and engage in considerable fictionalization and dramatization. Mostly shot on location and made quickly, artistic documentaries were compared with "special editions" of newspapers that reported same-day news.[38] By deploying both actors and nonactors who played themselves, the making of artistic documentaries also brought artists into closer collaboration with the working class, an approach encouraged since Mao Zedong's Yan'an talks in 1942.[39] More important, with the endorsement of exaggeration and imagination, these films enjoyed considerable formal fluidity and could involve fictional elements too. Indeed, these films were often called new art films (*xin yishu pian*), Great Leap films (*yuejin pian*), or documentary-style art films (*jiluxing yishu pian*), forgoing the distinction of "documentary" and "fiction" altogether.[40] Film studios welcomed this creative opportunity: in 1958 forty-nine artistic documentaries were produced, amounting to 47 percent of total film production; over twenty more followed in the next two years.[41]

Building Reservoirs with Film

There had been practical reasons for the perceived need to "document tomorrow": it's worth noting that both of the documentaries critiqued by He Jingzhi for their modest endings depicted the construction of reservoirs in the countryside. In the winter of 1957–58, huge campaigns were launched to mobilize villagers to build water conservancy and irrigation infrastructure. The goal was to rapidly increase the area of irrigated land, to boost grain production and support industrial expansion. In these constructions, labor mobilization was crucially important. Unlike in urban industries, where capital investment from the state drove production growth, the growth strategy in the countryside relied heavily on labor reorganization and mass mobilization. According to Nicholas Lardy, labor need for infrastructure construction provided the greatest impetus to the formation of people's communes at that time. As mentioned earlier, in 1957 and 1958, more than 100 million rural people were mobilized to do rural construction work. This nearly doubled China's total irrigated land area by the end of 1958.[42]

Labor mobilization for rural construction projects, however, was not easy. These projects were highly contested at the grassroots because they aimed at drastic and unprecedented transformations of the local environment where villagers lived and worked for generations. Receiving little capital investment from the state, these projects also relied on the villagers to perform long hours of backbreaking and often dangerous work with simple tools. Success stories and demonstrable benefits were needed to dispel doubts, minimize perceived risk, and encourage people to put in the hard labor for a better future. Yet in a nationwide campaign, infrastructure constructions happened simultaneously across the country. Most large constructions required significant time to complete. Even after completion, it would still take time for the benefits to manifest in agricultural output. The desire to "document tomorrow" arose from this mobilizational need in a production campaign meant to accelerate time. Instead of waiting for success stories to emerge in time, documentaries brought the future instantaneously into view to boost confidence in these massive infrastructure projects.

The Mediated Futures of the Ming Tombs Reservoir

A landmark construction completed in record time (January–June 1958), the Ming Tombs Reservoir mobilized hundreds of thousands of people laboring around the clock. Due to its proximity to Beijing and its spectacular natural setting, the site drew many writers and artists from the capital and became a media sensation. The construction was richly represented in photography, painting, music, literature, and film. Even the French photographer Henri Cartier-Bresson documented the reservoir construction in color photography when traveling through China that year.[43] At least three films were made and widely circulated about the construction of the Ming Tombs Reservoir between May and September 1958. A five-minute-long newsreel film, *State Leaders at Work with Us* (*Lingxiu he women tong laodong*), documented top state cadres, including Mao Zedong, Zhou Enlai, Zhu De, and Liu Shaoqi, working at the reservoir construction site along with other volunteers.[44] Besides the newsreel, two artistic documentaries were made: *Songs on the Reservoir* (*Shuiku shang de gesheng*), directed by Yu Yanfu and released by the Changchun Film Studio in June, and *The Caprice of the Ming Tombs Reservoir* (*Shisanling shuiku changxiangqu*), directed by Jin Shan and released by the Beijing Film Studio in September. Both were filmed at the reservoir before the construction's completion, and both sought to end on a satisfying success story.

Based on a real event adapted from reportage literature, *Songs on the Reservoir* told the story of a young village woman Lanxiang, who traveled to the Ming Tombs with her future father-in-law to visit her fiancé, a People's Liberation Army soldier volunteering on the construction site. Unable to find the soldier in such a large and congested place, and inspired by the spirit of voluntary work around them, the old man and the young woman plunged themselves into work. The loudspeaker on the site kept the family of three informed of one another's presence and achievements, before they finally met and a wedding was conducted for the two lovers on-site.

Shot on location before the construction's completion, *Songs on the Reservoir* sought to depict success by moving the end of the film to a smaller construction project at Lanxiang's home commune. An educated young woman,

Lanxiang went to the Ming Tombs not only to visit her fiancé but also to learn techniques to help her commune build its own irrigation system. The film's final ten minutes depicted the collective work of members of Lanxiang's commune in constructing a small reservoir near their village and celebrated its completion with ecstatic close-ups of water gushing into the fields. People from neighboring communes arrived to do what Lanxiang had done at the Ming Tombs: to learn how to build similar structures in their home area. Here the success story was not only the completion of the reservoir but the transmission of techniques and know-how from the Ming Tombs to countless communes, allowing its success story to be reproduced across rural China.

The other artistic documentary, *The Caprice of the Ming Tombs Reservoir*, similarly sought to demonstrate benefits from reservoir construction but took a different approach. While *Songs on the Reservoir* moved its ending from the Ming Tombs to Lanxiang's home commune, *The Caprice of the Ming Tombs Reservoir* stayed at the Ming Tombs but "documented tomorrow": it included a thirty-minute postscript depicting a splendid Communist world twenty years *after* the reservoir's completion.

Written by the veteran dramatist Tian Han originally as a thirteen-act musical drama and adapted into film, *The Caprice of the Ming Tombs Reservoir* is based on real people's real stories collected by the playwright on his field trips to the Ming Tombs. When writing, rehearsing, and adapting to cinema his play, Tian Han was aware of the many other literary, photographic, and cinematic representations of the reservoir and endeavored to compete with them in terms of the speed of production and the boldness of artistic imagination.[45] He wrote the play in nine days, and the China Youth Art Theater, under the direction of Jin Shan, began rehearsing it chapter-by-chapter as it was being written. Within a month, the play received its first audience, many of whom had worked on the construction site.[46] The production of the eighty-minute film adaptation took only thirty-seven days. To enact a heavier dose of revolutionary romanticism than previous representations, Tian placed the present moment in a grand sweep of history: the present, Tian Han believed, must be understood as both an overcoming of the past and a harbinger for the future.[47]

The film has three parts: a seven-minute-long prelude on the history of mass labor at the site, a fifty-minute-long main body depicting the present constructions at the dam, and a thirty-minute long section on the future. The film's status as an artistic documentary or artistic film gave license to its thoroughly hybrid text, which combines musical, melodrama, documentary, historical drama, and sci-fi all in one. The film begins with a prelude in the mode of historical drama: on his horse, Kublai Khan surveys the land with his Chinese engineer. The two decide to begin construction of the Grand Canal on the spot, and immediately amass a large number of poor laborers for the task. The following sequence fast forwards to the Ming dynasty and shows the Ming rulers on their horsebacks, coming to this area to identify a place for the imperial tombs and draft laborers for their construction. In both cases, coerced by arms-bearing soldiers into heavy labor, the laborers work under miserable conditions, and the ruling class pays no attention to the livelihood of the people. Documentary footage of floods, from indeterminate sources, is inserted here to show the extent of natural disaster and destitution of the population. The last shot of the prelude shows an old man in destitution praying to the sky for the intervention of the Dragon King. The camera moves slowly from the wrinkled face of the old man, upward to a sky indifferent to his plea, and then, in one continuous motion, the camera moves laterally to capture in its frame a red flag fluttering in the sky. While the traditional deities are irresponsive, the red flag of the Communist Party, located just as high as where the Dragon King would be, comes to the rescue and proves much more potent than the deities.

After this brief prelude on the past, the film goes into the musical mode, as it depicts the glorious construction of the reservoir in the present. It follows a group of intellectuals and artists as they visit the construction site, interview model workers, and observe each work team perform its work songs based on different local operatic traditions. Inspired by the enthusiasm among the workers on the site, the intellectuals and artists join the work teams, make sketches, and compose poetry on-site. Shot on location, and having actual model workers and their work teams play themselves and work and sing before the camera, this section also employs the documentary mode and incorporates documentary footage from the earlier newsreel, *State Leaders at Work with Us*.

The final thirty minutes of the film moves to depict the future in the sci-fi mode. Following the intertitle "Twenty years later," and accompanied by the bamboo and silk music of the fertile and prosperous Jiangnan region, the camera slowly passes through bamboo groves to enter the front gate of "Ming Tomb Communist Commune." Protagonists who had participated in the construction now reunite to celebrate the twentieth anniversary of the reservoir's completion. Their tour of the commune reveals a future full of miracles. A single tree bears all kinds of fruits—apples, pears, bananas, pineapples—year-round, all grains and vegetables grow and ripen regardless of the season, and pigs weigh a thousand pounds each. As developments in medicine have cured cancer, reversed aging, and prolonged life, most people look younger than they did twenty years before. Divisions no longer exist between mental and menial labor and between industry and agriculture: the commune operates steel and textile factories, as well as agricultural laboratories that minutely adjust the local weather and conduct research. The urban-rural difference has been eliminated, and intellectuals, workers, and peasants have been fully merged through intermarriage. Many nationalities from within China, and from socialist countries all around the world, live and work together at the commune. Everyone wears clothing that combines European and traditional Chinese styles, and the same mixture applies to architecture.

Besides being materially abundant and healthful, this future is full of advanced media technology. A television set occupies a central position at the outdoor reunion party. It's through the TV monitor that many of the commune's activities—such as the research labs, pig farm, and factories—are presented. Novel communication devices enable real-time long-distance video chats. As Taiwan had been recovered ten years previously, and rockets begin to fly to the Mars, communication devices that look remarkably similar to mobile phones and laptops of today enable video chat across long distances, connecting Taipei, Beijing, and the Mars-bound rocket in instantaneous communication.

A Media Ecology of Optimism

It's worth noting that some of the miracles depicted in the film—trees bearing all kinds of fruits, grains ripening in all the seasons, and tropical plants flourishing in the northern climate—were not groundless. They drew from widespread agricultural experiments at the time. After all, this was the time of the Green Revolution, when introduction of improved varieties of crops had in reality drastically increased agricultural—particularly grain—output in many places around the world. While the term *Green Revolution* was coined by William Gaud, director of the U.S. Agency for International Development (USAID) to refer to U.S.-led scientific farming programs in the postwar decades, recent works by Sigrid Schmalzer and Joshua Eisenman have shown that a parallel development happened in China, with improved varieties of grain raising output in the 1950s and further agricultural productivity gains in the 1960s and 1970s.[48] In the 1950s, Chinese agricultural science was also significantly influenced by the Soviet Union, where the Lysenko-Michurin doctrine had gained hegemony. Trofilm Lysenko, the Soviet agronomist, opposed Mendelian genetics and believed in the inheritance of acquired characters in plants and animals, that is, the ability of species to adapt to new environments and then pass the acclimatization to their offspring.[49] His advisory role in China in 1949 and the wide exhibition of Alexander Dovzhenko's biopic *Michurin* (1948) in China's early 1950s had brought a wave of grassroots breeding experiments in the early PRC.[50] Ivan Michurin, the Russian botanist, was reputed for creating new varieties of fruits that would thrive in extreme weather.[51] Numerous Michurin-inspired experiment groups were formed in Chinese schools and villages. Schoolchildren made attempts to cultivate higher yield, more adaptive breeds. Gardeners also attempted to create "gardens of a hundred fruits" by grafting various combinations of fruits and vegetables together.[52] In other words, the multispecies fruit tree and the "unseasonal" crops were not merely fantasies; they belonged to unfolding experiments that aimed to modernize agriculture at the time, both in China and elsewhere.

Experiments, however, have a large chance of failing. Even when they succeed, there can be negative consequences. The Green Revolution's legacies, particularly its heavy reliance on chemical fertilizers, have remained controversial. The Lysenko-Michurin theory, not heeding the genetic limitations in species' interactions with the environment, has long been discredited (though recent research in epigenetics called for a partial reassessment).[53] Experimentation lay at the heart of a production campaign as radical as the Great Leap Forward. More broadly, experimentation is foundational to the colossal attempt to bring about and sustain a socialist revolution. *The Caprice of the Ming Tombs Reservoir* and other mass media of the time imagined and magnified success stories of these ongoing experiments, making them palpably immediate and within reach, creating an environment of utmost optimism to energize mass participation.

Miracles were happening everywhere, and our ideas of what was possible must change, exclaimed the journalist Ye Mai in an article entitled "Fantasy and Reality," published in the *People's Daily* in August 1958. Ye recounted that in March earlier that year, he had seen a report in the *Hubei Daily* about a nineteen-year-old woman cotton-grower proposing to produce a thousand *jin* of cotton per *mu*.[54] "Even though that report provided detailed calculations of how many cotton plants she would plant, and how much cotton each plant would yield, ... in the end I was still, inevitably, suspicious. That just sounded like a fantastic dream!" However, just a few days after deeming this news mere fantasy, Ye found in the *People's Daily* that the cotton production record was newly set at 1,200 *jin* per *mu* in another county in Hubei. Quoting from numerous newspaper reports, Ye observed that miracles were happening on all fronts of agricultural production. "Things are changing so rapidly; they go entirely beyond normal expectations," Ye concluded. He decided to stop doubting these miracles but welcome them as unfolding realities of the Great Leap Forward.[55]

Newspaper articles, published sequentially, reinforced each other's credibility and competed with each other to deliver the most extraordinary news. Infused with revolutionary romanticism, photographers too participated in the making of a miraculous present by creating photo collages that celebrated oversized agricultural produce as a result of improved agricultural technique.[56] Cinema made its contribution to this unfolding media ecology of mutual reinforcement and competition. Yomi Braester has argued that political campaigns during the Mao-era were the most important "bearers of cinematic change" and could be considered as "akin to genres," as each campaign created certain unified expectations and iconographies that could be seen in documentary as well as fiction films, and in theater and other media.[57] The Great Leap Forward campaign generated a media avalanche where images of optimism reinforced each other and created stable generic expectations that had real life consequences: they affirmed successful futures and banished any doubt for failure.

The importance of mass media in sustaining optimism and coordinating mass action was acknowledged by both *Songs on the Reservoir* and *The Caprice of the Ming Tombs Reservoir*. In *Songs on the Reservoir*, the loudspeaker served as a lynchpin in the plot. Its instantaneous broadcasting coordinated production competitions and kept workers abreast of the construction's successful progress as a whole. *The Caprice of the Ming Tombs Reservoir* placed television and other screens of mediation at the center of the future. It was mainly through screen media that the film's protagonists, as well as its audience, witnessed the miracles that the Great Leap Forward would bring about (fig. 4.3).

Television was an emergent reality in China's 1958: the newly founded Beijing station transmitted to Beijing and its surroundings on May 1, in China's

4.3 Scenes from *The Caprice of the Ming Tombs Reservoir* (1958) depicting the reservoir area twenty years into the future. Through the TV monitor, featured prominently in the outdoor party, the visitors see the climate-control center and the gate to the textile factory that the commune operates. A tablet device enables long-distance video conversation with a scientist on a rocket to Mars.

first-ever TV broadcast. The technology and infrastructure for nationwide broadcasting, however, were still lacking at the time. *The Caprice of the Ming Tombs Reservoir*'s foregrounding of television as the next generation of mass media was poignant because cinema was exactly the medium to be leveraged to approximate television's instantaneous temporality and vast reach. Similar to rural construction works that relied on human labor rather than machine power to build infrastructure, film projectionists provided the human power to create an infrastructure of moving image distribution: they physically transported films across the country over difficult terrain, often by rudimentary means of transportation, bringing portable electric generators to power screenings in places not yet reached by electrification. This makeshift but highly effective assemblage of rapid dissemination allowed cinema to take millions of viewers on virtual tours of construction sites, as Lanxiang and other young people did in *Songs on the Reservoir*, so that they could be inspired by the success stories and replicate them where they were.

Cinema had since its early days been associated with the working class's "leisure time," offering workers both sensory acclimatization to and therapeutic innervation from industrial capitalism. During the Great Leap Forward, cinema was regularly shown on rural building sites, which replaced village squares as the new open-air film arena. There, leisure and work became unified/collapsed into one: people worked, sang, danced, and watched movies, all on the construction sites where the future would be born. County-level film projection teams toured reservoir construction sites in Fujian, Hubei, Shandong, Hebei, Zhejiang, and Anhui.[58] Film programs such as "new film week" brought artistic documentaries, fresh from the cutting table, to reservoir construction sites, where they were shown to tens of thousands of people in one screening.[59] Films were typically shown as double bills, and screenings often lasted until or beyond midnight. To accommodate large audiences, projectionists modified the projectors to allow projection onto multiple screens and developed special screens to show films in daylight, in order to avoid the drowsiness of night screenings after an exhausting day of work.[60]

Writing about cinema's revolutionary potential, Walter Benjamin exclaims, "Our taverns and our metropolitan streets, our offices and furnished rooms, our railroad stations and our factories appeared to have us locked up hopelessly. Then came the film and burst this prison-world asunder by the dynamite of the tenth of a second."[61] On the construction fields of rural China, cinema kept the successful future in view to validate and energize the construction. Sometimes cinema's *explosive* power became literal: after showing a double bill at one reservoir construction site, a film projection team in Shaanxi traveled for three hours overnight to reach another building site. There they used the electricity generator meant for film projection to power homemade explosives and blew up a mountain for reservoir building.[62]

Useful Pasts: Folk Technologies for a Chinese Modernity

While future-oriented, the Great Leap Forward also saw tremendous interest in folklore, mythology, and traditional arts and technologies. In *The Caprice of the Ming Tombs Reservoir*, the depiction of the communist future was a mixture of industrial and traditional aesthetics: the science labs followed a streamlined and functionalist aesthetic, yet the close-ups of fruits, grain, and pigs bore resemblance to traditional images of abundance like those in Chinese New Year prints. Another popular artistic documentary, *Huang Baomei* (dir. Xie Jin, 1958), set in a textile factory in Shanghai, with the model worker Huang Baomei acting herself as the protagonist, ended with women textile workers turning into the beloved folkloric figures of seven weaving fairies dancing by their power looms (fig. 4.4).

An extensive literature exists on the politics of folklore in modern China.[63] Lydia Liu has shown that engagements with folklore in China's twentieth century were an entangled history of colonial mimicry, cultural governance, nationalist construction, and revolutionary struggles, with folklore serving different political aims at different times.[64] While earlier ideas

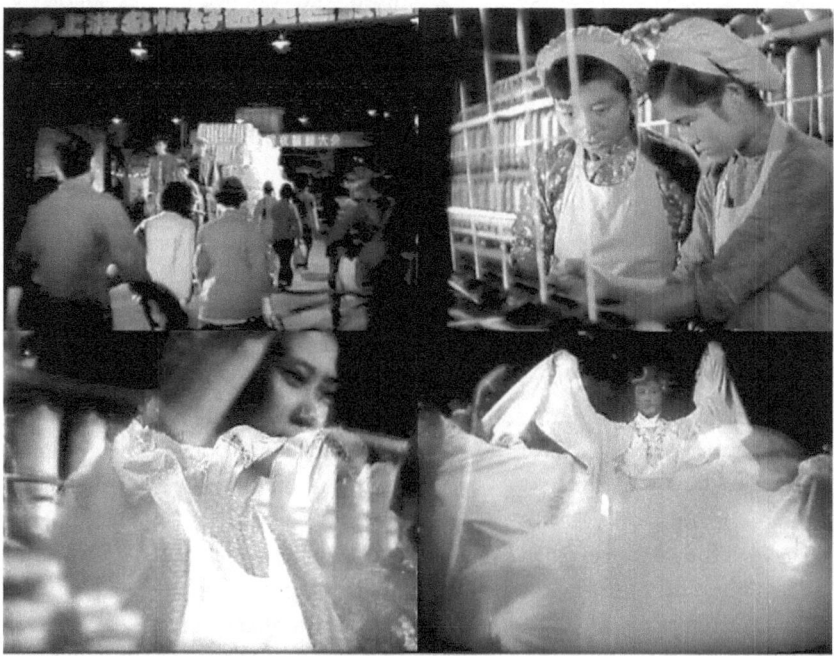

4.4 Scenes from *Huang Baomei* (1958). Textile workers enter the factory to work sleepless nights. Women turn into the weaving fairies while working.

on folklore—as authentic voices of the people and expressions of national identity—continued to operate during the Great Leap Forward, a new fascination arose from the idea that folklore and mythology were age-old storehouses of people's aspirations and inventive ideas, ready to be revived and realized in cultural and material productions of the present. As the journalist Ye Mai writes, "Myths such as Chang'e flying to the Moon, Hou Yi hunting the Sun, Nü Wa mending the sky with stones, and Sun Wukong riding on the clouds.... Weren't they forerunners to today's gigantic efforts to transform nature?"[65] Describing contemporary irrigation projects in his hometown, Ye argues that one could in fact find ideas, though unfinished and immature, in the legends circulating in the area about how to transform nature in this specific locale.

Since the folkloric register was understood as the language of the cultural grassroots through which the creativity of the masses could be released, the Great Leap Forward in agricultural and industrial productions was accompanied by the New Folksong Movement (Xinminge yundong) and the Peasant Painting Movement (Nongminhua yundong). Hundreds of thousands of peasant poets, songwriters, and painters emerged from these movements. In the New Folksong Movement, quotas were allotted to villages and counties in terms of how many folk songs must be collected and how many new peasant poets and songwriters must be "discovered." In the spirit of the Great Leap, the responses greatly surpassed the targets. Millions of new poems and folk songs were being written and collected, to the point that a paper shortage ensued. When delivering poetry submissions to the higher-level government, some county governments had to use large trucks or mobilize peasants to carry heavy loads of paper on shoulder poles.[66] In September 1959 a volume titled *Hongqi geyao* (Songs of the red flag), a collection of three hundred new folk songs and folk poems edited by writers Zhou Yang and Guo Moruo, was published. The book was meant to be comparable to the *Shijing* (*Book of Songs*), the earliest extant collection of songs and poems, which also contains about three hundred songs and poems and is part of the Chinese classical canon.

Out of the similarly massive Peasant Painting Movement emerged countless peasant artists, whose Great Leap–themed mural paintings covered village walls. Both the New Folk Song Movement and the Peasant Painting Movement borrowed heavily from traditional Chinese mythology to portray the daily miracles ushered in by the Great Leap Forward. One of the paintings, for example, showed a huge ear of corn, like a gigantic mountain, that blocked the path of the Money King, who used to fly above the mountains without any hindrance. Another painting portrayed the Eight Immortals crossing a river while sitting on a giant bean pod. These paintings began to form new canons. Professional painters copied and imitated (*linmo*) peasant paintings, treating them as socialist masterworks from the people.[67]

The productivity of folk materials was documented widely. A *People's Daily* article praised poems written by the masses for their formal incorporation of the rhythm of labor and the musicality of the spoken language. Because of their "simple, clear, and figurative" poetic language, these poems could spread more easily than poems written by intellectuals and could mobilize people most effectively. The author reported that reading and writing poetry had already helped workers increase production and argued that cultural productions at the grassroots could directly inspire people to be bolder and more optimistic about their work.[68]

Indigenous Iron and Steel: DIY Films for Backyard Furnaces

Given that folk materials were so productive, it should come as no surprise that the Great Leap Forward also saw a revival of folk technologies. The call for increasing the production of "native iron" (*tutie*) to support steel production began in December 1956, as the steel industry faced a shortage of imported iron.[69] By mid-1958 the state began to promote "indigenous" metallurgical methods and mass operation of "folk furnaces" (*tugaolu*). *Tu* literally means the soil and can also have extended meanings of "locally conceived, native and folk." In opposition to *yang* (literally, the ocean; also foreign and elite) in Mao-era scientific discourses, *tu* technology was valued as people's knowledge arising from practice. Harnessing such indigenous know-how was deemed important for a self-reliant and mass-based industrialization process.[70] To find *tu* technology, local cadres and technicians searched in historical archives for metallurgical technologies, sometimes finding documentation from the Ming and Qing dynasties.[71] New handbooks of metallurgical technology instructed on how to build folk furnaces, some said to date back to "China's ancient times."[72] These age-old practices were revived and revised for grassroots production of iron, copper, and even steel in the country.

Technical handbooks and manuals, however, were too difficult for the technically inexperienced to decipher. For such technologies to spread, visual technologies such as film, photography, and slide show proved indispensable. In September 1958 three film studios—Xinying, the August 1 Film Studio of the People's Liberation Army, and the Science and Educational Film Studio in Beijing—received an urgent request from the state to make instructional films on the building of backyard furnaces, "to propagate and spread the best techniques, so that tens of millions could learn these good technologies and begin to operate indigenous furnaces and flat furnaces nationwide."[73]

Upon receiving this task, the Xinying filmmaker Shi Mei consulted technical pamphlets but found them hard to decipher. "I couldn't understand the technical terms. . . . An engineer tried to teach us, but I barely understood it." If a filmmaker found these technical pamphlets difficult to comprehend, needless to say, they would be incomprehensible to the majority of people inexperienced with steelmaking. However, once she had been given a tour of an actual makeshift furnace near Beijing, she found producing steel easy. "After the head of the factory showed us around, I felt that making steel wasn't so mysterious. If we hadn't broken the mystique of steel making, who could have thought that in a simple brick house, one could make steel using iron scraps and other everyday raw materials?"[74]

Shi Mei's account illustrates just how important eyewitness accounts were for the spread of folk technologies. The films made by her and her colleagues would soon offer countless viewers the opportunity to observe backyard furnaces in operation on film. The filmmakers traveled to Henan, Hebei, Shanxi, Sichuan, Guizhou, and Sichuan to document a variety of locally conceived and historically inspired metallurgical technologies.[75] The films were short instructional films, each about ten minutes long. The making of these films took very little time, which meant that the filmmakers had no opportunity to verify the quality of metal produced from the furnaces. Xinying filmmakers shot three films in a day and a half and completed seven documentaries within twelve days.[76] The August First Film Studio shot a film in only three hours and completed five films altogether in less than two weeks.[77]

Held at the National Film Archive in Beijing, these films are inaccessible to researchers today, but one can get a sense of how they might have looked like from a widely circulated fifty-minute documentary entitled *Shenghuo de kaige* (Victorious song of life, 1958, dir. Gao Weijin and Wang Yonghong). Made by Xinying in September 1958, this film most likely used footage from these trips. It demonstrated how to look for mineral reserves in the vicinity, build a makeshift furnace, channel the hot metal liquid through ceramic conduits into molds, and finally, modify donkey or ox carts to transport products to nearby factories for further processing.

In chapter 3 I referred to Salomé Aguilera Skvirsky's idea of the "process genre" when discussing early CCP filmmaking in Yan'an. I showed that the film *Nanniwan*, documenting the production campaign in the Communist base area, could be understood as what Skvirsky calls the "process genre," which offered the viewers the opportunity to witness the transformative powers of human labor.[78] *Victorious Song of Life* was a film of "process genre" as well. Everything worked beautifully in the production process. Young people discovered mineral reserves on joyful hikes into the scenic mountains in the vicinity of their home. Fire was burning in the furnace, and the liquid metal was red and hot. The newly minted iron and copper bars proudly bore the name of the commune that made them (fig. 4.5). Documenting the building of furnaces at elementary schools, in factories, and by farmlands, these films were the YouTube DIY videos of yesterday. They put forth convincing visual evidence for

4.5 Scenes from *Victorious Song of Life* (1958) demonstrating how to work with backyard furnaces.

the efficacy of these folk technologies and called for nationwide emulation to build China's own industrialized future with them.

Class and Time: Wandering Intellectuals and Sleepless Labor

The Caprice of the Ming Tombs Reservoir featured a group of intellectuals visiting the construction site to learn from workers. Among them was a retrograde writer named Hu. In the film, Hu tries to interview a train driver who has just risked his life to stop a train accident on the construction site.

"Did you think of the consequences?" Hu asks. "You might have been injured, disabled, or killed."

"Everything happened in a few seconds; I had no time to think," answers the driver.

"You must have thought about it," Hu insists. "Maybe you have forgotten."

Upon hearing this, the train driver gets up impatiently, protesting that he has no time to talk and must return to his work.

The writer Hu will not let him go. "I have one more question for you. What were your happiest moments this past year?"

The train driver says loudly, "Being educated by the party."

"And what were your most unhappy moments?"

The train driver explodes with outrage. "I have nothing to be unhappy about," he yells furiously. "The only time when I feel unhappy is when I am asked such strange questions!"

In an otherwise upbeat film, this scene stands out as a rare moment where negative emotions are expressed. Here, the intellectual is rebutted for luring the worker to think in selfish terms. But why did the worker get so outraged by these questions?

Jacques Rancière defines aesthetics as "the distribution of the sensible."[79] An aesthetic marks certain things as self-evident, while shunning others as senseless. It determines what can be perceived and comprehended, and what cannot be. The politics of aesthetics is both inclusive and exclusionary: those who abide by the system of self-evident facts form a community with a common horizon of sensibility, while those who do not abide by it are banished from the community. Aesthetics delimits the community and determines its capacity: what it can feel, communicate, and do.

Rancière's discussion sheds light on the driver's outrage. Indeed, Hu's questions do not make *sense* to someone who operates within the temporality of the Great Leap Forward. To answer them requires taking a pause from time's breathless forward march and involves thinking about risk, failure, exhaustion, unfulfillment, all of which had been banished from the Great Leap Forward's timeline of optimism. Indeed, those who asked the questions were moodspoilers and time-wasters: they were intellectuals.

Intellectuals were seen to have a problematic relationship with time. Artistic documentary came into existence partly because filmmakers were deemed incapable of creating stories relevant to the changing times on their own. At a meeting with filmmakers in May 1958, the head of the Film Bureau, Chen Huangmei, described the problems facing intellectuals: "Our bodies have entered socialism, but . . . our hearts have remained in capitalism. . . . Time is moving forward, but [filmmakers] are lagging behind, hesitating, pacing back and forth, or even looking back nostalgically at things already rotting away." Intellectuals should have been society's vanguard, "serving as trumpeters in revolutionary marches."[80] But instead, intellectuals' deep enmeshment with capitalist and bourgeois thinking had made them hopelessly backward.

Like many other artistic documentaries of the time, *The Caprice of the Ming Tomb Reservoir* was as much a celebration of socialist labor as a conversion story for intellectuals. By the end of the film, most intellectuals are shown to join the working class—they work at the commune and have married workers and peasants. However, two backward intellectuals don't reform enough to make this conversion. The writer Hu made a hasty exit after his selfishness and disloyalty were exposed and never appeared in the film's segment on the future. The other intellectual was the biology professor Huang, who was doubtful about the miraculous labor productivity during the Great Leap Forward, deeming the production targets mathematically impossible to realize. Professor Huang is not entirely excluded from the Communist future: he is invited to the twentieth-anniversary celebration at the commune. Yet unlike the others who have benefited from improved medical sciences and look younger and healthier than they did twenty years before, Professor Huang appears significantly aged, with a full head of white hair, deep wrinkles, and a slouched back. "Yesterday's 'I' couldn't be pressed down, and it has come into conflict with today's 'I,'" he says of the internal conflicts that have plagued him in the past twenty years and prevented him from enjoying the true miracles of the Great Leap Forward. At the end of the film, as the rest of the people energetically party through the night, the old professor succumbs to the inertia of his body and falls asleep.

The working class didn't have the intellectuals' burden to reform themselves from their bourgeois ways; workers were the carriers of revolutionary temporality. Yet the working class also had its own burdens. They had little time to sleep. Overtime and extra shifts had been frequent as early as 1956, when the deadline to meet the production targets of the First Five-Year Plan approached. During the Great Leap Forward, overtime became normalized as workers were mobilized to work around the clock to create productivity surges.[81] Cinema helped perpetuate a culture of sleeplessness. Film screenings often ran between work shifts, or from end of work to around midnight. Reported experiments with daytime cinema to avoid drowsiness offered a glimpse into labor exhaustion. The prevalence of overtime, the reckless increase of production speed, and the general inexperience of a rapidly expanding labor force resulted in a sharp rise in reported workplace accidents. Meanwhile, the emphasis on reducing production costs led to cutbacks in workers' welfare, salary, and overtime pay.[82] The real wage for workers in Shanghai, for example, substantially declined between 1958 and 1960.[83]

On sleeplessness in late capitalism, Jonathan Crary writes, "24/7 is a time of indifference, against which the fragility of human life is increasingly inadequate and within which sleep has no necessity or inevitability. In relation to labor, it renders plausible, even normal, the idea of working without pause, without limits. It is aligned with what is inanimate, inert, or unageing."[84] Sleepless labor in China's "high socialism" reveals a fundamental contradiction in China's socialist experiment. Workers were supposed to rule the country and own the means of production. Yet despite the state's attempt to institute democratic management practices in factories, by the late 1950s these institutions' limits became increasingly clear, and labor interests remained subordinate to the developmental state's priority on industrial productivity and capital accumulation.[85] The Great Leap Forward was launched at a time of increasing labor unrest, when workers protested against stagnating wages, authoritarian assignments, and unsatisfactory working and living conditions, aggravated by the weakening of trade unions across the country.[86] Yet few of these contestations made it into cinema. The train driver's happiest moment was "being educated by the party," which placed him on the receiving and passive end of politics. Even when workers were portrayed as assuming active roles in managing production, as in *Huang Baomei*, "backward" voices and feelings were few and quickly abandoned in favor of a consensus for scoring further production surges. A few traces of labor discontent had existed in the published screenplay of *Huang Baomei*, such as a visibly distraught woman worker traveling by bus to work on a Sunday, but they are nowhere to be found in the completed film.[87]

In 1960 Xinying released a fourteen-minute documentary entitled *Flowers of Innovation Bloom Everywhere (Biankai gexinhua)*. This film introduced viewers to the various innovations made by workers during the Great Leap Forward. It began with a group of travelers arriving at a guesthouse in the northeastern city of Harbin. As all the rooms were filled, the hotel service staff quickly proceeded to make beds out of the tables and chairs in the game room, unfolding and refolding the furniture as if in a magic show. Every piece of furniture in the room, including bulletin boards standing against the wall, could be transformed into beds through a series of unfolding and refolding. The voice-over informed the audience, "This is not a magic show; all the furniture pieces have been made by the workers at the lodge themselves."

The rest of the film showcased three other places filled with marvels of technological innovation: a kindergarten, a grain store, and a restaurant, all located in Harbin. Using folding furniture built by the childcare workers themselves, the kindergarten had more than doubled its capacity and could flexibly transform a single room into multiple functional spaces, turning a bedroom first into a playroom and then a dining room. Both the grain store and the restaurant had installed machines to replace manual labor. At the grain store, which looked more like a spaceship, with the press of a few buttons, grain would automatically be weighed, loaded in dispensers, and released by a valve. At the restaurant, every kind of manual labor, including cooking, cleaning, taking orders, and delivering food to the table, had become automatic. The kitchen was filled with wonders of technology developed by the staff themselves, including mechanized dishwashers, and machines to slice meat and vegetable and make noodles and dumplings. Customers ordered food by pressing buttons on the table, sending the information to a monitor in the kitchen. The food was transported from the kitchen to the tables by a moving cart suspended from the ceiling of the restaurant.

Associated with magic shows since its earliest days, the film camera was the best medium to present the surprising transformations of the folding furniture, the miraculous workings of the automated kitchen, and, more generally, the magical everyday life promised by the Great Leap campaign.[88] Particularly mesmerizing here is the flexibility of these technologies, said to be conceived and crafted by the workers themselves, and the ease with which they can be manipulated to accommodate the changing everyday needs of communities. Meant to benefit collective spaces such as guesthouses, kindergartens, and restaurants, these technologies brought a sense of wonder to the state-promoted policies of communal childcare, communal dining halls, and centralized grain procurement and distribution.

The film was made in 1960, when the famine had begun to hit. While grain was dispensed automatically in the film, and a tasty meal created in the automated kitchen descended safely onto the center of the table from conveyor belts on the ceiling of the restaurant, food became scarce and out of reach for hundreds of millions of people in the country. Despite all the hard work that went into the Great Leap Forward, the production campaign ended tragically. National grain output plunged by 15 percent in 1959 and another 16 percent in the following two years.[89] The drop in agricultural yield was explained partly by the excessive rural labor input dedicated to infrastructure building, which meant fewer hours spent on agricultural production. Many irrigation projects had design issues, and what was successful elsewhere might not work well with the environment of a different locale. On the North China plain, inadequate drainage of many of the new waterworks resulted in increased soil salinity and decreased agricultural yield.[90] Industry collapsed in the cities.[91] Tens of millions of newly urbanized workers were resettled back to the countryside. The backyard furnaces turned out to be highly inefficient, leading to a tremendous waste of raw materials and to deforestation. In 1959 a quarter of the iron produced in the country was too poor in quality to be used in steel production.[92] The drop in grain output and excessive procurement were among the leading reasons for widespread famine between 1959 and 1961 in rural China, resulting in loss of life on the scale of tens of millions.[93]

As the first major setback to China's socialist experiment, the Great Leap Forward's overall failure and the subsequent Great Famine had devastating consequences. One could argue that the power struggles both at the center and at the grassroots that fueled the Cultural Revolution (1966–1976) had at least partly to do with grievances from this period, which were unequally distributed between urban and rural China, between the grassroots and the bureaucracy. This chapter has recounted the ways in which cinema, as a form of technologized media promoted by the state, propelled the Great Leap Forward as a productive force. Indeed, cinema was so deeply and widely entangled with practices of labor and technology at the time that it would be impossible to imagine the Great Leap Forward without it. Yet such a powerful media that fueled the Great Leap Forward had so spectacularly failed to register contending voices, and grasp risk, exhaustion, and possibilities of failure. Indeed, just when cinema had visualized the communist future so concretely, made it so palpable, just when films had traveled to construction sites to energize labor and spread technology to bring forth a new and better world, the communist future was slipping out of reach.

In chapter 3 I discussed how propaganda documentaries during wartime had focused on depicting "winning realities" to demoralize the enemy and strengthen the resolve of resistance. I proposed to engage with propaganda films ethically and politically, moving away from a simplistic treatment that presumed the existence of an "objective" truth and instead focusing on the power dynamics and the ethical accountability underlying propaganda production, to ask whose visions dominate, whose are excluded, and what are the political and ethical implications. The Great Leap Forward documentaries were propaganda films, too. They propagated "winning temporalities" that challenged the normativity of the clock time, promoted folk technologies as valuable forms of knowledge, and cultivated a commitment to a better future. Valuable for energizing a revolutionary project, the Great Leap temporalities nevertheless became exclusionary as they gained normativity. Documentary films associated dissenting experiences of uncertainty, risk, and exhaustion with political "backwardness" of intellectuals and the bourgeois class, while urging the working class to perform ever-intensifying labor at faster than clock time. Here the question of whose visions dominated and whose experiences were excluded not only had political and ethical implications but epistemological ones as well. Failure is integral to any experimentation, writes the biologist Stuart Firestein, and "we must make and defend a space for noncatastrophic failure, a place where failure can happen regularly."[94] As a campaign that could not afford to fail, the Great Leap Forward created a media ecology of optimism that shunned serious discussions of risk, contingency, and failure. On the surface, it seemed to have alleviated epistemological difficulties and enabled a unified striving; in effect, it intensified and escalated epistemological difficulties to disastrous levels.

In contrast to the well-represented Great Leap Forward, the Great Famine that followed left tens of millions dead and almost no images.[95] The heavily mediated Great Leap Forward and the scarcely mediated Great Famine alert us to media's imbrications in the energies and entropies of China's radical experiments. I'll continue to investigate these imbrications in the next chapter on the uncertainty of political knowledge, the persistence of class, and documentary crisis.

CHAPTER 5

THE UNCERTAINTY OF POLITICAL KNOWLEDGE

Documentary in Crisis

In the spring of 1963 Liu Shaoqi, then president of China, went on state visits to Indonesia, Myanmar, Cambodia, and Vietnam. In July of the same year a forty-four-minute color documentary film, *Chairman Liu Visits Indonesia* (*Liu Shaoqi zhuxi fangwen Yindunixiya*), was released and swiftly became a sensation nationwide. The film's admiring portrayal of Wang Guangmei accompanying her husband on the state visits left a deep impression on viewers. Retrospective accounts indicate that many were proud to see a woman participating in diplomacy, an arena that had been almost entirely dominated by men.[1] Even Chen Yinque, the learned historian and linguist who had lost his eyesight by the time of the film's release, became intrigued. In a poem written in the following year, Chen described the popular excitement around the film and the friendly relations between China and South Asian countries and speculated about political change.[2]

Two years later, in 1965, the Sino-Indonesian relationship ended with a U.S.-backed military coup in Indonesia, massacre of Indonesian Communists, and exodus of the Chinese diaspora there. The Cultural Revolution began the following year, and soon Liu Shaoqi and Wang Guangmei were denounced as capitalist roaders and traitors to the revolution. On April 10, 1967, a mass rally attended by some 300,000 people was held at Tsinghua University in Beijing. The Red Guards forced Wang Guangmei to dress as she had in the film: stockings, high-heeled shoes, a white hat, and the same *qipao* she had worn when visiting Indonesia. As the pearl necklace was too small to be visible to the massive audience attending the rally, a chain of Ping-Pong balls, each marked with

5.1 A rally at Tsinghua University in 1967 to condemn Wang Guangmei, who was dressed in the *qipao* she had worn when visiting Indonesia in 1963. A man with a film camera can be seen in the background. Photo source: Kuai Dafu and Mi Hedu, "Qinghua Pidou Wang Guangmei shimo," *Minjian lishi*, Universities Service Centre for Chinese Studies Collection, Chinese University of Hong Kong Library, http://mjlsh.usc.cuhk.edu.hk/Book.aspx?cid=4&tid=1364.

an X in black ink, hung around her neck, parodying the necklace she wore in the film (fig. 5.1).³

This real-life reenactment of cinema in front of a mass audience was only the beginning of a nationwide campaign to denounce the film and its protagonists, which lasted from the second half of 1967 to the end of 1968. The Central Cultural Revolution Small Group (Zhongyang wenge xiaozu) ordered a large number of copies of the film to be made and sent around the country and instructed local activists to organize denunciation rallies around screenings of the film.⁴ An outpouring of articles appeared in newspapers, condemning Liu Shaoqi and Wang Guangmei for their defection to the capitalist world and employing the film as evidence.⁵

This episode, chilling for both political and film histories of modern China, presents us with a moment of multiple crises, of international and domestic politics, and of documentary itself. How to make sense of this violent sequence of events, and how to think about documentary's participation in it? In the previous chapter I discussed cinema's entanglement with material productions in industry, agriculture, and infrastructure during the Great Leap Forward. In this chapter I continue the discussion on documentary's participation in the (un)making of Chinese socialism, focusing on its role in the production and dissemination of political knowledge (and doctrine) that identified "friends" and "enemies" in both international and domestic politics.

"Who are our enemies? Who are our friends? One can't be a revolutionary without being able to tell enemies apart from friends," Mao wrote as early as 1925 in "The Analysis of Social Classes in China."[6] These questions, however, are difficult to answer. Class analysis, the quintessential Marxist tool of political analysis, is powerful but never complete, as social groups are embedded in a web of power relations and interests that make categorization always partial. Furthermore, alliances, interests, class memberships, and even class categories themselves can profoundly shift during the revolutionary process. As I discussed in chapter 3 with regard to the forging of solidary relationships in the Communist base area of Yan'an, the proletariat in the Chinese revolution was not a preexisting category but was a desired political class that must be made through cultural operations of mutual learning between intellectuals and the masses in Yan'an—cadres, soldiers, peasants. The founding of the PRC ushered in rapid social transformations in the society and fundamentally altered the economic foundations underlying class formations. Would "enemy classes" such as capitalists continue to exist even when the economic foundations for them were no longer there? Would new class antagonisms form, and what would be their nature? And how would the proletariat develop as a political class during and after the socialist transformation? New complexities arose in the international realm, too. While the Soviet-led Socialist Bloc would be a natural ally given the ideological affinity, the tension between national interests and internationalist obligations, along with growing ideological differences after de-Stalinization, would eventually lead to hostilities in the bloc. Meanwhile, the newly independent nations of formerly colonized peoples, despite efforts at nonalignment, found their processes of decolonization entangled in Cold War bipolarism, making alliance with each other highly unstable and subject to drastic power shifts, such as in the case of Indonesia.

Looking at the political history at the time, one cannot but notice the profound entwinement between international and domestic politics during the PRC's first two decades. In the early 1950s the Korean War happened simultaneously with the first wave of domestic socialist transformation. In the late 1950s de-Stalinization across the Socialist Bloc informed China's Hundred Flowers Campaign and the Anti-Rightist Campaign, the latter an abrupt and punitive policy reversal of the former that caused widespread disillusionment and grief. The break with the Soviet Union happened at the same time as the resurgence of domestic class struggle in the early 1960s. The descent into violence during the Cultural Revolution occurred at the same time as China's bid for global revolutionary leadership following the Sino-Soviet split. It is beyond the scope of this chapter to trace these complex entwinements. Yet it's important to note that the events discussed earlier—the multiplication of enemies both internationally (Indonesia turning from friend to enemy overnight) and domestically (Liu and Wang condemned as enemies of the people)—happened sequentially not by accident, nor by simple causality. They were connected by complex force fields of international and domestic political dynamics and shaped by discursive practices that interpreted shifting political situations and gave verdict to political actors and lines of action. Put in another way, the contingent entanglements of domestic and international politics called for the formation of new political knowledge to comprehend them, while political knowledge, being formed to respond to changing political situations, further propelled domestic and international politics in certain directions in a dialectical process. And the fact that the same documentary film was involved both in the construction of the Sino-Indonesian relationship and in a forensic investigation into Wang and Liu's hidden "reactionary" nature suggests that documentary was an important discursive practice—and a mobilizing vehicle—that intervened in popular political response and knowledge formation.

As a Marxist-Leninist party, the CCP saw itself as the vanguard of the revolution, positioned at the center of political knowledge formation. Mao Zedong had articulated his politics of the mass line in epistemological terms: "In all the practical work of our Party, all correct leadership is necessarily 'from the masses to the masses.' This means: take the ideas of the masses (scattered and unsystematic ideas) and concentrate them (through study turn them into concentrated and systematic ideas), then go to the masses and propagate and explain these ideas until the masses embrace them as their own, hold fast to them and translate them into action, and test the correctness of these ideas in such action."[7] Since Yan'an, documentary had been seen as the "vanguard" in PRC filmmaking, and indeed there was a structural similarity between Mao's mass line and documentary production. Xinying's nationwide infrastructure stationed filmmakers in the provinces to film on the ground, while centralizing the overall planning of topics and postproduction in Beijing under party supervision. In other words, documentary filmmaking was very much a process of "from the masses, to the masses," the motto of the mass line. Meanwhile, filmmakers associated with the Xinying headquarters in Beijing were also responsible for overseas film missions, which allowed Xinying to cover both domestic and international news, shuttling political analysis across these two connected arenas in one institution.

This chapter discusses documentary's interactions with changing international and domestic politics in the first two decades of the PRC. In particular, I highlight three documentary "modalities of desire" in relation to the production of political knowledge: a cartographic tendency that maps friends and enemies in space, a forensic tendency to inscribe class (and enemy status) on the body, and a playful and transgressive tendency that counters the first two and insists on openness, experimentation, and the loosening of control. I borrow the term "modalities of desire" from Michael Renov, who has proposed four "fundamental tendencies"—or "modalities of desire"—that drive documentary practice and discourse: (1) to record, reveal, or preserve; (2) to persuade or promote; (3) to analyze or interrogate; and (4) to express. Renov carefully notes that these impulses are historically formed and vary across time and space.[8] The cartographic, forensic, and experimental impulses that I observe here have certainly been expressed in many other historical times and spaces, yet in the PRC context they arose as particular responses to particular political situations. At stake was the important question of how to imagine proletariat subjectivities and communities in the new socialist society.

Moving between international relations, domestic politics, and revolutionary epistemology, this chapter continues the book's broader aim to explore documentary as eventful media. As the first two decades of the PRC saw tremendous political change both domestically and internationally, periodization is particularly important. There was no single homogenous Maoist documentary. Instead, the forms and genres of documentary were being worked out as a constitutive part to historical change. I show that documentary served cartographic functions to orient viewers to new international and domestic terrains during the Korean War and created stable images of socialist unity when tension grew in the Socialist Bloc in the wake of de-Stalinization. I also demonstrate that a young generation of filmmakers, encouraged by the film critic Zhong Dianfei, sought new documentary aesthetics that moved away from the clear directionality of earlier documentaries and expressed a desire to explore, celebrate, and experiment with a new world that transcended old hierarchies and boundaries. Such aesthetics were denounced as "bourgeois" in the Anti-Rightist Campaign yet reemerged in the early 1960s in the sensuous and transgressive documentary *Chairman Liu Visits Indonesia*, the first cinema representation of the experimental "wife diplomacy," which, as I will discuss in depth, demonstrated the party's patriarchal tendencies and a gendered division of labor in diplomacy that demanded women to absorb the risk of liaising with ideologically different allies. In denunciation campaigns against this film and its protagonists at the height of the Cultural Revolution, cinema's important role in perpetuating reified classifications of social classes was manifested. Documentary had joined paintings, sculptures and artifacts presented in class education exhibitions to create archetypes of class struggle, providing behavioral templates and "seeing lessons" for the forensic detections of class enemies, and in time, enabling the violence of scapegoating, which had no chance of returning the society to any epistemological certainty but instead unleashed crises and devastations in all facets of political, social, and ethical lives.

In 1967, after reading a *People's Daily* article attacking him for being a capitalist roader, citing as evidence his approval in 1950 of a Hong Kong film, Liu Shaoqi lamented that "the internal struggles in the party had never been so frivolous." Confronting the multiple crises in international relations, domestic politics, revolutionary knowledge formation, and documentary, this chapter attempts a serious examination into what appeared as "frivolous politics."

Maps and Diagrams: Clarifying Friends and Enemies During the Korean War

On December 28, 1951, a fifty-six-minute documentary film, *Resist America and Aid Korea* (*Kangmei yuanchao*) was released with great fanfare. Directed by Xu Xiaobing, a veteran Yan'an filmmaker, and filmed by a team of more than fifty cinematographers on the battlefront in Korea, the film was simultaneously shown in all cinemas in China's forty-four largest cities as well as in factories, armies, and via mobile projection in the countryside. By February 12, 1952, just forty-seven days after its release, it had reportedly met more than ten million viewers nationwide, thanks to the tremendous promotional work performed by local cadres and cinemas.[9]

Praised by the *People's Daily* as the most important achievement in Chinese documentary filmmaking in the past several years,[10] the film begins with a map of the China-Korea border. "For more than 1,000 li (500 km) our territory borders that of the Democratic People's Republic of Korea," a male voice-over speaks. "Like lips and teeth, we live close to and rely on each other." The image of the map fades into a slow panning shot of the magnificent Changbai (Paektu) Mountain that stands at the border of China and Korea, and Heaven Lake, located at the mountain's summit caldera. A montage sequence follows the pan, further exploring the beauty of the mountain, the lake, and the Yalu River, which takes its source from the lake. As the camera captures snow-covered mountain peaks, pine trees in the valleys, and streams cascading down the mountain slope, the voice-over reads lines composed by the script writer and poet Ai Qing: "Like an untamable wild horse, the turbulent water from Heaven Lake crashes down the cliffs, races through hills, forests, valleys, and meanders across the plains in Northwestern Korea, until it flows into the Yellow Sea."

The Changbai Mountain range, Heaven Lake, and the Yalu River make up the bulk of the Sino-Korean border. In this beginning sequence, they are portrayed not as markers of separation and exclusion, but as a long stretch of connected and shared territory. This is decidedly different from how the thirty-eighth parallel is portrayed in a sequence about five minutes into the film. Beginning again with a map of the region, but this time featuring the thirty-eighth parallel drawn in tentative dotted lines, the sequence cuts abruptly to the newsreel footage of the American politician John Foster Dulles's visit to the military encampment at the thirty-eighth parallel. There is no soft transition between the shots to create a sense of connection and inclusion, nor any depiction of the region's natural environment. Instead, this sequence is composed of images shot exclusively in and around the trenches, thus portraying the thirty-eighth parallel as the thoroughly militarized zone that it is.

The sequence on the thirty-eighth parallel ends with yet another map: while inspecting the trenches, Dulles is seen to examine a map presented to him by South Korean officers. This shot is followed by an inserted map of the region, this time illustrating, with black arrows, strategies for the U.S. forces to attack China via Korea, making the map into a diagram of possible actions. Unlikely to be what Dulles was looking at, this map had been originally published in *Collier's*, an American weekly magazine, and made its way into a satirical cartoon in a newspaper in Tianjin, before being reprinted by the *People's Daily*.[11] Representing one of the most belligerent views in the United States, the map is incorporated into the film as revealing America's true aims in the war (fig. 5.2).

Spending the first six minutes of its running time alternating between maps and diagrams, on one hand, and the camera's onsite explorations on the other, *Resist America and Aid Korea* cues us to think about cinema—and in this case, documentary—as cartographic and diagrammatic, offering viewers the cognitive and affective support for geopolitical imaginations of the world and China's position in it. Maps and films are "coextensive" to each other, observes the film theorist Tom Conley: "A film, like a topographic projection, can be understood as an image that locates and patterns the imagination of its spectators. When it takes hold, a film encourages its public to think of the world in concert with its own articulation of space."[12] A diagram takes this articulation of space further by illustrating the force fields within the space: it plots possible movements, and by giving visibility to these possibilities, it further intensifies them, hence constituting a force of its own.

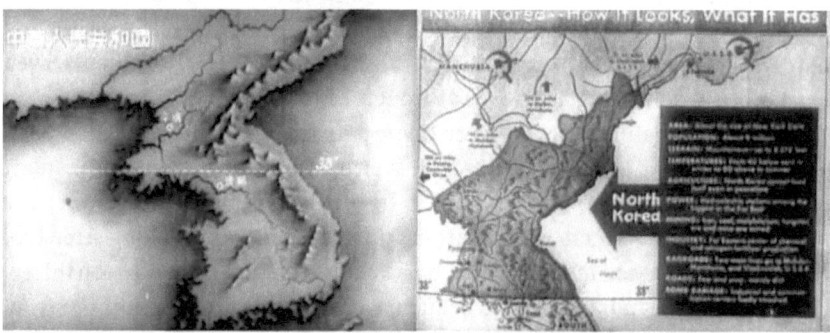

5.2 Uses of maps and diagrams in *Resist America and Aid Korea* (1951).

The outbreak of the Korean War was one of the most significant events in the postwar decades. Historians have argued that for the newly founded PRC, the war not only posed grave security issues on the border but also exerted impact on the domestic society at large.[13] The Communist government worried that America's entry into the war and dispatch of the Seventh Fleet to the Taiwan Strait might create anticipation among the Chinese population of a U.S.-supported attack from Taiwan. Such anticipation could hinder the implementation of new policies such as the land reform: peasants reportedly were too fearful of a comeback of the old regime to take advantage of these policies. With an increase in reported counterrevolutionary activities, the party was also anxious about losing control.[14] The CCP's decision to join the war might have to do with pressure from Moscow and concerns over border security, yet more important was its need to respond to the war in a way that could rally popular support and gain legitimacy at home. In other words, how this war was mediated to the Chinese public and how it inspired confidence in the party and in the new regime were of equal importance to how the war was fought on the battleground outside the Chinese border. As Hajimu Masuda writes about China's entry into the Korean War, "The point at issue is how people saw themselves, their history, and the outside world and how they behaved accordingly."[15]

It is in this context that *Resist America and Aid Korea*'s cartographic and diagrammatic value was put to good use. The film depicts the Sino-Korean border and the thirty-eighth parallel in strong contrast: the former goes along natural geographical contours that both sides share and is beautiful, open, and free. The latter is artificial, restricted, heavily militarized, and operating on principles of isolation and hostility rather than connection and codependence. It provides an ethical mapping to the space of conflict, contrasting the devastation caused by American air raids from the sky, with the Chinese Army's aid to Korean villagers on the ground. Countering the arrows of America's possible attack on the *Collier's* diagram, the camera marches *with* the Chinese Army and charges with them in crossfire, giving visibility to the military force that the army exerts on the battlefield. The camera also attends to other vectors of forces that map international support for North Korea. On the supply lines, trains pull in with supplies from international allies. In Chinese cities and throughout the countryside, students organize street rallies, and villagers travel with their animal-powered carts to contribute grain, dancing to the folk rhythms of hand drums. The film ends with the capture of Pyongyang on December 6, 1950, a success that not only had a significant impact on the war itself but also created greater confidence among the Chinese public in the new regime.

In chapter 3 I discussed *Victory of the Chinese People*, a Sino-Soviet coproduction that became a blockbuster in the autumn of 1950, on the first anniversary of the founding of the PRC. Released a year later, *Resist America and Aid Korea*'s comparable popularity demonstrates just how important documentary films were in the early years of China's socialist transition. The film was shown widely in cities and the countryside from 1951 to 1953 and at the battlefront in Korea, often with Chinese soldiers and Korean civilians watching it together.[16] The film was so influential that feature films used it in their plot design. For example, *Harvest* (*Fengshou*), a feature film released in 1953 by the Northeastern Film Studio, elaborated on the documentary's efficacy in resolving contradictions in a village in northeastern China. The film tells the story of villagers and cadres unable to come to an agreement on production targets, based on their different opinions on how realistic those targets are, given the village's limited land and water resources. One conservative village elder sees some younger villagers' request to raise production targets as ignorant and pompous and refuses to cooperate. Toward the end of the film, villagers sit down for an open-air screening of *Resist America and Aid Korea*. As the older villagers, who had never seen cinema before, marvel at the film's depiction of "concrete events" (*shizai de shi*), and as the villagers cheer for the Chinese soldiers finding their way in an unfamiliar terrain and accomplishing the impossible, the conservative village elder becomes transformed, and the disagreement about production targets is resolved. *Harvest* ends with a village more united than ever. Even villagers who had previously distrusted the state's capacity to create a socialist system and continued to sell their produce in the private commodity market now want to join the campaign to produce for the state.

Between 1950 and 1953, besides the Korean War, Chinese filmmakers also engaged in cross-border filmmaking in Vietnam during the First Indochina War. *Vietnam in Resistance* (*Kangzhan de Yuenan*) was codirected by Chinese and Vietnamese filmmakers and released in 1952.[17] These films identified clear friends and enemies for the Chinese public in the international realm. Meanwhile, documentary films such as *Special Report on the Three-Anti and Five-Anti Campaigns* (*Sanfan wufan teji*, 1951) also informed viewers of campaigns to purge domestic enemies. The suppression of counterrevolutionaries in 1950 and the Three-Anti and Five-Anti Campaigns in 1951 and 1952, targeting cadre corruption and the private sector, were certainly party responses to perceived domestic issues, yet they also coincided with the white terror in Taiwan, McCarthyism in the United States, and other purges of "internal enemies" across the board in both camps of the emerging Cold War, pointing to the intimate relationship between authoritarianism and Cold War geopolitics. I will return to this issue of the production and persecution of internal enemies later in the chapter.

Peaceful Coexistence and Zhou Enlai as Mediator

Perceived at its onset as a possible prelude to another world war, the Korean War wound down in the summer of 1953. CCP leaders were relieved that a general war had been deterred. Mao Zedong attributed this to the existence of a vast "intermediary zone" (*zhongjian didai*) composed of former colonies and semi-colonies in Asia, Africa, and Latin America, which hindered American domination. Zhou Enlai also noted America's unreliable alliances with countries in Europe and the Asia Pacific, with most of them unwilling to cooperate with the United States in an expanded war.[18] As the CCP had consolidated its control of the country and domestic policies began to pivot toward ensuring the fulfillment of the first five-year plan, China's foreign policy shifted to the principle of "peaceful coexistence," articulated by Zhou Enlai at the Geneva Conference of 1954 and reiterated at the Bandung Conference of 1955.

A gathering of five "big powers" (the Soviet Union, the United States, Britain, France, and China) aimed at resolving the Korean War and the Indochina War, the Geneva Conference was the PRC's first participation in a significant international diplomatic event. Zhou Enlai, who served as both premier and foreign minister at the time, led a delegation of more than two hundred people to Geneva in April 1954. Zhou was an experienced negotiator and mediator with a long-standing interest in drama and cinema—he had been an amateur actor when studying at the Nankai High School in Tianjin in the 1910s and helped build the Yan'an film unit in the late 1930s. At the Geneva conference Zhou expertly managed China's public image. The Chinese delegation's official diplomatic speeches were clear and principled, while its presence overall at the conference exuded openness, flexibility, and cultural sophistication. Zhou made arrangements to ship antiques and classical furnishings from China to decorate the Grand Mont-Fleur estate at Versoix, where the Chinese delegation stayed for the three-month duration of the conference, and where many of Zhou's meetings with diplomats and journalists took place.[19] He also adjusted the Chinese delegation's attire, adding more light-colored suits to their dark-colored wardrobe, to meet the international spotlight with a more youthful and lighthearted appearance.

Cinema contributed to building China's public image in Geneva. The Chinese delegation hosted three screenings there. The first screening was of a color documentary film entitled *The National Day 1952* (*1952nian guoqing yuebing*). As the film involved a military parade, it received critical reviews by American journalists as indicating "rising militarism" in China.[20] To counter this negative impression, Zhou subsequently hosted two screenings of *The Butterfly Lovers* (*Liang Shanbo yu Zhu Yingtai*, 1953), a color film adaptation of a Yue opera play telling a tragic love story. A regional opera from Zhejiang, Zhou's ancestral province, the Yue opera was well-known for its all-female cast, beautiful costumes, and a soft and flexible (*rou*) aesthetics both in music and in performance. The theater scholar Jin Jiang has discussed this aesthetics of *rou* as a "feminine aesthetics," built on the performing bodies of the all-female cast.[21] Introduced as the "Romeo and Juliet of China," the film was a tribute to youth and free love and was well-received in Geneva. A copy of the film was sent to Charlie Chaplin, who lived near Geneva at the time, in exile from the United States for his sympathetic views toward communism. Enthralled by the film, Chaplin met with Zhou and the actress Fan Ruijuan, who acted the male lead Liang Shanbo in the film and had traveled to Geneva upon Zhou's request after attending the Karlovy Vary International Film Festival in Czechoslovakia. I will return to this feminine aesthetics in a later section when I discuss "wife diplomacy," which placed Wang Guangmei under both limelight and scrutiny.

The Geneva conference was a media event in China. The *People's Daily* reported Zhou's activities with text and photographs, often with multiple news items daily. Filmmakers from Xinying accompanied the Chinese delegation for the entire duration of the conference and documented Zhou's meetings and activities. Newsreel films on the conference enjoyed cinema runs nationwide. Professional, religious, and other social groups organized rallies and signed open letters to support the ending of the Indochina War, which Zhou helped mediate, and the principle of "peaceful coexistence," which Zhou put forth at the conference. While the Geneva conference allowed Chinese readers and viewers to see China on the world stage serving a mediating role to end the wars, China's participation at the Bandung Conference a year later, also made into a documentary, entitled *The Bandung Conference* (*Wanlong huiyi*, 1955), gave visibility to the nonalignment movement in which China was a valued member.

Having fought the Korean War, mediated peace negotiations in Geneva, and built solidarity with newly independent, formerly colonized states at Bandung, the PRC by the mid-1950s had stabilized its revolutionary identity and geopolitical position. Meanwhile, the domestic socialist transformation continued. The first five-year plan was being implemented. New social relations had also been established. It was at this time of optimism that young documentary filmmakers at Xinying began to experiment with new forms of documentary.

Lost in Play: "Bourgeois" Tendencies in Documentary

In the previous chapter I discussed the Xinying filmmaker Shi Mei and her involvement in making Great Leap documentaries that taught the techniques of building backyard furnaces. In 1958, a year before Shi was tasked with making those instructional films, she had written an essay on bourgeois tendencies in documentary filmmaking. "Since the spring of 1956, the struggle between two lines at the thought front has become sharpened," Shi wrote.

> In the creative thoughts of news and documentary film workers, there has also been a two-line struggle. One line upholds the principle that art should serve politics and the proletariat, and uses newsreel and documentaries as a weapon

to fight for the party and for the people, and to serve socialist construction. Another line disengages with politics, is uninterested in the lives and struggles of the working people, and uses the work only to express personal bourgeois sentiments and to gain individual recognition. This means that news and documentary films in effect serve the interest of the capitalist class.[22]

In Shi's account, the bourgeois line of documentary filmmaking came into being in 1954, when Zhong Dianfei—a film critic who would later be labeled as a "Rightist" in the Anti-Rightist Campaign in 1957—served as the editor-in-chief of the studio. This tendency grew more prominent in 1956, during the Hundred Flowers Campaign. Filmmakers who exhibited this tendency no longer produced documentary films that the masses would need, as Shi Mei wrote, because these films no longer praised the worthy and opposed the incorrect. "What do working people need news and documentary films for? First, they want it to serve socialist construction and socialist thought education. Most important, it should directly represent working people's lives and struggles. It should praise thoughts and deeds of progressive people, so that people can learn from them. It should also criticize backward thoughts and deeds, so that people know what to oppose." In fact, not only did these films fail to offer orientations of right and wrong, they actively promoted an aesthetics of "losing oneself" and "intoxication." Shi took as an example a script entitled *White Clouds Deep in the Mountains* (Shenshan baiyun), submitted by an unnamed filmmaker but rejected by the studio. The film was ostensibly about a team of young workers on an excavation mission in the mountains in Sichuan, searching for mineral reserves to be used for the country's industrialization. Instead of prioritizing the team's important work, however, the script emphasized how entranced these young people were by the natural environment. Not concentrating on their work, the excavation team was constantly distracted by the mountain scenery and by the wild animals they encountered. In fact, the filmmaker stated clearly in the script the intention to let "the camera lens lead the viewers to experience being lost and intoxicated." Such experiences of disorientation and inebriation, Shi wrote, "absolutely failed to correspond to the thoughts and feelings of the proletariat, or the thoughts and feelings of the young people in our time."[23]

The film sector had been a major arena of ideological struggle since the founding of the PRC, with frequent campaigns against ideologically "problematic" films. In the early 1950s these denunciation campaigns targeted only feature films, particularly those made by private studios in Shanghai (before the studios were nationalized in 1953).[24] Documentary production had few problems in the first years of the PRC because it had a much stronger revolutionary pedigree: as I wrote in chapter 3, Yuan Muzhi had initiated documentary in Yan'an as the foundation for a new cinema for the revolution, and filmmakers trained in Yan'an and at the Northeastern Film Studio—the CCP's first fully functioning film studio—had documented the CCP's path to victory. After 1949 documentary production was centralized and based in Beijing. Even though cinematographers were stationed in the provinces to shoot footage in a timely manner, all editing was done in Beijing. It is fair to say that documentary had always been under closer party supervision than its fiction-based counterpart: it was celebrated as the vanguard of cinema, not just for its speedy production and proximity to social change, but also for its close association with the party.

Beginning in the mid-1950s, however, Xinying began to see changes in its production, as the overall political situation changed. The threat of open warfare was reduced. Chinese society also moved into a relatively stable period of peacetime construction. Class differences were drastically reduced as industries and businesses became nationalized. By 1956, even the CCP leadership believed that class conditions had fundamentally changed in the country, and the class background assigned to each individual and family upon the PRC's founding might have been made obsolete. Meanwhile, a younger generation of filmmakers who had not experienced Yan'an or the Civil War came of age and started innovating the documentary form to suit the new times. One aspect of this innovation was precisely a desire to freely move, explore, and celebrate a new world where old hierarchies and boundaries had been removed.

Shi Mei's essay mentioned another documentary film entitled *Plum Flower, Spring Rain, and Jiangnan (Xinghua chunyu Jiangnan)*. Unlike *White Clouds Deep in the Mountains*, which was never made, this color documentary was directed by Gao Zhongming and Zhang Mengqi and released in 1957 just before the Anti-Rightist Campaign came into full force. This was the first documentary to be labeled as a "poisonous weed," that is, detrimental to socialist construction and needed to be "weeded out." Described by Shi as displaying a "dark and decadent style," the film was in fact a "rural symphony," structured as a one-day journey through rural Jiangnan, a fertile region south of the Yangtze River on China's east coast. Beginning and ending with shots of luminous morning and evening clouds, it is a love song to the sun, the rain, and the rivers and streams that nourished the many life forms found in the region: plants, fish, silkworms, birds, farm animals, and people.

The film does depict a variety of work, from farming and fishing to raising silkworms and embroidery, yet indeed in these depictions one also finds in abundance what Shi Mei called "distractions." When filming professional embroiderers at work, for example, the camera becomes mesmerized by the woman embroiderers' agile hands, and the shifting light and shadow created by the sunlight and the moving tree branches in the courtyard where the embroiderers are seated. The hands and the sunlight seem to work together on the embroidery, creating beautiful patterns on the fabric, and the female voice-over reminds the viewers that the work is collaboratively accomplished by the workers and the environment and thus is life-giving: "The generous bosoms of Jiangnan's spring fields help the sowers nourish the seeds for the harvest; its beautiful scenery, like paintings, inspire the imagination of the young woman embroiderers."

In this film, the spring is sensuous. The same voice-over invokes many senses as it guides the viewer to have a sensorial experience of the spring, from how the breeze feels on the skin to how the spring fields smell ("an intoxicating fragrance hovers on every field"). The spring is also capacious. Loved by all, it also allows everyone to experience it differently. As the camera attends to different work performed by different people—fishers, farmers, the old and the young, men and women—and the rich plant and animal lives under their care, the voice-over says, "Spring, how the people love you . . . how they love everything glorious about you! And in people's hearts, they also hold their own springs, and everything about themselves in their springs." Deeply poetic, the segment depicting an afternoon drizzle in the film reminds one of Joris Ivens's early work, *Rain* (1929), though, in contrast to Ivens's urban setting, this film is set in the countryside, where the rain hovers over fields and creates ripples in fishponds, and the voice-over stresses again the experience of rain as belonging to the people themselves in their daily practices of labor and enjoyment: "When it comes to the familiarity with the sentiment of the spring rain, who could compare to the fisherwomen of Jiangnan?"

The film could still be called cartographic, if we consider cartography broadly, as Tom Conley understands it, to be the creation of spatial experiences within the film text. The spatial experience in this film, however, was very different from the clear demarcation of two parties in struggle in *Resist America and Aid Korea*. Instead, the space constructed by the film is freed from boundaries and directionality and is therefore conducive to multisensory experiences, to the integration of work and life, and to wandering, immersion, and exploration (fig. 5.3).

In other films made at Xinying in this period, one finds a similar energy of joy, freedom, and experimentation. The talented filmmaker Chen Guangzhong, who would make *An Inch of Time Is Worth an Inch of Gold* in 1959, a film discussed in detail in the previous chapter, made his directorial debut in 1954. Entitled *Forever Young (Yongyuan nianqing)*, the film begins with ducks and other birds bathing in the morning sun and a group of young people taking their morning jog along the river. "The earth has woken up!" A male voice-over exclaims, "This is just one morning in a thousand mornings. But viewers, what you are seeing is the new scenes of life of our nation." Speaking in first-person as the filmmakers, the voice-over continues: "We have named the film *Forever Young* because we abhor the premature graying of old age. We proclaim: not only politically but also in everyday life and spirit, our people belong forever to a new people!"

5.3 Scenes from *Plum Flower, Spring Rain, and Jiangnan* (1957).

Forever Young features the various kinds of popular sports that Chinese urban and rural residents engage in after work: dancing, bicycling, gymnastics, even parachuting. If the camera in *Plum Flowers, Spring Rain, and Jiangnan* is entranced by the lushness of the environment where various forms of life flourished together, in *Forever Young* the camera is fascinated by the beauty of human bodies in free movement within a communal setting. Sports in this film do not follow an industrial aesthetic that turns synchronized body movements into what Siegfried Kracauer would call a "mass ornament." Instead, these sports combine the communal and the personal into an exhilarating experience of dynamism, competence, and bodies taking and making space together. The film's camera movements and editing are attuned to the spontaneous formations and coordination of body movements on football fields, in group dances, and at volleyball matches. The camera follows workers at a bicycle factory in Shanghai as they ride the bicycles—the products of their own labor—out of the city into the countryside and allows viewers to join the workers' fun when they stack themselves onto a single bicycle, each performing a balancing act in response to others' positions and movements on the moving bike. In another scene at an open-air volleyball match, a ball is knocked out, but the camera follows it as it hits a chicken pen. This shot was criticized by Jiang Yunchuan, an older generation filmmaker who had been the director for the film, but whose work trip to Moscow allowed Chen to finish the film on his own. For Jiang, this shot conveyed no deeper meaning but was simply a "trick" to entertain the audience. Indeed the film was similarly criticized, overall, as low-brow entertainment (*diji quwei*).[25] Yet the shot of the chicken pen, considered in relation to the film's overall aesthetic of play, is not meaningless. It conveys that missing the target is allowed, and the game is still fun even when a ball is called out and a team does not score. While Shi Mei criticized the "bourgeois" films made at Xinying in this period as being disinterested in work—which for Shi was the defining characteristic of the proletariat—films such as *Plum Flowers, Spring Rain, and Jiangnan* and *Forever Young* were in fact redefining what work should be in the socialist period. Work and play should become united in socialism to allow the flourishing of life (fig. 5.4).

Based on his interviews with documentary filmmakers active in the mid-1950s, the filmmaker and scholar Zhang Tongdao has used the term *documentary new wave* to refer to the experiments of this period, drawing a direct analogy to the French New Wave, which emerged around the same time. Zhang writes, "Young filmmakers at the studio gathered around Zhong Dianfei, just like the French New Wave filmmakers gathered around Bazin. They listened to music, watched performances, told stories, and vigorously discussed film aesthetics."[26]

Zhong Dianfei, whom Zhang Tongdao compared to Bazin and whom Shi Mei named in her essay as responsible for encouraging the bourgeois tendency in documentary filmmaking, was an important film critic. By the time of Shi Mei's writing, he had already been labeled the biggest "Rightist" in the film sector, for his polemic article entitled "The Gongs and Drums of Cinema" (Dianying de luogu), published during the Hundred Flowers Campaign in 1956. In the article, Zhong took issue with the idea of *gongnongbing* cinema (worker, peasant, and soldier cinema). The meaning of the term, Zhong observed, was too vague. "It could be interpreted as 'cinema serving workers, peasants, and soldiers,' or that cinema could only depict workers, peasants, and soldiers. Judging from how the term has been practiced, its dogmatism and factionalism are clear." Zhong pointed out that the dogmatic understanding that cinema could only depict workers, peasants and soldiers had led to a reduction in film production and an overly narrow range of topics. Zhong astutely observed that this vagueness had been exploited by factional politics in the film studios: the fact that all pre-1949 films had been designated "petty bourgeois cinema" resulted in the convenient sidelining of many talented filmmakers and actors, whose pre-1949 experiences working for commercial film studios now made them suspect for their "capitalist" tendencies.[27]

5.4 Scenes from *Forever Young* (1954).

Coming of age in Yan'an, Zhong had an impeccable revolutionary background and participated in the investigation to denounce *The Life of Wu Xun* in 1951.[28] Yet he did not rest on his privilege but instead spoke out for marginalized film artists whom he believed had been wrongly designated the "bourgeois class" and excluded from *gongnongbing* cinema. Calling such exclusions a disrespect for the people, "pushing people a thousand *li* away" (*ju ren yu qianli zhi wai*), Zhong argued that this exclusion created huge problems for the development of cinema. Citing meager attendance numbers for recent films, he observed that cinema was losing its most fundamental connection, namely, that to its audience. The masses—especially workers in the urban areas, where Zhong's data came from—had found *gongnongbing* films wanting. Zhong's article was meant to beat the "gongs and drums," to make noise, alerting the PRC's cultural bureaucracy to the dire need to enrich filmmaking.

Working at Xinying in 1954, Zhong brought to, and developed at the studio some of the ideas that he later elaborated in "Gongs and Drums," and his encouragement for aesthetic innovation fell on willing ears. Besides experimenting with film form, filmmakers at Xinying also began to use documentary for social critique. Zhong had been involved in the filmmaker Lü Ban's experiments with satirical comedies, which had been politically risky but seemed safer after the Soviet thaw had resulted in a rise in satirical comedies in the Soviet Union.[29] Xinying filmmakers made documentary satires, too. Chen Guangzhong made *Pretty but Not Solid* (*Hua er bu shi*) in 1956 during the Hundred Flowers Campaign, critiquing the costly and superficial designs in new buildings in Beijing. Liu Deyuan, a filmmaker from a slightly older generation, also joined in. His film *The Customers' Troubles* (*Guke de fannao*) documented an "exhibition on the quality of everyday industrial products" (*riyong gongyepin zhiliang zhanlanhui*) held in Beijing in July 1956 that exposed the low quality of some industrial products in the country. From leaking washbasins, exploding thermos bottles, and shrinking and fading fabrics to broken shoes, the film unsparingly named factories, poked fun at the faulty products they put on the market, and critiqued their insufficient quality control.

It is worth noting that the three filmmakers discussed so far in relation to this new wave of documentary filmmaking—Gao Zhongming, Chen Guangzhong, and Liu Deyuan—all came from former colonies. Gao Zhongming (born in 1929) and Chen Guangzhong (born in 1930), the two young filmmakers who directed *Plum Flowers, Spring Rain, and Jiangnan* and *Forever Young*, respectively, hailed from Hong Kong and Taiwan. Both spent their early teenage years as refugees in the mainland: Gao's family fled Taiwan for Fujian to escape Japanese colonial rule, and Chen's family left Hong Kong for Guilin after the Japanese occupation in 1942. Both went back to their home region to study in the immediate postwar years and returned to the mainland to join the new People's Republic in 1949 out of patriotism and enthusiasm for the revolution. Both began their documentary film career in 1950, by learning from the older generation of filmmakers who spent their formative years in Yan'an during the Civil War. Born slightly earlier, in 1925, Liu Deyuan began his film career in 1944 as a cinematographer in the Japanese Manchurian Film Studio, trained further under Yuan Muzhi and the Yan'an veterans at the Northeastern Film Studio during the Civil War, and participated in the making of *Resist America and Aid Korea*, discussed earlier. These biographies alert us to the diverse film cultures that formed the personal backgrounds of Xinying filmmakers and contributed to filmmaking in the early PRC. This is a topic beyond the scope of the present book but offers opportunities for future research.

While this remarkable development in the mid-1950s saw only a handful of actualized films, and it may be an exaggeration to call it "a documentary new wave," as Zhang Tongdao suggests, there is no doubt that as China entered peacetime, the mid-1950s saw a growing confidence in the possibility of a new society, where the class struggle that had characterized previous societies would recede and be replaced by an increasingly boundless freedom enjoyed by all to explore new ways of being in community and in the world, from joyful communions with all life forms to the candid exposure of social problems. This development, unfortunately, was cut short by the Anti-Rightist Campaign of late 1957.

Filming Unity:
Mao Zedong's Interparty Visit to the Soviet Union

Released in 1958 by Xinying, *Congratulations* (*Zhuhe*), a thirty-one-minute color documentary, documented Mao Zedong's visit to Moscow in November 1957. It opens with a panorama of Moscow's majestic architecture bathed in the morning sunlight. "On the fortieth anniversary of the October Revolution, the hearts of all peace-loving people in the world are longing for the Soviet Union, for Moscow," a female voice-over intones in the soundtrack. The next sequence depicts the arrival of Mao and the Chinese delegation, greeted by Nikita Khrushchev, the head of the Communist Party; Kliment Voroshilov, the head of state; other Soviet officials; and a large number of people's representatives.

Compared to the new wave films discussed in the previous section, this film was in every way different. While it spends considerable screen time featuring the Moscow landscape, it structures the pleasure of spectatorship around familiarity and recognition, rather than exploration of the unknown. The camera shows little interest in exploring the city as a dynamic space of its own; rarely does it move through and interact with Moscow's built environment. Instead, it frames iconic sites of Moscow, such as the Kremlin, Red Square, and the Tomb of the Unknown Soldier, in static long shots, rendering them into meticulously composed, two-dimensional tableau images that appeared spectacular and were conducive to easy recognition.

These stable images on the screen were made at a time when the Socialist Bloc was experiencing significant instability. In February 1956 Khrushchev's secret speech at the Twentieth Congress of the Communist Party of the Soviet Union (CPSU) marked the beginning of de-Stalinization and sent shock waves across the bloc. As ruling Communist parties had drawn from Stalinist methods of authoritarian rule, de-Stalinization brought instability to their claims of legitimacy. In Poland and Hungary, popular protests erupted in October and November 1956. In the Soviet Union, Khrushchev experienced major challenges to his leadership just months before Mao's visit to Moscow, mounted by high-ranking party officials such as Georg Malenkov and Vyacheslav Molotov, who sought but failed to restore Stalinist policies. In China, the political liberalization of the Hundred Flowers Campaign of 1956 and 1957 could be seen as a measure of de-Stalinization. Meant to address contradictions between the party and the people, particularly the issue of increasing bureaucratization and the rise of a bureaucratic elite, the Hundred Flowers Campaign came to an abrupt reversal in June 1957, when the party began to crack down on dissent. The ensuing Anti-Rightist Campaign left many intellectuals brutally punished, displaced, and disillusioned. As mentioned earlier, the experiments with documentary form at Xinying came to a halt during the campaign. The critic Zhong Dianfei was condemned as a "Rightist" and didn't return to film criticism until after the Cultural Revolution.

Mao visited Moscow in November 1957 to attend the celebration of the October Revolution's fortieth anniversary and the Conference of World Communist and Workers' Parties, which followed the anniversary celebration. Representatives from sixty-four Communist parties worldwide attended the conference, among which twelve were ruling parties, making this event the largest gathering of world Communists since the birth of Marxism. The conference was meant to be an occasion for Communist parties to discuss problems openly and attempt to reach a renewed consensus within the Socialist Bloc.[30] None of the tensions and difficulties, however, could be seen in the film. The film represents the Conference of World Communist and Workers' Parties not as a forum of substantive discussion but as a spectacle of consensus, filled with prolonged rounds of clapping and ending with a long sequence of delegates signing the joint declaration. The solemn act of signing it, when repeated twelve times on camera by twelve representatives from various socialist states, commands a particular power of collective strength, even though, in fact, historians have since deemed the Moscow Declaration of 1957 a document without binding power and plagued by ambiguities.[31] In addition, differences, whether national or cultural, were minimized in the film. The delegates wear socialist attire, devoid of national and cultural markers. The film contains no display of linguistic diversity or barriers to communication: all acts of translation are erased. Singing and dancing are heavily featured to evade linguistic heterogeneity. At the end of the film, a grand party is held. A Chinese singer in military uniform sings a Russian song in Chinese with accompaniment by the Moscow Symphony Orchestra and Chorus. As the song continues in the soundtrack, images of Red Square in Moscow and the Gate of Heavenly Peace in China, both lit up by fireworks, appear and are intercut, cinematically merging the two national symbols into one connected space.

These images of stability and unity were considered desirable, as there was a perceived need in the Cold War environment for the Socialist Bloc to appear unified and strong, lest manifested vulnerabilities might offer enemies opportunities to attack. In chapter 3 I discussed war propaganda documentaries and the logic of presenting "winning realities." This logic remained pertinent in the eyes of the CCP leadership. Mao had deemed Khrushchev's denunciation of Stalin as a highly "imprudent act" that weakened the unity of the Socialist Bloc and invited sabotage from the enemies in the West.[32] The CCP's public response to Khrushchev's de-Stalinization efforts, published in the *People's Daily*, aimed not at reflecting on Stalin's errors but at defending the socialist enterprise against its enemies.[33] Another *People's Daily* editorial, published in December 1956, berated protests in Poland and Hungary as resulting from successful imperialist infiltration that aimed to "hinder the unity of the international Communists."[34]

While there were good reasons to emphasize certainty, stability, and unity at the time, the erasure of uncertainty, instability, and difference had huge costs as well. As *Congratulations* was being made, the Great Leap Forward began in the earnest. I discussed documentaries during the Great Leap in depth in chapter 4, but it is important to note here that the unison of Great Leap films—their unanimous acceleration of labor time, propagation of untested technology, and erasures of labor discontent and critique of the production campaign—would not have materialized if the Anti-Rightist Campaign hadn't curtailed documentary's critical and explorative function. Indeed, as the unfolding of China's revolutionary project brought the society into increasingly uncertain waters from the mid-1950s onward, Chinese documentary, as well as the Chinese Communist project, stumbled over the crucial question of how to mediate political relationality and knowledge formation amid such epistemic uncertainties and persisting Cold War threats.

"Wife Diplomacy" as Experiment

A great deal had happened between *Congratulations* and *Chairman Liu Visits Indonesia*, with which I began this chapter. Relations between China and the Soviet Union deteriorated soon after Mao Zedong's visit to Moscow in 1957. In 1960 the Soviets unilaterally withdrew all Soviet experts working in China. Meanwhile, the Great Leap Forward, launched in 1957, was overall a devastating failure. The famine that followed after the Great Leap Forward cost millions of lives. Heated and bitter contestations among the CCP top leadership broke out about what went wrong. Top officials such as Mao, Zhou Enlai, and Liu Shaoqi made self-criticisms at the seven-thousand-person meeting in January 1962 for the mistakes made during the Great Leap Forward. Mao ended his tenure as the head of the state and passed the position to Liu Shaoqi. The early 1960s saw a period of experimentation and reorientation. Liu Shaoqi and Deng Xiaoping took charge of the country's economy in 1961. Institutions deemed unworkable were abolished, such as communal dining halls. Economic policies respecting locally specific conditions helped restore agricultural productivity.[35]

The practice of combining documentary and fiction during the Great Leap Forward, which I discussed in chapter 4, also came to an end. In March 1959 and May 1960 the CCP's Central Propaganda Bureau organized two meetings to discuss documentary production, and on June 1, 1961, the June First Directive was issued to emphasize documentary's difference from fiction, a corrective to the practice of artistic documentary during the Great Leap Forward. "Newsreel and documentary must strictly follow the principle of entirely truthful, entirely real people and real events," stated the directive. "This is the most basic characteristic that differentiates newsreels from feature films. Newsreels and documentary films will lose value entirely if they do not follow this principle."[36] This new emphasis on documentary's grounding in real life encouraged filmmakers to follow the events, people, and environment they found before their cameras, rather than to lead them.

Meanwhile, the early 1960s saw changes in China's international position. The break with the Soviet Union made it necessary for China to strengthen its United Front with its Asian neighbors, in order to counter U.S. anti-Communist activities in Asia and compete with Moscow for political influence in the developing world. It was in this new circumstance that the practice of "wife diplomacy" became institutionalized. On December 20, 1960, Foreign Minister Chen Yi convened a meeting for the wives of state officials to encourage them to engage in diplomatic work. At the meeting, a wives' working group was founded, with Chen Yi's wife, Zhang Qian, serving as its leader. A year later, in December 1961, a meeting on "wife diplomacy" work was again convened at the Ministry of Foreign Affairs. Deng Yingchao, a revolutionary in her own right who was married to Zhou Enlai, spoke about her discomfort at being addressed as a "wife," yet "due to changes in the international environment," she argued, "it became necessary to use this identity in international work."[37] Such work, as described by Deng Yingchao, included communicating with top government officials; exchanging gifts on personal occasions, including marriages of state leaders' children; organizing tea parties and other gatherings at diplomat residences; and the like.

Women's role in diplomacy has been long noted. Feminist scholar Cynthia Enloe shows that state governments had traditionally relied on women as "symbols, consumers, workers, and emotional comforters" to build masculinized interstate diplomatic relationships. Since statesmen and diplomats—traditionally men—need to cultivate trust and confidence between them, women, with their traditional roles as homemakers, supposedly could create a congenial space for men to know one another "man to man."[38] In the PRC, Communist women such as Deng Yingchao were very much aware of the problems of "wife diplomacy," yet this practice had always been an aspect of PRC diplomacy, even though it wasn't officially institutionalized until 1960. In a training session on diplomatic work held in Beijing in 1950, the Soviet experts who led the training suggested that the wives of diplomats not take on any other administrative work but offer full-time help to their husbands' work. This suggestion was rejected by the majority of Chinese women cadres, in whose opinion the role of a full-time "wife" not only negated the principles of women's liberation but carried with it a strong "bourgeois" connotation. A collective protest by the female cadres ensued and was pacified only after Zhou Enlai's and Deng Yingchao's intervention. Deng in particular argued that as women exert powerful influences on their husbands, befriending wives of other countries' diplomats could help ease interstate relationships, and therefore "wife diplomacy" offered an effective unofficial avenue for diplomatic work.[39]

After the Geneva Conference of 1954 and the Bandung Conference of 1955, the PRC strengthened its relationships with nonsocialist nation-states in the "intermediary zone," and women served important roles in forming and maintaining these relationships. When discussing Zhou Enlai's film screenings at the Geneva Conference in 1954 earlier in this chapter, I commented on the "feminine aesthetics" of the Yue opera film *The Butterfly Lovers*, which helped affectively communicate China's position of "peaceful coexistence." Emily Wilcox's research on dance diplomacy shows that PRC's dance exchanges with other Asian countries in the 1950s and early 1960s "emphasized equality and exchange, employing a structure of interaction that foregrounded mutual learning over self-presentation," thus performing the Bandung spirit of mutual respect and equality among newly independent nation-states.[40] It's worth noting that the Yue opera had an all-female cast, in dance diplomacy women dancers were in the majority, and "wife diplomacy" also flourished in this period. "Diplomatic wives" were told to "treat the 'apolitical' and 'vulgar' interests of the majority of foreign wives in [bourgeois] culture, fiction and attire with patience" and "respect the cultures and customs of the place where you are."[41] Given the permission to be more tolerant and flexible, women became the affective media that bridged differences and brought ideologically heterogeneous nation-states together.

Apparently conservative, and rejected by women cadres numerous times in early and late 1950s, "wife diplomacy" demonstrated the party's patriarchal tendencies as well as women's real contributions to international relations as mediators that mended ideological rifts and class differences.[42] Indeed, one could observe a gendered division of labor in the diplomatic work of the time, with the men firmer, more distant, and adhering to revolutionary identities, and the women, while abiding by key political principles, nevertheless more flexible, less imposing, and more open to form personal relationships. This gendered division of labor in diplomacy put women in the risky business of building the United Front with short-term allies while denying them participation in situations where ideological differences either were negligible or must be openly reckoned with. In the 1950s "diplomatic wives" were almost never permitted to attend interparty meetings between the CCP and other Communist parties, for reasons of "confidentiality" (*baomi*). Only in the 1960s, as the ideological gulf between China and other Communist parties widened, did Zhang Qian, the aforementioned leader of the wives working group, endeavor to extend "wife diplomacy" to interparty relations, with the aim of expanding women's participation in diplomacy.[43]

Even though "wife diplomacy" had been practiced since the beginning of the PRC, it hadn't been represented in mass media until after its institutionalization in 1960. It granted Mao's wife Jiang Qing her first public visibility: it was during the visit of Sukarno's wife, Hartini, that the first photo of Mao and Jiang Qing since the founding of the PRC was released in 1962.[44] Wang Guangmei's visit to Indonesia was the first time that the wife of a PRC head of state accompanied her husband on an overseas visit. The visit, captured on camera and made into a documentary, represented the work of "wife diplomacy" in great detail. Different from Mao's austere interparty visit to Moscow, Wang and Liu's visit to Indonesia was a sensual exploration of the country's beautiful sceneries, of personal encounters and interpersonal relationships, and the limelight was on the woman rather than the man.

The Cinematic Form of "Wife Diplomacy"

Chairman Liu Visits Indonesia follows a chronological structure similar to that of *Congratulations*. The film begins with the arrival of Liu, Wang, and the Chinese delegation at the Jakarta airport, where state ceremonies are conducted. The camera then follows the Chinese delegation's daily public activities in Indonesia. Similar to *Congratulations*, the film ends with the signing of a declaration to successfully conclude the visit. Yet despite the structural similarity, *Chairman Liu Visits Indonesia* was filmed very differently from *Congratulations*. In contrast to the static and predictable camerawork in the latter, the camera in this film is curious and sensual, particularly attentive to eye contact, mutual acknowledgment, and collective play. Wang Guangmei and the "wife diplomacy" that she practiced are not just the content of the film; they shape its form as well.

In *Congratulations*, Mao Zedong is greeted upon arrival by an orderly crowd at the airport. The camera's attention on these people is short and instrumental: it is interested only in capturing images of "representatives" of the people, devoting one shot to government officials, one shot to workers, and other shots to women, children, journalists, and so on. The arrival of Liu and Wang in Indonesia is filmed differently. A handheld camera stays with the Indonesian crowd waiting at the airport. People talk among themselves, make contact with their hands and bodies, poke fun at one another. The camera, shooting at the eye level, positions itself as part of the crowd and observes, with curiosity and patience, how people act informally and relationally with one another. Liu and

Wang's arrival prompts an alternation of point-of-view shots between Liu, Wang, and the Indonesians greeting them, as Liu and Wang descend the boarding stairs and become part of the crowd. These camera-mediated moments of sustained eye contact foreground the pleasure of intersubjective acknowledgment and exchange, which are rarely present in *Congratulations*.

Throughout the film, the attention to eye contact is sustained. The handheld camera often performs 180-degree pans to capture eye contact between Chinese guests and their Indonesian hosts. Around twenty-two minutes into the film, for example, the Chinese delegation is invited to the Bogor Palace, one of the six presidential palaces in Indonesia, to have afternoon tea with Sukarno's wife Hartini. At the palace, a group of Indonesian young women dressed in colorful traditional dress lines up to greet the Chinese guests. The handheld camera walks alongside the Chinese delegation and simulates the point of view of the delegation by panning over the girls' faces one after another. At the end of the queue, a young woman wearing flowers in her hair and holding a plate of flowers catches the attention of the camera. It slows down to have prolonged eye contact with her and then, within the same shot, makes a 180-degree turn, assuming the young woman's point of view. Then we see Wang Guangmei, looking in the direction of the girl and making direct eye contact with the camera, smiling.

Besides eye contact, the camera evokes other senses, such as smell, touch, taste, and sound, to offer a full-bodied experience of Indonesia's natural and cultural landscapes. In the botanical garden, the camera records, in a single long take, Liu Shaoqi, Wang Guangmei, and Chen Yi taking turns to lean over and breathe in the fragrance of a new species of iris. At Bogor Palace, it captures Liu Shaoqi's curious examination of a tray of alluring tropical fruits, and Wang Guangmei's tactile study of Indonesian traditional block printing on fabric. Lounging around, Liu Shaoqi, Sukarno, and Chen Yi enjoy cigars together, and in a concert featuring Indonesian performance art and music, each Chinese guest is given an *angklung*, a traditional Indonesian musical instrument made of bamboo, and is taught to play a song collectively. Liu Shaoqi, Chen Yi, and other state leaders are depicted in an endearing moment of learning and play.

Documenting "wife diplomacy" in action, the film is centered on the women rather than the men. Wang Guangmei is the absolute star in the film. Her gigantic photo portrait graces main streets in Jakarta, together with portraits of Liu Shaoqi and Sukarno. To commemorate her visit, at Sukarno's suggestion a new species of iris is named after her. The "wife" wasn't just tagging along in a diplomatic encounter: her presence changed the mode of interaction and made it intensely personal and occasionally transgressive. Acting as the affective mediator, Wang is often seen sitting between Sukarno and her husband, charmingly conversing with both men. At one point, when having their photos taken together, Sukarno indicates that his wife, Hartini, should change positions with

Wang, such that Wang stands next to Sukarno, while Hartini takes the arm of Liu Shaoqi. This mixed pairing, Sukarno with Wang, and Liu Shaoqi with Hartini, appears multiple times in the film thereafter. Meanwhile, with the tolerance and openness associated with "wife diplomacy," the camera seems to have forgotten its usual task of political messaging. The film devotes only two cursory shots to the site of the Asian-African Conference in Bandung, where Zhou Enlai had elaborated on his principle of peaceful coexistence in 1955. Only one shot is given to another important symbol of Third World politics, the Sukarno Sports Stadium, which in 1963 would host the first Games of the New Emerging Forces as a Third World alternative to the Olympic Games.[45] In contrast, the camera devotes considerable space to religious relics and folk rituals. The 1,200-year-old Buddhist ruin of Borobudur appears extensively, as do folk religious rituals and masked shamanic dances. The camera also doesn't spare effort in exploring the Bogor Palace, despite its past as the residence of the Dutch governors-general, admiring its graceful statues, lotus pond, botanical garden, and greenhouse full of blooming tropical flowers, and showing the Chinese delegation relaxing in its gilded rooms, bantering with Sukarno. All these scenes would have repercussions a few years later.

An Inculpatory Rerun

The internal struggles in the party had never been so frivolous.

—Liu Shaoqi, 1967

Four years after its initial release, *Chairman Liu Visits Indonesia* reentered circulation in 1967. This time, the film was labeled as a "poisonous weed" and renamed *Criminal Liu Visits Indonesia* (*Liuzei fangwen yindunixiya*). The film was reedited, and a denunciatory voice-over was added to its soundtrack. A large number of copies were made and sent around the country, to be used at mass rallies to denounce Liu Shaoqi. An outpouring of articles appeared in newspapers, condemning Liu Shaoqi and Wang Guangmei for their capitalist ways.

This reversal had to do with complex events that had happened in China and Indonesia in the interim years. In October 1965 junior army officers associated with the Indonesian Communist Party (PKI) staged a coup aimed at liquidating the pro-Western Indonesian Army high command. The coup failed, and the counteractions from the right-wing military commanders led to the bloody suppression of the PKI, the overthrow of the left-leaning Sukarno government, the breakdown of diplomatic relations with China, and the restoration of Indonesia's close ties with the same Western powers that Sukarno had wished to move away from by building the nonalignment movement. This crisis in the Sino-Indonesian relationship resulted in both countries recalling ambassadors, anti-Chinese riots in Indonesia, and the exodus en masse of Indonesian Chinese back to China.[46] Meanwhile, in China, the Cultural Revolution began in 1966. Liu Shaoqi was denounced as the party's No. 1 "Capitalist Roader" in 1967, and by 1969 he had been expelled from the Chinese Communist Party, stripped of all party positions, and left to die in Kaifeng.[47]

The purge of Liu Shaoqi was the largest and most important of the Cultural Revolution, leading to the persecution of tens of thousands of Liu's supposed "followers." Cinema was deeply implicated in this purge. The first direct attack on Liu came in the form of film criticism. Qi Benyu's article "Patriotism or National Betrayal: On the Reactionary Film *Inside Story of the Qing Court*" was broadcast on the Central People's Radio Broadcasting Station on the night of March 31, 1967, and published in the *People's Daily* the following day. Retrospectively considered the death knell for Liu, the article began with a criticism of *Inside Story of the Qing Court*, a Hong Kong production that had been shown in China's major urban centers in 1950, nearly two decades earlier. The article pointed out that at the time of its release, Mao Zedong had instantly recognized the film's counterrevolutionary and traitorous nature and wished to launch a campaign to criticize the film. However, Mao's wish had been thwarted by the counterrevolutionary forces in the party led by Liu Shaoqi, who claimed that the film was patriotic. Liu's favoring of the film sufficiently revealed his traitorous nature, argued Qi. After accusing Liu of being a "spokesman for imperialism, feudalism, and the reactionary bourgeoisie" and an "imperialist comprador," the article concluded: "You are a fake revolutionary, an opponent to revolution. You are simply a Khrushchev sleeping right next to us."[48]

Liu Shaoqi's reaction to Qi's accusation was one of anger and bewilderment. "The internal struggles in the party had never been so frivolous" was his comment to his family after reading Qi's article.[49] This "frivolous" struggle, however, quickly escalated. Soon afterward, the plan to utilize *Chairman Liu Visits Indonesia* to denounce Liu Shaoqi was formed. The idea was suggested by staff at the Central Newsreel and Documentary Film Studio in a meeting with Jiang Qing in the spring of 1967. Jiang Qing agreed to the staff's proposal to re-edit the documentary on Liu's visit to Indonesia. At the same meeting, Jiang Qing also directed the staff to remove images of Liu Shaoqi from *Chairman Mao Inspects Red Guards* and to screen the airbrushed version together with the renamed *Criminal Liu Visits Indonesia* for the purpose of contrast.[50]

The inculpatory version of the film can no longer be recovered, yet one can gather what the version might have been like from the many articles published to condemn the film and the couple. Calling it "a colossal exposure," "a criminal record," or "a self-confession" of the couple's deeply hidden capitalist ways and capitulationism, these articles used scenes in the film as solid evidence of Liu's crimes.[51] I quote some at length here to show the extent of the "close-reading" applied to the film.

Yao Dengshan and Zhao Xiaoshou, cadres at the Foreign Ministry, wrote:

> When visiting Indonesia, [Liu] never mentioned Chairman Mao or Chairman Mao Thought. Everywhere he distinguished himself and broadened his own influence. Seeing enormous portraits of himself and Wang XX hanging everywhere, hearing people shouting "Long Live Chairman Liu," he happily accepted all and was proud of himself ... as if he had been the supreme leader of China.
>
> [Liu] never mentioned in his visit the struggles against American imperialism, against revisionism, ... he never said one word about establishing and broadening an international United Front against America.... From the documentary, it was clear that [Liu] never thought much of the anti-imperial, anti-feudal struggles of the Indonesian people. On the contrary, he praised the Indonesian capitalist elite [Sukarno] to the skies, branding him a "national hero of Indonesia," "great fighter against colonialism in the world." ... He also spread antirevolutionary ideas similar to Khrushchev's "peaceful coexistence" and "peaceful transition." ... These revisionist poisons he spread in Indonesia were like anesthesia, which made people less alert and greatly helped the militants on the right.
>
> The documentary film showed the intimate relations between [Liu] and the reactionaries in Indonesia.... The film showed him cheerfully shaking hands with [Abul Haris] Nasution, the murderer whose hands were soaked in the blood of Indonesian people. How close they were! His wife did not stay behind either. She grabbed the feudal lord of Yogyakarta and the head of the secret police to pose for a photo together, saying, "We feel safe as long as the two of you are here!"
>
> From the documentary, one can see how enchanted Liu was by the decadent and rotten capitalist life. He and Wang spent the whole day hanging out like ghosts with Indonesian capitalists, drunken with luxuries and wine, giving in to all kinds of ugly and clownish behaviors. In order to please the Indonesian capitalists, Wang dressed like a devil, with a necklace hanging on her neck, selling all her charms. She even asked to be shown around the licentious palace bedroom of the No. 1 Indonesian capitalist [Sukarno], and [Liu] walked in as well. Finding no shame in all this, Liu even boasted that he had lived nine days like a "president" in Indonesia. "We never had such a fanfare when we got married," he said, "this was like a make-up wedding." Such a person smells not like a Communist, but a capitalist rotten to the core, and a Khrushchevesque clown![52]

Ge Zhongbo, reportedly a worker at the Beijing Stamp Factory, wrote:

> The reactionary film *Visit Indonesia* completely exposed what [Liu] loved and hated. Please look, . . . [Liu] loved whatever the antirevolutionary capitalists loved. At the handicraft exhibition in Yogyakarta, he was so impressed with the gold and silver jewelry the Indonesian antirevolutionaries robbed off the people that he didn't even want to leave. He indulged in the rotten capitalist lifestyle, flirting with the capitalists and their wives and daughters all day long. . . . In the nine days in Indonesia, the Chinese Khrushchev clearly expressed his love and hatred with his words and behavior. He loves capitalism and the capitalist lifestyle, and hates socialism and the revolutionary struggles of people all over the world.[53]

Another writer, Chen Mou, wrote:

> When visiting the Tangkuban Perahu volcano, [Sukarno] deliberately took off Liu's straw hat and put it on his own head, saying, "When Khrushchev came here, he also wore this kind of hat." Criminal Liu not only happily agreed but also took off [Sukarno]'s little black hat and put it on his own head. [Sukarno] pointed at Liu and said with gusto, "You have become a Muslim." Upon hearing this, Liu was all smiles.
>
> At a welcome party, Liu Shaoqi and his wife, Wang XX, attending as "president" and "president's wife," took up Indonesia's musical instrument the *anklung* and gleefully played anti-Communist, anti-China, and antipeople noise with the antirevolutionary capitalists. Every Chinese feels anger and hatred upon seeing these images.[54]

From these commentaries, one can get a sense of what the denunciative version of the film was like. The original film does not include scenes of Wang and Liu visiting the bedroom of Sukarno, Wang having photos taken with the head of the secret police, or Liu and Sukarno bantering with each other about their hats. These moments were possibly additional footage inserted into the film. Jiang Qing, at the aforementioned meeting with Xinying filmmakers in 1967, had asked if the rest of the footage from Liu and Wang's visit to Indonesia had been destroyed. "No, we still have some left" was the answer she received. It was likely that additional footage was edited into the film.[55] We also know that a new voice-over was added to the film's soundtrack, which might have added anachronistic and retrospective contexts for the film, identifying some of the Indonesian state officials by name and informing the audience of their subsequent roles in suppressing the PKI in 1965. The comparison between Liu Shaoqi and Khrushchev can be found in almost all the articles. Both were denounced for their compromises with America and with the capitalist world order, and Liu had by then been condemned as "China's Khrushchev." Many commentaries discuss specific scenes in a Soviet documentary film, *N. S. Khrushchev in the U.S.A.*, made in 1959 on the occasion of Khrushchev's visit to the United States. It was conceivable that at some denunciation rallies, the Soviet film may have been shown together with *Criminal Liu Visits Indonesia*, to present evidence of commonality between Khrushchev and Liu.

It's also important to note, however, that many other media—photography, cartoons, pamphlets and big-character posters—were involved in multiplying the inculpatory images and narratives associated with Liu and Wang's Indonesia visit. Tani Barlow has offered an excellent treatment of the campaign to condemn Liu and Wang in Red Guard publications in 1967, which included a great deal of inculpatory narratives and caricatures of the couple's Indonesian trip.[56] *Film Criticism* (*Dianying pipan*), a Red Guard publication based in the city of Tianjin, released an entire issue devoted to "completely smashing to pieces the reactionary documentaries *Liu Shaoqi Visits Indonesia* and *N. S. Khrushchev in the U.S.A.*" This issue included an assortment of film stills from the latter. Khrushchev was seen in the photos to be lusting over food and American Hollywood actresses, while his wife was holding arms with Dwight Eisenhower.[57] In other words, if in the Great Leap Forward many media forms, including cinema, created a media ecology of optimism, then the same happened during the Cultural Revolution. The documentary film on Liu and Wang's visit to Indonesia spurred endless media (re)productions of images and narratives, contributing to a media ecology of class struggle that characterized the onset of the Cultural Revolution.

The Forensics of Class and a Frivolous Politics

Even though denunciative images and narratives of Liu and Wang's Indonesia trip proliferated in many popular media forms, the documentary film was singularly referred to as the originary evidential document for the couple's crimes. The idea that the film camera could capture and magnify one's unconscious behavior and allow detection of their crimes wasn't new. As apparatuses of record-keeping and revelation, photography and cinema have been used by modern legal institutions to establish guilt and innocence since their earliest days. For Walter Benjamin, the invention of photography was "no less significant for criminology than the inventing of the printing press is for literature."[58] Photography and cinema participate in criminological investigations by supplying evidence—capturing a crime scene, for example—or as a means to identify and track a criminal. Aided by these new technologies, the "modern detective," writes Tom Gunning, relies on the "observation of trifles," discerning signs of criminality by "focusing on marks that the criminal might not be aware of or would find difficult or impossible to conceal," and by "capturing the criminal in an act of unconscious revelation."[59] Indeed, early filmmakers such as Dziga Vertov reveled in cinema's ability to catch people "unawares," which he believed would get to the real truth, hence the slogan *kinopravda* (film truth).[60] The Hungarian film theorist Béla Balázs, writing in the 1920s, praised the cinematic close-up of facial expressions as "lyrical" and "polyphonic," capable of revealing a person's innermost "soul."[61]

The use of photography and cinema in criminology, as Gunning points out, must be coupled with a system of classification that can translate image into information.[62] It was the transformation of ideas of class and class analysis in PRC's early decades that supported the assertion that Liu Shaoqi and Wang Guangmei's behaviors abroad, when recorded, could help reveal their capitalist nature.

Earlier in the chapter I quoted from Mao Zedong's article in 1925 that used class analysis to tell enemies apart from friends in the revolutionary process. Prior to 1949, the CCP relied on class analysis to achieve its victories. In the immediate years after 1949, to facilitate socialist policies, the party implemented a complex system of class designations that classified the majority of the Chinese population into more than sixty classes by 1952.[63] This classification system was difficult to apply, as people's social and economic backgrounds were often too complex to be encapsulated by one class designation. Neither was it expected to persist for long, as rapid transformation into a socialist economy would remove the economic foundations for class divisions, change power structures in the society, and make these classifications increasingly irrelevant. Indeed, as Yiching Wu reports, by 1956 the CCP leadership had reasons to believe that the class situation in China had changed sufficiently to render the class system obsolete. In a speech in 1956, Deng Xiaoping admitted that the classification of classes "has lost or is losing its original significance." Mao Zedong, too, acknowledged that "class contradictions within our country have already been *basically* resolved," and that new political analysis was needed for new circumstances under socialism.[64]

Political instability within the Socialist Bloc and ongoing Cold War hostilities, which I discussed in relation to Mao Zedong's Moscow visit, might be among the reasons why the CCP felt the need to keep the system of class identification, and the emphasis on class struggle, in place despite the society's economic foundations had been radically changed. In "On the Correct Handling of Contradictions Among the People," a speech delivered in February 1957 during the Hundred Flowers Campaign but edited and published after the Anti-Rightist Campaign had begun in June 1957, Mao argued that class struggle would persist during socialist construction. "Class struggle is by no means over," he declared. "The class struggle between the proletariat and the bourgeoisie, the class struggle between the various political forces, and the class struggle between the proletariat and the bourgeoisie in the ideological field will still be protracted and tortuous and at times even very sharp. The proletariat seeks to transform the world according to its own world outlook, and so does the bourgeoisie. In this respect, the question of which will win out, socialism or capitalism, is not really settled yet."[65] This new conception of socialist class struggle, Rebecca Karl observes, was no longer based on economic relations but on ideology, "where class was more a question of revolutionary consciousness and activism than a socioeconomic category."[66]

In the wake of the Great Leap Famine, party leadership further resorted to class analysis to reckon with what had gone wrong. The failure of the Great Leap Forward had many factors. In chapter 4 I discussed the contribution of media politics and practice to the failed production campaign. Among the CCP's top leaders, including Mao and Liu, a shared assessment was that class enemies had penetrated the party bureaucracy, though the two had different takes on which levels of bureaucracy were affected: Liu blamed hidden enemies and cadres at the village level for sabotage and corruption, while Mao increasingly thought that the entire bureaucratic system might have been infested with revisionism, which had already sent the Soviet Union on a path of no return. In the early 1960s, alongside more accommodating economic policies and "wife diplomacy," there was an increasing emphasis on class struggle, highlighted by Mao Zedong's call to "never forget class struggle" in September 1962 and the subsequent Socialist Education Movement aimed at identifying class enemies and cleaning bad elements out of the bureaucracy.

If in 1957, in the mainly urban Hundred Flowers and Anti-Rightist Campaigns, Mao spoke about class in relation to ideology, with the Socialist Education Movement targeting a much broader society, including rural China, class status became further linked to one's manifested behavior and attitude toward the regime. Work teams sent by Beijing, pioneered by Liu Shaoqi and Wang Guangmei, moved into villages to investigate the true class status of local cadres, activists, and commune members according to their behaviors, resulting in what Patricia Thornton describes as a "massive reshuffling" in local societies, with many condemned as "class enemies" for minor behavioral deviations. A gulf widened between "actual lived experience of rural residents and the officially sanctioned discourse on the meaning of class struggle," Thornton observes. "Once untethered from its basis in objective material conditions, preserving or improving one's revolutionary class status over time required regular, even daily, public demonstration or expression of support for the party line."[67]

The adherence to and intensification of the old discourse of "class struggle" in the early 1960s not only created struggle where there was none but also obscured the changing nature of contradictions in the society. It created cognitive fallacies that readily identified new emergent contradictions in social life as life-and-death struggles against hidden class enemies who not only infiltrated the country but were also linked up with enemies from outside the country. These scenarios of class struggle were so removed from lived realities that representing them became a problem for documentary. It was easier to stage such struggles in fiction films, such as *Never Forget* (*Qianwan buneng wangji*, 1964), which told the fictional story of an urban worker falling under consumerist influence from his mother-in-law, who as a previous shop owner had been a member of the exploitative class. As drama such as these was not readily available for the documentary lens, documentary filmmaking during the Socialist Education Movement relied increasingly on class education exhibitions. It was through remediating and animating these exhibitions with moving image and sound effects that documentary created the archetypes of class struggle not found in real life.

Organized around the country, class education exhibitions mobilized the masses to collect artifacts of class exploitation from pre-1949 times and organized lessons and activities around their exhibition.[68] While each exhibition, organized by local governments, used highly site-specific narratives and relied on local collections and excavations, documentary films allowed specific class education exhibitions to circulate nationwide on film. *Forget Not Class Bitterness, and Remember a Blood Ocean of Grievances* (*Buwang jieji ku, yongji xuehai chou*, 1965), for example, documented a class education exhibition in the Shandong Province. *Rent-Collection Courtyard* (*Shouzu yuan*, 1966) documented a class education exhibition in Sichuan that turned the home of the landlord Liu Wencai into a museum of the horrors of the old society. Both films offered lessons of class exploitation through objects: luxury goods that showcased the decadence of the exploitative classes, weapons and military objects that the landlords used to suppress peasant revolt, and account books and documents of economic exploitation. *Forget Not Class Bitterness* also documented storytelling by former victims, and *Rent-Collection Courtyard* featured the famous 114 life-sized sculptures that depicted the landlord's cruelty and the peasants' misery and revolt.[69] The downcast eyes, firm facial expressions, clutched fists, and emancipated bodies wrapped in ragged clothing—sculpted in clay and magnified and animated by close-ups and camera movements—provided the template of what the revolutionary class looked like. With relaxed and well-fed bodies and clad in silk, the class enemies possessed jewelry and other valuables, their decadent lives portrayed in sculptures, paintings, and caricatures on display in the exhibitions too.

In his study of evolving cinematic realisms in Chinese cinema, Jason McGrath observes that the aesthetics of cinema shifted to "an even more formalized state" during the Cultural Revolution. This shift, which culminated in the "theatrical stasis" of model opera films in the late 1960s and early 1970s, brought "an unmooring of form from reality." Pushing the melodramatic mode to its limits, the stylized model opera performances created polarized stereotypes and transcendental truths almost entirely removed from lived experiences. Such a stereotypical representation not only "threatens to become a mere surface itself, a superficial appearance that in fact reveals nothing."[70] It also brings the revolution to a "standstill" by corroding revolution's dialectical and immanent qualities. McGrath's insights resonate with what I discuss here. While McGrath associates this extreme formalist shift primarily with the model opera films made in the later years of the Cultural Revolution, I add that similar formalist tendencies had happened in documentary earlier, in the years leading to the Cultural Revolution, when documentary remediated exhibitions, paintings, and sculptures to support the political doctrine of the persistence of old class enemies when the actual contradictions in the society had in fact changed nature. In this capacity, documentary provided templates for politically correct language and behavior and circulated these superficial markers of class designations widely, thereby strengthening the behavioralist approach to class: it became beneficial to follow these behavioral templates for political survival.

After returning from their trips to Southeast Asia in 1963, Liu Shaoqi and Wang Guangmei spearheaded the Socialist Education Movement. Wang in particular headed investigative work teams to rural China in November 1963 and to the Tsinghua University in 1966. Tani Barlow, in her extensive treatment of the denunciation campaign against Wang Guangmei, has offered a detailed account of Wang's activities at Tsinghua, especially her heavy-handed punishments of student radicals, which created substantial grievances. While the contradiction here was between elite cadres such as Wang, who enacted party normativity, and radical students, who wished to break these rules, what in the end became staged in the denunciation campaign, was a reenactment of the Indonesian trip with Wang in her summer *qipao*, sun hat, and the chain of Ping-Pong balls parodying the pearl necklace. Barlow points out that this strategy, developed by a student radical named Kuai Dafu together with Jiang Qing, was meant to put Wang's "feminine performance on trial; it raised questions about the appropriate performance of Chinese womanhood on a global stage."[71]

By then "wife diplomacy" had ended. An ambiguous practice at best, "wife diplomacy" asked Communist women to perform the "diplomatic wife." Their job was inherently transgressive, meant to tread uncertain political waters and build affective and personal relationships between states with different political systems and differently positioned in the force field of the Cold War. As discussed earlier in the chapter, this practice was clearly patriarchal, yet it did draw real contributions from women who participated, and its accommodation of allies with political difference did follow the Bandung spirit of mutual respect and peaceful coexistence. Yet Cold War instability and domestic strife resulted in a general perception among the CCP leadership that domestic and international enemies were multiplying. The CCP's class analysis, failing to adjust to the revolutionary changes that had taken place in the country, became ever more forensic. As class markers became increasingly superficial and arbitrary, everyone's revolutionary identity was in doubt, which fueled more stringent disciplining and fiercer display of revolutionary credentials. The traditional dress of the *qipao*, having been worn by Communist women through the 1950s, now became a class marker. Women, who put their revolutionary identity at risk by answering the call for "wife diplomacy," now served as scapegoats to superficially restore epistemological certainty when political knowledge was in deep crisis.

Media was of great importance in political struggles. Access to and control of media must be fought for: even Mao Zedong did not have as much media access as he wanted. One of Qi Benyu's accusations against Liu Shaoqi was that Liu, and the intellectuals under him, controlled the media and obstructed Mao's attempt to launch a campaign against a reactionary film.[72] Meanwhile, exclusion from and exposure to media were among the immediate punishments awaiting a fallen leader. The first thing that Liu's staff noticed after his fall from power was that his access to party media had been blocked: he no longer was included in any internal circulation of CCP documents.[73] Positive images of Liu no longer appeared in public. According to the instructions that Jiang Qing gave to Xinying in 1967, Liu's image was to be airbrushed out of *Chairman Mao Inspects Red Guards*, the newsreels documenting Mao's inspections of the Red Guards in the summer and autumn of 1966 before the next printing of the newsreels.[74] While positive images of Liu were excluded from media, negative images of Liu and his wife appeared in big-character posters, cartoons, and denunciative reruns of films. Photographic and cinematic documentation were part of the humiliation that the couple underwent. Wang Guangmei's interrogators forced her into the silk *qipao* that she had worn in Indonesia and hung a necklace of Ping-Pong balls around her neck, upon which "she was photographed."[75] Xinying also recorded Liu's and Wang's respective struggle sessions in Beijing.

Chairman Liu Visits Indonesia, widely seen in 1963 and now in rerun, played a crucial role in energizing the mass indignation toward Liu and Wang as class enemies, and Wang as a failed Communist woman. Cinematic replay typically offers viewers the pleasurable experience of recall, and here it brought in the thrill of detective work, as viewers were guided by the voice-over to examine the minute details in the film forensically for traces of behavioral deviancy caught unawares by the cinematic medium. As the Socialist Education Campaign had already trained the viewing public in the high-stakes activity of performing and detecting class belonging through attitude, behavior, and dress code, applying the same behavioral norms to Liu and Wang, at the top of the bureaucratic hierarchy, gave the added pleasure of iconoclasm.

In 1967 denunciation rallies and meetings condemning Liu and Wang swiftly spread across China. Gathering footage from a large number of mass rallies condemning Liu, documentary films such as *Lift the Flag of Political Criticism and Bravely March Forward* (*Gaoju geming pipan de qizhi fenyong qianjin*, 1967) offered "how-to" guides on staging an anti-Liu rally. Decorated with self-made revolutionary icons and placards and animated by singing and dancing performances and a chorus of slogans, each rally was a showcase of creative variations on the same set of symbols and rhetoric. In these rallies, a large number of local cadres were purged and denounced as Liu's associates. I will discuss the rehabilitation of Liu and his supposed associates in chapter 6.

Documentaries on China's international relations amounted to more than a third of the documentaries and newsreels made in China between 1949 and 1979.[76] These included films documenting mutual international visits by state officials, visits and performances of international artistic delegations in China and Chinese delegations abroad, and films reporting on world affairs and revolutionary struggles in allied countries. Besides screening widely in China for a domestic audience, they often served as official gifts to other national states and generated further diplomatic events when presented and screened overseas, as the screenings were often attended by top state officials, well-known artists, and Chinese ambassadors.[77] These films allowed Chinese viewers to experience sovereignty by watching their own leaders operating on the international stage as the equal of those of other countries. They took viewers on virtual journeys, satisfying the curiosity of the majority of viewers who had little chance to travel outside the country. Many also documented exhibitions and performances by Chinese and foreign artists. More important, they represented China's relationships with other forces in the world, from animosity to allyship.

This chapter's limited space doesn't do justice to this rich body of films and China's varied and changing relationships with different parts of the world. Instead, it attempts to reflect on a moment of crisis by thinking through documentary's participation in both international relations and domestic politics at the time. I've shown that in documentaries one finds both a cartographical desire to map friends and enemies and impart political knowledge, and a playful desire to explore the newness of the postrevolutionary society and disrupt existing categories. These two tendencies could have formed a dialectical process of learning that would contribute to a revolutionary epistemology grounded in experience. Yet as political stability became threatened by internal and external factors in the late 1950s, experiments in documentary were curtailed. As perceived enemies multiplied, documentary representations of interparty relationships relied on static and iconic images to create a sense of stability. In the wake of the Great Leap Famine, while women involved in "wife diplomacy" contributed an aesthetics of flexibility to China's relationship with allied friendly states such as Indonesia and to the form of diplomatic documentary, the resurgence of class struggle put a countervailing pressure on documentary, moving it away from exploration of what was emergent and eventful and marrying it to the exhibition of (obsolete) class archetypes. As class analysis became increasingly based on behavior and appearance, struggles became fierce, while politics became attenuated to "frivolous" forensics. Documentary entered a crisis, along with crises in political relationalities and revolutionary epistemology. The next chapter will examine documentary's engagement, in the post-Mao decade, with grassroots and party-led efforts to rehabilitate the wrongly accused and mend social divisions. It was through participating in political rehabilitation and experimenting with television as the exciting new media of the day that documentary rehabilitated itself as an eventful and empathetic medium, building communities and attuned to change.

CHAPTER 6

REHABILITATION

Documentary in the Post-Mao Decade

On September 9, 1976, Mao Zedong passed away. Less than a month later, members of the radical faction in the CCP leadership, including Mao's widow, Jiang Qing, were arrested. Over the next few years, a nationwide "cleansing" (*suqing*) campaign purged a large number of power-holders who had gained government positions during the Cultural Revolution. Subsequently, a massive "rehabilitation" (*pingfan*) process was launched to reverse the verdict for millions of people who had been labeled and persecuted as rightists and counterrevolutionaries. The Cultural Revolution ended, and the post-Mao era began.

This chapter examines new developments in documentary cinema and its participation in political changes during the post-Mao decade (1976–1988). I discuss, in the early post-Mao period, documentary's participation in the square (the Tiananmen mass protests of 1976), in the courtroom (the Gang of Four trials), and at the state funeral (Liu Shaoqi's rehabilitation and memorial service). These were among the central locations where mourning—here understood as open inquiries into, and reckonings with, the losses of the past—was organized. Combining amateur photography and audio recordings with moving images, the Xinying filmmakers repositioned documentary in the midst of the people to capture spontaneous political action. While the state tried to regulate mourning with the help of funerary rituals, documentaries subverted such stabilization and refused to put the past to rest. Used in the courtrooms, in biographical documentaries for rehabilitated leaders, and in documentaries reassessing historical events, archival footage destabilized existing master narratives, fueled historical imagination, and brought about a historiographic reorientation.

As the decade went on, documentary production began to move to television, the new medium of China's reform era. I discuss new forms of television documentary that emerged from an intensified exchange of moving images between Chinese and international television networks, particularly those that explored China's long trade routes and rich waterways as sites of historical and cultural sedimentation: *Silk Road* (*Sichou zhilu*, 1980), *Stories of the Yangtze* (*Huashuo changjiang*, 1983), *Stories of the Grand Canal* (*Huashuo yunhe*, 1986), and the landmark documentary *River Elegy* (*He shang*, 1988). These television documentaries, as I will show, were powerhouses for formal innovation. The "storytelling" format, experimented with great success in *Stories of the Yangtze*, moved poetically between deep geological time, dynastic histories, and contemporary times, excavating the Yangtze's rich depository of material and cultural remnants to fire historical imagination. The dialogical format of the storytelling gained further reflexivity and interactivity in *Stories of the Grand Canal*. As a historical water infrastructure connecting the state in Beijing to the southern provinces, the Grand Canal became a model for the new medium of television and its infrastructural roles to mediate between different sectors in the society, including the people and the state bureaucracy. The chapter ends with a discussion of the controversial landmark documentary series *River Elegy*. Using archival footage from historical documentaries (some discussed in earlier chapters), along with spectacular aerial and ground footage from the Yellow River and its surrounding areas, *River Elegy* brought the decade's mournful pathos and bold historiographical reorientation into culmination. I focus on the tension between its singular male voice-over expressive of a renewed vanguardism among intellectuals to create alternative master narratives of China's historical development and its open-ended montage that brought the unfinished business of mourning into view. Overall, I argue that documentary in the post-Mao decade "rehabilitated" itself as a more democratic, reflexive, interactive political medium befitting its longtime status of the "vanguard" of cinema, building much-needed connectivity in the society, while challenging the extent of rehabilitation sanctioned by the party state.

"A Second Liberation": The Work of Rehabilitation

Initiated in late 1977, rehabilitation became one of the most important political processes for Chinese society between 1978 and 1982. Deng Xiaoping was rehabilitated in July 1977. In late 1978 the Third Plenum passed the party decision to "reverse all unjust verdicts." Following that resolution, millions of people, dead or living, were rehabilitated. Victims and their families received various kinds of compensation, including return of confiscated property and unpaid salary, death benefits, and improvements in housing and job assignments. Many returned to work.

The CCP's rationale for the rehabilitation efforts was multifarious. The restoration of bureaucratic control and the reopening of universities required the return of competent cadres and intellectuals who had been removed from their positions during the Cultural Revolution. Rehabilitation would enable their return to work. More important, however, rehabilitation was necessary "emotional work" to "regain people's hearts," as a *People's Daily* editorial argued. The editorial was written under the supervision of Hu Yaobang, who chaired the Organization Department of the Central Committee of the CCP and was a passionate advocate for complete rehabilitation. It compared the Cultural Revolution with the Stalinist purges in the Soviet Union during the 1930s and suggested that the CCP learn an important lesson from Soviet history. When purging the party of antirevolutionary elements, Stalin "made many mistakes" and did not sufficiently correct them or adequately rehabilitate the wrongly accused cadres. This neglect led to a large number of party members and masses harboring anger and grievances against the party, making them susceptible to revisionist ideas in the future, the article argued. Therefore the CCP had to bravely correct all past wrongs, or the people's pent-up anger would make future governance difficult.[1]

Documentary was an integral part of the rehabilitation efforts. Every major rehabilitation led to filmmaking. These films were used to "give form to rehabilitation (*shi "pingfan" xingxianghua*) and were greatly popular," writes film historian Fang Fang.[2] In rehabilitation, documentary experimented with new film forms, new historiographic practices, and new attention to political spaces, actions, and record-keeping.

Cameras on the Square: The April 5 Movement

Released in 1979, the forty-six-minute *Raise Your Eyebrows and Draw Your Sword* (*Yangmei jian chujiao*, hereafter *Draw Your Sword*) is a film on the rehabilitation of the April 5 Movement and its participants. The movement refers to the spontaneous mass protests in Tiananmen Square between late March and early April 1976 to commemorate the death of Premier Zhou Enlai. With its title drawn from a poem by an anonymous poet that circulated in poster form in the square, the film was one of the most important documentaries of the late 1970s. It made unprecedented use of crowd-sourced amateur photography and on-location sound recordings and foregrounded the important roles played by photographers, filmmakers, and the synch-sound film technology in recognizing and communicating the will of the people.

Considered a caring leader and a sane and pragmatic voice in the top leadership, Zhou evoked an outpouring of grief in the country upon his passing on January 8, 1976. Mourning activities, however, were discouraged by the government under the control of the radical faction. Before Zhou's death, the radicals had attacked him for his alleged role in bringing the more liberal-minded Deng Xiaoping back to party leadership in 1975. After Zhou's death, they launched a new round of attacks on him and Deng, prohibited commemorative activities for Zhou, and ordered mass denunciations of Deng to be organized nationwide.[3] Articles remembering Zhou Enlai could not be published. A documentary film made on Zhou's funeral, which I will discuss later in the chapter, was banned and prevented from being released.

The radicals' attempt to restrain expressions of grief and prohibit displays of mourning backfired. People were led to spontaneous collective action, and a movement began to take shape. As April 5 is the traditional Qingming Festival for the remembrance of the dead, on March 23 a wreath of white paper flowers dedicated to the memory of Zhou Enlai appeared at the foot of the Monument to the People's Heroes in Tiananmen Square. The Beijing municipal government immediately removed the wreath, which prompted angry responses from the people. Over the following days, tens of thousands of people went to the square with handmade wreathes and posters of poetry and essays, which they placed at the foot of the monument, mourning Zhou and protesting against the radicals' suppression of the people's will. On April 4, the day before the Qingming Festival, about 100,000 people gathered in the square, and around the same number showed up the next day. Having already been clearing away wreaths and posters and making arrests, the Beijing municipal police finally organized a major assault. About ten thousand armed police and militia entered the square on the night of April 5, beating and arresting the demonstrators. Further arrests were made over the next days. In total, more than three hundred people were imprisoned, and the movement was labeled "counterrevolutionary."[4] *Draw Your Sword* reconstructed a day-by-day chronology of events in the square during the protests.

Tiananmen Square had seen many mass gatherings throughout the early decades of the PRC. At the beginning of the Cultural Revolution, Red Guards packed the square eight times to be inspected by Chairman Mao and his comrades. Each gathering and inspection generated newsreel films, whose swift circulation in the country drew more Red Guards to Beijing and to the square to be inspected. The April 5 movement, however, had no such blessings from a powerful top leader, nor was it sanctioned by the party. For this reason, the movement would not have been documented at all on film, if it were not because Chen Jinshu, a woman filmmaker at the Central Newsreel and Documentary Film Studio (Xinying), after having gone to the square and, inspired by the protest, rushed back to the studio and organized her colleagues to document the movement in secret. The filmmakers took a few cameras to the square and filmed on its fringes on and off for three or four days without reporting to the studio. Afterward they hid the film reels instead of sending them to be processed, as they waited for a better time to bring them to public attention.[5] After the movement was rehabilitated in November 1978, this footage came to light and contributed to the making of the film. The fact that the filmmakers had to shoot in secret and managed to do so only at the fringes of the square meant that other image sources were needed. It was amateur photographers who came to the filmmakers' assistance.

According to art historian Wu Hung, the Tiananmen Movement of 1976 was a turning point for Chinese photography.[6] Hundreds of amateur photographers took tens of thousands of photographs during the two-week-long protests in the square. Some photographers were arrested and imprisoned and their photographs confiscated. Others hid the negatives. In 1977 two of the photographers, Wang Zhiping and Li Xiaoping, began to build an underground network to collect and compile photos on the protests into a single volume. At the time, the "Gang of Four" had been arrested, but the April 5 Movement had not yet been rehabilitated. Wang and Li worked secretly and organized a seven-member editorial committee to select photographs. Hundreds of photographers sent in prints. The movement was rehabilitated in November 1978, and the volume of photographs, titled *People's Mourning* (*Renmin de huainian*), was published in January 1979. It contains more than five hundred photographs selected from between twenty thousand and thirty thousand different prints.[7] Working with Wang, Li, and other photographers, whose names are in the film's credits, *Draw Your Sword* includes many of the photos published in *People's Mourning*.

To Whose Norms We Perform: Cameras in the Midst of People

In chapter 5 I discussed the impact of the various political campaigns—the Anti-Rightist Campaign, the Socialist Education Movement, and the Cultural Revolution—on filmmaking. As one's class affiliation became gradually unhinged from one's economic situations and tied to behavior and attitudes, the film camera, carrying the normative authority of the state, became an apparatus by which people would put on the best performances of themselves as socialist subjects. The question, of course, is what is an acceptable "socialist subject," and who are involved in creating this norm. April 5 was a movement to defy existing scripts and reassert the collective norm-setting agency of the people. This extraordinary act created a new political aesthetics on the square, which could be captured only by cameras positioned in the people's midst.

The use of amateur photography in PRC documentary was unprecedented; Xinying always used film footage from its own correspondents. By using amateur photographs from the square, *Draw Your Sword* drew from spontaneous record-keeping actions by the people. Many photographs used in the film are reproductions of poems, essays, and elegies written on flower wreaths and posters. As these were in danger of being removed and destroyed by the authorities overnight, many people came to the square with pens and paper to copy poems and essays by hand, and those who had cameras used them as a faster means of reproduction. Besides keeping a record of people's written expressions and handmade objects of mourning, photographers were also attracted to the emotional intensity in the square. Many photos captured facial expressions and gestures of the body in close-ups (fig. 6.1). The photographic close-up, for the early film theorist Béla Balázs, is particularly good to express what cannot yet be articulated verbally. "To say nothing is by no means the same as having nothing to say," Balázs writes. "Those who remain silent can still be overflowing with things to say, which, however, can be uttered only in forms, pictures, gestures and facial expressions."[8] People came to the Tiananmen Square spontaneously, with many different kinds of grievances. The square offered a space where pent-up emotions could be shared, and political demands could be articulated through emergent public discourse. Amateur photography became the record-keeper of this unfolding formation of collective politics.

Besides amateur photography, the film used moving images and sound recordings from the square, secretly recorded by Xinying filmmakers. Diegetic sound had been rarely included in documentary films up to this point.[9] In this film, on-location sound recordings were not only included but in a "raw" form.

6.1 Expressions of emotion on Tiananmen Square in *Draw Your Sword* (1979).

Most likely taped by a hidden recorder, the sound recordings were muffled and noisy, with voices of public speech and poetry reading coming in and out of audible range. Also of poor quality were the images shot by Xinying filmmakers with a handheld camera from a moving vehicle on the periphery of Tiananmen Square. Shaky, out of focus, with abrupt zooms, the camera registered spontaneous movements in the square from the sidelines, its viewfinder trembling with excitement.

The heavy use of amateur photography and the inclusion of secretly recorded, poor-quality moving images and sound give the resulting film an aesthetic of spontaneity and make it look very different from the official documentaries that Xinying had been making since its founding. Making films for the party, Xinying filmmakers typically had the privilege of occupying the best filming positions and organizing performance before the cameras. Now, however, these filmmakers were in a similar position as the amateur photographers—both were participating and filming this momentous event out of their own volition as political actors, and both were aware of the risk and meaning of this act. Indeed, both the amateur photographers and the Xinying filmmakers had used their cameras to highlight other acts of image-making and record-keeping in the square (fig. 6.2). Photographers took photos of people copying poetry and essays from posters and of other photographers at work. The fugitive moving camera also repeatedly found photographers in its viewfinder: a lone photographer in the crowd, or a cluster of photographers precariously standing on the top of a lamppost (fig. 6.3).

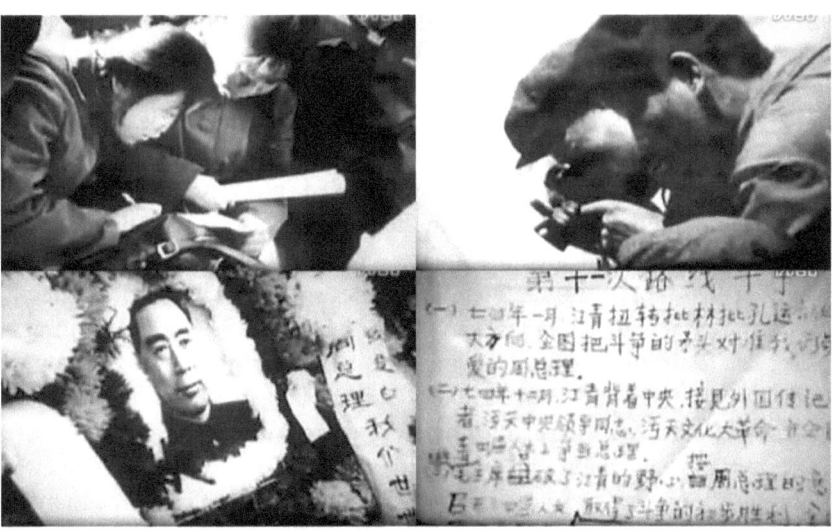

6.2 Keeping records of the objects of mourning on the square in *Draw Your Sword*.

6.3 Blurry images at the edge of the square, taken by a fugitive moving camera from a moving vehicle in *Draw Your Sword*. The camera discovers a number of photographers standing on a lamppost (*bottom left*) and zooms in on them (*bottom right*).

Meanwhile, the film also exhibited a remarkable sensitivity to the positionality of the camera, and to the accountability of the filmmaking process. A few reenactments were made after the rehabilitation to supplement the moving footage shot on the sly. These reconstructed scenes, however, were carefully marked as reenactments. The reconstructed scene of the police assault on protestors, for example, was shot on reversal (positive) film. When printed, the images were inverted and appeared like film negatives. This special visual effect not only caricaturized the assault but also informed the audience that the scenes were not actual footage. The film also included interviews conducted after the rehabilitation with participants in the movement, such as members of the workers' militia who cleared the square, and service staff who witnessed the planning of the police assault. Interviews all begin with the interviewee directly facing the camera and stating clearly his or her name, profession, and workplace, as if testifying in court. The medium-shot framing and the eye contact that was maintained between the interviewee and the camera allow the viewer to come into a face-to-face, and therefore more trusting, relationship with the interviewee. In the midst of one interview, the film camera moved away from the interviewee to a close-up of the sound recorder and the tape that was moving inside it, drawing attention to the filmmaking as a mediated process open to the viewer's scrutiny (fig. 6.4).

6.4 Interviews with workers and the attention to the recording apparatus.

Refusing to end with celebration, the film returns, in its final sequence, to the moving images of a trembling and out-of-focus Tiananmen Square, shot by Xinying filmmakers' fugitive cameras in 1976. The film's final image is an unstable zoom shot onto the photographers standing precariously on a lamppost in the square to document the April 5 Movement. This sequence is both foundational and unsettling. Xinying filmmakers asserted through this cinematic replay that their loyalties lay with the people, and that the interpretation of what was revolutionary ultimately rested with the people, whose collective action served as an impetus for rehabilitation. Indeed, an earlier sequence in the film reminds viewers that the people persistently called for the rehabilitation of the April 5 Movement between 1976 and 1978, rather than it being a benefit from above. With an openness to destabilized images and inaudible expressions, a rigorous demarcation between spontaneous happenings and reenactments, and a sensitivity to their chosen positionality to stand with the people, the Xinying filmmakers saw in the trembling moving images and the photographers on a lamppost the political and ethical foundations of their practice.

Cameras at Court: The Gang of Four Trials

The rehabilitation of the April 5 Movement was a major event that celebrated the power of people's collective political agency. Around the time the movement was rehabilitated, many young people returned to the cities from the countryside, where they had spent the final years of the Cultural Revolution. Political discussions filled the unofficial publications that mushroomed at the time. Thousands of posters appeared on a long brick wall in the Xidan District in central Beijing, in which people freely expressed their political views. In December 1978 Wei Jingsheng, then an electrician at the Beijing Zoo, penned an essay "The Fifth Modernization" on a poster, arguing that China should pursue democratization in addition to the four modernization goals proposed by the CCP in industry, agriculture, science and technology, and national defense. Such spontaneous political mobilization at the grassroots level challenged the party's methods of rule and called for more political power to the people at all levels of the society. As the situation unfolded, the party—itself going through rapid change during that time—began to reinstate law and order. The Democracy Wall Movement lasted for about a year before the authorities shut it down. Wei Jingsheng was also arrested and later imprisoned.

In 1980 Deng Xiaoping indicated that the examination of past events should stay at the level of rough outlines rather than getting into the historical details (*yicu bu yixi*), to avoid radical revisions of official histories.[10] Meanwhile, two events took place: the Gang of Four public trials, and Liu Shaoqi's rehabilitation. Both were aimed at relieving mass grievances while limiting mass engagement to forms prescribed by the party. Both events were broadcast on television and made into documentaries.

Taking place between November 20, 1980, and January 25, 1981, the Gang of Four trials were part of the CCP's effort to reestablish an institutionalized justice system.[11] Being political in nature, the trials were far from fair. As Alexander C. Cook writes, "The selective prosecution of politically palatable defendants, the retroactive application of laws, the numerous procedural irregularities, the wide-spread assumption of guilt, the limited opportunities for defense, the strongly pedagogical tone—these elements rightly contributed to the impression that the Gang of Four trial used the barest of legal trappings to conceal a raw demonstration of political power." Nevertheless, Cook argues that these trials must be considered seriously because they served important pedagogical functions. These didactic trials "teach history lessons . . . and honor the memory of victims and survivors by providing a solemn public space in which anguished remembrance could take the form of legally probative testimony."[12]

The Gang of Four trials gained high visibility thanks to daily television broadcasts of selected sessions and wide circulation of documentary films on the trials. As the new mass media of the post-Mao period, television profoundly affected Chinese documentary filmmaking, which I will address at length later in the chapter. For now, it suffices to say that both the television broadcasts and the documentary films, as audiovisual dispatches from the courtroom, reached millions around the country. They showcased the workings of the reinstated legal system, mobilized archival materials, including audiovisual recordings, and promoted a new political culture of justice based on legal institutions rather than direct mass political action.

A ten-minute documentary, *Indictment Sent to the Lin and Jiang Group* (*Qisushu songda Lin Jiang jituan*), was released in 1980. The film documents clerks from the Special Court of the Highest People's Court delivering the indictment to the defendants at Qincheng Prison before the case opened. Set entirely in a small office, with the clerks sitting at the right side of the room and the defendants separately entering through a door at the left, the camera records the simple interactions between each defendant and the clerks, as the defendant is handed the indictment, told about his or her rights, and given a receipt to sign. The routine is conducted six times for the six defendants, including the "Gang of Four" and two others. There is no voice-over. The only sound in the film is the synched sound from the interactions between the court clerks and the defendants, recorded on location. The camera position also changes little during the ten minutes. The film's minimalist mise-en-scène and lack of emotional color were thoroughly choreographed. According to the prison guard Li Hong, the guards had practiced the delivery of the indictment for nearly half a month before the event.[13]

A Trial by Nine Hundred Million People (*Jiuyi renmin de shenpan*, 1980), an eighteen-minute film documenting the opening of the trial, begins with a sequence studying an empty courtroom just before the court opens. Specially designed for this public trial by Qiu Shaoheng, a legal adviser to the court who had served as a delegate to the Far Eastern War Crimes Tribunal in Tokyo in April 1946, the courtroom was a spatial manifestation of the legal institutions strengthened after the Cultural Revolution.[14] The camera explores the courtroom's layout, moving from the imposing red-and-gold state emblem hanging above the judges' bench; down to the empty rows of seats and the wooden name plates indicating the seating positions of the chief justice, associate justice, chief procurator, deputy chief, and others; and, finally, to the docks where the defendants would sit, at the lowest place in the courtroom.

The rest of the film records the announcement of the opening of the trial, the entrance of the defendants one by one, and the lengthy reading of the indictment, which takes up most of the screen time. When the chief and deputy chief of the Special Procuratorate read aloud the indictment, besides observing the defendants' reactions, the camera also takes a special interest in the audience. Those who attended the opening of the trial were carefully selected people's representatives from each province and autonomous region, as well as families of victims, including the widows of the persecuted party leaders Liu Shaoqi, He Long, and Luo Ruiqing.

Attentive but silent and manifesting little emotion, this audience represented a different concept of mass participation in the pursuit of justice from that of the past. Here, the people no longer acted directly in condemnation, denunciation, interrogation, and punishment. Instead, they gave the power of action to the court and legal professionals. The film ends with two long shots of the courtroom, one from the front and the other from the back, simulating two different viewing positions: that of the legal professionals sitting in the front of the courtroom, and that of the observers sitting in the audience. Ending the film with a long shot of the courtroom from the perspective of the audience, the film highlights observing and witnessing institutional justice as a form of new historical agency that replaces "the right to violent revolution," sanctioned previously.

Audiovisual Evidence at Court

Documentaries of the public trial featured the prison, the court, and the professional processes of justice in these institutions. Meanwhile, archival documentary footage was also included among items of evidence presented at the court. During the individual trials, 873 items of evidence—including testimonies, archival documents, and other verifiable traces from the past—were shown in court.[15] Equipped with a projector and an audio player, the court projected photograph slides and played audio recordings and documentary film clips. In an article for the *Newsletter of Archival Science*, Liu Tielin of the PLA Archives wrote passionately about the use of archival materials during the public trials. Liu was among the many archivists who gathered documents from archives to support the drafting of the indictments for the public trials. "Every written report, every article, every film, photograph, and audio or video recording left records of truth on paper, film, and magnetic tapes," Liu wrote. "These historical records are the true evidence of all the criminal activities. Even though the criminals tried everything to destroy documents that might harm them, history couldn't be erased or changed. In front of hundreds of pieces of historical evidence that refuse to show mercy to anyone, the criminals have no other choice but lower their heads and acknowledge their crimes."[16]

In his article, Liu described how archival documents, including audiovisual materials, were used in the court proceedings. For example, Jiang Qing had initially denied her role in Liu Shaoqi's persecution, but she had no choice but to acknowledge her crime after the court showed her own signature on documents instructing the persecution and played audio recordings of her own denunciation of Liu in a public speech in September 1968. Wang Hongwen's involvement in the largest violent factional fight in Shanghai, on August 4, 1968, was ascertained by clips from a documentary film. Audio and visual evidence was particularly favored in the investigation, for it was seen to be more authentic that written documents. For example, in 1967 the Red Guards tortured to death Professor Zhang Zhongyi of Beijing Normal University, an alleged associate of the fallen Liu Shaoqi, in order to extract a confession. The dying professor gave false statements, which were recorded both on paper and in audio recordings. What the recording could capture but the written documents could not was the extent of torture involved in the interrogation. The incoherent, cracked voice of the confessor was that of a dying man in severe pain. Liu Tielin argued that the truth of the past stubbornly lived on in these traces. He described the potency of historical evidence as "knives thrust at the heart of the enemy, and bombs exploding into the enemy's camp." It was through these historical documents that "the original face of our party and country's history could be maintained."[17]

Using audiovisual materials as evidence was certainly nothing new. In the introduction of this book I already discussed Grierson's choice of the word *documentary* as connected to the dominance of the "document" in professions of law, science, and history writing in Euro-America at the time. In chapter 5 I also discussed the historical use of cinema in forensic examination, and in mass denunciation campaigns to detect "capitalist sentiments." The renewed emphasis on the evidentiary use of documents around the Gang of Four trial, along with enhanced practices of courtroom witnessing and cross-examination, contributed to the post-Mao transition to an institutionalized justice system. Of course, documents themselves do not guarantee truth. Much depends on the interpretation. As mentioned earlier, this trial was in fact a "show trial" with a great deal of procedural irregularities. Yet the emphasis on the use of documents and cross-examination in reckoning with history continued through the post-Mao decade. The use of archival footage became increasingly prevalent in the documentary film culture of the time, as a way to reassess and disturb existing historiography. I will return to this point later in the chapter.

The Limits of Rehabilitation: Laying Liu Shaoqi to Rest

On May 17, 1980, the Great Hall of the People in Beijing was packed to capacity for a memorial service that came eleven years too late. More than ten thousand people attended the ceremony, and millions watched the event's live broadcast on television. Dominating the stage was a giant black-and-white photographic portrait of the former state president, Liu Shaoqi. The photograph, roughly 3 meters high and 2.3 meters wide, framed the face of a gray-haired Liu in the frontal head shot of an official portrait. Stripped of all positions and Communist Party membership, Liu died in 1969 after suffering torture and solitary confinement. Now he looked on quietly from a photographic image that had not been seen in public for thirteen years (fig. 6.5).

6.5 Scenes from *Long Live the Memory of Comrade Liu Shaoqi* (1980): the rehabilitation ceremony for Liu Shaoqi.

For a long time, observers of China had thought that it would be too risky for the CCP to rehabilitate Liu Shaoqi, who had been framed as the antithesis of what the Chinese Communist Party stood for, and whose negative image, just like the positive image of Mao Zedong, had to be preserved to maintain the legitimacy of the Communist regime.[18] However, by the end of the 1970s, it became clear that Liu had to be rehabilitated. The wider society called for it: letters from ordinary citizens urged it, and big-character posters on Beijing's Democracy Wall did as well. Liu's purge affected tens of thousands of people nationwide who were persecuted as Liu's associates and supporters. These people could not be fully rehabilitated if Liu remained guilty. The CCP had also begun to revive Liu's moderate economic policies, which meant that it became untenable to leave Liu condemned as a "capitalist roader."[19]

In February 1980 the Party's Fifth Plenum passed the resolution for Liu Shaoqi's rehabilitation. Two documentaries, the forty-minute *Comrade Liu Shaoqi Forever Lives* (*Liu Shaoqi tongzhi yongchui buxiu*, 1980) and the eighty-minute *Comrade Liu Shaoqi, the People Remember You* (*Shaoqi tongzhi renmin huainian nin*, 1980), were released in the same year and screened widely throughout the country. The first recorded Liu's memorial service; the second was a biographic documentary, recounting Liu's revolutionary career through a compilation of archival footage of his activities during his lifetime.

The return of Liu's images was an extraordinary event. As I discussed in chapter 5, exclusion from the media was one of the immediate punishments for a fallen leader. Photographs of Liu had been systematically cleansed from Chinese media and public spaces after his downfall in 1967. His official portraits, once ceremoniously hung next to those of Mao Zedong, were removed and destroyed. Films with positive images of Liu were recalled and banned from further exhibition. Those that were too important to recall and ban, such as the popular newsreels documenting Mao's inspection of the Red Guards, went through painstaking reediting so that Liu's images were completely purged before the next printing. In 1980 viewers responded to the return of Liu's image with excitement and relief. A commentator in a film journal wrote, "Comrade Liu Shaoqi was the greatest victim in the Cultural Revolution. Lin Biao and the Gang of Four imposed on him all kinds of 'crimes,' wanting to erase completely his image in history. However, historical facts can't be erased. History must be written by the people, who have their own evaluations of a person's achievements and mistakes." He went on to describe his feelings upon seeing Liu's images again after twelve years: "When I saw him on the film screen . . . I was so excited! It felt as if I had not been watching a film, but had been seated next to him, seeing and listening to him in person."[20] Another author in the same issue of the journal wrote a poem to celebrate the return of Liu's image.[21]

While viewers celebrated the return of Liu's image as a "victory of history," his rehabilitation was carefully managed and largely centered on proving his innocence from the alleged crimes. Inquiries into his persecution and into the ideological differences within the top leadership of the party were very limited. The rehabilitation ceremony was framed as a belated state funeral. Funerary rituals were used traditionally to create unity among mourners and domesticate grief through prescribed behaviors.[22] Starting in 1976, the first generation of top Communist leaders gradually passed away. By 1980 the convention to mourn deceased top officials with two documentaries—one funeral and the other biographic—had been formed, with borrowings from the Soviet Union and Republican China precedents.[23] The funeral documentary allowed the public to join the rituals of laying a statesman to rest, and the biographic documentary constructed the person's legacy according to the party's evaluations. Liu's televised state funeral and the two documentaries remembering him were meant not to revisit the case of his purge, but to restore him to the pantheon of revolutionaries, and to bring a quick closure to the political struggle that had brought calamity on him and many of his alleged associates.

Unsettling State Funerals

As part of the state ritual, funeral and biographical documentaries followed certain conventions. Funeral films would begin with commemoration activities held all over the country, followed by the state memorial service where the official elegy would be read. Biographical films would retrace the person's revolutionary career with the help of historical photographs and archival footage. Like a traditional ritual, these films' conventionality was meant to regulate emotions. Yet filmmakers often bent the conventions, in which cases the films' affective impact became particularly intense.

One such example was the eighty-one-minute color documentary, *Long Live the Memory of Premier Zhou Enlai* (*Jing'aide Zhou Enlai Zongli yongchui buxiu*), released on January 8, 1977, one year after Zhou passed away. The film had been banned by the radicals after Zhou's death in 1976, and its release in 1977 was deeply gratifying to everyone who admired, indeed loved, the late premier. Copies of the film were in such high demand that some cinemas even sent people to line up in front of Xinying overnight to secure a screener.[24] The film's emotional impact and artistic merit can be compared to Dziga Vertov's *Three Songs of Lenin* (1934), a film made for the tenth anniversary of Lenin's death, which incorporated Lenin's funeral footage and his moving images when alive. Besides filming the people's grief at Zhou Enlai's funeral and Deng Xiaoping's official elegy of the late premier, the Zhou film includes a seven-minute sequence depicting a spontaneous gathering of millions of people lining up on the Chang'an Avenue (Avenue of Everlasting Peace), waiting in below freezing temperatures for hours to bid farewell to Zhou. As the van carrying Zhou's coffin drives slowly by, a camera filming from a moving vehicle pans across the grieving crowd standing in tears and silence. The long takes of the endless crowd (covering every inch of an avenue famed to be ten *li*, or five kilometers, long) are intercut with close-ups of faces of all ages, whose tearful eyes follow the movement of the van in the anguished desire to see their beloved premier one more time, a desire that only photography and cinema could now satisfy. The film shows that immediately after Zhou's body was cremated, Zhou's photographic portraits were given out to the people who came to pay their respects. The staff wipe their tears while rolling up Zhou's portrait, and the receivers clench the posters with their wet fingers, creating a tear-soaked, affective circulation of Zhou's image. Another ten-minute sequence, placed at the end of the film, features moving images of Zhou from the 1920s to the 1970s, bringing the beloved leader back to life for the viewer. Unprecedented in earlier funeral films, these two sequences affirmed the power of photographic and moving images to continue the material existence of the deceased premier and build affective communities through his memory, even though Zhou was demonstrably no more: his ashes were soon to be scattered from the air.

Zhou's funeral film assured viewers of the preservation of his memory and answered their desire to see him again by resurrecting the premier with moving images. Liu Shaoqi's funeral film, *Long Live the Memory of Comrade Liu Shaoqi*, in contrast, had no such affirmation or resurrection. Meant to be a ritual to lay the dead to rest, Liu's funeral film was so unsettling and ritually incorrect that it stood in the way of the closure the party had sought to achieve. Liu died in Kaifeng, Henan Province, in November 1969, after being severely tortured and denied medical care, and he was quickly cremated under the pseudonym Liu Weihuang. For a long time the whereabouts of his ashes were a mystery. After Liu was rehabilitated, his remains were finally located in a government office in Zhengzhou, the capital city of Henan. In addition to documenting Liu's state funeral at the Great Hall of the People, the camera accompanied Liu's widow, Wang Guangmei, and son Liu Yuan on their visit to Kaifeng, where Liu spent his last days, and filmed them receiving Liu's ashes at a ceremony from Zhengzhou city officials.[25] While the rest of the film was shot mostly by fixed cameras in the well-rehearsed conventions of a state funeral, these scenes in Kaifeng were filmed with a handheld camera, which stayed close to Liu's family members and captured their deeply emotional journey. The camera walks with Wang Guangmei as she enters the room where Liu Shaoqi had died and weeps, clutching the pillowcases that Liu used in the final days of his life; it records the transfer of Liu's ashes from the Zhengzhou officials to Liu's family and witnesses the bereavement of the family as they kiss and caress the box of ashes. Besides the return of Liu's ashes, the film includes another scene documenting the ceremony in which Liu's ashes are scattered in the ocean, according to his wishes (fig. 6.6).

Ashes had never been included in funeral films. Zhou Enlai's ashes were also scattered, but it was done secretly and quietly, to avoid intensifying people's grief.[26] Zhou's funeral film represents the scattering of his ashes with aerial shots of beautiful landscapes: mountains, rivers, and fields, on which a small

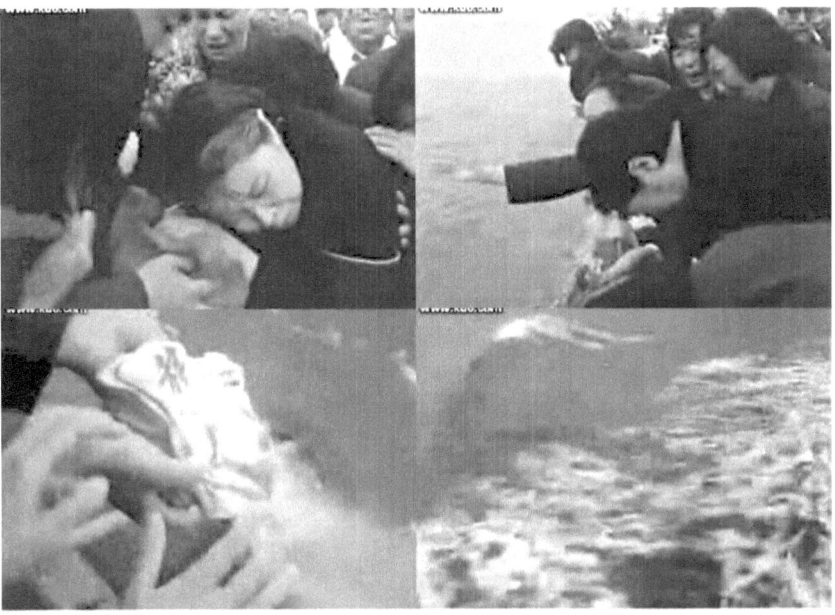

6.6 Scene from *Long Live the Memory of Comrade Liu Shaoqi*: scattering Liu Shaoqi's ashes in the sea.

airplane (where the camera was located, and from where the ashes would be scattered) occasionally leaves an elusive shadow. In the case of Liu Shaoqi, however, his funeral film ends with the actual scattering of his ashes. The camera in this scene is handheld again, and it boldly frames Liu's white ashes, wrapped in red silk, in a close-up. It also films the grieving family aboard a warship, holding handfuls of Liu's ashes and letting the ocean wind blow them away into the water. Rocked by ocean waves, these scenes are unstable and disquieting. They emphasize the irrevocability and injustice of Liu's death and stand out in stark contrast to the ritual stability of a state funeral.

Even though Liu's images returned to public view, there was a general feeling that his persecution during the Cultural Revolution had not been sufficiently dealt with. Liu's biographic film, *Comrade Liu Shaoqi, the People Remember You*, recounts Liu's life from birth to 1965, leaving out the years of the Cultural Revolution entirely. The limits in official historiography on Liu Shaoqi and the Cultural Revolution were to be contested later in the landmark documentary released in 1988, *River Elegy*. Before turning to that film, however, two concurrent developments must be discussed at length, namely, the increasing use of archival moving images in historical documentaries and the rise of television documentary.

Documentaries and the Historiographical Reorientation

As discussed in association with the Gang of the Four trials, archival documents, including audiovisual documents, played an important role in the early years of the post-Mao era as the party reinstituted the rule of law. Through the 1980s, archival film footage also played an increasingly important role in facilitating a historiographical reorientation.

Biographical documentaries were the earliest films to make extensive use of historical footage. As mentioned earlier, each rehabilitation of important Communist leaders led to a biographical documentary production. After the rehabilitation process drew to an end, production of biographical documentaries continued. Xinying produced *The Songs of the Pioneers* (*Xianquzhe zhi ge*, 1981), on the lives of early Chinese Communists, to commemorate the sixtieth anniversary of the founding of the party. In the following year, the August First Film Studio also made a series of biographical films titled *Glorious Achievements* (*Guanghui yeji*), each showcasing one PLA marshal.[27] As the decade progressed, more biographical films were made of important historical figures in the arts and literature, such as the writers Lu Xun and Ba Jin and the actor Zhao Dan. Politicians in the progressive wing of the Nationalist Party, such as Liao Chengzhi and He Xiangning, and activists among overseas Chinese communities such as Chen Jiageng were also featured in biographical documentaries.[28]

Biographies followed historical figures in their networked interactions with others; these personal journeys and stories enriched historical narratives, and some pushed the boundaries of official historiography.

With the success of biographical documentaries, Xinying filmmakers took on documentary treatments of significant events in modern Chinese history. In 1984, as China and the UK prepared to sign the Joint Declaration of Hong Kong's return to China, Xinying started the production of a 390-minute, eight-episode documentary film series, *Chronicle of the Modern Era* (*Jindai chunqiu*), an epic treatment of Chinese history between the Opium Wars and the founding of the PRC. The overarching narrative foregrounded China's struggles to modernize the country in the face of Western and Japanese imperialist encroachment. Each episode, released separately as stand-alone documentary films between 1984 and 1989, brought previously obscured historical events and figures to visibility.

In an interview conducted in 1986, after one of the episodes, "The Beacon Fire of Resisting Japan" (*Kangri fenghuo*), won major awards in the country, the director He Zhongxin spoke of this documentary series as an attempt to "return to history its original face," a slogan associated with early 1980s rehabilitation efforts. "History is history—it's what has already happened. We must insist on the principle of historical materialism, to return to history its original face. We can't distort, nor can we fabricate," He was quoted as saying.[29] *Chronicle of the Modern Era* mobilized a substantial amount of archival material, including footage from a number of films I have discussed in this book, such as Lai Manwai's *A Record of the National Revolutionary Army's War on Sea, Land, and Air* (1927, re-edited by Lai in 1950), Cheng Bugao's *Battle of Shanghai* (1932), Lai Manwai's *War of Resistance in Songjiang and Shanghai* (*Songhu kangzhan jishi*, 1937), and other wartime propaganda documentaries made out of Chongqing and Yan'an. These archival images, as He Zhongxin indicated in the interview, brought visibility to historical events whose existence had been previously denied. Using archival documentary footage, "The Beacon Fire of Resisting Japan" acknowledged the Nationalist Party and its troops' contributions to the War of Resistance, which had been written out of PRC official history. Another episode, on the Northern Expedition, gave screen time to Nationalist military commanders including Chiang Kai-shek, who had not been depicted in any positive light since 1949. Qing modernizers such as Zeng Guofan and Li Hongzhang and liberal intellectuals such as Hu Shi all had screen presence and received positive evaluations for their contributions to China's modernization efforts.[30] Certainly, this historiographic reorientation had a lot to do with the party's "reform and opening" agenda. By the early 1980s the CCP had already articulated the "One Country Two Systems" policy for Hong Kong and Taiwan and was actively building rapport with overseas Chinese communities who served as mediators for international trade and collaboration.

While China's own moving image archive had been mobilized to revise the country's foundational historical narratives, footage exchange with overseas media companies allowed Chinese viewers to view international archival footage side by side with the Chinese footage. Between 1987 and 1988, as later episodes of *Chronicle of the Modern Era* were still being made, a new TV documentary miniseries composed entirely of archival footage, entitled *Today in History* (*Lishishang de jintian*), was aired on CCTV to great popularity. This program was an adaptation of *One Day*, a program CCTV had acquired in 1985 from the British television company Visnews (renamed Reuters Television in 1994). *One Day* assembled archival images of important events that had happened on each day of the year for different years across history. CCTV reedited the program by inserting archival footage from twentieth-century Chinese history. Each episode of *Today in History* was only three minutes long. The program was broadcasted daily after the seven o'clock evening news on CCTV between October 1, 1987, and September 30, 1988.[31]

Assembling archival footage of events with no apparent connection except for having happened on the same day of the year, *Today in History* was in fact following a commonplace narrative trope in commercial television, not so different from the "parade of the world" infotainment in American newsreels, as discussed in chapter 2. Indeed, indiscriminate collections of historical images may create a spectacle of history without revealing the underlying structures of historical development. Chinese viewers, however, enthusiastically received this mode of historical engagement. Within two months of broadcasting, the program became the third most watched program in China.[32] As an archivist from Yangzhou wrote in the journal *Archive and Construction*: "Many of the images [in *Today in History*] have appeared in books, journals, and films, and I have seen them before. They are not new images. However, day after day, I eagerly wait to watch every episode and regret it when I miss one. Why is that?" He went on to answer his own question: "By using time as the thread to weave together history, the film broke up old thematic frameworks. It made histories intersect each other, and allowed viewers to see amazing similarities and connections between historical events. . . . No longer was history just about class struggle."[33]

Archives are always selective.[34] Which images are made and which are preserved depended on many structural and contingent factors. The 1980s saw the reuse of a great deal of archival documentary footage; much came from documentaries that this book has discussed in earlier chapters. To what extent can archival footage return to history its "original face," as He Zhongxin believed? Documentaries, as discussed throughout the book, are not reflections of reality but "eventful" mediations. They create and strengthen relationships, capture and inscribe what is emergent and yet nameless, and intervene into material and symbolic (re)productions in the society. When taken out of production contexts, moving images from the archives, much like photographs or artefacts, arouse imagination and interest in the complex historical processes that gave rise to the moments of the images' inscription. While these historical processes cannot be recovered from the images alone, these images' metonymic power, that is, their ability to refer beyond themselves to larger processes of history, returns a sense of mystery and wonder to historical imagination, pushing against a reductionist official historiography that focused on class struggle alone. As more and more archival images, made by various political forces over the twentieth century, began to populate rehabilitation films, historical documentaries, and TV programs such as *Today in History*, they began to fuel popular interest in history and support a substantial historiographic reorientation.

Television Documentary: Reinventing an Interactive, Reflexive, and Democratic Medium

I mentioned in passing the importance of television when discussing the Gang of Four trials and Liu Shaoqi's rehabilitation ceremony, both broadcast on television in 1980; *Today in History* was also a television program. After its founding in 1953, Xinying had been the PRC's center for documentary. Yet by the 1980s its central position was no more. Instead, China Central Television (CCTV) replaced Xinying to become the largest producer and exhibitor of documentaries. The rise of television documentary brought substantial development to documentary form and to documentary's engagement with history and with the present.

Silk Road and the Democratic Tendency of Television

As mentioned in chapter 4, China launched its first television broadcast at the height of the Great Leap Forward in 1958, though at that time the new Beijing TV station could broadcast to only a small area around Beijing, and with no infrastructure or technology to support a nationwide television network at the time, cinema became leveraged to approximate television's speed and reach. During the 1960s and 1970s the country's television infrastructure grew moderately, and by the end of 1976 all provinces and autonomous regions except Tibet had a television station. Despite the small number of television sets (one television set for every 1,600 people), 36 percent of the population enjoyed some form of TV coverage through communal viewing.[35] The reform era of the late 1970s and 1980s saw rapid growth in television ownership and programming. The Beijing Television Station, which had begun broadcasting in 1958, was renamed China Central Television in 1978. In 1980 it broadcast major public trials (such as those of the Gang of Four) and rehabilitation ceremonies (such as that of Liu Shaoqi) to viewers around the country. By the end of the decade, in 1988, television had become a dominant mass media, with more than 600 million viewers nationwide.[36]

As the most prominent new medium for the reform era, television not only allowed instantaneous and simultaneous distribution of audiovisual materials to viewers around the country but also brought Chinese documentary filmmaking into an expanded international market. Since rebuilding its relationship with the United States in the early 1970s, China had gradually opened up to countries and regions on the other side of the iron curtain. The need for international and Chinese TV stations to fill air time, and the intense mutual interest between China and the rest of the world as China "opened up," resulted in voluminous exchanges of moving images. TV networks in Euro-America and Japan eagerly sought documentary content from China to satisfy their viewers' curiosity about the country. As Chinese TV production had been sporadic and irregular in the late 1970s, to answer international demand for content and support China's policies of reform and opening up, documentary filmmakers needed to quickly learn to produce for television and for an international market. State-sponsored study tours sent CCTV documentarists to Europe, North America, and Africa to learn audience preferences and industry standards.[37] CCTV also sought coproduction with international TV stations. Such exchanges in time gave rise to serialized TV documentaries that allowed new experimentation with documentary form.

CCTV's first international collaboration was with NHK, Japan's public broadcasting company, on the documentary series *Silk Road* in 1980. It was a substantial undertaking: eleven Chinese and nineteen Japanese filmmakers spent twenty-one months filming in China together.[38] For postproduction, the two sides shared footage but separately edited two different versions of the program to suit their respective domestic audience. NHK's thirteen-episode TV series was a resounding success in Japan and internationally, generating a handsome profit and lasting international interest in the "Silk Road."[39] CCTV's fifteen-episode series, in contrast, did poorly in China, due to low TV ownership, irregular programming, and the lack of a television culture in 1980.[40] Yet even though the Chinese series did not achieve domestic popularity, the impact of this collaboration cannot be overstated. The Japanese filmmakers brought the most up-to-date filming technologies on the trip. They used specialty film stock for extreme weather conditions and made stunning aerial shots with their more advanced cameras. More important, Chinese filmmakers were introduced to NHK's well-tested, standardized production and publicity practices. The coproduction was not unlike a crash course in television documentary.

"Though television is young and not as mature as cinema, its capacity to represent broad topics isn't so different from film; in fact, television representation can even be bolder, with more possibilities," wrote Wang Jiyan, a young lecturer at the television department of the Beijing Broadcast Institute who participated in the *Silk Road* collaboration with NHK and published his musings in a series of articles in 1980–1983. Wang observed that compared to cinema, the seriality of television not only enabled the unfolding of more complex narratives and allowed for more sustained engagement with a topic but also made the production more democratic, as the relatively self-contained nature of each episode allowed a larger number of filmmakers to work together in a more decentralized fashion. Another democratizing aspect of television was its embedment in the viewers' everyday lives. By close-reading the Japanese version of *Silk Road*, Wang discussed how slow-paced long takes, instead of rapid montage sequences, are more suitable to television documentary, as they can better accommodate distracted home viewing. This, Wang added, is not simply a pragmatic strategy but is indicative of the "aesthetic ideas" (*meixue sixiang*) of television documentary, which should impart on the viewers "a sense that they are watching everyday life."[41]

Documentary Interactivity and Reflexivity in the River Stories of the Mid-1980s

In 1980 *Silk Road* had failed to generate much public interest in China. The situation was entirely different in 1983, when a twenty-five-episode TV documentary series, *Stories of the Yangtze* (*Huashuo Changjiang*, hereafter *Yangtze*), achieved great popularity and an astounding 40 percent viewer rate among Chinese viewers. Three years later the thirty-four-episode *Stories of the Grand Canal* (*Huashuo Yunhe*, hereafter *Grand Canal*) was also immensely popular. The Chinese TV documentary had come of age.

The popularity of these two series had a great deal to do with formal innovations that brought interactivity and reflexivity to documentary. A runaway success when broadcast, *Yangtze* had begun as a failed collaborative project between Japan's Sada Planning Company (owned by the singer Sada Masashi) and CCTV. The footage was filmed by Japanese filmmakers between 1980 and 1983. The Sada Company invested in costly aerial cinematography, which produced spectacular birds-eye views of most of the Yangtze's extensive river basin. Yet overall the filming was touristic and lacked thematic focus. With Sada unable to follow through with the postproduction, CCTV filmmakers found themselves left with a massive amount of spectacular but fragmentary footage, to which they needed to bring a sense of coherence.

The ingenuous format of "storytelling" came about as a solution to this problem. Actors Chen Duo and Hong Yun were brought into the studio to serve as "storytellers." They spoke directly to the camera in studio or produced voice-overs to accompany the moving images. Their narration was penned by CCTV producer Chen Hanyuan, who had majored in Chinese literature in college.

Complete with literary flourishes, the narration provided historical depth and cultural meaning to breathtaking images of the Yangtze River. The informal, chatty format of "storytelling" also allowed the narration to move freely between temporal registers, from commenting on the formations of mountains and glaciers in deep geological time, to narrating the political, cultural, and technological histories of a region that spanned millennia.

As discussed previously, the increased usage of archival footage during public trials, rehabilitation, and historical documentaries had unsettled existing historical narratives and fueled new historical imagination. *Yangtze* did not use archival footage, yet the Yangtze River was an extraordinary site of historical and cultural sedimentation, from its geological formations and biosphere, to the large number of historical sites and local traditions, to the endless legends, classical poetry, paintings, and material cultures that produced the river landscape with rich layers of cultural meaning. In other words, the Yangtze River is an archive in itself, holding a wealth of remnants from material and cultural productions of the past two millennia. These remnants are what Corey Byrnes calls "traces," or *ji* 跡. The Chinese character means footprints but is also etymologically connected to the *ji* of record-keeping and documentary.[42] Not unlike archival footage or photography, these historical traces point beyond themselves to the broader processes of mediation that gave rise to their production. And *Yangtze* invigorated these traces through its transmedial aesthetic of "storytelling" in television documentary. Language and narrative—both in the written titles and in the voice-over—came into palpable interaction with image and sound. Classical poetry, in calligraphy, appeared as titles on moving images. Voice-overs complemented aerial shots of the river basin with fantastical stories from traditional operas and local legends. Reassembling cultural resources of the past without imposing a strong historical narrative, the meandering storytelling of *Yangtze* recalls the documentary innovations pursued by young Xinying filmmakers in the mid-1950s, particularly the poetic documentary *Plum Flowers, Spring Rain, and Jiangnan*, also filmed along a river, which I discussed at length in chapter 5. Whereas in the mid-1950s the Xinying filmmakers' experiments were cut short, television documentary in the 1980s became the main powerhouse for formal innovations. The popularity of *Yangtze* encouraged further experiments with the storytelling format, bringing further interactivity and reflexivity to television documentary.

Yangtze's storytelling format was so successful that the storytellers Chen Duo and Hong Yun became household names after the series aired. In 1986 the two appeared in another television documentary series, *Grand Canal*. If in *Yangtze* the storytelling was still heavily scripted and largely a one-way communication from the storytellers to the viewer, in *Grand Canal* it acquired further dialogical, interactive, and reflexive qualities and began to intervene in the politics of the present. *Silk Road* and *Yangtze* were collaborations with Japanese companies; *Grand Canal* was produced entirely by CCTV. The production began in 1984, and thirty-four episodes of twenty minutes apiece, including a "preface" and an "epilogue," were made. The series was broadcast weekly for nine months, between March 1986 and January 1987, to great popularity.

Unlike the naturally formed Yellow and Yangtze Rivers, the Grand Canal is an artificial human construction. Throughout the documentary series, Chen Duo and Hong Yun compare the canal to the Great Wall. "The Great Wall and the Grand Canal are the two largest engineering projects designed and executed by the Chinese in human history," exclaims Hong Yun with pride. A note of ambivalence can be discerned in this comparison. After all, massive constructions such as the Great Wall and the Grand Canal involved a tremendous amount of labor and heavy human costs. They were built with people's "blood, flesh, and sweat," says Chen Duo.

As state infrastructure, the Grand Canal connected China's major rivers to create a network for water transportation, strengthening the state government's capacity to influence regional economies, and facilitating the circulation of goods and people and the formation of regional markets at the same time. Complex relationships between the state and the society were formed around the canal's construction, maintenance, and use. Flowing through towns and villages and contributing to their high population density and vigorous commercial activity, the canal was built for all kinds of water traffic (unlike the Yangtze and Yellow Rivers, whose turbulent stretches are prohibitive for small boats). For this reason, the canal was accessible and hummed with human activity. "On the boats traveling along the canal, people are born; they come of age, form families, and spend their whole lives on the canal," Hong Yun reflects over a montage of different kinds of boats on the canal and the people traveling in them. In symbiotic relationship with the towns and villages along it, the canal is a site of everyday life and work.

Like the canal, television is also a state infrastructure that enables networked connectivity across the country. It is also developed and powered by the work of many people: producers, actors, critics, and, most important, viewers. This analogous relationship underpinned the strong reflexivity with which the series approached its own production process, alongside its explorations of the canal's functions as state infrastructure and its embedment in everyday life.

The series includes a prefatory episode entitled "The Front and the Back" (*Qianqian houhou*). With the same twenty-minute running time as the other episodes, it offers a behind-the-scenes look at the production itself. The episode begins with the commotion on the ground caused by aerial filming, as people gathered to watch the camera-bearing helicopter with curiosity. In *Yangtze*, Japanese filmmakers relied heavily on aerial cinematography to create a disembodied bird-eye's view of the Yangtze River in its rich geographical context. The focus was on the river; no attention was given to how aerial shots were made. In contrast, *Grand Canal* foregrounds aerial cinematography's interactive relationship with what was being filmed and shares with viewers the various kinds of work and contingency that underlay its process. Hong Yun and Chen Duo discuss the heavy rain and flood in South China that grounded the helicopters, and the crew's worries about the accruing rent. In northern China, where the weather permitted departure, a handheld camera follows the cinematographers' preparations. Cui Yanmin, a female cinematographer, is seen buckled into her seat next to the helicopter's door. As the helicopter begins its ascent, the storytellers urge the viewers to imagine what it is like to film from an open aircraft door. "Imagine sitting on a chair tied to the outside of a window on the twentieth floor, and looking down," one says. "The wind is strong no matter how fast or slow you fly. There is always a feeling of risk," says the other. "If someone tells you that she has no worries on her mind, it wouldn't be true. She must feel a bit uneasy thinking about the signature she just put on the life insurance contract."

Throughout the discussion of anxiety and risk, the helicopter is the center of attention. It ascends, hovers, and circles, while the viewer is led to imagine how the cinematographer sitting in it might feel and the kind of work she must perform. In chapter 4, when discussing documentaries during the Great Leap Forward, I observed the lack of concern about work-related risk, sleep deprivation, and disability. In contrast, the makers of *Grand Canal* took the corporeality of labor very seriously. The anchors discuss aerial cinematography as embodied work, for which one first has to deal with one's fear of heights. "Succumbing to the fear, your heart palpitates, eyes blur, legs give away, and hands tremble. Shutter speed, distance, depth of field, and composition—all of these are out of the question!" The only way to get crisp, clean images is to forget the fear by focusing on the work: "Once we start working, we just don't think too much about it!" Only when this discussion draws to an end do viewers finally get to see the stunning aerial cinematography, accomplished by Cui, of the Great Wall and the Grand Canal. By then, the viewers have been prepared to see these images differently, not as disembodied, birds-eye points of view, but as enabled by many factors, from technology and weather to the embodied and technical work of the cinematographer.

Throughout the series' thirty-four episodes, this sustained attention to the belabored process of filmmaking went far beyond aerial cinematography. The series gives screen time to those who supported the production, from local cadres, script writers, editors, grips, to museum staff who enabled the filming of objects in the local museum collections. One scene shows ten staff members of the Zhejiang Provincial Museum holding up an eighteen-meter-long scroll of a Qing dynasty painting for the cinematographer to film. In the epilogue, the two anchors thank a large number of writers and consultants who contributed to the production and present handwritten pages filled with the names of people who supported the production in some way. "These are lists of all the people with whom we contacted and who helped us," Hong Yun says. "All of them are part of our production crew."

This unprecedented level of reflexivity about the production process was matched by the series' interactivity with viewers. Street interviews along the canal were unscripted and featured a variety of northern and southern dialects, with a spontaneity that reminds one of Jean Rouch and Edgar Morin's cinéma vérité documentary, *Chronicle of a Summer* (1961). Two episodes (nos. 21 and 23) were devoted to discussing issues raised in the viewer letters the program had received. Episode 21 focuses on water pollution, a severe problem raised by many viewers. The anchors read excerpts that criticize the series for showing only beautiful images of the canal. "The real situation that I saw with my own eyes, that left the deepest impression, wasn't the local customs, or the human achievements of the canal's construction, or the cultural artifacts and historical sites, but the canal's pollution and destruction," one viewer from Sichuan writes. Acknowledging that the viewers' "concerns were much broader than the visions provided by our lens," Chen Duo asks, "What kind of attitude should our camera take?" He answers his own question: "It must report both the good and the bad."

Indeed, considerable screen time was spent in episodes 21 and 23 on exposing pollution on the canal, showing pollutants being poured into the water and the oil, foam, and trash that cover the water surface. The episodes also include interviews with affected households, factory workers, and cadres in local and central governments. The anchors observe that many letters from viewers express the wish for the TV program not to just "discuss action on paper" (*zhishang tanbing*), but to engage in direct actions to "move things along" (*tuidong*). In response, the anchors assure the viewers that their letters are taken seriously: "[These letters] are what we rely on when making the program."

Grand Canal signaled a maturation of television documentary as a reflexive and interactive medium. It invited viewers into its production process, was willing to be held accountable to viewers' criticism, and was conscious and proud of the multiplying effect of its eventfulness: it reported on many events organized by various social groups, from trivia shows and kayak competitions to cultural productions such as painting exhibitions and concerts, that came into being in response to the series. More important, the television documentary was seen as infrastructure—not unlike the Grand Canal itself—that could bring the party state and the people into inclusive and constitutive interaction, this time focusing on the people's needs and experiences, rather than the party's ideological identities. Soon, television's mediating role would be further explored in a landmark documentary, *River Elegy* (1988).

The Unfinished Business of Mourning: *River Elegy*

River Elegy, a six-episode TV documentary series, was released on CCTV in June 1988 and immediately became a sensation nationwide.[43] The series was originally a collaboration between CCTV and NHK on a documentary about the Yellow River, following the success of *Yangtze*. After the filming concluded in 1986, NHK promptly edited the footage into a ten-episode series *The Great Yellow River* (*Daikōga*), broadcast in Japan in the same year. CCTV, however, did not bring out the Chinese version until two years later.

Whereas previous river films depicted the Yangtze and the Grand Canal as hometown rivers that sustained everyday lives and local cultures, *River Elegy* began with deaths on the Yellow River. Its first episode, "Searching for Dreams" (*Xun meng*), begins with a small, inflatable raft trying to navigate the turbulent waves of the Yellow River. This was newsreel footage of an expedition undertaken by young Chinese rafters in June 1987, during which seven lives were lost. The rafters embrace one another, pose for photos, and set off in the rafts, quickly succumbing to the waves. "It was reported that these young Chinese rafters decided to take the risk in order to compete with a contending American rafting team and be the first to raft the Yellow River in its entirety," the narrator explains, and he goes on to say that such risk-taking could never be understood by an American athlete. "If a Chinese team were the first to raft the entirety of the Mississippi, no American would have opposed it," the narrator says, quoting from the American rafting athlete Ken Warren, who reportedly made the comment. "Mr. Warren couldn't connect today's rafting expeditions with Western warships storming into China's rivers and seaports more than one hundred years ago. Chinese young people, on the other hand, cannot forget."[44]

Accompanying the narrator's voice is a montage sequence intercutting between a wide range of historical footage and contemporary images. It starts with archival footage of a navy battle, most likely historical footage of the Russo-Japanese War, discussed at length in chapter 1. The historical bombardment of navy ships cuts to the contemporary Chinese rafters beginning their ill-fated expedition, and Chinese men's soccer and women's volleyball teams in their respective games. As devastated Chinese soccer fans weep and riot after their national team loses yet another game, the voice-over comments, "This is a nation that psychologically can't bear to lose again." The women's volleyball team beats the United States to win another championship, yet as the players break down in tears and embrace one another to celebrate the victory, the voice-over says apprehensively, "What would happen if they were to lose next time?"

The montage sequence continues. A long queue of young people wait in front of the American Embassy for visas to leave China. Overseas Chinese wielding expensive cameras arrive in tour groups. Historical footage appears again—colonial officers patrolling the streets of Beijing, Sun Yat-sen's revolutionary army in a military parade from Lai Manwai's 1927 film, Red Guards shouting with joy at Tiananmen Square being inspected by Chairman Mao in 1966, and tearful faces on the long Chang'an Avenue in Beijing, where people gathered to bid a last farewell to Zhou Enlai in 1976 (from *Draw Your Sword*). Ending this sequence are two images superimposed on each other: Red Guards marching under the banner of "The Proletarian Cultural Revolution," and a wooden plow pulled by oxen digging into the soil. The narrator comments, "Hidden behind these phenomena is the grief of the nation's soul. This grief has to do with the fact that [our] civilization has declined."

Exemplifying the series' overall aesthetics, this montage sequence brought archival footage from nearly a century of wars and destruction and the Cultural Revolution into clashing juxtapositions with contemporary images of grief, distress, and disorientation. In documentary films made before 1988, one can find hardly any documentary images from the Cultural Revolution, either in biography films or in television programs such as *Today in History*. Although the producers of *Today in History* had initially hoped to include images of events during the Cultural Revolution in the program, not a single one was used in the show during the entire year of its running.[45] Here these historical images reappeared. Furthermore, *River Elegy* did not use these archival materials to build biographies, as in the rehabilitation films of the early 1980s, or to rewrite specific historical events, as in the historical documentaries of the mid-1980s. Like the earlier river documentaries, it was interested in excavating historical sediment, yet it no longer relished the riches of regional histories and cultures like *Yangtze* or dealt with concrete social problems such as water pollution like *Grand Canal*. Instead, it aimed for a sweeping cultural critique of the Chinese civilization to find the "deep structures" of the society responsible for the repeated failures of modernization and cyclical recurrences of destruction. The iconoclastic impulse of this critique was clear. The Great Wall and the Grand Canal were praised as major achievements of the Chinese people in *Grand Canal*. *River Elegy* presented them instead as manifestations of tyrannical rule and coercive mass labor. The Yellow River, like the Yangtze, has been considered one of China's mother rivers, yet it was portrayed in *River Elegy* as despotic and cyclically violent, with deadly floods that devoured its own children. The images of Liu Shaoqi's family reclaiming and scattering his ashes to the ocean reappeared in the fifth episode, "Mindful of Potential Perils" (*Youhuan*). The narrator comments: "Liu Shaoqi's white bones and ashes certainly demonstrate the incredible cruelty of the Cultural Revolution and the tragedy of our times. However, looking at his individual fate alone cannot reveal to us the origin of the tragedy."

River Elegy insisted that serious reflection on history was necessary in order to imagine the society's future, and this resonated with a society that had yet to fully reckon with the gains and losses from its socialist past, while already caught up in the deepening anxieties of the reform era. According to Su Xiaokang, one of *River Elegy*'s writers, by the late 1980s an anxiety that China might enter another tragic crisis had surfaced. The year 1988, a dragon year in the Chinese zodiac, was one complete zodiac cycle from the previous dragon year of 1976, when Mao Zedong had passed away and the Cultural Revolution had come to an end. As 1988 approached, Su wrote, rumors began to spread that another round of disaster was about to hit China, and people rushed to the stores to purchase firecrackers to fend off evil spirits.[46]

There were indeed many reasons for anxiety. An era of reform and opening up, the 1980s saw heated contestations over the direction and extent of reform at the party center, among intellectuals, and in the society at large. While the CCP in general supported reform—though the top leadership was divided on how to go about it—the party saw stability as a precondition for development and did not hesitate to crack down on dissent when its authority was challenged. In October–December 1983, the CCP launched the Anti–Spiritual Pollution Campaign to strengthen censorship and punish intellectuals who reinterpreted Marx or engaged in non-Marxist political theories. In response to the first major student protests in the reform era from December 1986 to January 1987, the CCP initiated the Anti–Bourgeois Liberalization Campaign, and the then party secretary Hu Yaobang resigned over accusations of "taking a laissez-faire attitude towards bourgeois liberalization."[47] Intellectuals, with memories of the Anti–Rightist Campaign and the Cultural Revolution still fresh in their minds, were wary of these campaigns in the new era. In 1986, in a collection of essays, the veteran writer Ba Jin called for the building of a museum dedicated to the Cultural Revolution to prevent it from happening again: "Some people say, happening again? That's impossible. I want to ask, 'Why is it impossible?' These years I have repeatedly thought this question over. I want to get a clear and certain answer, is it possible, or not? Only then I will stop having nightmares." Ba Jin went on to describe his fears during the Anti–Spiritual Pollution Campaign, which punished a number of intellectuals for critiquing "socialist alienation," advocating humanism and other supposedly non-Marxist political and economic theories, and strengthened party control over freedom of expression and the reform process in general. This, Ba Jin wrote, reminded him of the years leading to the Cultural Revolution: "It's not true that there is no soil or climate today to breed a second Cultural Revolution; on the contrary, it seems that all conditions are ready for it. If the aforementioned 'less than one month' [referring to the Anti–Spiritual Pollution Campaign] had lasted a bit longer, or had doubled or tripled its scale, then the situation might have gotten out of hand. After all, there are many people who could profit from a Cultural Revolution."[48]

Besides a periodic resurfacing of political campaigns to tighten ideological control, other reform policies created new contradictions in the broader society. With the restructuring of the state enterprises beginning in 1984, job security and welfare for urban workers began to be attenuated, and income inequality was on the rise. The introduction of market mechanisms in a state-planned economy brought inflationary pressure, while the dual-track price system allowed power-holders at different levels to exploit the difference between a commodity's (lower) price in the planned economy and its (higher) price on the market, fostering widespread corruption. These developments brought new conflicts of interests between different departments within the bureaucracy, between the localities and the center, and between different social strata reaping unequal benefits from the reform process.[49] It also intensified disagreements on the direction and pace of reform at the party center, between reformers such as Zhao Ziyang and Deng Xiaoping, who were eager to push through thorough market reform, and leaders such as Chen Yun, who believed that the market should not overtake the primacy of socialist planning.[50] As people began to question "the legitimacy of the redistribution of benefits that was proceeding in the name of the reform . . . as well as the legitimacy of the course of the redistribution process itself," which Wang Hui argues provided the impetus to the Tiananmen protests in 1989, the government's attempt to liberalize commodity prices in the summer of 1988 resulted in a wave of panic buying, bank runs, high inflation, and worker protests all over the country.[51]

In such a historical conjuncture, *River Elegy*'s bold iconoclasm and critique must have been exhilarating to viewers. Within just a month of the documentary's premiere, the writers Su Xiaokang and Wang Luxiang, the director Xia Jun, and CCTV received thousands of letters from viewers from all walks of life—students, teachers, doctors, soldiers, unemployed youth, retirees. Many letters were composed immediately after the letter-writer had watched an episode, often in the middle of the night. "It's five minutes after midnight on June 19. I had waited for a long time to watch 'Light of Inspiration' (*Lingguang*), the second [sic] episode of *River Elegy*, and now, having watched it, I couldn't fall asleep. Since television came to China, there has never been such a wonderful program," wrote one viewer.[52] Another viewer wrote about the anguish she had felt as a long-time Communist Party member. "Since the age of sixteen, I had devoted myself to the grand cause of anti-Japanese resistance and liberating the whole of humankind. . . . However, the cause now has turned into ashes. . . . What have I done right? What have I done wrong? Why have things turned out so terribly? How will people in the future judge us?" Praising the boldness of the filmmakers to take on these hard questions, the same writer questioned why CCTV changed the broadcasting time of the series from around eight o'clock for the first episode to near midnight for the later episodes. "Why do you place this gem at a corner, not giving it the attention it deserves? Is it true that you actually don't want people to see it?" She ended the letter by requesting a rerun of the series at an earlier hour, so all would have a chance to watch it.[53]

Critics writing at the time marveled at *River Elegy*'s mobilization of montage to construct historical narratives. Its juxtaposition of disparate historical phenomena was thought to ignite historical imagination across a longer time span and allow viewers to think about multiple social and cultural factors simultaneously. "The images in *River Elegy*, when seen on their own, were very commonplace.... Scattered across thousands of years and tens of thousands of kilometers, all the people and historical events in these images seemed to have nothing to do with each other. However, when they were edited together, they exploded into such intense intellectual brilliance and emotional power," wrote one critic.[54] "*River Elegy* didn't mechanically assemble images together. Rather, the assembling was done in such a way that it revealed what was hiding behind the history and buried in the depths of the social organizations and cultural psychologies of the Chinese people.... It was as if we didn't just drift down the Yellow River on the surface, but went all the way to the riverbed, dug out the soil that had accumulated there for thousands of years, and took a good look," wrote another.[55]

Over the years, *River Elegy* has been rightly critiqued for its culturalist approach and binary constructions that pitted what it called the "yellow" Chinese civilization—the poverty and stagnation of the yellow earth, the cyclical crises of the Yellow River, and the subservience to despotism in dragon worship—against the "blue" Western civilization of seafaring, industrial capitalism, and democracy. Jing Wang observes that *River Elegy* betrayed an intense elite nostalgia for a bygone golden age of the Chinese Empire, and that the narrator's "vision for the future is helplessly and unconsciously embedded in the same rhetoric of imperialistic nationalism [that it criticizes]."[56] Xiao Liu points out that *River Elegy*'s culturalist analysis not only drew from the Orientalist stagnancy thesis but was also heavily indebted to the influence of postwar modernization theory, which had "successfully explained the 'superiority' of the West as that of culture, concealing the history of colonial expansion accompanying the rise of capitalism."[57] Both Wang's and Liu's analyses point to the temporal conundrum, or, in Liu's words, "the strange loops," in which Chinese intellectuals, earnestly seeking solutions for the country, were nevertheless caught. Attempting to reckon with the problems both of the Mao era and of the reform process, the writers of *River Elegy* became enmeshed in a "modernization" discourse that both looped them back to the "self-strengthening" nationalism in the early twentieth century and pushed them toward the late Cold War development of neoliberalism.

As I mentioned earlier, documentary filmmakers had attempted to bring more interactivity and reflexivity to television and reinvigorate documentary as a medium to reconstitute the party and the people by giving priority to the varied lived experiences of the people. *River Elegy* shifted away from the dialogical and reflexive and instead adopted a singular, male, and authoritative narrative voice. Instead of listening to the people, the documentary series featured interviews with almost exclusively intellectuals. Jin Guantao, a writer and consultant for *River Elegy*, expressed his enthusiasm for television as a new medium for enlightenment: "The enormous influence of *River Elegy* in the country shocked me. It showed me how much the Chinese people needed ideas, just like the dried-up Yellow Earth needed rain." If the cultural enlightenment of the past relied on books, newspapers, and magazines, Jin wrote, intellectuals of today should make use of television to create a new culture.[58] The characterization of the people as dried yellow earth waiting for ideas to be bestowed from above can be found throughout *River Elegy*, and particularly in the inclusion in the series of sequences from feature films such as *Yellow Earth* (1984) and *Old Well* (1985) that depicted deity workshop and dire poverty in rural China.

This vanguardism wasn't new: we have seen it in the first chapter of this book, as intellectual as political and technocratic elites in late Qing and early Republican periods resorted to media practices such as photography and cinema to support their cultural and political leadership. During the Maoist period, intellectuals' roles were redefined. They became the mediator between the party and the masses, and their work was meant to support a dialectical, mutually constitutive relationship between the two. As I discussed in chapter 5, this mediation came to a severe crisis. In the 1980s this mediation work was, to some extent, on the mend, and television played an important role in such mending, or rehabilitation. Yet the contestations between the party and the intellectuals over directions of change continued. *River Elegy*, in effect, brought the intellectual back to its traditional leadership position, bypassing and replacing the party in its authoritative positioning.

River Elegy, however, is more than its narrative voice. The empathetic and astute critic Jing Wang has observed that "*He shang* is not just a verbal construct. It also speaks to us through the camera. And as a visual representation, it is able to transcend the ideological enclosure determined by the written text."[59] The immense popularity of the series among Chinese viewers at the time also confirms a remarkable affective power, which I argue derived from *River Elegy*'s commitment to the unfinished business of mourning, rather than its proposal of easy solutions to China's complex problems.

Commenting on the ethical imperative to care for justice beyond the living present, Jacques Derrida observes that to learn to live a good life means to learn to live with specters, including those who are already dead and those who are not yet born. Specters are not docile: they are strange, out-of-control creatures who mark a past that refuses to conform to any simple narrative or any imposed timeline of history: "Haunting is historical, to be sure, but it is not dated, it is never docilely given a date in the chain of presents, day after day, according to the instituted order of a calendar." A spectral moment, then, forces open existing historical narratives, gives ethical weight to both the past and the future in the economy of time and raises questions that have been repressed.[60] Taking inspiration from Derrida, Alessia Ricciardi proposes a "poetics of mourning" as a new strategy to represent the past. She argues against Freud's pragmatic view regarding mourning: "Freud's account of the working-through of loss adopts a pseudo-pragmatic tone that presupposes a certain indifference to the value of a past that the reality principle eventually must declare nonexistent." While Freud believes that mourning should aim at disentanglement and forgetting, Ricciardi argues otherwise. The "poetics of mourning," according to Ricciardi, "neither upholds any myth of progress through forgetting, nor affirms a unique genealogical path back to the past through nostalgia. It insists instead on openness to different levels and components of loss. . . . [It] seeks not to deny or disguise the strangeness of the past, but in fact to visualize it critically and thus to greet it with ethical attention."[61]

It is on the point of how to mourn that the voice-over of *River Elegy* and its powerful montages of historical images diverged. The voice-over, similar to the Freudian position, advocated for a severing of the past based on what it considered to be the "reality checks": the supposed decline of the world's "agrarian" civilization, and the ultrastable system of feudalism and tyrant worship that supposedly underlay Chinese political traditions. The series' engagement with historical and contemporary footage, however, did a different work of mourning. Shining flashlights on the past, it acknowledged the profound losses that had occurred on many levels and throughout China's revolutionary century and brought these fragments from the past into montage to illuminate one another. The beginning montage sequence, discussed at length earlier, is a good example, with its evocations of previous wars and revolutions, juxtaposition of Chinese nationals leaving and overseas Chinese returning, and superimposition of images from the Cultural Revolution and from rural poverty (both of which the Red Guard generation experienced as they participated in struggles in the cities before being sent to the countryside for reeducation). All these are put together to testify to the complex tempo-spatial multiplicities that engulfed not only the unfolding of Chinese revolutions but also the profound experiences and memories that underlay these radical social changes as their impetus and aftermath. The coexistence of narrative enclosure at the level of the voice-over and open illumination at the level of image in *River Elegy* help us reconsider what made *River Elegy* a landmark documentary.

I began this book with documentary's emergence in the early twentieth century. In the post-Mao decade, some of the historical moving images we encountered in the earlier parts of the book returned to visibility, as filmmakers made use of archival footage to expand historical imagination, keeping the past alive and its interpretation open. In a decade when the constitutive relationship between the party and the people underwent substantial change, documentary, having now increasingly moved to television, played an important role in creating a more democratic, interactive, and reflexive media culture that supported more inclusive political and social lives. Throughout this eventful decade of rehabilitation, reform and opening, the party's authority over the interpretation of the past and its control over the directions for future change were intensely contested. Even though the intellectuals, aided by the new media of television, became more vocal with their political visions in *River Elegy*, documentary media in this decade drew most energy from the grassroots. From the amateur photography in the April 5 Movement in 1976, to audiences' enthusiastic interactions with rehabilitation documentaries and television programs, the people played an extremely active role in shaping the development of documentary media through the post-Mao decade, and the documentary camera, with increasing spontaneity, responsiveness and boldness, stayed in their midst.

EPILOGUE

Notes on Chinese Independent Documentary

In less than a year after *River Elegy*'s broadcast, the Tiananmen Movement of 1989 erupted. Around the same time, new documentary practices also emerged. Now commonly referred to as "Chinese independent documentary cinema," this new documentary was first practiced in the late 1980s and early 1990s by filmmakers associated with state-run television stations, such as Wu Wenguang, Chen Xiaoqing, Duan Jinchuan, and Li Hong, who had access to high quality video and editing technologies for their own projects. The situation began to change in the late 1990s to the early 2000s, when increasing availability of digital technologies gave rise to a vibrant unofficial film culture. Online film forums disseminated screening information more easily among film fans and offered spaces for film discussion and criticism. Unofficial screening venues mushroomed in galleries, cafes, personal studios, and homes, and pirated video discs allowed residents in urban China to access world cinema like never before. As more and more filmmakers made use of DV cameras and personal computers for independent productions, the early 2000s saw a flourishing of unofficial film festivals where filmmakers and audiences began to gather. The first festivals—China Independent Moving Image Exhibition (Zhongguo duli yingxiang zhan) and the Beijing Queer Film Festival—appeared as early as 2001. The Nanjing Independent Film Festival (CIFF) and the Yunfest in Yunnan, both founded in 2003, and the Beijing Independent Film Forum, founded in 2006 and later renamed the Beijing Independent Film Festival, became the most important showcases for independent documentary in the first decades of this millennium. The Li Xianting Film Fund, headed by the art critic Li Xianting with funds donated by Chinese contemporary artists, not only ran the Beijing festival but also financed productions, liaised with film clubs around the country, and operated a summer film school from its office in the Song Village (Songzhuang) near Beijing.[1]

The Li Xianting Film Fund was where I first became acquainted with Chinese independent documentary. I was a regular at Songzhuang's film festivals and summer film schools between 2009 and 2013 and experienced the incredible creative energy and exhilaration so palpable at these gatherings. Of course, I also witnessed police surveillance and cancellation of selected screenings in earlier festivals, and aggressive raids and closures as time went on. By the mid-2010s most festivals had been forced to close. The CIFF in Nanjing persisted until its closure in early 2020, after prolonged periods of difficulty. The loss of physical exhibition spaces, however, coincided with the emergence of online streaming platforms where independent documentary has migrated and experienced further transformation and diversification.

From the end of the 1980s to the present, Chinese independent documentary has built an impressive repertoire and history of its own. Film scholars, including myself, have closely followed and written about the rich offerings of independent documentary. We have participated in its development not only as researchers, but also as critics, curators, allies, and fellow filmmakers. As the aim of this book is to offer a history of Chinese documentary up to the late 1980s, just before the emergence of independent documentary, I will use this epilogue to briefly comment on these recent developments and reflect on how this book's excavation of China's documentary tradition can help us better understand contemporary documentary. Readers interested in independent documentary can learn more about it from my more substantive writings elsewhere, as well as a large body of excellent scholarship on the topic.[2]

Documentary, as this book has shown, was a medium closely related to political initiatives throughout China's twentieth century. As an eventful medium, documentary participated in the unfolding of events large and small, shaping their inscription, interpretation, and entry into public memory. It mediated political relationalities and networks and helped form technical, political, and historiographic knowledge. Central to documentary's mediations were questions about inclusion and exclusion: who was included in, or excluded from, the political communities that could shape the directions of social and political change, and whose knowledge became valued or obscured in the society's (re)productive processes.

As the "vanguard" of cinema, documentary in the Mao era meant, *in principle*, to facilitate the dialectical relationship between the masses and the party, not only to aid in their mutual constitution, but also to facilitate a collective formation of knowledge and priorities to direct the unfolding of the revolution. In practice, as I discussed in chapters 4 and 5, this dialectical relationship experienced severe crises, manifested by increasing exclusivity of who could be considered part of the "masses," what was permitted in party–people interaction, and the reification of old class categories that obscured, rather than clarified, new contradictions in the society. The Cultural Revolution encouraged the "masses" to challenge the "party," yet by that time, both the masses and the party had become exclusionary and crises-ridden entities, entwined with the crises of mediation that underlay their constitution.

Documentaries of the 1980s, as I discussed in chapter 6, tried to mend the party–people relationship. They participated in rehabilitation campaigns, institutionalization of justice, and historiographic reconstruction. Documentary filmmakers used television as an infrastructure to pursue dialogical, reflexive, and interactive filmmaking, further strengthening documentary's mediating potential and bringing documentary into the midst of lived experience. *River Elegy*, with its authoritative voice-over and expert interviews, broke away from this emphasis on dialogical relationship and lived experience, yet its mobilization of historical and contemporary footage nevertheless populated the screen with documentary images from across the twentieth century, which carried with them, as this book has argued, an eventfulness: positions, relationships, networks, radical aspirations, historical irregularities, and multivalence. The end of the 1980s, however, saw this decade-long effort to reconfigure the party–people relationship came to a disappointing and sorrowful end. The Tiananmen Movement in the spring and summer of 1989 was a deeply mournful, aspirational and multifaceted reckoning by the people with the party, a true event whose message was too new to be named. The violent shattering of this reckoning meant the shattering of the party–people relationship.

Independent documentary, having emerged after the suppression of the Tiananmen protests in 1989 and developed in the post-1989 political ecology, no longer mediated party–people relationships. This refusal to take on this particular work of mediation was among the most substantial meanings of the "independence" in independent documentary. If documentary filmmakers in the Mao era, and even in the 1980s, had encountered their filmed subjects as emissaries from the party state, independent filmmakers after 1989 abandoned such an identity. Documentary became a personal (but still political) act.

This transformation brought substantial benefits. No longer bound by reified official ideology, the personal turn allowed documentary to be more attuned to what was around the camera, to the here and now. The relationship across and around the camera now became interpersonal, which brought a degree of equality between the filmmaker and the filmed subject. It allowed interactions facilitated by the camera to become more spontaneous, dialogical, even confessional and confrontational. Documentary could now reach into difficult spaces in personal lives and perform the work of inquiry and therapy. Autobiographical documentaries exploring family life and broader socialization emerged to further develop documentary's ability to interrogate as well as mend relationships in everyday life and reflect on the political, social, and historical formations of (inter)subjectivities. In chapter 6 I discussed the unfinished business of mourning, which motivated a great deal of documentary filmmaking at state film studios and television stations in the decade after the end of the Cultural Revolution. The personal turn of independent documentary allowed filmmakers to further explore how personal experiences and interpersonal relationships were connected with larger historical circumstances and public memory. If, in the 1980s, documentaries made in the state system began the process of mourning but couldn't carry it through due to restrictions imposed by the party, then independent documentary continued the work of reckoning with the past, this time by investigating the past's varied legacies in personal lives of the present. Scholars have also commented on Chinese independent documentary's persistent interest in dealing with taboo topics and social exclusions, and in giving visibility to marginalized communities.[3] Independent documentary's engagement with the social margins challenges the coercive and oppressive hegemonies found in contemporary Chinese society, which Erin Y. Huang calls, with a productive indeterminacy, "neoliberal postsocialist."[4]

The personal turn of independent documentary was, of course, not without cost. Documentary filmmakers in earlier periods of the twentieth century had almost always worked with political forces that had power to make social and political change. Not mediating the party–people relationship was a conscious choice by independent filmmakers, a resounding vote of no confidence in the party-state. Yet this choice also meant that independent documentary not only had no support from the state but was placed under increasing censorship, which significantly limited the reach of its influence. In the 1990s and early 2000s, with no possibility for legal distribution in the country, independent documentary had a small viewership, mostly composed of audiences at overseas film festivals, as well as Chinese urban middle-class audiences in Beijing, Shanghai, Guangzhou, and other large cities where independent documentary had a small presence in galleries and film clubs. This marginalized position led to a political and ethical impasse, especially for those films that exposed social injustices among marginalized and oppressed people. If documentary's exposure of injustices and sufferings could not reach a substantial Chinese public and foster social change, were they simply providing spectacles of suffering for the consumption of the privileged few? As I've written elsewhere, such uncertainties regarding the meaning and purpose of filmmaking have since troubled the interpersonal relationship between filmmakers and their subjects and sustained heated debates on documentary ethics by filmmakers and film critics.[5]

Around the early to mid-2000s, thanks to a series of developments, independent documentary began to reach a wider public. First, pirated films, including

Chinese independent documentary titles such as Wu Wenguang's *Bumming in Beijing* (*Liulang Beijing*, 1990), Yang Li'na's *Old Men* (*Laotou*, 1997), and Wang Bing's award-winning *The West of the Tracks* (*Tie xiqu*, 2002), became more readily available. Shops selling pirated films on VCD and DVD mushroomed all over China, in big cities as well as small towns. This was how Chinese independent cinema, including fiction films, such as Jia Zhangke's and Zhang Yuan's early films, gained its first mass audience. Wu Wenguang's *Fuck Cinema* (*Cao tamade dianying*, 2005) documented how pirate film stores helped support the cinephilia in this period. Further expanding the viewership was online downloading, which had become a possibility in the early 2000s, thanks to P2P file-sharing software such as emule.

More important, the early 2000s was also a time when more and more activist groups came into being around various issues, such as labor protection, citizen rights, environmental activism, and the fight for equal rights for LBGTQ communities. These activist networks, aided by the internet, as Guobin Yang has shown, began to create sites where political forces for social change could be cultivated.[6] By plugging into these networks, independent documentary gained new political relevance as well as expanded and meaningful viewership. Between 2004 and 2009, documentary became increasingly embedded in social activism, from Hu Jie's *In Search of Lin Zhao's Soul* (*Xunzhao Linzhao de Linghun*, 2005), to Ai Xiaoming's films covering topics such as date rape, village elections, and the plight of HIV/AIDs patients in rural China, to Hu Jie, Ai Xiaoming, and Ai Weiwei's collaborations on a series of documentaries supporting citizen investigations into schoolchildren casualties during the Wenchuan earthquake of 2008.[7] By the late 2000s documentary had allied with many other activist initiatives. Wu Wenguang's Village Memory Project, launched in 2009, uses cinema as a mediator for local memories and as a facilitator for village self-governance. The project has since cultivated prolific young filmmakers such as Zou Xuping and Zhang Mengqi, who have made multiple films in their home villages and combined filmmaking with social work. In Yunnan, the environmental film project From Our Eyes (*Xiangcun zhi yan*) began operation in 2007 and has since trained countless amateur filmmakers (many from non-Han backgrounds) to use the video camera to document environmental change in their villages and collect indigenous ecological knowledge. In 2008 Cui Zi'en, the queer activist and filmmaker, made *Queer China, "Comrade" China* (*Zhi tongzhi*), depicting a large network of queer activists in action. As documentary entered activist networks, its eventfulness became multifold: it strengthened and expanded these networks, energized conversations, and began to form network-specific knowledge to propel the future development of activism. It was no coincidence that independent documentary began to run into more severe problems with government authorities shortly after its activist turn: police surveillance and shutdowns had been sporadic and selective in the 2000s but became more frequent and severe toward the late 2000s, leading to film festival closures and massive reduction of physical gathering space for independent documentary in the 2010s. By then, however, the era of online streaming was already dawning.

In the past decade, documentary has moved onto digital platforms. The independent documentary filmmaker Cong Feng has coined the concept of "social compound eye" (*shehui fuyan*) to describe the "participatory social cognition" that the internet now affords. Even though no one's personal experience is "objective," Cong writes, when people upload videos of what they see, they create materials that "can be compared to each other, complement each other, and can verify, supplement and revise [our understandings] of the overall reality." As "the relay of seeing, and the uniting of perspectives," the social compound eye brings personal visions together to "form a seeing that's at the level of the society, a kind of trustworthy 'just vision' about social realities and history, a kind of revealing perspective that combines facts and truth."[8] Indeed, in China, "relays of seeing" happen almost daily, as people share videos in their WeChat groups and through their Weibo accounts, often reposting in a race with censors who seek to restrict the circulation of "sensitive" materials that could destabilize state authority. A collective and collaborative epistemology, however, is not easy to form. Everywhere the digital sphere has fueled fierce political polarizations. What one sees daily online, and in which community the seeing happens, is shaped by operations of digital capitalism, state surveillance, as well as online activism.

Cong's social compound eye brings to mind the proposal by feminist scholars Sarah Harding and Donna Haraway to create a "strong objectivity" with "situated knowledges." Instead of giving in to the illusion created by modern visual technology, imbricated in militarism, capitalism, colonialism and male supremacy, that one can "[see] everything from nowhere," Haraway proposes that we return embodiment, specificity, partiality, and difference to our understanding and practice of vision. All eyes, including our own organic ones, are active perceptual systems with specific materiality and embodiment, which offer "partial [ways] of organizing world." This partiality must be acknowledged and understood in its specificity in order for a collective and collaborative epistemology based on "situated knowledges," that is, "partial, locatable, critical knowledges," to take hold.[9]

This book has located and investigated documentary's specific entwinement with broader (re)productive processes in the society, its networking capacities and mediation of political relationalities, its radical proposals and hegemonic operations, and the inclusions and exclusions inherent in its constitution of political communities and formation of knowledge. All these have now moved to the online environment, underlain by even more complex and changing structures of power, technological affordances, and everyday media practices.

As I conclude this book, the COVID-19 pandemic has kept Chinese cities under prolonged lockdown. The digital sphere has replaced the square, the street, and other public spaces to become the most vibrant arena where political contestations take place. How documentary will transform in the postpandemic world is yet to be seen, but one thing is certain: for its eventfulness and its situated inquiries into how the world is, and what to be done about it, documentary will continue to be a privileged medium in movements seeking political and social change.

NOTES

Introduction

1. Yasuhiko Yamaguchi, "Tokubetsu kikaku-ten 'magofumi Umeya Shōkichi to Nagasaki' ni yosete" (Preface to the "Sun Yat-sen, Nagasaki, and Shōkichi Umeya" special exhibition) (Nagasaki: Nagasaki Prefecture Cultural Promotion Division, 2012), http://tabinaga.jp/tanken/view.php?hid=20120111191005.
2. "Shina hito to Machitaza ryūgakusei no kakumei enzetsu," *Toyo hinode shinbun* (East ocean sunrise news), November 28, 1911, 3.
3. Kim Fahlstedt, "Marketing Rebellion: *The Chinese Revolution* Reconsidered," *Film History* 26, no. 1 (2014): 87.
4. Umeya's story will be told in detail in chapter 1. See notes to that chapter for references to existing literature on his career and friendship with Sun Yat-Sen.
5. Rebecca Karl, *China's Revolutions in the Modern World: a Brief Interpretive History* (London: Verso, 2020), 2.
6. Substantial scholarship exists on Chinese independent documentary. Examples include Chris Berry, Lü Xinyu, and Lisa Rofel, eds., *Chinese New Documentary Movement: For the Public Record* (Hong Kong: Hong Kong University Press, 2010); Paul G. Pickowicz and Yingjin Zhang, eds., *Filming the Everyday: Independent Documentaries in Twenty-First-Century China* (Lanham, Md.: Rowman & Littlefield, 2017); Luke Robinson, *Independent Chinese Documentary: From the Studio to the Street* (London: Palgrave Macmillan, 2013); Zhen Zhang and Angela Zito, *DV-Made China; Digital Subjects and Social Transformations After Independent Film* (Honolulu: University of Hawaii Press, 2015); Matthew D. Johnson, Keith B. Wagner, Kiki Tianqi Yu, and Luke Vulpiani eds., *China's iGeneration: Cinema and Moving Image Culture for the Twenty-First Century* (London: Continuum, 2014); Ying Qian, "Power in the Frame: China's Independent Documentary Movement," *New Left Review* 74 (March–April 2012),

105–23. For more references to scholarship on independent documentary, see the notes for the epilogue.

7. For a long time, Mao-era documentaries, deposited in the archives of the Central Newsreel and Documentary Studio, were inaccessible for scholarly research. The situation, however, began to change in recent decades. In China's flea markets, a considerable number of Mao-era documentary titles have surfaced. In 2009 private film collectors began to sell DVD copies of these documentaries. These DVDs are rough to watch, since the collectors have only rudimentary means of digitization: they digitize their collections of film reels by projecting them onto a white surface and recording the projection with a digital camera. Since 2010, discovering nostalgic value of Mao-era films and trying to promote "red" culture and nationalism as a cohesive of the "harmonious society," the CCTV began a program entitled "Nostalgic Cinema" (Huaijiu yingyuan), devoted entirely to regular screenings of Mao-era films including both features and documentaries. Film fans immediately recorded these films with home DV recorders, uploaded low-resolution copies online, and put high-resolution copies on sale through online shopping sites. I have benefited from the increasing availability of documentary films from the Mao-era online and have also worked with private collectors in Chengdu and Shanghai.

8. China-based film scholar Lü Xinyu, in her seminal study of new documentary from the 1980s to the early 2000s, shows that practitioners of Chinese new documentary had defined themselves against Mao-era works, which they considered fake, empty, and exaggerated propaganda. Lü Xinyu, "Rethinking China's New Documentary Movement," in *Chinese New Documentary Movement: For the Public Record*, ed. Chris Berry, Lü Xinyu, and Lisa Rofel (Hong Kong: Hong Kong University Press, 2010), 17–19. Yingchi Chu's book-length study of PRC documentary also characterizes Mao-era documentary as dogmatic. The book is an excellent guide to film-related policies, though without analyzing films, her conclusion that the films were dogmatic has more to do with the materials she has used for the study, namely, the party documents that spelled out the "dogmatic formula," than with the films themselves.

9. Bill Nichols, *Representing Reality: Issues and Concepts in Documentary* (Bloomington: Indiana University Press, 1991), 12.

10. For Grierson's discussion on documentary, see John Grierson, "First Principles of Documentary," in *The Documentary Film Reader*, ed. Jonathan Kahana (Oxford: Oxford University Press, 2015), 217–25. Also see Brian Winston, *Claiming the Real II Documentary: Grieson and Beyond* (London: British Film Institute, 2009), 11.

11. Bill Nichols, *Speaking Truth with Film: Evidence, Ethics, Politics in Documentary* (Berkeley: University of California Press, 2016), 14.

12. Philip Rosen, *Change Mummified: Cinema, Historicity, Theory* (Minneapolis: University of Minnesota Press, 2001), 237.

13. Winston, *Claim the Real II Documentary*, 14; Lorraine Daston and Peter Galison eds., *Objectivity* (New York: Zone Books, 2007), 17–54.

14. Rosen, *Change Mummified*, 249.

15. Charles Musser, "Problems in Historiography: The Documentary Tradition Before Nanook of the North," in *The Documentary Film Book*, ed. Brian Winston (London: British Film Institute, 2013), 119–26.

16. Nichols, *Speaking Truth with Film*, 14.

17. See Louis Althusser, *On the Reproduction of Capitalism: Ideology and Ideological State Apparatuses*, trans. G. M. Goshgarian (London: Verso, 2014).

18. Martin Jay, *Downcast Eyes: The Denigration of Vision in Twentieth-Century French Thought* (Berkeley: University of California Press, 1994), 149–210.
19. See Jonathan Crary, *Technique of the Observer: On Vision and Modernity in the Nineteenth Century* (Cambridge, Mass.: MIT Press 1992); Jonathan Sterne, *The Audible Past: Cultural Origins of Sound Reproduction* (Durham, N.C.: Duke University Press, 2003), 87–136.
20. See Janet Walker and Diane Waldman, "Introduction," in *Feminism and Documentary*, ed. Diane Waldman and Janet Walker (Minneapolis: University of Minnesota Press, 1999), 1–36, for a comprehensive and inspiring survey of feminist scholarship on documentary.
21. Jane M. Gaines, "Political Mimesis," in *Collecting Visible Evidence*, ed. Jane M. Gaines and Michael Renov (Minneapolis: University of Minnesota Press, 1999), 93.
22. In China, *jilu*, as in documentary film, was written as either 記 or 紀 in the 1930s and 1940s and only as 紀 afterward. For a comprehensive history of Japanese early documentary film, including *kiroku eiga* and the various other names used in Japan, such as *bunka eiga*, a translation of the German term *kulturfilm*, and *dokyumentarī*, a transliteration of documentary, see Abé Mark Nornes, *Japanese Documentary Film: The Meiji Era Through Hiroshima* (Minneapolis: University of Minnesota Press, 2003).
23. Yingjin Zhang has shown that Chinese cultural elites had considered entertainment cinema as a lowly trade in the 1920s. Yingjin Zhang, "Introduction: Cinema and Urban Culture in Repubilcan Shanghai," in *Cinema and Urban Culture in Shanghai, 1922–1943*, ed. Yingjin Zhang (Stanford, Calif.: Stanford University Press, 1999), 5.
24. Film scholar Emilie Yueh-yu Yeh argues that besides the established genealogy of *yingxi* (shadow play), which strongly associates Chinese early cinema with theater, there are alternative genealogies—such as *yinghua* (shadow picture), which Yeh explores in the context of southern China—that can help us recover cinema's close connection to other forms of projected image (such as lantern slides) and to institutional settings where these projected images were screened. Emilie Yueh-yu Yeh, "Translating Yingxi: Chinese Film Genealogy and Early Cinema in Hong Kong," in *Early Film Culture in Hong Kong, Taiwan and Republican China: Kaleidoscopic Histories*, ed. Emilie Yueh-yu Yeh (Ann Arbor: University of Michigan Press, 2018), 20, 39. For vernacular modernism, see Zhang Zhen, *An Amorous History of the Silver Screen: Shanghai Cinema, 1896–1937* (Chicago: University of Chicago Press, 2005), chap. 1. For political modernism, see Weihong Bao, *Fiery Cinema: The Emergence of an Affective Medium in China, 1915–1945* (Minneapolis: University of Minnesota Press, 2015), 17–26.
25. Vinzenz Hediger and Patrick Vonderau, eds., *Films That Work: Industrial Film and the Productivity of Media* (Amsterdam: University of Amsterdam Press, 2009); Devin Orgeron, Marsha Orgeron, and Dan Streible, eds., *Learning with the Lights Off: Educational Film in the United States* (Oxford: Oxford University Press, 2012); Haidee Wasson, *Everyday Movies: Portable Film Projectors and the Transformation of American Culture* (Oakland: University of California Press, 2021).
26. A great deal of scholarly literature points us to thinking about historical new media, including Lisa Gitelman, *Always Already New: Media, History and the Data of Culture* (Cambridge, Mass.: MIT Press, 2008); John Durham Peters, *Marvelous Clouds: Toward a Philosophy of Elemental Media* (Chicago: University of Chicago Press, 2015); Shaoling Ma, *The Stone and the Wireless: Mediating China, 1861–1906* (Durham, N.C.: Duke University Press, 2021); and others.

27. John Guillory, "Genesis of the Media Concept," *Critical Inquiry* 36, no. 2 (2010): 341–42.
28. Guillory, 346.
29. Bernhard Siegert describes this shift of focus as moving beyond Michel Foucault's concept of the "historical a priori" toward the idea of the "technical a priori." Bernhard Siegert, "Introduction," in *Cultural Techniques: Grids, Filters, Doors, and Other Articulations of the Real* (New York: Fordham University Press, 2015), 4. Examples include Brian Larkin, *Signal and Noise: Media, Infrastructure, and Urban Culture in Nigeria* (Durham, N.C.: Duke University Press, 2008); Peters, *The Marvelous Clouds*; Melody Jue, *Wild Blue Media: Thinking Through Seawater* (Durham, N.C.: Duke University Press, 2020); Yuriko Furuhata, *Climate Media: Transpacific Experiments in Atmosphere Control* (Durham, N.C.: Duke University Press, 2022); and others.
30. Eva Horn, "There Is No Media," *Grey Room* 29 (2007): 8.
31. Thomas Elsaesser, *Film History as Media Archaeology: Tracking Digital Cinema* (Amsterdam: University of Amsterdam Press, 2019), 21, 19.
32. Brian Winston, "Introduction: The Documentary Film," in *The Documentary Film Book*, ed. Brian Winston (London: British Film Institute, 2013), 10.
33. Bill Nichols, *Introduction to Documentary*, 2nd ed. (Bloomington: Indiana University Press, 2010), 31–32.
34. Selmin Kara and Daniel Marcus, "Introduction: Situating Contemporary Documentary," in *Contemporary Documentary*, ed. Daniel Marcus and Selmin Kara (London: Routledge, 2016), 1.
35. Patricia Zimmermann and Helen De Michiel, *Open Space New Media Documentary: A Toolkit for Theory and Practice* (New York: Routledge, 2018), vii.
36. V. I. Lenin, "Where to Begin," in *Lenin: Collected Works* (Moscow: Foreign Language Publishing House, 1961), 5:13–24, https://www.marxists.org/archive/lenin/works/1901/may/04.htm. Originally published in *Iskra*, no. 4 (May 1901).
37. Liang Qichao, "Lun baoguan youyi guoshi" (On the benefits of the press to state affairs), *Shiwu bao* (Contemporary affairs), no. 1 (1896): 1–2.
38. Elizabeth J. Perry, *Anyuan: Mining China's Revolutionary Tradition* (Berkeley: University of California Press, 2012), 5
39. Nick Knight, "Mao Zedong and the Peasants: Class and Power in the Formation of a Revolutionary Strategy," *China Report* 40, no. 1 (2004): 64; Arif Dirlik, "The Predicament of Marxist Revolutionary Consciousness: Mao Zedong, Antonio Gramsci, and the Reformulation of Marxist Revolutionary Theory," *Modern China* 9, no. 2 (1983): 193–94.
40. Lin Chun, "Mass Line," in *Afterlives of Chinese Communisim: Political Concepts from Mao to Xi*, ed. Christian Sorace, Ivan Franceschini, and Nicholas Loubere (Canberra: ANU Press and London: Verso, 2019), 122–23. For Maoist epistemology, see Aminda Smith, "The Living Soul of Mao Zedong Thought," in *Chinese Ideology*, ed. Shiping Hua (London: Routledge, 2021), 151–67.
41. Dirlik, "Marxist Revolutionary Consciousness," 199.
42. William H. Sewell Jr., *Logics of History: Social Theory and Social Transformation* (Chicago: University of Chicago Press, 2005), 100.
43. Sewell, 101.
44. Alain Badiou, *Philosophy and the Event*, trans. Louise Burchill (Cambridge: Polity, 2013), 9–10; Adrian Johnston, "Courage Before the Event: The Force of Affects," *Filozofski vestnik* 14, no. 2 (2008): 126.

45. For the concept of the campaign film, see Yomi Braester, "The Political Campaign as Genre: Ideology and Iconography During the Seventeen Year Period," *Modern Language Quarterly* 69, no. 1 (March 2008): 119–40.
46. The idea of "situatedness" here is inspired by Sandra Harding, *The Science Question in Feminism* (Ithaca, N.Y.: Cornell University Press, 1986); and Donna Haraway, "Situated Knowledges: The Science Question in Feminism and the Privilege of Partial Perspective," *Feminist Studies* 14, no. 3 (Autumn 1988).
47. Thomas Waugh, *The Conscience of Cinema: The Work of Joris Ivens, 1926–1989* (Amsterdam: University of Amsterdam Press, 2016), 195.
48. Badiou, *Philosophy and the Event*, 329.
49. Antonio Gramsci, *Prison Notebooks*, ed. and trans. Quintin Hoare and Geoffrey Nowell-Smith (New York: International, 1971), 55n. Quoted in Dirlik, "Marxist Revolutionary Consciousness," 204–5.
50. Raymond Williams, *Marxism and Literature* (Oxford: Oxford University Press, 1977), 113.
51. Nichols, *Representing Reality*, 3.
52. Tom Gunning, "Before Documentary: Early Nonfiction Films and the 'View' Aesthetic," in *Uncharted Territory: Essays on Early Nonfiction Film* (Amsterdam: Stichting Nederlands Filmmuseum, 1997), 17.
53. Selected titles include *The Great Land Reform* (Weidade tudi gaige, 1953), *Stepping on the Road to Life* (Tashang shenglu, 1949), and *The Transformation of Flower Girls* (Yanhua nüer fanshengji, 1950).
54. Tani Barlow, *In the Event of Women* (Durham, N.C.: Duke University Press, 2022), 215–16.
55. Jason McGrath, "Cultural Revolution Model Opera Films and the Realist Tradition in Chinese Cinema," *Opera Quarterly* 26, no. 2–3 (Spring–Summer 2010): 372.
56. Alain Badiou, "The Cultural Revolution: The Last Revolution?," trans. Bruno Bosteels, *positions: east asia cultures critique* 13, no. 3 (Winter 2005): 481–54.
57. Nico Baumbach, "Jacques Ranciere and the Fictional Capacity of Documentary," *New Review of Film and Television Studies* 8, no. 1 (2010): 67. The italics are my own.
58. Patricia Zimmerman, *Documentary Across Platforms: Reverse Engineering, Media, Place, and Politics* (Bloomington: Indiana University Press, 2019), 2.

1. Emergence

1. *Kiroku eiga* didn't become the predominant way of referring to documentary film until after World War II. Other names include *bunka eiga* and *dokyumentarī*.
2. Michel Foucault, *The Archaeology of Knowledge*, trans. A. M. Sheridan Smith (London: Routledge Classics, 2002), 3–6.
3. Michel Foucault, "Nietzsche, Genealogy, History," in *The Foucault Reader*, ed. Paul Rabinow (New York: Pantheon, 1984), 84.
4. *Jilu* is composed of two characters, *ji* 紀 and *lu* 錄. Both are common characters with frequent usage through recorded Chinese history. According to the earliest Chinese dictionary, *Shuowen jiezi*, dated from the second century, *ji* refers to the practice of sorting, counting, and knotting silk threads, used as a mnemonic method. Besides the idea of recording and inscribing, *lu* also means to collect (*cai*) and acquire (*qu*).

5. For a survey of the field of decolonize thinking, see Walter D. Mignolo, "Preamble: The Historical Foundation of Modernity/Coloniality and the Emergence of Decolonial Thinking," in *A Companian to Latin American Literature and Culture*, ed. Sarah Castro-Klaren (Malden, Mass.: Blackwell, 2008), 12–32. Also see Tani Barlow, "Introduction: On 'Colonial Modernity,' " in *Formations of Colonial Modernity in East Asia*, ed. Tani Barlow (Durham, N.C.: Duke University Press, 1997), 1–20.
6. Zhong Dafeng, "Lun 'yingxi' " (On "shadow play"), *Beijing dianying xuebao* 2 (1985), 55–56; Chen Xihe, "Zhongguo dianying meixue de zairengshi—ping yingxi jubeng zuofa" (Rethinking Chinese film aesthetics: On the writing of filmscripts), *Dangdai dianying* 1 (1986): 82–90.
7. Emilie Yueh-yu Yeh, "Translating Yingxi: Chinese Film Genealogy and Early Cinema in Hong Kong," in *Early Film Culture in Hong Kong, Taiwan and Republican China: Kaleidoscopic Histories*, ed. Emilie Yueh-yu Yeh (Ann Arbor: University of Michigan Press, 2018), 20.
8. Exemplary works include Zhang Zhen, *An Amorous History of the Silver Screen: Shanghai Cinema, 1896–1937* (Chicago: University of Chicago Press, 2005); and Weihong Bao, *Fiery Cinema: The Emergence of an Affective Medium in China, 1915–1945* (Minneapolis: University of Minnesota Press, 2015).
9. Zhong Dafeng, "Lun 'yingxi,' " 57–58.
10. Yingjin Zhang, "Introduction: Cinema and Urban Culture in Republican Shanghai," in *Cinema and Urban Culture in Shanghai, 1922–1943*, ed. Yingjin Zhang (Stanford, Calif.: Stanford University Press, 1999), 5. Zhang is among the few film scholars who have introduced the Commercial Press's filmmaking activities to English-language scholarship. See Yingjin Zhang, *Chinese National Cinema* (New York: Routledge, 2004), 20–21.
11. Yeh, "Translating Yingxi," 34–39.
12. Paul Virilio, *War and Cinema: The Logistics of Perception*, trans. Patrick Camiller (London: Verso, 1989), 85.
13. Virilio, 86–87.
14. Antoine Bousquet, *The Eye of War: Military Perception from the Telescope to the Drone* (Minneapolis: University of Minnesota Press, 2018), 2.
15. For reprographic technologies that allowed woodblock prints to be produced en masse and with texts, see John Clark, "Indices of Modernity: Changes in Popular Reprographic Representation," in *Being Modern in Japan: Culture and Society from the 1910s to the 1930s*, ed. Elise K. Tipton and John Clark (Honolulu: University of Hawai'i Press, 2000), 27–28.
16. Benjamin A. Elman, "Optical and Cognitive Illusions: The MIT Visualizing Cultures Controversy in Spring 2006," *positions: asia critique* 23, no. 1 (2015): 19, 28, 20.
17. Wu Hung, *Zooming In: Histories of Photography in China* (London: Reaktion Books, 2016), 7.
18. The Chinese state had long printed official newspapers (*dibao*) to circulate information across the empire's vast bureaucracy, while suppressing unofficial circulations of government-related information beyond its bureaucratic ranks. Yet this information monopoly by the state crumbled in the mid- to late nineteenth century, first in the newly opened treaty ports, which curtailed the Qing's ability to exert social control in the foreign settlements, and later across the country, due to increasing domestic pressure for political reform and transparency. See Joan Judge, *Print and Politics:"Shibao" and the Culture of Reform in Late Qing China* (Stanford, Calif.: Stanford University Press, 1996), 19–20; Barbara Mittler, *A Newspaper for China: Power, Identity, and*

Change in Shanghai's News Media, 1872-1912 (Cambridge, Mass.: Harvard University Asia Center, 2004), 2-3; and Xiantao Zhang, *The Origins of the Modern Chinese Press: The Influence of the Protestant Missionary Press in Late Qing China* (London: Routledge, 2007), 43-44.

19. Laikwan Pang, *The Distorting Mirror: Visual Modernity in China* (Honolulu: University of Hawai'i Press, 2007), 10; Mittler, *A Newspaper for China*, 43-117; Bao, *Fiery Cinema* 2005. Also see Leo Ou-Fan Lee, *Shanghai Modern: The Flowering of a New Urban Culture in China, 1930-1945* (Cambridge, Mass.: Harvard University Press, 1999); and Zhang Zhen, *An Amorous History of the Silver Screen: Shanghai Cinema, 1896-1937* (Chicago: University of Chicago Press, 2005).
20. Ge Gongzhen, *Zhongguo baoxue shi* (History of Chinese journalism) (1927; Shanghai: Shanghai Guji chubanshe, 2014), 82-87.
21. Weipin Tsai, "The First Casualty: Truth, Lies, and Commercial Opportunism in Chinese Newspapers During the First Sino-Japanese War," *Journal of the Royal Asiatic Society*, 3rd series, 24, no. 1 (2014): 145-63.
22. Liang Qichao, "Lun baoguan youyi guoshi" (On the benefits of the press to state affairs), *Shiwu bao* (Contemporary affairs), no. 1 (1896): 1-2.
23. Liang Qichao, "Lun Zhongguo zhi jiangqiang" (On the growing strength of China), *Shiwu bao*, no. 31 (1897), quoted in Rebecca Karl, *China's Revolutions in the Modern World* (New York: Verso, 2020), 13.
24. Paula Harrell, *Sowing Seeds of Change: Chinese Students, Japanese Teachers, 1895-1905* (Stanford, Calif.: Stanford University Press, 1992), 1-2.
25. James R. Ryan, *Photography and Exploration* (London: Reaktion Books, 2013), 7-10; Charles Musser, "The Travel Genre in 1903-1904: Moving Towards Fictional Narrative," *Iris* 2, no. 1 (1984): 47-60; Tom Gunning, "'The Whole World Within Reach': Travel Images Without Borders," in *Virtual Voyages: Cinema and Travel*, ed. Jeffrey Ruoff (Durham, N.C.: Duke University Press, 2006), 25-41.
26. Gunning, "'The Whole World Within Reach,'" 30, 31.
27. Abé Markus Nornes, *Japanese Documentary Film: The Meiji Era Through Hiroshima* (Minneapolis: University of Minnesota Press, 2003), 3.
28. Gunning, "'The Whole World Within Reach,'" 33.
29. Cheng Yu, *Bingwu riben youji* [Traveling in Japan in 1906] (China: n.p., 1907), https://babel.hathitrust.org/cgi/pt?id=uc1.aa0002266211&view=1up&seq=276.
30. Cheng, "Preface," *Bingwu riben youji*, n.p.
31. Walter Benjamin, *The Work of Art in the Age of Its Technological Reproducibility, and Other Writings on Media*, ed. Michael W. Jennings, Brigid Doherty, and Thomas Y. Levin; trans. Edmund Jephcott et al. (Cambridge, Mass.: Belknap Press of Harvard University Press, 2008), 23-25.
32. Jay David Bolter and Richard Grusin, *Remediation: Understanding New Media* (Cambridge, Mass.: MIT Press, 1999), 56.
33. Yi Gu, "What's in a Name? Photography and the Reinvention of Visual Truth in China, 1840-1911," *Art Bulletin* 95, no. 1 (2013): 120, 121, 128. For a book-length discussion on the importance of technical images in Chinese traditional texts of all kinds, see Francesca Bray, Vera Dorofeeva-Lichtmann, and Georges Métailié eds., *Graphics and Text in the Production of Technical Knowledge in China: The Warp and the Weft* (Leiden: Brill, 2007).
34. Gu, "What's in a Name?," 130. This specific album contains 110 images of the war.
35. Gu, 128. For a discussion on the rise of "objectivity," concurrent with the development of the technology of photography, in the mid- and late nineteenth century and the

epistemic virtues associated with objectivity, see Lorraine Daston and Peter Galison, *Objectivity* (New York: Zone Books), 27–42.
36. *Sheying* became a commonly recognizable word for photography around 1911, though it had been occasionally used previously as well. Gu, "What's in a Name?," 120.
37. Cheng, "Preface," n.p.
38. For discussions on this episode, see David Der-Wei Wang, *The Monster That Is History: History, Violence, and Fictional Writing in Twentieth-Century China* (Berkeley: University of California Press, 2004), 20; and Michael Berry, *A History of Pain: Trauma in Modern Chinese Literature and Film* (New York: Columbia University Press, 2008), 28–32.
39. Lu Xun, "Preface to the First Collection of Short Stories, 'Call to Arms,'" in *Selected Stories of Lu Hsun*, trans. Yang Hsien-yi and Gladys Yang (Beijing: Foreign Languages Press, 1960), 2–3. Cited and translation modified by Rey Chow, *Primitive Passions: Visuality, Sexuality, Ethnography, and Contemporary Chinese Cinema* (New York: Columbia University Press, 1995), 4.
40. Ari Heinrich, *The Afterlife of Images: Translating the Pathological Body Between China and the West* (Durham, N.C.: Duke University Press, 2008), 154–55.
41. Friedrich Kittler, "A Short History of the Searchlight," trans. Geoffrey Winthrop-Young, *Cultural Politics* 11, no. 3 (2015): 385.
42. Chenshu Zhou, "Literature by Other Mediums: Revisiting Lu Xun's Preface to Outcry," *positions: east asia cultures critique* 29, no. 2 (2021): 381.
43. Lu, "Preface," 2–3.
44. Zhang Deming and Ding Xiao, "Jiawu zhanhou qingchao haijun de chongjian" (Rebuilding the Qing navy after the 1895 war), *Qishi cankao* (Qing history review), no. 40 (2012), http://www.qinghistory.cn/qsck/363264.shtml.
45. Zhang Deming and Ding Xiao, "Jiawu zhanhou qingchao haijun de chongjian."
46. Feng Qing, *Zhongguo jindai haijun yu riben* (Chinese modern navy and Japan) (Jilin: Jilin daxue chubanshe, 2008), 86.
47. Komatsu Hiroshi, "Some Characteristics of Japanese Cinema Before World War I," trans. Linda C. Ehrlich and Yuko Okutsu, in *Reframing Japanese Cinema: Authorship, Genre, History*, ed. Arthur Nolletti Jr. and David Desser (Bloomington: Indiana University Press, 1992), 238.
48. Nornes, *Japanese Documentary Film*, 4. Nornes reports that more than ninety titles of Russo-Japanese War films were listed in a Japanese film catalog in 1910.
49. Nornes, 4.
50. Ueda Manabu, "Nichirosensō to eiga" (The Russo-Japanese War and cinema), in *Eiga to sensō—toru yokubō / miru yokubō* (Cinema and war: The desire to shoot / the desire to see), ed. Okumura Masaru (Tokyo: Shinwasha, 2009), 36–37.
51. Yuan Xiluo, "Wang shenghu shequ chutong kuaijian jinshuishi huodong xiezhen ji" (On capturing moving pictures of the completion ceremony of the Chutong torpedo ship in Kobe), *Shen bao*, July 13–15, 1906. I was alerted to Yuan's serialized essays by Li Zhen, "1906nian 'chutong kuaijian jinshuishi' huodong xiezhen yiqi shijuewenhua yiyi" (The moving image of "the completion ceremony of the Chutong torpedo ship" in 1906 and its significance in visual culture), *Journal of Beijing Film Academy*, no. 6 (2019).
52. Yuan, July 13, 2.
53. Yuan, July 13, 2.
54. Yuan, July 14, 2.
55. Yuan, July 14, 2.

56. Komatsu Hiroshi, "Transformation in Film as Reality (Part One): Questions Regarding the Genesis of Nonfiction Film," trans. A. A. Gerow, *Documentary Box* 5 (1994): 3–4. Quoted in Aaron Gerow, *Visions of Japanese Modernity* (Berkeley: University of California Press, 2010), 49.
57. Nornes, *Japanese Documentary Film*, 8, 11–12.
58. Xi, "Zhishi kaiyan huodong yingxi" (Men of ideals begin to screen moving shadow plays), *Shen bao*, July 31, 1906, 9.
59. Xi, "Kaiyan huodong yingxi" (Screening moving shadow plays), *Shen bao*, August 4, 1906, 10.
60. "Xiezhu haijunhui jianzhang" (Brief bylaws of the Society for Assisting the Navy), *Shen bao*, August 31, 1906, 17.
61. Kang Youwei (pseud. Ming Yi), "Gongmin zizhi pian" (On self-government by the citizenry), *Xinmin congbao* (New people's miscellany), no. 7 (1902): 28.
62. See Sally Borthwick, *Education and Social Change in China: The Beginnings of the Modern Era* (Stanford, Calif.: Hoover Institution Press, 1983), 87–103.
63. Gao Jun, *Qingmo quanxuesuo yanjiu: yi baoshanxian wei zhongxin* (End-of-Qing institutions for encouraging education: Focusing on Baoshan County) (Shanghai: Shanghai cishu chubanshe, 2013), 158. Also see "Tichang tongsu jiaoyu" (Promoting popular education), *Shen bao*, April 27, 1907, 19.
64. Yasuhiko Yamaguchi, "Tokubetsu kikaku-ten 'magofumi Umeya Shōkichi to Nagasaki' ni yosete" (Preface to the "Sun Yat-sen, Nagasaki, and Shōkichi Umeya" special exhibition) (Nagasaki: Nagasaki Prefecture Cultural Promotion Division, 2012), http://tabinaga.jp/tanken/view.php?hid=20120111191005&offset=10; "Shina hito to Machitaza ryūgakusei no kakumei enzetsu," *Toyo hinode shinbun* (East ocean sunrise news), November 28, 1911, 3.
65. Film historian Kim Fahlstedt has identified an unattributed eleven-minute film preserved at the Library of Congress as an incomplete copy of this film, but I don't agree with his identification upon close examination. Fahlstedt, "Marketing Rebellion: The Chinese Revolution Reconsidered," *Film History* 26, no. 1 (2014): 80–107.
66. Kosaka Ayano, *Kakumei o purodyusu shita nihonjin* (The Japanese who produced a revolution) (Tokyo: Kodansha, 2010), 31–33, 36–38.
67. Kosaka Ayano, *Nagasakijin Umeya Shōkichi no shōgai* [The Nagasaki man Umeya Shōkichi's career] (Nagasaki: Nagasaki Bunkensha, 2012), 31–32.
68. Peter B. High, "Umeya Shōkichi: The Revolutionist as Impresario" (Nagoya University, n.d.), 119–22, https://www.lang.nagoya-u.ac.jp/proj/socho/mirai/mirai-high.pdf.
69. Kosaka, *The Nagasaki Man*, 53.
70. High, "Umeya Shōkichi," 124.
71. Kosaka, *The Nagasaki Man*, 53.
72. High, "Umeya Shōkichi," 124.
73. Tom Gunning, "Early Cinema as Global Cinema," in *Early Cinema and the "National,"* ed. Richard Abel, Giorgio Bertellini and Rob King (Eastleigh, UK: John Libbey, 2016), 14–15.
74. Umeya Shōkichi, preface to *Katsudō shashin Hyakka hōten* [A treasured encyclopedia of moving pictures] (self-pub., 1911), http://dl.ndl.go.jp/info:ndljp/pid/853860.
75. Kosaka, *The Nagasaki Man*, 54–56.
76. Fahlstedt, "Marketing Rebellion," 87.
77. Nornes, *Japanese Documentary Film*, 6.
78. "Shina hito to Machitaza ryūgakusei no kakumei enzetsu," *Toyo hinode shinbun*, November 28, 1911, 3.

79. Bao, *Fiery Cinema*, 52, 42. Also see Xinyu Dong, "The Laborer at Play: 'Laborer's Love,' the Operational Aesthetic, and the Comedy of Inventions," *Modern Chinese Literature and Culture* 20, no. 2 (Fall 2008), 1–39.
80. "Pi Chengyu shechang zhizao tongsu jiaoyu yingpian chengqing li'an ying zhaozhun" (Approval of Cheng Yu's application to establish a factory to manufacture popular educational films), *Jiaoyu gongbao* 5, no. 3 (December 31, 1918): 131–32.
81. Sun Jiansan, *Sun Mingjing jishi sheying yanjiu* [Sun Mingjing's documentary photography] (Hangzhou: Zhejiang sheying chuban she, 2018), 1:32.
82. Tian Yi, "Huodong yingpian jiaoyushang de shiyong" (The practical use of moving cinema for education), *Progress* 4 (1913): 64–74; Da Ke, "Kexue wanneng ji: Huodong yingxi ke zhu toupiao" (Science is omnipotent: Moving cinema can help voting), *Progress* 6, no. 5 (1914): 97; Han Sheng, "Huodong dianying yongwei guiding gongzuo chengji zhi qitan" (The intriguing tale of moving cinema's use for standardizing work output), *Xiehe journal* 4, no. 25 (1914): 5–7.
83. Liao Weici, "Huodong yingxi yu ziran kexue zhi guanxi" (The relationship between moving cinema and the natural sciences), *Kexue* (Science) 2, no. 10 (1916): 11. Liao's preface is followed by his translation of excerpts from Leonard Donaldson, *The Cinematograph and Natural Science: The Achievements and Possibilities of Cinematography as an Aide to Scientific Research* (London: Ganes, 1912). Widely cited by scholars of early cinema, Donaldson's book highlights the use of films in scientific investigation and exploration, particularly for teaching surgery, as operations could be recorded on film to allow students' experiential learning.
84. Daston and Galison, *Objectivity*, 27–30, 39–40.
85. Lisa Cartwright, *Screening the Body: Tracing Medicine's Visual Culture* (Minneapolis: University of Minnesota Press, 1995), 3.
86. Oliver Gayken, "The Cinema of the Future: Visions of the Medium as Modern Educator, 1895–1910," in *Learning with the Lights Off: Educational Film in the United States*, ed. Devin Orgeron, Marsha Orgeron, and Dan Streible (Oxford: Oxford University Press, 2012), 71.
87. See Katie Day Good, "Sight-Seeing in School: Visual Technology, Virtual Experience, and World Citizenship in American Education, 1900–1930," *Technology and Culture* 60, no. 1 (2019): 98–131.
88. Zhang Zhen, *An Amorous History of the Silver Screen*, 119; Bao, *Fiery Cinema*, 42.
89. In 1917 Henry Doherty, owner of a silk mill in New Jersey, visited Hangzhou and showed an industrial film to Chinese agricultural school students to explain how Japanese and Italian silk producers had improved the quality of raw silk for mechanized silk processing. In 1918 an American consular officer traveled to Wuxi to lecture on new technologies for the production of silk and flour and promised to lend more industrial films to further educate locals. Kashia Amber Arnold, "U.S. Silk Imports During World War I: Contextualizing U.S.–Japanese Relations, Munitions Production, and Wartime Substitution," unpublished paper, University of California, Santa Barbara, n.d., 7–8, https://labor.history.ucsb.edu/sites/secure.lsit.ucsb.edu.hist.d7_labor/files/sitefiles/Kashia%20Arnold%20WWI%20Silk%20Imports.pdf. Also see "Meiguo sishang zaihang zhi zhouxuan" (American silk merchants' activities in Hangzhou), *Shen bao*, May 24, 1917, 10; "Wuxi" (News from the city of Wuxi), *Shen bao*, December 24, 1918, 7.
90. "Yanshuo meiguo zuijin zhi qingxing" (Talks on contemporary American affairs), *Shen bao*, October 18, 1918, 10. The American consulate also lent industrial films to Tsinghua University for screenings. See *Qinghua zhoukan*, no. 161, 1919, 7.

91. "Mei siye gonghui zhi gaoyi" (The lofty friendship from the American Silk Business Association), *Shen bao*, October 2, 1919, 10.
92. Zhang Wei, "Changwei yushan yu shangwuyingshuguan" (Nagao Uzan and the Commercial Press), in *Minjian yingxiang* (Vernacular moving images), ed. Ma Changlin (Shanghai: Tongji daxue chubanshe, 2013), 2:183; "Shanghai shangwu yinshuguan tezhi tongsu jiaoyu zhi buzhupin huandeng yingpian" (Lantern slides specially made by Shanghai Commercial Press to aid popular education), *Shi bao*, April 5, 1914, 1. Quoted in Huang Dequan, *Zhongguo zaoqi dianying shi kaozheng* (Evidential studies on Chinese early cinema) (Beijing: Zhongguo dianying chubanshe, 2012), 87.
93. "Wei zizhi yingpian zhun mianshui chengwen" (Application on tax exemption for self production of films), *Shangwu yinshuguan tongxunlu*, May 1919. Quoted in Matthew Johnson, "International and Wartime Origins of the Propaganda State" (Ph.D. diss., University of California, San Diego, 2008), 117–18.
94. Xiao Chunfang, "Shangwu yinshuguan dianying yewu xiaoshi yuanyin yanjiu" (A study of the reason for the disappearance of the Commercial Press's filmmaking venture), *Journal of Beijing Film Academy*, no. 4 (2012): 93.
95. "Fenshao cuntu zhi disiri" (Burning remaining opium for the fourth day), *Shen bao*, January 21, 1919, 10.
96. At the annual meeting of the Chinese Professional Education Association in 1918, for example, lantern slides made by the association were shown alongside films made by the Commercial Press. "Zhonghua zhiye jiaoyushe tongxun: dianying" (China professional education association notice: Film), *Shen bao*, May 4, 1918, 11.
97. The Commercial Press contracted an American cinematographer from the YMCA in Shanghai to make a three-part newsreel. The film was sold to a Japanese distributor through the games' institutional connections. Efforts were also made to send the film to the Philippines. "Shishi caiji guonei zhi bu" (Selection of news: Domestic section), *Lai fu*, no. 159 (June 1921): 11–12.
98. Xiao, "A Study of the Reason for the Disappearance," 95.
99. Wang Xifeng, "Diyici zhifeng zhanzheng qian de dianbaozhan" (War of telegraph before the first Zhifeng war), *Journal of Liaoning Normal University, Social Science Edition*, no. 2 (2008): 120–23. I thank Fuyin Shen for alerting me to telegraph's importance and this reference.
100. Huang Jianmin, "Sun Zhongshan de yingxiang yu xingxiang yanjiu chutan" (Initial explorations on Sun Yat-sen's cinematic image), in *Shijie Shiyexia de Sun Zhongshan yu zhonghua minzu fuxing: jinian Sun Zhongshan xiansheng dancheng 150zhounian guoji xueshu tantaohui lunwenji* (Sun Yat-sen and the revival of the Chinese nation in international perspective: An international academic conference to commemorate the 150th anniversary of Mr. Sun Yat-sen's birth), no. D (2016): 154–55, http://www.sunyat-sen.org/html/yjcg/szsyj09.pdf.
101. Wu Yigong ed., *Shanghai dianying zhi* (Shanghai film chronicle) (Shanghai: Shanghai shehui kexueyuan chubanshe, 1999), 462. Li Zongren appeared in Sanmin Film Company's *Gemingjun zhanshi* (A history of Revolutionary Army's battles, 1927). See Wang Xiaohua, "Zaoqi yingxiang ziliao duiyu huzheng dang'an yi yanjiu lishi zhi zuoyong" (Early cinema's role in archival cross-checking and historical research), in *Zhongguo zaoqi jilu dianying yu guomin geming yingxiang dang'an* (Chinese early documentary cinema and the image archive of the Nationalist Revolution), ed. China Film Archive (Beijing: Zhongguo guangbo dianshi chubanshe, 2012), 36. Bai Chongxi appeared in *Beifa wanchengji* (The completion of the Northern Expedition, 1928), directed by Wang Yuanlong and Wang Cilong and produced by the Dazhonghua baihe

266   1. Emergence

      Film Company. It was a cinematic reconstruction of one of the major battles that led to the successful completion of the Northern Expedition. Bai lent his soldiers to play both themselves and the enemy army. See Wu Yigong ed., *Shanghai dianying zhi*, 462, http://www.shtong.gov.cn/node2/node2245/node4509/node15254/node16773/node63939/userobject1ai111747.html, accessed January 15, 2012.

102. *War on Sea, Land, and Air* screened at the Palace Cinema for four days before moving to the Victoria Cinema (New Central Cinema) on December 2, 1928, for another three days. Advertisements in *Shen bao* ended on December 4, 1928.

103. "Guomin gemingjun hailukong dazhan ji" (A record of *National Revolutionary Army's war on sea, land, and air*), *Shen bao*, December 1, 1928, 28, and December 4, 1928, 25.

104. "A Record of *National Revolutionary Army's War on Sea, Land, and Air*," November 11, 1928, 25; December 1, 1928, 28; and November 25, 1928, 28 (for quote).

105. "A Record of *National Revolutionary Army's War on Sea, Land, and Air*," December 1, 1928, 28.

106. Lai collaborated with Brodsky to make two short fiction films: a comedy skit, *Tou shaoya* (Stealing a baked duck) and a costume play, *Zhuangzi shiqi* (Zhuangzi tests his wife), a morality tale with the ancient Chinese philosopher Zhuangzi (third century BCE) and his disloyal wife as protagonists. Never a radical, Lai turned to Chinese traditional morality tales for resources—such as the loyalty of wife to husband—to support devotion to a patriarchal nation-state.

107. Feng Qun, *Li Minwei ping zhuan* (Annotated biography of Li Minwei) (Beijing: Wenhua yishu chubanshe, 2009), 58–59.

108. In 1923 Lai traveled to Japan to document Chinese sportsmen's performance at the Far Eastern Championship Games and worked with Mei Lanfang to film five of his modernized Peking opera performances. See excerpts from Lai's diary in Yu Xiaoyi and Lai Shek, eds., *Zhongguo dianying de tuohuangzhe Li Minwei* (The pioneer of Chinese cinema Lai Manwai) (Wuhan: Changjiang wenyi chubanshe, 2005), 122.

109. Yu Xiaoyi and Lai Shek, 123–24.

110. The original film from 1928 is no longer extant, destroyed in Japanese bombings of Shanghai in 1938. What remains are fragments from two later versions, both re-edited by Lai Manwai himself—first in 1940, at the height of the Second Sino-Japanese War, and then in 1950, just after the Nationalist Party moved to Taiwan after the Chinese Communist Party declared victory on the mainland. In 1940 Lai changed the title to *Xunye qianqiu: jianguoshi zhi yiye* (Lasting victories: A page in the founding of the nation) and added a female narrative voice to the soundtrack. The 1950 version replaced the female voice-over with a male voice but left the images untouched. Sixteen minutes of the 1940 version and thirty-four minutes of the 1950 version remain today. My analysis is based on the 1950 version, preserved at the Hong Kong Film Archive. The extant copies of the film bear traces from multiple historiographical acts by Lai Manwai to adjust the film to suit changing political situations in China. Yet there is still good reason to believe that the 1950 version bears considerable similarity to the silent version, completed in 1928. All footage in the film had been shot prior to the completion of the original film. Lai spent only one day in 1940 re-editing the film, which means that besides recording and adding a voice-over, he couldn't have significantly altered the images. The 1950 version is different from the 1940 version only by the newly recorded voice-over. The fact that the film included mostly portraits for the conservative faction of the Nationalist Party suggest that some figures might have been erased during re-editing in 1940 or 1950.

111. "Juchang xiaoxi" (Theater news), *Shen bao*, November 29, 1928, 22.

112. "A Record of *National Revolutionary Army's War on Sea, Land, and Air*," *Shen bao*, December 1, 1928, 28.
113. Teresa Castro, "Aerial Views and Cinematism, 1898–1939," in *Seeing from Above: the Aerial View in Visual Culture*, ed. Mark Dorrian and Frédéric Pousin (London: Tauris, 2013), 119.
114. Lynne Kirby, *Parallel Tracks: The Railroad and Silent Cinema* (Durham, N.C.: Duke University Press, 1997), 2.
115. Dziga Vertov, *Kino-Eye: The Writings of Dziga Vertov*, ed. Annette Michelson, trans. Kevin O'Brien (Berkeley: University of California Press, 1984), 17.
116. Audrey Linkman, *The Victorians: Photographic Portraits* (London: Tauris Parke Books, 1993), 46.
117. "A Record of *National Revolutionary Army's War on Sea, Land, and Air*," *Shen bao*, December 1, 1928, 28.
118. A complete copy is no longer extant. What remains are twelve film reels that have only recently been identified as constituting a longer documentary on Feng. See Chen Mo, "Women kandaole shenme, women ruhe kan," in *Chinese Early Documentary Cinema and the Image Archive of the Nationalist Revolution*, ed. China Film Archive, 8, note 1.
119. Yu Xiaoyi and Lai Shek, *The Pioneer of Chinese Cinema*, 125, 124.

2. Bombs and Seafarings

1. S. A. Smith, *Like Cattle and Horses: Nationalism and Labor in Shanghai, 1895–1927* (Durham, N.C.: Duke University Press, 2002), 168.
2. Xu Bibo, "Jilupian 'wusa huchao' paishe jingguo" (Making the documentary *The May Thirtieth Shanghai Movement*), *Zhongguo dianying*, no. 5, 1957, 62.
3. Xu Bibo, 62.
4. See "Xuejie zuori xiaoxi" (Yesterday's news from the universities), seventh item in "Can'an yijinghou zhi shanghai zuoxun" (News received yesterday from Shanghai), *Shen bao*, June 23, 1925, 9. Also "Jiuji bagong gongren xiaoxi" (News on strike relief), *Shen bao*, August 1, 1925, 13.
5. Xu Bibo, "Jilupian 'wusa huchao' paishe jingguo," 62; Fei Jingbo, *Zhejiang dianying jishi 1908–1990* (Chronicle of Zhejiang cinema) (Hangzhou: Zhejiang guji chubanshe), 11.
6. Laikwan Pang, *Building a New China in Cinema: The Chinese Left-wing Cinema Movement, 1932–1937* (Lanham, Md.: Rowman & Littlefield, 2002), 9. For the hard versus soft cinema debate, see Zhang Zhen, *An Amorous History of the Silver Screen: Shanghai Cinema, 1896–1937* (Chicago: University of Chicago Press, 2005), 267–74.
7. No Chinese film studios attempted to make regularly released newsreels until 1933, when the state-run Central Film Studio (Zhongyang dianying sheying chang) in Nanjing collaborated with the United China Film Studio (Lianhua) to bring out a weekly news program. Zhi, "Meizhou qingbao: Lianhua yu Zhongyang dangbu hezuo xinwenpian" (Weekly information: Lianhua collaborates with the central office of the party on news films), *Lianhua huabao* 1, no. 23 (1933); 1; "Lianhua meizhou chuban xinwenpian yijuan" (Lianhua releases a reel of news films weekly), *Lianhua huabao* 1, no. 22 (1933), 1.
8. John Grierson, "First Principles of Documentary," in *Grierson on Documentary*, ed. Forsyth Hardy (New York: Praeger, 1971), 145, 201, 146.

9. Joseph Clark, *News Parade: The American Newsreel and the World as Spectacle* (Minneapolis: University of Minnesota Press, 2020), 25–26.
10. Ying Zhu, *Chinese Cinema During the Era of Reform: The Ingenuity of the System* (Westport, Conn.: Praeger, 2003), 191.
11. Ying Zhu, 194.
12. Cheng Bugao, "Xinwen yingpian tan" (On news films), *Mingxing tekan*, no. 5 (1925): 1.
13. "Amateur Gets Film of Disaster at Sea," *Exhibitor's Trade Review*, May 9, 1925, discusses this incident and the production of the newsreel by International Newsreel.
14. Clark, *News Parade*, 20.
15. As explained in chapter 1, we now have a re-edited version made by the filmmaker in 1940.
16. "Meishang sanyingpian gongsi lianhe shequ rijun baoxing xiezhen" (Three American film companies collaborate on filming Japanese acts of violence), *Shen bao*, February 19, 1932, 2.
17. Terry Ramsaye, "Fox and Hearst Newsreels Give Full Report of Shanghai Battle," *Motion Picture Herald*, March 5, 1932, 16. The paper printed separate advertisements for both Fox Movietone news and Hearst Metrotone news. Hearst Metrotone relied on Fox Movietone sound systems, and the article seems to suggest that the production was done by the same team of filmmakers.
18. Robert Littell, "A Glance at the Newsreel," *American Mercury*, November 1933, 264, 271. Quoted in Clark, *News Parade*, 53.
19. Ramsaye, "Fox and Hearst Newsreels," 16.
20. Clark, *News Parade*, 118.
21. Clark, 103.
22. Advertisement spread for Hearst Metrotone newsreels on the Battle of Shanghai, *Motion Picture Herald*, March 5, 1932, 46–47.
23. "War in China," *Motion Picture Herald*, March 26, 1932, 39.
24. "'Shanghai zhanshi' gongying" (Premiere of *Chronicle of the Battle of Shanghai*), *Shen bao*, May 16, 1932, 16, 18; "Gegonsi jingzheng shezhi zhi huzhan yingpian" (The Battle of Shanghai films that all companies are competing to make), *Diansheng ribao*, July 8, 1932, 2. The Huichong Film Studio, according to this report, used footage from non-Chinese filmmakers, though their sources remained unknown. The Jinan Film Studio's *Blood of Shanghai* (*Songhu xie*) was said to include fake battle scenes in the second half of the film.
25. "Shijiulujun guangrongshi" (The glorious history of the 19th Route Army), film advertisement, *Shen bao*, July 6, 1932, 23. The advertisement ran from July 6 to 11, and then again from August 23 to 25.
26. "Gegonsi jingzheng shezhi zhi huzhan yingpian," 2.
27. "Guopian gongsi zhi mangmu" (The blindness of domestic film companies), *Diansheng ribao*, July 9, 1932, 2.
28. "Gegonsi jingzheng shezhi zhi huzhan yingpianxu" (The Battle of Shanghai films that all companies are competing to make, continued), *Diansheng ribao*, July 9, 1932, 2.
29. Cheng Bugao, *Yingtan yijiu* (Old memories of the film arena) (Beijing: Zhongguo dianying chubanshe, 1983), 20–34.
30. "Shanghai zhi zhan" (The Battle of Shanghai), film advertisement, *Shen bao*, August 4, 1932, 22.
31. "Zhandi qingtian" (Romance on the battlefield), *Dianying yuebao*, no. 4, 1928, 17–19.

32. "'Zhandi Ergunü' yishu xinwenpian" (*Two Orphan Girls on Battlefield* is also a news film), *Kaimaila* (Camera), no. 82, 1932, 1. Also see "War in China (Educational): Enlightening, Timely," *Motion Picture Herald*, March 26, 1932, 39.
33. "Shanghai zhi zhan," 22.
34. "Zuo chenguang shiying 'Shanghai zhi zhan' pingfan" (Yesterday's test screening of *Battle of Shanghai* at the Chenguang Theater: Ordinary), *Dianying ribao*, July 23, 1932, 1, 2.
35. "'Shanghai zhi zhan' zengying cishu" (More screenings for *Battle of Shanghai*), *Shen bao*, August 5, 1932, 14.
36. Pang, *Building a New China in Cinema*, 9, 198, 201, 202.
37. Charles Laughlin, *Chinese Reportage: The Aesthetics of Historical Experience* (Durham, N.C.: Duke University Press, 2002), 2, 12, 81, 10.
38. Cheng Bugao, "Kuangliu" (Torrent), *Xiandai dianying* (Modern cinema), no. 1 (March 1933): 22.
39. Cheng Bugao, *Yingtan yijiu*, 7.
40. Cheng Bugao, 8.
41. Weihong Bao, *Fiery Cinema: The Emergence of an Affective Medium in China, 1915–1945* (Minneapolis: University of Minnesota Press, 2015), 167–72.
42. From Le Giornate del Cinema Muto Catalog, cited by Yiman Wang, "From Word to Word-Image: Film Translation of a 'Sketchy' Chinese Short Story 'Spring Silkworm,'" *Literature/Film Quarterly* 33, no. 1 (2005): 43.
43. Cheng Bugao, *Yingtan yijiu*, 1–2.
44. Tom Gunning, "Before Documentary: Early Nonfiction Films and the 'View' Aesthetic," in *Uncharted Territory: Essays on Early Nonfiction Film* (Amsterdam: Stichting Nederlands Filmmuseum, 1997), 17.
45. Sun Jiansan, *Zhongguo dianying, ni buzhidao de naxie shier* (Beijing: Shijie tushu chuban gongsi, 2010), 6.
46. "'Chunchan' zuotanhui," in *Sanshi niandai zhongguo dianying pinglun wenxuan* (A selection of film criticism from 1930s China), ed. Chen Bo (Beijing: Zhongguo dianying chubanshe, 1993), 250.
47. Ling He, "'Chuncan' zaijiantao" (A reappraisal of *Spring Silkworm*), *Shen bao dianying zhuankan* (*Shen bao* film supplement), October 10, 1933. Quoted in Yiman Wang, "From Word to Word-Image," 43.
48. Huang Jiamo, "'Chunchan' zhi jiantao" (Critiquing *Spring Silkworm*), *Maodun yuekan* (Contradiction monthly) 2, no. 3 (1933): 122.
49. Liu Na'ou, "Ping 'chunchan'" (Commenting on *Spring Silkworm*), *Maodun yuekan* 2, no. 3 (1933): 120.
50. "'Chunchan' zuotanhui," 255, 251.
51. See Yi Gu, "What's in a Name? Photography and the Reinvention of Visual Truth in China, 1840–1911," *Art Bulletin* 95, no. 1 (March 2013): 120–38.
52. Charles Laughlin, "One Day in China," in *A New Literary History of Modern China*), ed. David Der-wei Wang (Cambridge, Mass.: Harvard University Press, 2017), 420–26.
53. "'Chunchan' zuotanhui," 251.
54. Pang, *Building a New China in Cinema*, 39.
55. Shen Xiling, writing as Ye Chen, "Guanyu dianying de jige yijian" (Several views on film), *Shalun* (Siren), no. 1 (June 16, 1930): 45–50. Quoted in Pang, *Building a New China in Cinema*, 38, 37.
56. Pang, *Building a New China in Cinema*, 39.

57. For the prominence of the 16mm film in China's educational film movement of the 1930s, see Hongwei Thorn Chen, "Building the Nation on 16mm: Film Formats and the Institutionalization of Cinema Portability in 1930s China," *Journal of Chinese Cinemas* 16, no. 1 (October 2022): 40–57.
58. "Amateur Cinema League Organizes Contests at 'Y,'" *China Press*, January 25, 1930, 4.
59. Masaru, "Sōkan no ji" (Inaugural essay), *Amachua shinema* (Amateur cinema), Shanghai, January 1930, 1. I thank Noriko Morisue for directing me to National Film Archive of Japan's holding of this surviving publication by the Amateur Cinema League in Shanghai.
60. Masuo, "Dai Shanhai o se kage ni shita 16miri Eiga" (16mm films set within the backdrop of the Great Shanghai), *Amachua shinema*, January 1930, 2.
61. Ginma, "Shoho ga mono gen'ya" (Preliminary words), *Amachua shinema*, January 1930, 4.
62. "Plan to Organize Amateur Film Group in Shanghai," *Shanghai Times*, October 9, 1934, 8.
63. Liang Cheng, "Xiaoxing dianyinglun 1: xuyan" (On small-scale cinema 1: Prelude), *Min bao*, September 11, 1934, 8.
64. Liang Cheng, "Xiaoxing dianyinglun 3" (On small-scale cinema 3), *Min bao*, September 13, 1934, 6.
65. Liang Cheng, "Xiaoxing dianyinglun 9" (On small-scale cinema 9), *Min bao*, September 20, 1934, 8.
66. Liang Cheng, "Xiaoxing dianyinglun 14" (On small-scale cinema 14), *Min bao*, September 26, 1934, 8.
67. Liang Cheng, "Xiaoxing dianyinglun 16" (On small-scale cinema 16), *Min bao*, September 28, 1934, 8. Also, "Xiaoxing dianyinglun 17," *Min bao*, September 30, 1934, 10; "Xiaoxing dianyinglun 21," *Min bao*, October 5, 1934, 9.
68. In existing literature, the film was said to be entitled *Man Who Has a Movie Camera*. Yet the actual title frame in the film seems to suggest that it doesn't have a name but is simply labeled in both Japanese and English as "A Film by Man Who Has a Movie Camera."
69. Liu studied French in the Jesuit Aurora University in Shanghai in 1924 and then decided to return to the city in 1928 after a short trip back to Japan in 1926.
70. In Taiwan a club for amateur filmmakers shooting in 9.5mm had been founded in November 1924. It held monthly members' meetings and two exhibitions of members' films per year and was a member club to the Pathé Cinema network in Japan. See Li Daoming, "Liu Na'ou de dianying meixueguan: jiantan tade jiludianying 'chizhe sheyingji de nanren'" (Liu Na'ou's film aesthetics: A brief discussion on his documentary *Man Who Holds a Film Camera*), in *Liu Na'ou Guojiyantaohui lunwenji* (International conference proceedings on Liu Na'ou) (Taipei: Guojia Taiwan wenxueguan, 2005), 155.
71. The issue also included a report from the first meeting of the organizers, which included representatives from the Eastman-Kodak company. Advertisements of Kodak products were printed in the issue, too.
72. Scholarly treatments of Liu Na'ou's film theories include Zhang Zhen, *An Amorous History of the Silver Screen*, 269–83; Weihong Bao, *Fiery Cinema*, 175–82; Victor Fan, *Cinema Approaching Reality: Locating Chinese Film Theory* (Minneapolis: University of Minnesota Press, 2015), 75–108; and Ling Zhang, "Rhythmic Movement, the City Symphony and Transcultural Transmediality: Liu Na'ou and *The Man Who Has a Camera* (1933)," *Journal of Chinese Cinemas* 9, no. 1 (2015): 42–61.

73. Liu Na'ou, "Yingpian yishulun" (On film art), originally printed in *Dianying zhoubao* (Film weekly), nos. 2, 3, 6, 7, 8, 9, 10, 15 (July 1–October 8, 1932). Reprinted in *Liu Na'ou quanji: Yingxiangji* (The complete collection of Liu Na'ou: Film volume), ed. Kang Laixin and Xu Qinzhen (Tainan: Tainanxian wenhuaju, 2001), 268.
74. Lin Zhengfang, "Wenming Kaihua—yige rishi taiji wenhuaren de dianxing" (Civilizing: A typical case of a Taiwanese intellectual under Japanese rule), in *Liu Na'ou Guojiyantaohui lunwenji*, 79–80, 85–86.
75. The quote in the epigraph to this section is from Liu Na'ou, "Yinmu shang de jingse yu shiliao" (The sceneries and poetic materials on screen), originally printed in *Wenyi huabao*, no. 1 (1934): 65–66, reprinted in *Liu Na'ou quanji*, 334.
76. Liu Na'ou, "On Film Art," 265–67, 271–72.
77. Liu Na'ou, "Kaimaila jigou—weizhijiaodu jinenglun" (Camera apparatus—the functions of position and angle), originally published in *Xiandai dianying*, no. 7 (June 15, 1934), reprinted in *Liu Na'ou quanji: yingxiangji*, 313–14, 324, 327.
78. Liu Na'ou, "Guanyu zuozhe de taidu" (On the attitude of the author), originally published in *Xiandai dianying*, no. 5 (October 1, 1933), reprinted in *Liu Na'ou quanji: Yingxiangji*, 303–4.
79. Liu Na'ou, "Guanyu zuozhe de taidu," 303.
80. For early PRC scholarship on soft film, see Chen Jihua, Li Shaobai, and Xin Zuwen, *Zhongguo dianying fazhanshi* (History of the development of Chinese cinema) (Beijing: Zhongguo dianying chubanshe, 1963). For reappraisals, see Zhang Zhen, *An Amorous History of the Silver Screen*, 244–97; Weihong Bao, *Fiery Cinema*, 173–82; and Victor Fan, *Cinema Approaching Reality*, 75–108.
81. Fan, *Cinema Approaching Reality*, 76, 77, 89, 95.

3. Winning Realities

1. For wartime cinema, see Weihong Bao, *Fiery Cinema: The Emergence of an Affective Medium in China, 1915–1945* (Minneapolis: University of Minnesota Press, 2015), 265–374; and Poshek Fu, *Between Shanghai and Hong Kong: The Politics of Chinese Cinemas* (Stanford, Calif.: Stanford University Press, 2003).
2. Brett Gary, *The Nervous Liberals: Propaganda Anxieties from World War I to the Cold War* (New York: Columbia University Press, 1999), 4.
3. Philip M. Taylor, *Munitions of the Mind: A History of Propaganda from the Ancient World to the Present Era*, 3rd ed. (Manchester, UK: Manchester University Press, 2003), 3.
4. Bao, *Fiery Cinema*, 300, 268, 314.
5. Bill Nichols, "Axiographics: Ethical Space in Documentary Film," in *Representing Reality: Issues and Concepts in Documentary* (Bloomington: Indiana University Press, 1991), 76–103.
6. Thomas Waugh, *The Conscience of Cinema: The Work of Joris Ivens, 1926–1989* (Amsterdam: University of Amsterdam Press, 2016), 195.
7. Rossen Djagalov, *From Internationalism to Postcolonialism: Literature and Cinema Between the Second and Third Worlds* (Montreal: McGill-Queen's University Press, 2020), 180.
8. Sally J. Scholtz, *Political Solidarity* (University Park: Pennsylvania State University Press, 2012), 6.

9. For solidarity as a challenging relationship that requires reflexivity on power relations, see Katie Boudreau Morris, "Decolonizing Solidarity: Cultivating Relationships of Discomfort," *Settler Colonial Studies* 7, no. 4 (2017).
10. Zheng Yongzhi, "Kangzhan yinianlai zhi dianying shiye" (Film work in a year of war of resistance), *Wen zhong* (Shanghai) 1, no. 4–5 (1938): 27.
11. Zheng Yongzhi, 27.
12. Zheng Yongzhi, "Kangjiandianying zhizuo gangling," *Zhongguo dianying* (Chinese cinema) (Chongqing) 1, no. 1 (1941): 20.
13. Xu Suling, "Jilu dianying zhi gujia" (Evaluating documentary cinema), *Zhongguo dianying* 1, no. 1 (1941): 38–39.
14. Zheng Yongzhi, "Kanjiandianying zhizuo gangling," 19.
15. Zheng Yongzhi, "Quanguo de yinse zhanshimen qilai!" (Rise up, silver solders of the country!), *Kangzhan dianying* (Cinema of War of Resistance), no. 1 (1938): 7.
16. Zheng Yongzhi, "Kanjiandianying zhizuo gangling," 19.
17. James Leibold, *Reconfiguring Chinese Nationalism: How the Qing Frontier and Its Indigenes Became Chinese* (London: Palgrave Macmillan, 2007), 122.
18. Hsiao-ting Lin, *Modern China's Ethnic Frontiers: A Journey to the West* (London: Routledge, 2011), 17–18.
19. Lin, 37.
20. For a study of the South China Society, see Liang Luo, *The Avant-Garde and the Popular in Modern China: Tian Han and the Intersection of Performance and Politics* (Ann Arbor: University of Michigan Press, 2014), 60–102.
21. Zheng Junli, "Zheng Junli yishu chuangzuo nianbiao" (Zheng Junli's artistic work by the year), in *Zheng Junli quanji* (The complete works of Zheng Junli), ed. Li Zhen (Shanghai: Shanghai wenhua chubanshe, 2017), 8:213.
22. Zheng Junli, "Xiandai Zhongguo dianying shi" (History of modern Chinese cinema), in Li Zhen, *Zheng Junli quanji*, 1:3–54. The concept of indigenous film is used throughout the piece.
23. Zheng Junli, "Women zenme zhizuo minzu wansui" (How we made *Long Live the Nation(s)*), in Li Zhen, *Zheng Junli quanji*, 4:45.
24. Lin, *Modern China's Ethnic Frontiers*, 55–56.
25. Du Zhongyuan, *Sheng Shicai yu Xinxinjiang* (Sheng Shicai and the new Xinjiang) (Chongqing: Shenghuo shudian), 1938.
26. Zhao Dan was arrested and imprisoned in Xinjiang when Sheng Shicai turned against the Soviet Union in 1942.
27. Han Shangyi, "He Zheng Junli zai daxibei pai 'minzu wansui'" (Filming *Minzu wansui* with Zheng Junli in the Northwest), in *Minzu wansui: Zheng Junli riji 1939–1940* (Minzu wansui: Zheng Junli's diaries 1939–1940), by Zheng Junli (Shanghai: Shanghai wenhua chubanshe, 2013), 1.
28. Zheng Junli's diary, May 9, 1939; Zheng Junli, *Minzu wansui*, 41.
29. Bao, *Fiery Cinema*, 305.
30. Zheng Junli, *Minzu wansui*, 56.
31. Zheng Junli, 27.
32. Waugh, *The Conscience of Cinema*, 205.
33. Waugh, 205, 209.
34. Zheng Junli, *Minzu wansui*, 355.
35. Paul Rotha, *Documentary Film* (London: Faber and Faber, 1936), 117. Quoted in Zheng Junli, "Women zenme zhizuo 'minzu wansui'" (How did we make *Minzu wansui*), in Li Zhen, *Zheng Junli quanji*, 4:46. Zheng Junli most likely read Roman Karman in

translation. Ka Erman (Roman Karmen), "Jiludianying sheyingshi de xiuyang," trans. Su Fan, *Zhongguo dianying* (Chongqing) 1, no. 1 (1941): 38–43.
36. Rotha, *Documentary Film*, 116–17, 118. Part of this is also quoted in Zheng Junli, "Women zenme zhizuo 'minzu wansui,'" 46.
37. Zheng Junli, *Minzu wansui*, 355–56.
38. Zheng Junli, 356–57.
39. Zheng Junli, 357.
40. Zheng's film plan was submitted to Ma Bufang. Zheng Junli, 47.
41. Zheng Junli, "Xibei gongzuo riji" (Work diaries in the Northwest), in Li Zhen, *Zheng Junli quanji*, 8:99.
42. "Lu Zhonglin dian Jiang Zhongzheng" (Telegraph from Lu Zhonglin to Jiang Zhongzheng), August 11, 1938, Jiang Zhongzheng zongtong wenwu (President Jiang Zhongzheng archive), file 002, Academia Historica, Taiwan, https://ahonline.drnh.gov.tw/index.php?act=Display/image/1049244T=5=e1Q#e4F.
43. Zheng Junli, *Minzu wansui*, 68, 75.
44. Zheng Junli, 73.
45. Zheng Junli, 359. Xikang is in present-day Sichuan and Tibet.
46. Zheng Junli, "Minzu wansui gongzuo taiben" (*Minzu wansui* working script), in Li Zhen, *Zheng Junli quanji*, 4:13–14.
47. Zheng Junli, "Zheng Junli zibian nianbiao," in Li Zhen, *Zheng Junli quanji*, 8:224.
48. Thomas Waugh, "*The 400 Million* (1938) and the Solidarity Film: Halfway Between Hollywood and Newsreel," *Studies in Documentary Film* 3, no. 1 (2009): 9–10.
49. Personal communication with Zheng Dali, son of Zheng Junli, July 30, 2017.
50. Cao Shuming, "Minzu wenti zai sulian" (The issue of nationalities in the Soviet Union), *Sulian xinxian zhuanji* (A special issue on the new Soviet constitution), *Zhongsu wenhua zazhi* (Chinese and Soviet cultures magazine) 2, no. 1 (1937): 115–20; Zhao Kang, "Sulian minzu goucheng zhi gaikuang" (Survey of the composition of Soviet nationalities), *Zhongsu minzu wenti bijiao yanjiu teji* (A special issue comparing Chinese and Soviet nationalities questions), *Zhongsu wenhua zazhi* 2, no. 6 (1937): 135–40.
51. Jean Rouch, *Cine-Ethnography*, trans. Steven Field (Minneapolis: University of Minnesota Press, 2003), 99.
52. Cheng Jihua, "Yuan Muzhi yu xinwenjilu dianyin" (Yuan Muzhi and news and documentary film), in *Women de zuji* (Our footprints), ed. Zhang Jianzhen (Beijing: Zhongyang wenxianchubanshe, 2002), 1:9.
53. Yin Can, "Yuan Muzhi daizhe sheyingji cong diren houfang lai datan jiludianying yu bianqu juyun" (Yuan Muzhi arrived from the enemy's hinterland with a film camera, discussing at length documentary cinema and the drama movement in the [Communist] base areas), *Zhongguo dianying* (Chinese cinema) (Chongqing) 1, no. 2 (1941): 51.
54. For the work of the Workers' International Relief (WIR) in cinema, see Vance Kepley, "The Workers' International Relief and the Cinema of the Left, 1921–1935," *Cinema Journal* 23, no. 1 (Autumn 1983): 7–23. The Workers Film and Video League in the United States later split into Nykino and Frontier Film Group.
55. Waugh, *The Conscience of Cinema*, 222–24.
56. Waugh, 219.
57. Cheng Jihua, "Yuan Muzhi yu xinwenjilu dianyin," 7.
58. Mao Zedong, "Talks at the Yan'an Forum of Literature and Art," in *Modern Chinese Literary Thought: Writings on Literature 1893–1945*, ed. Kirk Denton (Stanford, Calif.: Stanford University Press, 1996), 460, 464, 467.
59. Mao Zedong, 460, 470, 473, 475.

274   3. Winning Realities

60. Cheng Jihua, "Yuan Muzhi yu xinwenjilu dianyin," 12–13.
61. Wu Zhuqing and Zhang Dai, *Zhongguo dianying de fengbei: Yan'an dianyingtuan de gushi* (Monument of Chinese cinema: Story of the Yan'an Film Troupe) (Beijing: Renmin University Press, 2008), 93–101.
62. Wu Benli, "Huainian dangde xinwenjilu dianying kaituozhe—Yuan Muzhi, Wu Yinxian" (Remembering the pioneers of the party's news and documentary cinema: Yuan Muzhi and Wu Yinxian), in Zhang Jianzhen, *Women de zuji*, 2:1071; Qian Xiaozhang and Zhang Jianzhen, "Jilupian 'Nanniwan' de dansheng" (The birth of the documentary *Nanniwan*), *Bainian chao*, no. 5 (2012): 30.
63. Chen Yung-fa, "The Blooming Poppy Under the Red Sun: The Yan'an Way and the Opium Trade," in *New Perspectives on the Chinese Communist Revolution*, ed. Tony Saich and Hans van de Ven (London: Routledge, 2015), 270.
64. Mark Selden, *The Yenan Way in Revolutionary China* (Cambridge, Mass.: Harvard University Press, 1971).
65. This is the original order of the film as indicated by the filmmakers' retrospective accounts. See Qian Xiaozhang and Zhang Jianzhen, "Jilupian 'Nanniwan' de dansheng," 29. This order was modified in the reprint of the film in 1961, with the celebratory sequence on agricultural production and Mao's calligraphy occurring at the end of the film, after the soldiers were shown to engage in agricultural production and military training.
66. Qian Xiaozhang and Zhang Jianzhen, 27–28.
67. Salomé Aguilera Skvirsky, *The Process Genre: Cinema and the Aesthetics of Labor* (Durham, N.C.: Duke University Press, 2020), 2, xiv.
68. Wu Benli, "Shenqie huannian Qian Xiaozhang tongzhi" (Remembering deeply Comrade Qian Xiaozhang), in Zhang Jianzhen, *Women de zuji*, 2:1085.
69. Qian Xiaozhang and Zhang Jianzhen, "Jilupian 'Nanniwan' de dansheng," 26.
70. Wu Benli, "Huainian dangde xinwenjilu dianying kaituozhe—Yuan Muzhi, Wu Yinxian," 1072–73.
71. Cheng Jihua, "Yuan Muzhi yu xinwenjilu dianying," 21.
72. Cheng Jihua, 23–24.
73. Between May 1947 and October 1948 in its temporary location in Hegang, the studio hosted three programs that trained more than 250 filmmakers. When the studio moved back to Changchun after the Communists gained control of the city, it organized larger training programs between February and August 1949 that trained 460 filmmakers. Cheng Jihua, 22–23.
74. Ka Erman, "Jiludianying sheyingshi de xiuyang," 38–43.
75. Han Kechao, "Canjia liaoshen zhanyi 'heishan zhujizhan'" (Participating in the Black Mountain Blockade, the Battle of Liaoshen), in Zhang Jianzhen, *Women de zuji*, 1:310–11.
76. The killed cinematographers were Wang Jingan, Yang Yinxuan, and Zhang Shaoke. Zhang Jianzhen, "Zhongguo xinwen jiludianying de shoufen kanwu—'xinwen sheying tongxun'" (The first publication of Chinese news and documentary film—*News Cinematography Circular*), http://www.cndfilm.com/special/jlysh/20130814/103116.shtml, accessed October 18, 2020.
77. Lei Ke, "Sui baiwan xiongshi guojiang paisheji" (On filming the million heroes crossing the river), in Zhang Jianzhen, *Women de zuji*, 1:326.
78. The four battles that were reenacted were the Battles of Liaoshen, Huaihai, Pingjin, and Crossing the Yangtze (*Dujiang*).

79. Interview with Wu Benli, in Fang Fang, *Zhongguo jilupian fazhan shi* (A history of the development of Chinese documentary) (Beijing: Zhongguo xiju chubanshe, 2003), 215.
80. Fang Fang, 164, 165, 215.
81. Sylvia Sasse, "Reenacting Revolution? Theater and Politics of Repetition," in *The Russian Revolution as Ideal and Practice: Failures, Legacies and the Future of Revolution*, ed. Thomas Telios, Dieter Thomä, and Ulrich Schmid (New York: Springer, 2019), 39.
82. Frederick C. Corney, *Telling October: Memory and the Making of the Bolshevik Revolution* (Ithaca, N.Y.: Cornell University Press, 2004), 76.
83. Sasse, "Reenacting Revolution?," 38.
84. David C. Gillespie, *Early Soviet Cinema: Innovation, Ideology and Propaganda* (London: Wallflower Press, 2000), 45.
85. Dziga Vertov, "The Essence of Kino-Eye" (1925), in *Kino-Eye: The Writings of Dziga Vertov*, trans. Annette Michelson (Berkeley: University of California Press, 1984), 50, 48.
86. Vertov, "On Kinopravda," in *Kino-Eye*, 45.
87. Yuri Tsivian, *Lines of Resistance: Dziga Vertov and the Twenties* (Bloomington: Indiana University Press, 2005), 152.
88. Vertov was denounced as following a "documentalism" that was too naturalistic and dispassionate to be revolutionary. For the campaign against "documentalism" targeting Vertov and other filmmakers, see Graham Roberts, *Forward Soviet: History and Non-fiction Film in the USSR* (London: Tauris, 1999), 93–104. For Eisenstein's *October* serving as historical footage, see Gillespie, *Early Soviet Cinema*, 45.
89. Jeremy Hicks, *Dziga Vertov: Defining Documentary* (New York: Tauris, 2007), 88.
90. I. Nazarov, "Jilupian zhong de zhenshixing" (Authenticity in documentary), *Dianying yishu yicong* (Film art in translation), no. 1 (1953): 53, 58, 57.
91. R. Grigoriev, "Lun jilupian de juben" (A discussion of documentary filmscripts), *Dianying yishu ziliao congkan* (Film art resources), no. 3 (1952): 11.
92. Beijing dianying zhipianchang xingzheng chu (Beijing Film Studio Administrative Unit), ed., *Yijiuwuling nian gongzuo zongjie ji yijiuwuyi nian gongzuo fangzhen yu renwu* (Work summary of year 1950 and direction and tasks for year 1951) (Beijing, 1951), 3. Quoted in Matthew Johnson, "International and Wartime Origins of the Propaganda State: The Motion Picture in China, 1897–1955 (Ph.D. dissertation, University of California, San Diego, 2008) 409.
93. Chen Bo, "Huiyi Wa'erlamofu zai Zhongguo" (Recalling Varlamov in China), *Zhongguo dianying*, November–December 1957, 106.
94. Yang Yuanying, *Beiying jishi* (A chronicle of the Beijing Film Studio) (Beijing: Zhongguo dianying chubanshe, 2011), 31.
95. Xu Wenming and Yang Xi, "Zhongguo renmin de shengli yu Jiefangle de zhongguo: Xinzhongguo chuqi jilu dianying de yunzuo Shijian yu guojia rentong" (The victory of the Chinese people and liberated China: The practice of documentary film and national identification in the early PRC), *Dianying xinzuo* (New works on film), no. 3 (2018): 37–43.
96. Zhang Tongdao, *Dianyingyan kan zhongguo* (Seeing China with the kino-eye) (Beijing: Zhongguo guangbo dianshi chubanshe, 2016), 94–95.
97. Edward Tyerman, *Internationalist Aesthetics: China and Early Soviet Culture* (New York: Columbia University Press, 2021), 143.

98. C. Martin Wilbur and Julie Lien-ying How, *Missionaries of Revolution: Soviet Advisers and Nationalist China, 1920–1927* (Cambridge, Mass.: Harvard University Press, 1989), 424.

4. When Taylorism Met Revolutionary Romanticism

1. Hu Feng, "Shijian kaishi le" (Time has begun), *People's Daily*, November 20, 1949, 7.
2. Hannah Arendt, *On Revolution* (New York: Viking, 1965), 21.
3. Kimberley Ens Manning and Felix Wemheuer, "Introduction," in *Eating Bitterness: New Perspectives on China's Great Leap Forward and Famine*, ed. Kimberly Ens Manning and Felix Wemheure (Vancouver: UBC Press, 2011), 3–4.
4. In November 1957 Mao Zedong visited the Soviet Union to participate in the celebration of the fortieth anniversary of the October Revolution and the Conference of World Communist and Workers' Parties. During the conference, following Nikita Khrushchev's announcement that the Soviet Union would surpass the United States in both industrial and agricultural production within fifteen years, or the duration of three Five-Year Plans, Mao made the announcement that China would surpass Britain in the same amount of time. For more on this visit, see chapter 5.
5. For the economic rationale of the Great Leap Forward, see Maurice Meisner, *Mao's China and After: A History of the People's Republic*, 3rd ed. (New York: Free Press, 1999), 204–14.
6. On Mao's voluntarist beliefs, see Richard D. Baum, "Red and Expert: The Politico-Ideological Foundations of China's Great Leap Forward," *Asian Survey*, September 1964, 1048–57.
7. Wei Li and Dennis Tao Yang provide statistical evidence in "The Great Leap Forward: Anatomy of a Central Planning Disaster," *Journal of Political Economy* 113, no. 4 (2005): 840–77. For other studies that reached similar results, see also Manning and Wemheuer, "Introduction," 10.
8. Cheng Jihua, "Yuan Muzhi yu xinwen jilu dianying" (Yuan Muzhi and news and documentary film), in *Women de zuji* (Our footprints), ed. Zhang Jianzhen, Zhang Mengqi, and Guan Minguo (Beijing: Zhongyang wenxian chubanshe, 2003), 3, no. 1:25–26.
9. Cheng Jihua, 27.
10. Lin Shaoxiong and Chen Jianfeng, *Yishixingtai de xingxiang zhanshi: jishi yingpian fazhan yu zhizhengdang de wenhua celue* (Visual manifestation of ideology: Development of documentary cinema and cultural strategies of the ruling party) (Shanghai: Shanghai renmin chubanshe, 2009), 218.
11. Huang Mei, "Xin Zhongguo dianying shiye de xunsu fazhan" (The rapid development of new China's cinematic enterprise), *People's Daily*, October 30, 1959. After 1962 a large number of provincial-level film studios closed, leaving only Zhujiang, Emei, Xi'an, Neimeng, Xinjiang, Yunnan, and a few others in ethnic-minority regions in operation. See Shan Wanli, *Zhongguo jilu dianying shi* (History of Chinese documentary cinema) (Beijing: Zhongguo dianying chubanshe, 2005), 191.
12. Chris Berry, *Postsocialist Cinema in Post-Mao China: The Cultural Revolution After the Cultural Revolution* (New York: Routledge, 2004), 32; Huang Mei, "Xin Zhongguo dianying shiye de xunsu fazhan."
13. Huang Mei, "Xin Zhongguo dianying shiye de xunsu fazhan."

14. Shan Wanli, *Zhongguo jilu dianying shi*, 179.
15. Shan Wanli, 178. See also Ding Jiao, "Xinwen jilu dianying yongyuan zuo shidai de jianbing" (News films are always vanguards of the times), *People's Daily*, August 24, 1960, 7.
16. Yang Jinyong, "Cong jianli sheying qudui dao sheying jizhezhan de licheng" (The journal from setting up district teams for cinematography to founding correspondents' stations), in Zhang Jianzhen, Zhang Mengqi, and Guan Mingou, *Women de zuji*, 3, no. 1:68–70.
17. Shan Wanli, *Zhongguo jilu dianying shi*, 181.
18. Mary Ann Doane, *The Emergence of Cinematic Time: Modernity, Contingency, the Archive* (Cambridge, Mass.: Harvard University Press, 2002), 4.
19. Miriam Bratu Hansen, *Cinema and Experience: Siegfried Kracauer, Walter Benjamin, and Theodor W. Adorno* (Berkeley: University of California Press, 2012), 107.
20. Some of Frank B. Gilbreth's film clips can be seen at the Moving Image Archive, http://archive.org/details/OriginalFilm, accessed on May 8, 2012.
21. Scott Curtis, "Images of Efficiency: The Films of Frank B. Gilbreth," in *Films That Work: Industrial Film and the Productivity of Media*, ed. Vinzenz Hediger and Patrick Vonderau (Amsterdam: University of Amsterdam Press, 2009), 89.
22. Han Sheng, "Huodong dianying yongwei guiding gongzuo chengji zhi qitan" (The intriguing tale of moving cinema's use for standardizing work output), *Xiehe Journal* 4, no. 25 (1914): 5–7.
23. Wang Guangyan, *Wenhua chuanbo yu meijie yanjiu* (Studies of cultural transmission and media) (Wuhan: Central China Normal University Press, 2016), 150–64.
24. Judith A. Merkle, *Management and Ideology: The Legacy of the International Scientific Management Movement* (Berkeley: University of California Press, 1980), 107.
25. N. Lebenov, ed., *Danglun dianying* (The party on cinema), trans. Xu Guming (Beijing: Shidai chubanshe, 1951), 25, 26, 29, 34, 37–41.
26. Li and Yang, "The Great Leap Forward," 845.
27. For a fascinating account of how work discipline and time became inculcated in the mindset of workers during the Industrial Revolution, see E. P. Thompson, "Time, Work-Discipline, and Industrial Capitalism," *Past & Present*, December 1967, 56–97.
28. In issues of the *People's Daily* published in 1949 and the 1950s, one can find numerous critical reports on cadres and workers whose negligence regarding keeping time caused delays in meetings, public events, and coordinated work schedules, indicating the importance of training for time discipline. Examples include Huang Mei, "Jiaqiang shijian guannian, kaihui yao zhunshi!" (Strengthen the sense of time and attend meetings on time), *People's Daily*, April 15, 1950; and Du Zhunqing, "Yunshu liangshi bushou shijian, zaocheng renli wuli shunshi" (Lack of time discipline in grain transportation resulted in losses of labor and substance), *People's Daily*, July 26, 1950.
29. In the early PRC, trade unions were among the most energetic organizers of film screenings, with their own mobile film units traveling to factories, mines, and small towns where there was a sizable worker population. Cinema became the quintessential entertainment for workers: the screenings were so profitable that union projection teams competed with one another as well as government teams for audience. *Dianying fangying* published letters from union film exhibitors on the problem of competition. See Zhou Yongxiang, "Why Always Creating Difficulties for Film Projection Teams of the Workers' Union?," *Dianying fangying* (Film exhibition), no. 7 (1957): 3–5.
30. Judith A. Merkle, *Management and Ideology: The Legacy of the International Scientific Management Movement* (Berkeley: University of California Press, 1980), 113.

278   4. When Taylorism Met Revolutionary Romanticism

31. Ying Qian, "The Shopfloor as Stage: Production Competition, Democracy, and the Unfulfilled Promise of 'Red Flag Song,'" in "Re-imagining the Chinese Worker: Media and Cultural Politics from Revolution to Reform," ed. Wanning Sun, *China Perspectives*, special issue, June 2015, 7–14.
32. Karl Marx, "The Economic and Philosophical Manuscripts of 1844," in *Karl Marx: A Reader*, ed. Jon Elster (Cambridge: Cambridge University Press, 1999), 39 (italics in original).
33. Karl Marx, "Comments on James Mill," in Elster, *Karl Marx*, 34 (italics in original).
34. Quoted in Ding Jiao, "Xinde tansuo: geming xianshi zhuyi yu geming langman zhuyi xiang jiehe de chuangzuo fangfa ruhe zai xinwen dianying zhong tixian" (New explorations: How to manifest the creative method of combining revolutionary realism and revolutionary romanticism in news films), *Dianying yishu* (Film art), October 1958, 5.
35. For a discussion on how revolutionary romanticism might apply to documentary filmmaking, see the January 1958 issue of *Dianying yishu* for a cluster of articles.
36. Zhou Yang, "Xinminge kaituole shige de xindaolu" (New folk songs opened new paths for poetry), *Hongqi* (Red flag), no. 1 (1958); Guo Moruo, "Langman zhuyi he xianshi zhuyi" (Romanticism and realism), *Hongqi*, no. 3 (1958).
37. Ding Jiao, "Xinde tansuo," 6.
38. Yan Jizhou, "Women xuechao de cai bieren yuanyi chima?" (Would others be willing to eat the dishes we are learning to make?), in "Zuotan Jiluxing yishupian" (Discussion on documentary art films), *Zhongguo dianying* (Chinese cinema), no. 4 (1959): 38.
39. Mao Zedong, "Talks at the Yan'an Forum on Literature and Art," in *Modern Chinese Literary Thought: Writings on Literature, 1893–1945*, ed. Kirk Denton (Stanford, Calif.: Stanford University Press, 1996), 458–84.
40. Yan Jizhou, "Women xuechao de cai bieren yuanyi chima?," 38.
41. Shan Wanli, *Zhongguo jilu dianying shi*, 193.
42. Nicholas Lardy, "The Chinese Economy Under Stress, 1958–1965," in *The Cambridge History of China*, vol. 14: *The People's Republic*, part 1, *The Emergence of Revolutionary China, 1949–1965*, ed. Roderick MacFarquhar and John K. Fairbank (Cambridge: Cambridge University Press, 1987), 364.
43. See Henri Cartier-Bresson, "Red China Bid for a Future," *Life*, January 5, 1959, 44–61. The photos are also available at pro.magnumphotos.com/Catalogue/Henri-Cartier-Bresson/1958 /CHINA-The-Great-Leap-Forward-1958-NN142462.html.
44. Filmed, edited, and completed within a few days, the documentary film *Leaders Working with Us* was widely distributed and was featured predominantly in the popular film biweekly *Dazhong dianying* in July 1958. In that issue, the cover was a color photograph of Mao Zedong working at the dam. Black-and-white film stills of Liu Shaoqi, Zhou Enlai, and Zhu De working on the site were printed on the third page of the magazine. *Dazhong dianying* (Cinema for the masses), no. 13 (July 11, 1958).
45. Tian Han wrote a review of *Songs on the Reservoir*, commending the film for its timely adaptation of a literary reportage from the construction site, which Tian himself had also consulted when writing his own play. He also praised the film's efforts to "adopt revolutionary romanticism to the screen," lauding a well-executed dialogue between two old workers in the film as comprising the reservoir's past, present, and future seen from the perspective of the working class. See Tian Han, "Rang 'Shuikushang de gesheng' changbian quanguo" (Let "Songs on the Dam" be sung all over the country), *Dazhong dianying*, no. 14 (July 26, 1958): 7.

46. Li Zhiyan, *Tian Han chuangzuo ceji* (Side observations of Tian Han's creative process) (Chengdu: Sichuan wenyi chubanshe, 1994), 118. Also see Paola Iovene, *Tales of Futures Past: Anticipation and the Ends of Literature in Contemporary China* (Stanford, Calif.: Stanford University Press, 2014), 21.
47. Tian Han, "Rang 'Shuikushang de gesheng' changbian quanguo," 7.
48. See Sigrid Schmalzer, *Red Revolution, Green Revolution: Scientific Farming in Socialist China* (Chicago: University of Chicago Press, 2016); and Joshua Eisenman, *Red China's Green Revolution* (New York: Columbia University Press, 2018).
49. See Loren Grahm, *Lysenko's Ghost: Epigenetics and Russia* (Cambridge, Mass.: Harvard University Press, 2016).
50. Hua Shu, "Sulian nongye zhuanjia zai zhongguo" (Soviet agricultural experts in China), *People's Daily*, November 11, 1954, 2.
51. Liu Baiyu, "Jinhuang de pingguo" (Golden apples), *People's Daily*, April 14, 1958, 8.
52. Wei Wenhua, "Xiangcun xiaoxue yizhi hua" (A flower among rural elementary schools), *People's Daily*, April 13, 1959, 6.
53. Grahm, *Lysenko's Ghost*, 1.
54. 1 *jin* equals 0.5 kilo. 1 *mu* is roughly 0.165 acre.
55. Ye Mai, "Huanxiang yu zhenshi" (Fantasy and reality), *People's Daily*, August 8, 1958.
56. Jie Li, *Utopian Ruins: A Memorial Museum of the Mao Era* (Durham, N.C.: Duke University Press, 2020), 125-34.
57. Yomi Braester, "The Political Campaign as Genre: Ideology and Iconography during the Seventeen Years Period," *Modern Language Quarterly* 69:1 (March 2008), 140, 126.
58. "Wei zhishui, zhishan, zhitu fuwu, faxing fangying zhanxian chuzheng desheng" (To serve water, mountain, soil control, the first victories on the distribution and exhibition front), *Dianying fangying*, no. 1 (1960): 2-4.
59. Lao Zhuang, "Gongdi juban xinpian zhanlan zhou" (A week of new films held on construction sites), *Dianying fangying*, no. 7 (1958): 21.
60. For experiments with exhibiting films simultaneously on multiple screens and in daylight, see Li Mifang, "Baizhou dianying fangyicai, Gexin yuanli tianxinhua" (The marvelous colors of daylight cinema, the new flowers in the garden of innovation), *Dianying fangying*, no. 12 (1960): 28-30; and Ya Xuan, "Zheshe lutian dianying" (Reflected open-air cinema), *Dianying fangying*, no. 12 (1960): 30. For developing screens that allowed for projection films in daylight, see Lu Xinya, "Baizhou dianying" (Daytime cinema), *Dianying jishu* (Film technology), no. 7 (1957): 29-30; and Zhang Shiyuan, "Woshi ruhe kaizhan fangying jishu gexin de" (How I innovated in film-exhibition techniques), *Dianying fangying*, no. 4 (1960): 23.
61. Walter Benjamin, "The Work of Art in the Age of Mechanical Reproduction," in *Illuminations: Essays and Reflections*, ed. Hannah Arendt, trans. Harry Zohn (Boston: Houghton Mifflin, 2019), 188.
62. Fang Yunguang, "Zhandou zai shuili gongdishang de lueyang fangyingdui" (Lueyang film projection team fighting on reservoir construction fields), *Dianying fangying*, no. 2 (1960): 17-18.
63. Chang-tai Hung, *Going to the People: Chinese Intellectuals and Folk Literature, 1918-1937* (Cambridge, Mass.: Harvard University Press, 1985).
64. See Lydia H. Liu, "Translingual Folklore and Folklorics in China," in *A Companion to Folklore*, ed. Regina F. Bendix and Galit Hasan-Rokem, (Chichester, UK: Wiley, 2012), 190-210.
65. Chang'e, Hou Yi, Nü Wa, and Sun Wukong are all figures from legends circulating in traditional China. Ye Mai, "Huanxiang yu xianshi," 6.

66. Xue Bing, *Feng cong minjian lai* (Wind comes from amid the people) (Jinan: Shandong huabao chubanshe, 2009), 102, 103.
67. Wu Xueshan, "'Chao xianshi'" 'Liangjiehe' yujing xia de dayuejin nongminhua" ("Surrealism" peasant paintings in the context of "Two Combinations" during the Great Leap Forward), *Qinghua meishu*, July 2012, 78–87.
68. Shao Quanlin, "Women de wenxue jinru le xinde shiqi" (Our literature has entered a new era), *People's Daily*, October 6, 1958, 7.
69. "Quanguo shougongye hezuo zongshe haozhao zengchan tutie mibu gangtie yuanliao buzu" (The National Handicrafts Cooperative calls for an increase in indigenous iron production to supplement raw material shortage for steel industry), *People's Daily*, December 27, 1956, 2.
70. Schmalzer, *Green Revolution, Red Revolution*, 35–36.
71. *Zhonghua renmin gongheguo difangzhi fujian shengzhi yanjin gongye zhi* (China local historical records: The province of Fujian, history of the metallurgical industry) (Fuzhou, 2001), 108.
72. An Yanling, *Jinshu gongyi xue: Jinshu yanlian* (Metallurgical technology) (Beijing, 1959), 1:65.
73. The film studios were the Central Newsreel and Documentary Studio, the August First Film Studio of the PLA, and the Science and Education Film Studio in Beijing. Shi Mei, "Guangrong de shiming: wei gangtie er zhan!" (A distinguished mission: Fighting the battle for steel and iron), *Dazhong dianying*, no. 20, October 26, 1958, 22.
74. Shi Mei, 22.
75. "Shi'er bu jilu dagao gangtie duanpian jijiang quanguo shangying" (Twelve short films documenting the great steel-making will be shown soon nationwide), *Dazhong dianying*, October 11, 1958, 27.
76. Shi Mei, "Guangrong de shiming," 22. Six out of the seven Xinying films were named after a folk technology, such as *Dixia tugaolu* (Underground indigenous furnace), *Shangcheng tugaolu* (Indigenous furnace from Shangcheng), and *Chengangshi tugaolu* (Chengang-style indigenous furnace). Titles of films made by the August 1 Studio included *Tufanglu liantie* (Making iron with indigenous square furnaces) and *Shouyao xiaozhuanlu liangang* (Making steel with small hand-operated rotating furnaces). "Shi'er bu jilu dagao gangtie duanpian jijiang quanguo shangying," 27.
77. "Shi'er bu jilu dagao gangtie duanpian jijiang quanguo shangying," 27.
78. Salomé Aguilera Skvirsky, *The Process Genre: Cinema and the Aesthetics of Labor* (Durham, N.C.: Duke University Press, 2020), xiv.
79. Jacques Rancière, *The Politics of Aesthetics*, trans. Gabriel Rockhill (London: Bloomsbury, 2013), 7.
80. Chen Huangmei, "Zai dianying yuejinhui shang de fayan" (Speech at the meeting to discuss the Great Leap Forward in cinema), in *Zhongguo dianying yanjiu ziliao: 1949–1979* (Research materials for Chinese cinema, 1949–1979), ed. Wu Di (Beijing: Wenhua yishu chubanshe, 2006), 198.
81. Yiching Wu, *The Cultural Revolution at the Margins: Chinese Socialism in Crisis* (Cambridge, Mass.: Harvard University Press, 2014), 100–101.
82. Jackie Sheehan, *Chinese Workers: A New History* (New York: Routledge, 1998), 90, 55–57.
83. Wu, *Cultural Revolution at the Margins*, 99.
84. Jonathan Crary, *24/7: Late Capitalism and the Ends of Sleep* (London: Verso, 2013), 9–10.
85. For discussions of the party's efforts at creating democratic institutions at workplaces and these institutions' limitations, see Sheehan, *Chinese Workers*, 13–46.

86. Industrial unrest became prominent by the end of 1956 and continued through the first half of 1957. See Sheehan, *Chinese Workers*, 47; François Gipouloux, *Les cent fleurs à l'usine: Agitation ouvrière et crise du modèle soviétique en Chine, 1956-1957* (Paris: Diffusion, 1986), 189; and Perry, "Shanghai's Strike Wave of 1957," 1-27. On the weakening of the trade unions, see Sheehan, *Chinese Workers*, 13-46; and Wu, *Cultural Revolution at the Margins*, 99.
87. Chen Fu and Ye Ming, "Fangwen Huang Baomei" (Visiting Huang Baomei), *Zhongguo dianying*, no. 8 (1958): 61-67.
88. For the connection between early cinema and magic shows, see Matthew Solomon, *Disappearing Tricks: Silent Film, Houdini, and the New Magic of the Twentieth Century* (Champaign: University of Illinois Press, 2010).
89. Li and Yang, "Great Leap Forward," 841.
90. Lardy, "Chinese Economy Under Stress," 370.
91. Light industrial output decreased by 9.8 percent in 1960, by 21.6 percent in 1961, and by another 8.4 percent in 1962. Heavy industrial output declined by 46.6 percent in 1961 as compared with 1960, and by another 22.2 percent in 1962 over 1961. See Kenneth Lieberthal, "The Great Leap Forward and the Split in the Yenan Leadership," in *Cambridge History of China*, ed. MacFarquhar and Fairbank, 14:318. Statistics are cited from Ma Hong, "Jinji tiaozheng he fazhan sudu" (Economic adjustment and speed of development), *People's Daily*, December 29, 1981, 5.
92. Mao Jianxin, "'Dayuejin' yundong zhongde gongye 'jishu geming'" (The "revolution of industrial techniques" during the "Great Leap Forward" movement), *Jiangsu daxue xuebao (shehui kexue ban)* (Journal of Jiangsu University [social science ed.]), July 2013, 41-47.
93. Li and Yang, "Great Leap Forward," 840-77; James Kai-sing Kung and Justin Yifu Lin, "The Causes of China's Great Leap Famine, 1959-1961," *Economic Development and Cultural Change* 52 (2003): 51-73. For other studies that reached similar results, see also Manning and Wemheuer, "Introduction," 10.
94. Stuart Firestein, *Failure: Why Science Is So Successful* (Oxford: Oxford University Press, 2016), 1, 17.
95. For a discussion on searches for images from the famine, see Jie Li, *Utopian Ruins*, 139-47.

5. The Uncertainty of Political Knowledge

1. Young women adored Wang Guangmei's graceful appearance in the *qipao*, the pre-1949 fashion. Antonia Finnane, *Changing Clothes in China: Fashion, History, Nation* (New York: Columbia University Press, 2008), 227.
2. Hu Wenhui, *Chen Yinque shijian shi* (Guide to Chen Yinque's poetry and letters) (Guangzhou: Guangdong renmin chubanshe, 2008), 1188.
3. "The Trial of Liu Shao-ch'i's Wife, 10 April 1967," in *The People's Republic of China, 1949-1979: A Documentary Survey*, vol. 3, *The Cultural Revolution*, part 1, ed. Harold C. Hinton (Wilmington, Del.: Scholarly Resources, 1980), 1699-1700. See also Finnane, *Changing Clothes in China*, 227.
4. "Zhongfa (68), No. 160," in *Wuchanjieji wenhua dageming wenjian huibian* (Collection of documents from the Great Proletariat Cultural Revolution), ed. Hubei Geming Weiyuanhui (Hubei Provincial Revolutionary Committee), vol. 3 (Wuhan, 1969).

5. In the *People's Daily*, four articles expressing condemnation were published on July 13, 1967. Another four were published on August 11, 1967. One more article appeared on September 13, 1967, three on November 27, 1968, six on December 1, 1968, and two on December 12, 1968.
6. Mao Zedong, "Zhongguo shehui gejiji de fenxi" (The analysis of social classes in China), in *Mao Zedong Xuanji* (Collected works of Mao Zedong) (Beijing: Renmin chubanshe, 1991), 1:1.
7. Mao Zedong, "Some questions concerning leadership", *Selected Works*, v. 3, 119, quoted in *Quotations from Mao Tsedung* (Beijing: Peking Foreign Language Press, 1966), https://www.marxists.org/reference/archive/mao/works/red-book/ch11.htm.
8. Michael Renov, "Towards a Poetics of Documentary," in *Theorizing Documentary*, ed. Michael Renov (New York: Routledge, 1993), 21, 23. For the place of desire in revolutionary cinema, see Ban Wang, *The Sublime Figure of History: Aesthetics and Politics in Twentieth-Century China* (Stanford, Calif.: Stanford University Press, 1997).
9. "Wenhua shenghuo jianping: ying zhongshi dianying de xuanchuan gongzuo" (Short commentary on cultural life: We should pay attention to film publicity work), *People's Daily*, February 12, 1952, 3.
10. "Zhu jilupian 'Kangmei Yuanchao' zai quanguo fangying" (Celebrate the nationwide exhibitions of documentary 'Resist America and Aid Korea'), *People's Daily*, December 28, 1951, 1.
11. Hajimu Masuda, *Cold War Crucible: The Korean Conflict and the Postwar World* (Cambridge, Mass.: Harvard University Press, 2015), 180.
12. Tom Conley, *Cartographic Cinema* (Minneapolis: University of Minnesota Press, 2007), 1–2.
13. Chen Jian, *China's Road to the Korean War: The Making of the Sino-American Confrontation* (New York: Columbia University Press, 1994), 128; Masuda, *Cold War Crucible*, 139, 123–26.
14. Masuda, *Cold War Crucible*, 128, 123–25.
15. Masuda, 194.
16. Jiang Zhuzhi, "'Kangmei Yuanchao' zai chaoxian qianxian," *Dazhong dianying* (Mass cinema), no. 3 (1952): 38–39.
17. For Chinese documentary filmmaking in Vietnam, see Zhang Yun, "Yuenan renmin zai shengli daolu shang: jieshao yingpian 'Kangzhan de Yuenan'" (The people of Vietnam on the road to victory: Introducing "Vietnam in Resistance"), *Dazhong dianying*, no. 7 (1952): 6–7, a special issue showcasing this film.
18. Shu Guang Zhang, "Constructing 'Peaceful Coexistence': China's Diplomacy Toward the Geneva and Bandung Conferences, 1954–55," *Cold War History* 7, no. 4 (2007): 510–11.
19. Zhang, 514–15.
20. Lanjun Xu, "The Lure of Sadness: The Fever of 'Yueju' and 'The Butterfly Lovers' in the Early PRC," *Asian Theatre Journal* 33, no. 1 (Spring 2016): 119.
21. Jin Jiang, *Women Playing Men: Yue Opera and Social Change in Twentieth-Century Shanghai* (Seattle: University of Washington Press, 2011), 231.
22. Shi Mei, "Jilupian Zhong de zichanjieji qingxiang" (The bourgeois tendency in documentary), *Zhongguo dianying* (Chinese cinema), no. 6 (1958): 12.
23. Shi Mei, 13.
24. See Wang, *Revolutionary Cycles in Chinese Cinema*. The book centers on a number of campaigns targeting "problematic" films spanning early 1950s to late 1970s.
25. Zhang Tongdao, *Dianyingyan kan zhongguo* (Seeing China with the kino-eye) (Beijing: Zhongguo guangbo dianshi chubanshe, 2016), 116.

26. Zhang Tongdao, 114.
27. Zhong Dianfei, "Dianying de luogu" (The gongs and drums of cinema), *Wenyi bao* 23 (December 1956): 3–4. This article followed and contributed to a discussion on film production that had begun with twenty-four articles published in the Shanghai-based newspaper *Wenhui Daily*.
28. Wang, *Revolutionary Cycles in Chinese Cinema*, 35.
29. Wang, 72.
30. For a study on the Moscow conference of 1957 and its aims, see Zhihua Shen and Yafeng Xia, "Hidden Currents During the Honeymoon," *Journal of Cold War Studies* 11, no. 4 (Fall 2009): 74–117.
31. Shen and Xia, 105. Shen and Xia argue that in the end, each party used the Moscow Declaration according to its own interpretation, whenever conflicts arose with other parties, and the document became no more than a mere scrap of paper.
32. Zhang Shude, *Miyue de jiesu: Mao Zedong yu Heluxiaofu juelie qianhou* (The end of the honeymoon: Before and after the split between Mao Zedong and Khrushchev) (Beijing: Zhongguo qingnian chubanshe, 1999), 90.
33. "Guanyu wuchanjieji de lishi jingyan" (On historical experiences of proletariat dictatorship), *People's Daily*, April 5, 1956, 1.
34. "Zailun wuchanjieji de lishi jingyan" (The second discussion on the historical experience of proletariat dictatorship), *People's Daily*, December 29, 1956, 1.
35. Frederick C. Teiwes, with Warren Sun, *China's Road to Disaster: Mao, Central Politicians, and Provincial Leaders in the Unfolding of the Great Leap Forward, 1955–1959* (London: Sharpe, 1999), 216.
36. Quoted in Chen Huangmei, *Dangdai Zhongguo dianying* (Contemporary Chinese cinema) (Beijing: Zhongguo shehui kexue chubanshe, 1989), 2:24, 25.
37. Quoted in "Deng Yingchao lingxian furen waijiao, waijiaobu zhaokai furen gongzuo huiyi" (Deng Yingchao leads wife diplomacy, the Ministry of Foreign Affairs convenes meeting on wife diplomacy), *People's Daily* (overseas edition), December 14, 2010, http://news.xinhuanet.com/politics/2010-12/14/c_12876315.htm. For a photo of all the participants at the meeting on "wife diplomacy" in 1960, see http://www.picturechina.com.cn/bbs/thread-154878-1-1.html.
38. Cynthia Enloe, *Bananas, Beaches, and Bases: Making Feminist Sense of International Politics* (Berkeley: University of California Press, 2001), xxii, 97.
39. Jiang Huajie, "Geming waijiao de zhangli: guanyu xinzhongguo furen waijiao de lishi kaocha (1950–1965)" (The tension within revolutionary diplomacy: Historical investigations on wife diplomacy in new China (1950–1965)), *Zhonggong dangshi yanjiu*, no. 5 (2016): 37.
40. Emily Wilcox, "Performing Bandung: China's dance diplomacy with India, Indonesia and Burma, 1953–1962," *Inter-Asia Cultural Studies* 18, no. 4 (2017): 519.
41. Jiang Huajie, "The Tension Within Revolutionary Diplomacy," 38, 40.
42. Jiang Huajie, 37.
43. Jiang Huajie, 37, 42.
44. Roderick MacFarquhar, *The Origins of the Cultural Revolution*, vol. 3, *The Coming of the Cataclysm, 1961–1966* (New York: Columbia University Press, 1997), 399.
45. In 1962, when Indonesia hosted the Asian Games, it denied visas to participants from Israel and Taiwan for political reasons. To retaliate, the International Olympic Committee suspended Indonesia's participation in the Olympic Games. Subsequently, Indonesia decided to initiate the first Games of New Emerging Forces as an alternative to the Olympics for Third World nations.

284   5. The Uncertainty of Political Knowledge

46. David Mozingo, *Chinese Policy Toward Indonesia, 1949–1967* (Ithaca, N.Y.: Cornell University Press, 2004), 250.
47. See, among others, Lowell Dittmer, *Liu Shaoqi and the Chinese Cultural Revolution* (New York: Sharpe, 1998); and Roderick MacFarquhar and Michael Schoenhals, *Mao's Last Revolution* (Cambridge, Mass.: Harvard University Press, 2006).
48. Guo Jian, Yongyi Song, and Yuan Zhou, *The A to Z of the Chinese Cultural Revolution* (Lanham, Md.: Scarecrow, 2006), 121–22; Qi Benyu, "Aiguo zhuyi haishi maiguo zhuyi: ping fandong yingpian *qinggong mishi*" (Patriotism or national betrayal: On the reactionary film *Inside Story of the Qing Court*), *People's Daily*, April 1, 1967, 1.
49. Zhang Yang and Zhang Jianxiang, *Zhongguo xiandaishi* (Chinese modern history) (Xi'an: Shaanxi shifan daxue chubanshe, 1988), 2:186.
50. Jiang Qing, "Jiang Qing tongzhi jiejian zhongyang xinwen jilu dianying zhipianchang he bayi dianying zhipianchang geming qunzhong daibiao shi de jianghua" (Comrade Jiang Qing's talk when meeting the revolutionary masses from the Central Newsreel and Documentary Film Studio and August First Film Studio), in *Jiang Qing tongzhi jianghua xuanbian: 1966.2–1968.9* (internal circulation) (Wuhan: Hubei Renmin Chubanshe, 1969), 156–57.
51. Respectively, Guo Xiande, Zhang Honglin, and Li Huiming, "Yifu gongzei zuilian" (The portrait of a traitor to the workers), *People's Daily*, December 1, 1968, 6; Chen Jianmin, "Dadao 'touxiang zhuyi' de chuigushou" (Down with the proponent of "capitulationism"), *People's Daily*, August 11, 1967, 4; Zhang Chunxi, Tao Jiashan, and Ma Haoliu, "Geming wuzhuang bu ke diu" (Don't throw away revolutionary armed forces), *People's Daily*, December 1, 1968. According to the *People's Daily*, Guo, Zhang, and Li were workers at the Beijing Central Food Factory; Chen was a soldier stationed in Beijing; and Zhang, Tao, and Ma were members of the PLA Air Force.
52. Yao Dengshan and Zhao Xiaoshou, "Zai guojishang tuixing touxiang zhuyi de huochouju—chi fandong jilu yingpian *Fangwen Yindunixiya*" (The living farce of promoting defeatism in the world: Critiquing the reactionary film *Visit Indonesia*), *People's Daily*, July 13, 1967.
53. Ge Zhongbo, "Ai he hen—chi fandong yingpian *Fanwen Yindunixiya*" (Love and hatred: Critiquing the reactionary film *Visit Indonesia*), *People's Daily*, August 11, 1967.
54. Chen Mou, "Dixiufan de zougou, shehuizhiyi de pantu" (Running dog for the imperialists, revisionists, and antirevolutionaries, traitor to socialism), *People's Daily*, November 27, 1968, 6.
55. Jiang Qing, "Jiang Qing tongzhi jiejian," 156–57. Upon the suggestion to use this film as denunciative material, Jiang Qing asked, "Didn't you say that the rest of the footage had been destroyed?" Staff at the Central Newsreel and Documentary Film Studio answered, "No, we still have some left." The re-edit used additional footage from the documentation of the visit.
56. See Tani Barlow, *In the Event of Women* (Durham, N.C.: Duke University Press, 2021), chap. 6.
57. "Heluxiaofu fangmei dianying jingtou jianji" (A collection of film stills from Khrushchev visiting America), *Dianying pipan*, published by Tianjinshi gongnongbing "za sanjiu" pipan ducao yingpian lianluozhan (Tianjin city worker peasant soldier correspondent office for "smashing the three olds" and criticizing poisonous weed films), no. 6 (August 1967): 3. I thank Yingchuan Yang for sharing this material with me, and directing me to the Hoover Institute archives, where this publication is held.
58. Walter Benjamin, *Selected Writings*, vol. 4, *1938–1940*, ed. Howard Eiland and Michael W. Jennings, trans. Edmund Jephcott et al. (Cambridge, Mass.: Belknap Press

of Harvard University Press, 2003), 27. Quoted in Tom Gunning, "Tracing the Individual Body: Photography, Detectives, and Early Cinema," in *Cinema and the Invention of Modern Life*, ed. Leo Charney and Vanessa R. Schwartz (Berkeley: University of California Press, 1995), 21.
59. Gunning, "Tracing the Individual Body," 24.
60. Dziga Vertov, "The Essence of Kino-Eye" (1925) and "Artistic Drama and Kino-Eye" (1924), in *Kino-Eye: The Writings of Dziga Vertov*, ed. Annette Michelson, trans. Kevin O'Brien (Berkeley: University of California Press, 1984), 50, 48.
61. Béla Balázs, *Early Film Theory: "Visible Man" and the "Spirit of Film,"* ed. Erica Carter, trans. Rodney Livingstone (New York: Berghahn Books, 2010), 34.
62. Gunning, "Tracing the Individual Body," 19.
63. Richard Curt Kraus, "Class Conflict and the Vocabulary of Social Analysis in China," *China Quarterly*, no. 69 (March 1977): 56
64. Quoted in Yiching Wu, *The Cultural Revolution at the Margins: Chinese Socialism in Crisis* (Cambridge, Mass.: Harvard University Press, 2014), 42.
65. Mao Zedong, "On the Correct Handling of Contradictions Among the People," https://www.marxists.org/reference/archive/mao/selected-works/volume-5/mswv5_58.htm, accessed October 13, 2021.
66. Rebecca E. Karl, *China's Revolutions in the Modern World* (New York: Verso, 2020), 128–29.
67. Patricia Thornton, *Disciplining the State: Virtue, Violence, and State-Making in Modern China* (Cambridge, Mass.: Harvard Asia Center, 2007), 133.
68. Denise Y. Ho, *Curating the Revolution: Politics on Display in Mao's China* (Cambridge: Cambridge University Press, 2018), 138–73. Haiyan Lee, *The Stranger and the Chinese Moral Imagination* (Stanford, Calif.: Stanford University Press, 2014), 197–242.
69. Denise Ho and Jie Li, "From Landlord Manor to Red Memorabilia: Reincarnations of a Chinese Museum Town," *Modern China* 42, no. 1 (2016): 3–37. Haiyan Lee, 197–242. Lee offers an excellent discussion on Maoist "class racism" when class became hereditary.
70. Jason McGrath, *Chinese Film: Realism and Convention from the Silent Era to the Digital Age* (Minneapolis: University of Minnesota Press, 2022), 201, 231, 236.
71. Barlow, *In the Event of Women*, 194–98.
72. Qi Benyu, "Aiguo zhuyi haishi maiguo zhuyi," 1.
73. Huang Zheng, *Liu Shaoqi de zuihou suiyue (1966–1969)* (The last years of Liu Shaoqi) (Beijing: Jiuzhou chubanshe, 2012), 109.
74. Jiang Qing, "Jiang Qing tongzhi jiejian," 156–57.
75. "Trial of Liu Shao-ch'i's Wife, 10 April 1967," 1699–1700.
76. This is estimated from an incomplete list of 1,780 documentary and newsreel film titles made during the period 1948–1979 that I have compiled.
77. The *People's Daily* regularly published news on such film exchanges, and such items were particularly frequent between 1960 and 1963. For example, on May 3, 1960, the paper reported that a documentary on the Nepali prime minister Bishweshwar Prasad Koirala's visit to China was shown in Kathmandu, and the prime minister himself attended the film. On December 25, 1963, the Chinese ambassador in Somalia presented to Somalia's prime minister Abdirashid Ali Shermarke a color film documenting his visit to China in August of the same year. The film was screened at the Chinese Embassy, and many of the highest government officials, including the prime minister himself, the minister of interior, and the minister of defense, attended the screening. On April 11, 1962, the Chinese ambassador in Ghana presented a documentary film to the Ghanian president Kwame Nkrumah on his visit to China in 1961.

The minister of news and broadcast took the gift and said that the film would be shown all over the country. On December 11, 1962, the Chinese ambassador in Cuba gave the documentary *Defending Cuba* (*Baowei guba*) to Fidel Castro. The film documented parades held in China in the beginning of November that year in support of Cuba during the Cuban Missile Crisis. In the 1950s, Soviet documentary and newsreel films on diplomacy were widely shown in China. These Soviet films and their means of circulation might have set the precedent for Chinese practices, though this linkage needs to be further examined. Examples include an article on March 13, 1956, entitled "Youyi de huaduo chuchu kai" (The flowers of friendship blossom everywhere), in which the writer Yuan Ying wrote about watching documentary films on Khrushchev's visits to India and Cambodia. These recordings of diplomatic events spur further diplomatic events.

6. Rehabilitation

1. "Pingfan yuanjia cuo'an de lishi jiejian" (Learning from history regarding rehabilitating wrong verdicts), *People's Daily*, November 20, 1978, 1.
2. Fang Fang, *Zhongguo jilupian fazhan shi* (The historical development of the Chinese documentary) (Beijing: Zhongguo xiju chubanshe, 2003), 289.
3. For details on the campaign against Deng Xiaoping and on Zhou Enlai's death, see Frederick C. Teiwes and Warren Sun, *The End of the Maoist Era: Chinese Politics During the Twilight of the Cultural Revolution, 1972–1976* (Armonk, N.Y.: Sharpe, 2007), 435–61.
4. Teiwes and Sun, 462–74.
5. Chen Jinshu, "Qinzhu zuiduo qinggan de *Yangmei jian chuqiao*" (*Drawing the Sword* where I poured the most emotion), Central Newsreel and Documentary Studio, http://www.cndfilm.com/20110322/104806.shtml.
6. Wu Hung, *Making History: Wu Hung on Contemporary Art* (Beijing: Timezone 8, 2005), 93.
7. *Renmin de daonian* (People's mourning) (Beijing: Beijing chubanshe, 1979).
8. Béla Balázs, *Early Film Theory: "Visible Man" and "The Spirit of Film,"* ed. Erica Carter, trans. Rodney Livingstone (New York: Berghahn Books, 2010), 9.
9. In 1980, writing about his experience working with the Dutch leftist filmmaker Joris Ivens, who was shooting his last film *A Tale of the Wind* (1988) in China, filmmaker Li Zexiang noted his surprise at Ivens's insistence on including diegetic sound in the film and observed that locational sound had rarely made it into Chinese documentaries up to then. Li Zexiang, "Duibai he shengyin jinru jilu dianying: yu Yiwensi yiqi gongzuo de diandi tihui" (Dialogue and sound entering documentary cinema: Some reflections on working with Ivens), *Shijie dianying* (World cinema), no. 4 (1980): 152–62.
10. Geremie Barmé, "History for the Masses," in Jonathan Unger, *Using the Past to Serve the Present: Historiography and Politics in Contemporary China* (Armonk, N.Y.: Sharpe, 1993), 262.
11. The Gang of Four were not the only ones standing trial. Among the accused were also five military officers who had allegedly attempted to assassinate Mao Zedong in 1971, and Mao's former secretary Chen Boda, who had been purged in 1970. Alexander C. Cook, *The Cultural Revolution on Trial: Mao and the Gang of Four* (Berkeley: University of California Press, 2016), 1.

12. Cook, 7, 8.
13. Alexander C. Cook, "Unsettling Accounts: The Trial of the Gang of Four" (Ph.D. diss., Columbia University, 2007), 74.
14. Cook, *The Cultural Revolution on Trial*, 68.
15. *People's Liberation Army Daily*, January 26, 1981, 1, quoted in Liu Teilin, "Zai lishi de tiezheng mianqian,—cong shengpan Lin Jiang fangeming jituan zhufan kan dang'an de pinzheng zuoyong" (Facing solid evidence of history: On the evidential function of archives in the trials of the antirevolutionary group of Lin and Jiang), *Dang'an xue tongxun* (Newsletter of archival science), no. 3 (1981): 31. Cook, *The Cultural Revolution on Trial*, 2, says that 651 items of evidence and 49 witnesses were presented.
16. Liu Tielin, "Zai lishi de tiezheng mianqian," 31–33.
17. Liu Teilin, 33.
18. Lowell Dittmer, "Death and Transfiguration: Liu Shaoqi's Rehabilitation and Contemporary Chinese Politics," *Journal of Asian Studies* 40, no. 3 (1981): 464.
19. Shi Cunzhen, ed., *Gongheguo lingxiu fengyun jishi* (Historical chronicles of leaders of the People's Republic) (Hohhot: Neimenggu renmin chubanshe, 1999), 3:485; Dittmer, "Death and Transfiguration," 464.
20. Chen Ruifeng, "Qianqiu gongguo ziyou renmin pingshuo: guankan daxing wenxian jilupian *Shaoqi tongzhi, renmin huainian nin* yougan" (The people evaluate historical merits: Reflections on the compilation documentary *Comrade Liu Shaoqi, the People Remember You*), *Dianying pingjie* (Film criticism and introduction), no. 5 (1980): 2–3.
21. Li Ge, "Shenqie de huainian: daxing jilupian *Shaoqi tongzhi, renmin huainian nin* guanhou" (Deep remembrance: After watching the documentary *Comrade Shaoqi, the People Remember You*), *Dianying pingjie*, no. 5 (1980): 3.
22. For Chinese funerary rites and their contribution to social hierarchy and cohesion, see James L. Watson and Evelyn S. Rawski, eds., *Death Ritual in Late Imperial and Modern China* (Berkeley: University of California Press, 1988).
23. The funeral films included titles such as *Weidade lingxiu he daoshi Mao Zedong zhuxi yongchui buxiu* (The Great Leader and mentor Chairman Mao Zedong forever lives, 1976, 12 reels); *Jing'aide Zhou Enlai zongli yongchui buxiu* (Dear Premier Zhou Enlai forever lives, 1976, 9 reels); and *Yongyuan huainian Zhu De weiyuanzhang* (Forever remember Committee Chairman Zhu De, 1977, 4 reels). Memory films included *Mao Zhuxi he women xinlianxin* (We are linked heart-to-heart with Chairman Mao, 1978, 4 reels); *Zhou Zongli he women zaiyiqi* (Premiere Zhou together with us, 1979, 4 reels); and *Zhu De weiyuanzhang huozai women xinli* (Committee Chairman Zhu De lives in our hearts, 1979, 6 reels). The practice of making both funeral and biographic films might have been an influence received from the Soviet Union. Both funeral and memory films were made after Lenin's passing. The first memory film of Lenin, *Leninskaia Kino-pravda* (Lenin's film-truth, 1925), was made on the first anniversary of his passing by the Soviet documentarian Dziga Vertov, who set out to make a number of such films about Lenin over the next ten years. See Jeremy Hicks, *Dziga Vertov: Defining Documentary Film* (London: Tauris, 2007), 13. Vertov's best-known film about Lenin was *Three Songs About Lenin* (1934), which memorializes Lenin on the tenth anniversary of his death. Lenin's funeral film was screened in Tianjin in 1924 and influenced how Sun Yat-sen's funeral was conducted and filmed in 1925. See Rudolf G. Wagner, "Ritual, Architecture, Politics, and Publicity During the Republic: Enshrining Sun Yat-sen," in *Chinese Architecture and the Beaux-Arts*, ed. Jeffrey W. Cody, Nancy S. Steinhardt, and Tony Atkin (Honolulu: University of Hawai'i Press, 2011), 223–78. On page 234, Wagner incorrectly identifies Lenin's funeral film (*Lie Ning*

chubinji) as Vertov's memory film *Leninskaia Kino-pravda*, which was actually released in 1925 for the first anniversary of Lenin's death. However, Wagner's article discusses in great detail and with insight the influence of Western (Soviet and American) state funerals on Sun Yat-sen's funeral, as the new republic had to search for new funeral rituals. The funeral film of Stalin, released in 1953, featured mourning crowds all over the Soviet Union as well as in other socialist countries, including a Tiananmen Square packed with Chinese mourners led by Mao Zedong himself. The funeral film of Mao in 1976 followed the format of that of Stalin, involving millions of mourners who gathered in Tiananmen Square and scenes of mourning all over China.

24. Fang Fang, *Zhongguo jilupian fazhan shi*, 289.
25. Huang Zheng, *Liu Shaoqi de zuihou suiyue, 1966–1969* (Liu Shaoqi's last years, 1966–1969) (Beijing: Zhongyang wenxian chubanshe, 1996), 249.
26. Wang Ximin and Hao Wenwei, *Gongheguo miwenlu* (Collection of secret news of the republic) (Beijing: Zhongguo guoji guangbo chubanshe, 1990), 156.
27. This series includes *Ye Jianying* (1983), *Liu Bochen* (1984), *Nie Rongzhen* (1985), and *Xu Xiangqian* (1986).
28. *Lu Xun zhuan* (Biography of Lu Xun, 1981), *Geming laoren He Xiangning* (A revolutionary elder: He Xiangning, 1982), *Chizi xin—huainian Liaogong* (Heart of a patriot: Remembering Liao Zhongkai, 1983), *Huaqiao qizhi Chen Jiagen* (A banner among Overseas Chinese: Chen Jiagen 1984), *Renmin yishujia Zhao Dan* (People's artist Zhao Dan, 1985), and *Ba Jin* (1987).
29. Hao Chunyang, "Huan lishi de benlai mianmu—fang *Jindai chunqiu* zong daoyan He Zhongxin" (Return to history its original face: Interview with He Zhongxin, director of *Chronicle of the Modern Era*), *Dianying pinglun*, November 1986, 10.
30. Fu Hongxing, "Xiezai jiaopian shang de lishi: tan xin Zhongguo wenxian jilupian de chuangzuo" (History written on film: A discussion of compilation documentary filmmaking in the new China), *Dangdai dianying* (*Contemporary cinema*), May 2000, 47–52. For the period 1977–1985, see 49–50.
31. Wang Ying, "*Lishishang de jintian* kaibo yilai" (Since *Today in History* began broadcasting), *Xinwen yu xiezuo* (News and writing), April 1988, 28.
32. Wang Ying, 28.
33. Zhang Daoyou, "*Lishishang de jintian* gei women de qishi" (What *Today in History* has shown us), *Dang'an yu jianshe* (Archive and construction), April 1989, 27.
34. Michel Foucault, *The Archaeology of Knowledge*, trans. A. M. Sheridan Smith (London: Routledge, 2002), 145.
35. Yuezhi Zhao and Zhenzhi Guo, "From Political Mobilization to Commercial Revolution: Television and the Contradictions of Chinese Reform," in *A Companion to Television*, ed. Janet Wasko (Malden, Mass.: Blackwell, 2005), 523.
36. Su Xiaokang and Wang Lu-hsiang, *Deathsong of the River: A Reader's Guide to the Chinese TV Series "Heshang,"* trans. Richard W. Bodman and Pin P. Wan (Ithaca, N.Y.: Cornell University Press, 1991), 65.
37. Fang Fang, *Zhongguo jilupian fazhan shi*, 308.
38. Wang Jiyan, "Shilun weirao dianshi texing zhizuo jiemu: cong dianshipian *Sichou zhi Lu* de bianji tese tanqi" (Producing content according to the specificity of television: On the special qualities of editing in *Silk Road*), *Xiandai chuanbo* (Modern communication), no. 3 (1983): 36.
39. Pei Yuzhang, "Xiezai *Sichou zhi lu* shezhi wanbi de shihou" (Notes upon the completion of *Silk Road*), *Xinwen zhanxian* (The news front), no. 10 (1981): 29.
40. Fang Fang, *Zhongguo jilupian fazhan shi*, 312.

41. Wang Jiyan, "Shilun weirao dianshi texing zhizuo jiemu: cong dianshipian 'sichou zhi lu' de bianji tese tanqi" (On making programs based on the specificity of television: Speaking from the editing of the television program *Silk Road*), *Xiandai chuanbo*, no. 1 (1983), 35–39.
42. Corey Byrnes, *Fixing Landscape: A Techno-Poetic History of China's Three Gorges* (New York: Columbia University Press, 2018), 18.
43. Su Xiaokang, "Longnian de beichuang" (The tragedy of the dragon year), in *Haiwai "heshang" da taolun* (Heated debates on *River Elegy* overseas), ed. Su Xiaokang and Cui Wenhua (Harbin: Heilongjiang chubanshe, 1988), 71.
44. A year before, a similar expedition on the Yangtze River had been attempted, also responding to plans by American rafting teams to raft on the Yangtze. While in both cases the American teams quit after ascertaining that the weather conditions were too dangerous, the Chinese rafters pushed on, losing ten lives on the Yangtze and seven lives on the Yellow River.
45. While viewers responded enthusiastically to *Today in History*, which grew to be among the top three most popular programs on television in 1988, the authorities grew more and more nervous over the program's popularity, fearing this free-form revisitation of recent history, without a master-narrative to rule over its meaning, might lead to social instability. *Today in History* was shut down on September 30, 1988, making its totally running time to be just a year, three months shorter than planned. Liu Jianming, *Dangdai xinwenxue yuanli* (Theory of contemporary journalism) (Beijing: Tsinghua University Press, 2003), 101.
46. Su Xiaokang, "Longnian de beichuang," 71.
47. Alexander V. Pantsov with Steven I. Levine, *Deng Xiaoping: A Revolutionary Life* (Oxford: Oxford University Press, 2015), 401.
48. Ba Jin, "Wenge bowuguan" (Cultural Revolution Museum), in *Wuti ji: Suixiang lu* (Records of random thoughts) (Beijing: Renmin wenxue chubanshe, 1986), 5:121.
49. Wang Hui, "The Year 1989 and the Historical Roots of Neoliberalism in China," trans. Rebecca E. Karl, *positions: east asia critique* 12, no. 1 (2004): 16–18.
50. Isabella M. Weber, *How China Escaped Shock Therapy: The Market Reform Debate* (London: Routledge, 2021), 227.
51. Wang Hui, "The Year 1989," 18–19; Weber, *How China Escaped Shock Therapy*, 252–53.
52. Hong Heng to CCTV, June 19, 1988, in *He shang lun* (Discussions on *River Elegy*), ed. Cui Wenhua (Beijing: Wenhua yishu chubanshe, 1988), 102.
53. Xiu Xinmin to CCTV, June 19, 1988, in Cui Wenhua, *He shang lun*, 113.
54. Wang Pin, "Minzu lishi wenhua de fansi" (Reflections on nation, history, and culture), *Guoji shangbao* (International business daily), July 2, 1988, in Cui Wenhua, *He shang lun*, 168.
55. Zhong Min, "Gandai yu beidao" (Admiration and mourning), *Shanghai wenhua yishu bao* (Shanghai culture and art weekly), July 15, 1988, in Cui Wenhua, *He shang lun*, 170.
56. Jing Wang, "*He shang* and the Paradoxes of Chinese Enlightenment," *Bulletin of Concerned Asian Scholars*, 23, no. 3 (1991), 24–25.
57. Xiao Liu, *Information Fantasies: Precarious Mediation in Postsocialist China* (Minneapolis: University of Minnesota Press, 2019), 126.
58. Jin Guantao, in "Tong renmin yiqi lai sikao" (Thinking together with the people) (collection of speeches at the *River Elegy* discussion forum), *Wenyibao* (Literature and art weekly), July 16, 1988, in Cui Wenhua, *He shang lun*, 143–44.
59. Wang, "*He shang* and the Paradoxes of Chinese Enlightenment," 31.

290   6. Rehabilitation

60. Jacques Derrida, *Specters of Marx: The State of the Debt, the Work of Mourning, and the New International*, trans. Peggy Kamuf (New York: Routlege, 2006), xvii, 4, xviii.
61. Alessia Ricciardi, *The Ends of Mourning: Psychoanalysis, Literature, Film* (Stanford, Calif.: Stanford University Press, 2003), 6, 9.

Epilogue

1. For video piracy, internet forums and the rise of unofficial cinema culture in the late 1990s and early 2000s, see Jinying Li, "Piracy, Cinema, and an Alternative Public Sphere in Urban China," *International Journal of Communication* 6 (2012): 542–63. For a discussion of independent film festivals and their closures, see Sabrina Qiong Yu and Lydia Dan Wu, "The China Independent Film Festival and Chinese Independent Film Festivals: Self-Legitimization and Institutionalization," in *Chinese Film Festivals: Sites of Translation*, ed. Chris Berry and Luke Robinson (New York: Palgrave Macmillan, 2017).
2. Scholarship on independent documentary has grown in recent decades. For a succinct overview, see Ying Qian, "Power in the Frame: China's Independent Documentary Movement," *New Left Review* 74 (March–April 2012), 105–23. Selected book-length studies include Lü Xinyu, *Ji lu Zhongguo: dang dai Zhongguo xin ji lu yun dong* (Beijing: Sheng huo, du shu, xin zhi san lien shu dian, 2003); Chris Berry, Lu Xinyu and Lisa Rofel eds., *The New Chinese Documentary Film Movement: For the Public Record* (Hong Kong University Press, 2010); Zhang Zhen and Angela Zito eds., *DV-Made China: Digital Subjects and Social Transformations After Independent Film* (Honolulu: University of Hawai'i Press, 2015); Matthew D. Johnson, Keith B. Wagner, Kiki Tianqi Yu, and Luke Vulpiani eds., *China's iGeneration: Cinema and Moving Image Culture for the Twenty-First Century* (London: Continuum, 2014); Dan Edwards, *Independent Chinese Documentary: Alternative Visions, Alternative Publics* (Edinburgh: Edinburgh University Press, 2015). Selected articles include Yiman Wang, "The Amateur's Lightning Rod: DV Documentary in Postsocialist China," *Film Quarterly* 58, no. 4 (Summer 2005): 16–26; Chris Berry, "Getting Real: Chinese Documentary, Chinese Postsocialism," in *The Urban Generation: Chinese Cinema and Society at the Turn of the Twenty-First Century*, ed. Zhen Zhang (Durham, N.C.: Duke University Press, 2007), 115–36; Yingjin Zhang, "Rebel Without a Cause? China's New Urban Generation and Postsocialist Filmmaking," in Zhen Zhang, *The Urban Generation*, 50–54; Luke Robinson, *Independent Chinese Documentary: From the Studio to the Street* (New York: Palgrave Macmillan, 2013). Meanwhile, the Chinese Independent Film Archive (CIFA), https://www.chinaindiefilm.org/, led by Sabrina Qiong Yu, Chris Berry, and Luke Robinson, is an excellent resource to delve into independent documentary.
3. This is observed in the majority of studies of Chinese independent documentary, some of which are listed in note 2. Jie Li has done excellent work on documentary's processing of history and its concerns for the social margins. See, for example, Jie Li, "Filming Power and Powerless: Zhao Liang's Crime and Punishment (2007) and Petition (2009)," in Zhang and Zito, *DV-Made China*, 76–96; Jie Li, "Virtual Museums of Forbidden Memories: Hu Jie's Documentary Films on the Cultural Revolution," *Public Culture* 21, no. 3 (2009): 539–49. On autobiographical documentary, see Qi Wang, *Memory, Subjectivity and Independent Chinese Cinema* (Edinburgh: Edinburgh University Press, 2014); and Kiki Tianqi Yu, *"MY" Self on Camera: First Person*

Documentary Practice in an Individualising China (Edinburgh: Edinburgh University Press, 2018).
4. Erin Y. Huang, *Urban Horror: Neoliberal Post-Socialism and the Limits of Visibility* (Durham, N.C.: Duke University Press, 2020).
5. Ying Qian, "Just Images: Ethics and Documentary Film in China," *China Heritage Quarterly*, no. 29 (March 2012), http://www.chinaheritagequarterly.org/scholarship.php?searchterm=029_qian.inc&issue=029.
6. Guobin Yang, *The Power of the Internet in China* (New York: Columbia University Press, 2009).
7. For an excellent analysis of independent documentary's embedment in grassroots activism in this period, see Sebastian Veg, *Min Jian: The Rise of China's Grassroots Intellectuals* (New York: Columbia University Press, 2019). Also see Ying Qian, "Working with Rubble: Montage, Tweets and the Reconstruction of an Activist Cinema," in *China's iGeneration: Filmmakers, Films and Audiences in a New Media Age*, ed. Matthew D. Johnson et al. (London: Continuum, 2014), 181–96.
8. Cong Feng, "On Social Compound Eye," trans. Liu Pei-An, Soft: DocLab, November 2011, https://soft-doc.com/?p=528.
9. Donna Haraway, "Situated Knowledges: The Science Question in Feminism and the Privilege of Partial Perspective," *Feminist Studies* 14, no. 3 (Autumn 1988): 575, 599, 583, 581, 584.

INDEX

aerial view: bombing from air in *The Battle of China* (1944, dir. Frank Capra), 112–13; Lai Manwai's aerial shot, 55; Liu Na'ou's aerial filming in Japan; the scattering of Zhou Enlai's ashes, 229; used in Sino-Japanese documentary coproductions of *Yangtze* (1983), 235; the labor of aerial shot reflected upon in *Grand Canal* (1986), 237–38
Ai Weiwei, 252
Ai Xiaoming, 252
Aleksandrov, Grigori, *October* (1927, codirected with Sergei Eisenstein), 139
Alptekin, Isa Yusuf, 117
Althusser, Louis, 6
amateur photography: active role in documenting the April 5 Movement, 217–19
amateur cinema: amateur filmmaking by Liu Na'ou, 85–86, 96–97, 100; small-scale filmmaking in the 1920s and 1930s, 82–83; amateur cinema league (Shanghai), 82–83, 270n59; film liberated from cinemas, 83–84; amateur film club (9.5mm) in Taiwan, 270n70.

See also *Liu Na'ou–Man Who Holds a Movie Camera*
Anti–Rightist Campaign (1957–1958): de-Stalinization and uncertainty, 178, 194; experiments with documentary form at Xinying halted during, 21, 151, 180, 194, 195, 196; *Plum Flowers, Spring Rain, and Jiangnan* labeled as a "poisonous weed" during, 188; political risk of feature film production, 151; Zhong Daifei named a "rightist" during, 187
April 5 Movement: chronicled in *Draw Your Sword*, 215, 216–17, 218, 221; documentary's participation in, 213, 218; new political aesthetics on Tiananmen Square created by, 217; rehabilitation of, 221–22; as a turning point for Chinese photography, 217; Zhou Enlai's passing, 216. See also *Raise Your Eyebrows and Draw Your Sword* (*Yangmei jian chujiao*)
Arendt, Hannah, 147
Arjia Rinpoche, 117
artistic documentary (yishuxing jilupian). *See* documenting tomorrow–artistic documentary (*yishuxing jilupian*)

Ba Jin, 230, 242
backyard furnaces: for making "native iron"(*tutie*), 168; instrumental films on how to make, 168–70, *170*
Badiou, Alain, 14–15, 17–18, 22
Balázs, Béla, 206, 218
Bandung Conference (1955): *The Bandung Conference* (*Wanlong huiyi*, 1955), documentary film by Xinying, 14, 186; cursory inclusion in *Chairman Liu Visits Indonesia*, 201
Bao Weihong, 75, 100, 103–4, 113.
Barlow, Tani, 205, 209
The Battle of China (1944, dir. Frank Capra), 112–13
Battle of Shanghai: advertisement for Hearst Metrotone newsreels, 68, 68; Cheng Bugao's covering of, 62, 73; Terry Ramsaye on newsreel production in, 66–67, 268n17; as a "watershed movement" for news films in China, 66–70. See also *Cheng Bugao-Battle of Shanghai*
Baumbach, Nico, 22
Beijing Film Studio, 141, 149
Beijing Queer Film Festival, 248
Benjamin, Walter, 36, 152, 165, 205
Berry, Chris, 255n1, 276n12, 290n1–2
Berry, Michael, 262n38
biographical documentaries: amateur filmmaking of Liu Na'ou, 85–86, 96–97, 100; autobiographical filmmaking in independent documentary, 250–51; *Comrade Liu Shaoqi, the People Remember You* (*Shaoqi tongzhi renmin huainian nin*, 1980), 226, 230; *Long Live the Memory of Comrade Liu Shaoqi* (*Liu Shaoqi tongzhi yongchui buxiu*, 1980), 226, 228–29, *229*; *Long Live the Memory of Premier Zhou Enlai* (*Jing'aide Zhou Enlai Zongli yongchui buxiu*, 1977), 228–29, 287n23; *The Songs of the Pioneers* (*Xianquzhe zhi ge*, 1981) by Xinying filmmakers, 230; *Three Songs of Lenin* (1934) by Dziga Vertov, 228, 287–88n23. See also *Liu Na'ou–Man Who Holds a Movie Camera*; rehabilitation
Bliokh, Yakuv, *Fishermen of the Caspian* (1949), 140; *Shanghai Document* (1928), 143–44

Bolter, Jay David, 36
Braester, Yomi, 163
Brodsky, Benjamin, 54, 266n106
Byrnes, Corey, 236

Cambodia: documentary films on Khrushchev's visits to India and Cambodia, 286n77; Liu Shaoqi's visit to, 176
The Caprice of the Ming Tombs Reservoir (*Shisanling shuiku changxiangqu*, dir. Jin Shan, 1958): as a conversion story for intellectuals, 170–72; foregrounding of television as the next generation of mass media, 164–65, *164*; future full of miracles depicted in, 161–62; industrial and traditional aesthetics mixed in, 166; optimism and mass action in, 163, *164*; production of, 159, 160–61; Tian Han's effort to "document tomorrow," 160–62
Cartier-Bresson, Henri, 159
cartography and cartographic cinema: orientation to international and domestic terrains by documentaries, 24, 180, 211; *Plum Flowers, Spring Rain*, and *Jiangnan*'s immersive (anti-)cartography, 183, 189; *Resist America and Aid Korea*'s cartographic value, 24, 182, 183, 189
CCTV (China Central Television): the founding of, 233. See also television
Central Newsreel and Documentary Film Studio (*Zhongyang Xinwen jilu dianying zhipianchang*). See Xinying
Central Cultural Revolution Small Group (*Zhongyang wenhua geming xiaozu*), 177
Chairman Liu Shaoqi Visits Indonesia (*Liu Shaoqi zhuxi fangwen Yindunixiya*, 1963): *Congratulations* compared with, 199–200; reediting as *Criminal Liu Visits Indonesia* (*Liuzei fangwen yindunixiya*, 1967), 201, 202–5; reenactment at a rally at Tsinghua University, 175–76, 177; reruns of, 210; Wang Guangmei's role as a "diplomatic wife" featured in, 21, 176, 180, 200–1

Chen Bo, on Varlamov's direction of documentary films, 141
Chen Duo and Hong Yun: narration of *Grand Canal*, 236–37, 238–39; narration of *Yangtze*, 235–36
Chen Guangzhong: hailing from Hong Kong, 193; *Forever Young* (*Yongyuan nianqing*, 1954) directed by, 189, 193; *Pretty but not Solid* (*Hua er bu shi*, 1956), 193
Chen Guangzhong-An Inch of Time Is Worth and Inch of Gold (*Yicun guangyin yicun jin*, 1959): inculcation of socialist modern temporality, 151–52; self-actualizing workers portrayed in, 153, 153, 156; on time management, 145, 148
Chen Huangmei, 150, 171
Chen Jianran-*The May Thirtieth Shanghai Movement* (*Wusa Huchao*, 1925): destruction in the bombing of Shanghai, 66; workers' protest and general strike in 1925 recorded in, 9, 60–61, 63, 64, 104
Chen Jinshu, 215–16
Chen Mou, 204
Chen Xiaoqing, 248
Chen Xihe, 28
Cheng Bugao: on American newsreel producers, 65; *Amorous History of the Silver Screen* (*Yinmu yanshi*, 1931), 78; leftward turn in filmmaking, 62
Cheng Bugao-*Battle of Shanghai*: as a box office hit, 71; docu-fiction, 72–73, 136; footage quoted in *Chronicle of the Modern Era*, 231
Cheng Bugao-*Spring Silkworm* (*Chun chan*, 1933): as a process film, 19, 76–78, 77, 131–32; bodies of water connected to liquidity of capital and commodity exchange, 94; as educational cinema, 80; as left-wing docu-fiction, 50, 73, 80; Mao Dun's (*Shen Yanbing*) novella *Spring Silkworm* adapted for its storyline, 75, 80; as a sketch (*sumiao*), 79; Xia Yan's collaboration on, 71, 75
Cheng Bugao-*Torrent* (*Kuangliu*, 1933): class struggle dramatized in, 76, 94; as left-wing docu-fiction, 62–63, 73–75; Xia Yan's collaboration on, 71, 74
Cheng Yu, application to build a factory to distribute educational films, 48–49, 50
Chinese Communist Party (CCP)-campaigns: Anti-Spiritual Pollution Campaign (October–December 1983), 242; Special Report on the Three-Anti and Five-Anti Campaigns (*Sanfan wufan teiji*, 1951), 184. *See also* Anti-Rightist Campaign (1957–1958); Hundred Flowers Campaign (1957–1958); Socialist Education Movement
Chinese Independent Film Archive, 290n1
The Chinese Revolution. See Umeya Shōkichi-*The Chinese Revolution*
Chronicle of the Modern Era (*Jindai chunqiu*, 1984–89), 231
Chu Yingchi, 256n8
Civil War (1946–1950), documentary filmmaking during, 14, 17, 103, 132–33, 134, 143, 143
class analysis and class struggle: the behavioral turn of class designations, 207–8; documentary creating class archetypes, 180; Mao Zedong's 1925 article on class analysis, 178; Mao Zedong's call to "never forget class struggle," 207; media ecology of class struggle, 205; *Never Forget* (*Qianwan buneng wangji*, 1964), 208
coloniality/modernity, 28, 260n5
Commercial Press: drama films made by, 51–52; educational filmmaking by, 8, 28, 48, 50–51, 59, 154, 260n10; loss of its films during the Japanese air raid on Shanghai (1932), 66, 71; making of *Yan Ruisheng* (1921) and *Red Beauty and Skeleton* (*Hongfen kulou*, 1921) facilitated by, 52
Cong Feng, on the "social compound eye" (*shehui fuyan*), 253
Congratulations (*Zhuhe*, 1958), Mao Zedong's visit to Moscow (November 1957) documented, 194
Cook, Alexander C., 222
Crary, Jonathan, 172
Cui Zi'en-*Queer China, "Comrade" China* (*Zhi tongzhi*), 252

Cultural Revolution: critique of Badiou's evaluation of, 22; enmeshment in Cold War geopolitics, 178–9; "formalist drift" in documentaries made during, 22, 208–9; as long-term consequence of the Great Leap Forward, 174; Liu Shaoqi and Wang Guangmei condemned at the height of, 21, 176–77, 202; Liu Shaoqi's lament of "frivolous politics," 181, 201, 202; Red Guards inspected by Mao in Tiananmen Square during, 216; historical images rarely included in documentaries in the 1980s, 241

De Michiel, Helen, 11
Democracy Wall Movement, 222, 226, 247
Deng Xiaoping: on avoiding historical details (*yicu bu yixi*) when examining past events, 222; in charge of the PRC's economy (1961), 196; mass denunciations of, 216; rehabilitation of (July 1977), 214
Deng Yingchao, "wife diplomacy" considered by, 197–98
Derrida, Jacques, 245–46
Djagalov, Rossen, 105, 106
Doane, Mary Ann, on cinema as a time-based medium, 151
docu-fiction. *See* Cheng Bugao–*Battle of Shanghai*; Cheng Bugao–*Spring Silkworm (Chun chan*, 1933); Cheng Bugao–*Torrent (Kuangliu*, 1933); documenting tomorrow–artistic documentary (*yishuxing jilupian*)
documentary defined: the Chinese term *jilu* (documentary), 7, 27, 58, 257n22, 259n4; John Grierson's definition provincialized, 5–7; multifaceted productivity of, 5, 9–10; as eventful media, 14.
documenting tomorrow: He Jingzhi's call for, 157; labor mobilizational for rural construction associated with, 158–59; logic or process film pushed to its limit by, 19
documenting tomorrow–artistic documentary (*yishuxing jilupian*): Ding Jiao on, 157; docu-fiction during the Great Leap Forward, 24, 146, 163–64; process film logic pushed to its limit by, 20; *Songs on the Reservoir (Shuiku shang de gesheng)*, 159–60, 164, 165, 278n8; *Split Mountains to Bring Water (Pishan yinshui*, 1958), 157; *Spring in the Mountains (Shanqu de chuntian*, 1958), 157; Zhou Enlai's suggestion of, 157.
Donaldson, Leonard, 49, 264n83
Dovzhenko, Alexander, *Michurin* (1948), 162
Draw Your Sword. *See Raise Your Eyebrows and Draw Your Sword (Yangmei jian chujiao)*
Duan Jinchuan, 248
Dziga-Vertov Group, 3

educational film: in Cheng Bugao's *Spring Silkworm*, 80; Cheng Yu's application to build a factory to distribute educational films, 48–49, 50; film production by the Commercial Press, 8, 28, 48, 50–52, 59, 154; importance of media to revolutionary endeavors, 2–3, 12–14; Lenin's ordering of educational films for labor retraining, 154–55; M. Pathé's educational focus, 46; pedagogical use of cinema in Europe and the U.S., 49–50; Chinese elites' interest in cinema's educational value, 49. *See also* Northeastern Film Studio (*Dongbei dianying zhipian chang*); popular education associations; process films; Socialist Education Movement
1895: cinema's invention in, 2, 26; reconfiguration of power dynamics in East Asia after the First Sino-Japanese War, 2
Eisenmen, Joshua, 162
Eisenstein, Sergei, *October* (1927, codirected with Grigori Aleksandrov), 139
Elman, Benjamin, 31
Elsaesser, Thomas, 11
events and eventfulness: actualization of revolutionary movements by documentary practices, 2–3; anti-event tendencies of documentary, 22; documentary as an eventful medium, 3, 4–5, 14–16, 22–23, 104, 253–54; propaganda

documentary production as eventful, 104–5, 143

The Fall of the Romanov Dynasty (dir. Esfir Shub, 1927), 53
Fan, Victor, 100, 270n72
Fang Fang, 215
Feng Yuxiang, 57–8.
Feng Yuxiang's Northern Expedition Work (Feng Yuxiang beifa gongzuo ji, 1929): Soviet training of filmmaker Zhao Yiyun, 57; warlord leadership on screen, 28, 53, 57
film diplomacy, 285–6n77
Firestein, Stuart, on failure, 175
First Opium War (1839–1842): China's earliest newspapers established after, 32; first known instance of photography in China, 31–32, 34
First Sino-Japanese War (1894–1895): annihilation of the Beiyang Fleet during, 38–39, 42; Cheng Yu's photographing of war trophies in Japan, 33–36, 35; Japanese propaganda and the "optical illusion," 31; mushrooming of political newspapers after, 32–3; searchlight featured in Japanese woodblock prints made during, 29–30
Flowers of Innovation Bloom Everywhere (Biankai gexinhua, 1960), 173–74
folklore and folk technologies: "folk furnaces" (tugaolu) built during the Great Leap Forward, 146, 168–69; *Hongqi geyao (Songs of the red flag)* edited by Zhou Yang and Guo Moruo, 167; revival during the Great Leap Forward, 166–67
Foucault, Michel, 27, 258n29

Gaines, Jane, 7
Gang of Four trials: archival materials—including audiovisual materials—used in the court proceedings, 224–25; *Indictment Sent to the Lin and Jiang Group (Qisushu songda Lin Jiang jituan,* 1980), 223; reels of "documentary evidence" at the trial of, 4, 25, 213; *Trial by Nine Hundred Million People (Jiuyi renmin de shenpan,* 1980), 223–24; TV broadcast of, 222
Gao Zhongming, 188, 193
Gao Zhongming–*Plum Flowers, Spring Rain, and Jiangnan (Xinghua chunyu Jiangnan,* 1957, codirected with Zhang Mengqi): aesthetic of play in, 190, 190–91; as alternative cartography, 189; Shi Mei's criticism of, 188–89, 191; Yangtze compared with, 236
Ge Gongzhen, 32
Ge Zhongbo, 204
Geneva Conference of 1954: *The Butterfly Lovers (Liang Shanbo yu Zhu Yingtai,* 1954, dir. Sang Hu and Huang Sha) screened at, 185–86, 198; *The National Day 1952 (1952nian guoqing yuebing,* 1952) screened at, 185; PRC's participation in, 185–86, 198; Zhou Enlai's soft diplomacy, 185, 198
Gerasimov, Sergei, 135, 141
gongnongbing cinema, 191
Gilbreth, Frank, time-motion study films, 153, 153, 155. *See also* Taylorism
Gramsci, Antonio, 18
Grand Canal (Stories of the Grand Canal, Huashuo yunhe, 1986), 214, 236–39
Great Leap Forward (1957–1960): devastating failure of, 148, 174–75, 196, 207; documentary and fiction combined during, 24, 146, 163–64, 196–97; first television broadcast launched during (1958), 233; *Flowers of Innovation Bloom Everywhere (Biankai gexinhua,* 1960), 173–74; growth in documentary cinema during, 150–51; instructional films for backyard furnaces, 20, 168–69; labor conditions during, 172–73; mass campaign to speed up industrialization, 147–48; scarcely mediated Great Famine subsequent to, 175; "winning temporalities" propagated in documentaries during, 175
Green Revolution: coining by William Gaud of USAID, 162; Lysenko-Michurin theory, 162–63
Grierson, John: documentary defined, 5–7, 225; excluding newsreel from documentary, 63–64

Grigoriev, R. "On the Documentary Screenplay," 141
Grusin, Richard, 36
Guillory, John, 10
Gunning, Tom, 19, 34, 46, 77–78, 205–6
Guobin Yang, 252
Guo Moruo, 157, 167

Hansen, Miriam Bratu, 152
Haraway, Donna, 253
hard (Marxist) versus soft (modernist) cinema debate: contribution of documentary to, 9, 23–24, 100; dismissal of soft film in early PRC, 272n80; modes of filmmaking on both sides compared, 62–63; revolution hard as well as soft, 101
Harding, Sarah, 253
He Jingzhi, 156–57, 158
He Zhongxin, 231, 232
Hong Yun. See Chen Duo and Hong Yun
Horn, Eva, 11
Hu Feng, "Time Has Begun," 147
Hu Jie, 252
Huang Baomei (1958, dir. Xie Jin): labor discontent minimized in, 173; textile workers turned into weaving fairies in, 166, 166
Huang, Erin Y., 251
Huang Jiamo, 78
Hundred Flowers Campaign (1956–1957): experiments with documentary form at Xinying during, 20–21, 187; and de-Stalinization, 178, 194; Zhong Dianfei's "The Gongs and Drums of Cinema" published during, 191

Inch of Time. See Chen Guangzhong–*An Inch of Time Is Worth an Inch of Gold* (*Yicun guangyin yicun jin*, 1959)
independent documentary: activist turn, 252–53; association with television, 248; DV and digital platforms, 248, 253; ethics, 251; independent film festivals, 248–49; personal turn, 250–51; piracy, 251–52; post-1989 refusal to mediate for the party, 23, 250; rise of, 4, 248–49, 290n1; taboo topics and social margins, 251, 290–91n3

Indictment Sent to the Lin and Jiang Group (*Qisushu songda Lin Jiang jituan*, 1980). See Gang of Four trials
Indonesia: U.S.-backed military coup in 1965, 176, 201–2. See also Bandung Conference (1955); *Chairman Liu Shaoqi Visits Indonesia* (*Liu Shaoqi zhuxi fangwen Yindunixiya*, 1963); "wife diplomacy"
infrastructure: construction of irrigation infrastructure during the Great Leap Forward, 158–59, 174; for documentary production in the PRC, 14, 149–51, 179; the Grand Canal as, 214, 237; Lenin's writing on the newspaper as revolutionary infrastructure, 12; media infrastructure, 11, 104, 258n29; for newsreel production (early twentieth century and wartime), 8, 64, 127; for television production and broadcasting, 165, 233; shared by early revolutionaries and filmmakers, 2; television as, 237, 239
Ivens, Joris: *400 Million* (1937), 105, 112, 125; Li Zexiang's observation on his *A Tale of the Wind* (1988), 286n9; meeting with Yuan Muzhi, 9; *Rain*, 92, 189; as a solidarity filmmaker, 9, 16; *Song of Heroes*, 125; *The Spanish Earth* (1937), 105, 125

Jiang, Jin, 185
Jiang Qing: arrest of, 213; public appearance in the context of "wife diplomacy," 199; meeting with Xinying filmmakers in 1967, 202, 204, 210; at court, 224. See also Gang of Four trials
Jiang Yunchuan, 191
Jia Zhangke, 252
jilu (documentary), etymological meanings associated with, 27, 259n4. See also documentary defined
Jin Guantao, 245

Kara, Selmin, 11
Karl, Rebecca, 207
Karman, Roman: his view on dramatization, 116, 272–73n35; short films made in Yan'an, 16–17; "The Cultivation of a Documentary Cinematographer," 133

Khanddorj, 117
Khrushchev, Nikita: depictions in Congratulations, 194; de-Stalinization, 194; documentary films of his visits to India and Cambodia, 286n77; Liu Shaoqi compared with, 202–5; Mao's criticism of Khrushchev's de-Stalinization efforts, 195–96; N. S. Khrushchev in the U.S.A (1959), 205
Kirby, Lynn, 55
kiroku eiga (documentary films): the Chinese term *jilu dianying* ("documentary film") derived from, 7, 26, 257n22, 271n1; filming of the Boxer Rebellion as the first *jiji eiga* (current events film) in Japan, 34
Kittler, Frederich, 38
Kobayashi Toshimitsu, *Our Army's Great Victory at the Night Battle of Pyongyang*, 30, 30, 31
Korean War: documentary's cartographic function in, 181–82; impact on domestic politics, 183. See also Resist America and Aid Korea (1951)
Kracauer, Siegfried, on mass ornament, 190

labor: artisanal filmmaking in Yan'an, 132; Chen Jianran's filming of workers' protests and general strike in 1925, 9, 60–61, 63, 64, 104; film screenings organized by trade unions, 277n29; inculcation of industrial temporality, 155–56; labor unrest prior to the Great Leap Forward, 172–73; Marx on labor alienation under capitalism, 155–56; process of silkworm farming in *Spring Silkworm*, 131–32; of rural construction, 158–59; Taylorist images of work routines, 146, 153–54, 156; Zheng Junli's substitution of labor for capital, 123. See also Chen Guangzhong–*An Inch of Time Is Worth an Inch of Gold* (*Yicun guangyin yicun jin*); *Huang Baomei* (1958, dir. Xie Jin)
Lai Manwai: background of, 54; collaborations with Benjamin Brodsky, 54, 266n106; filming of the Northern Expedition, 54, 266n110; general strike in Shanghai filmed by, 59; *War of Resistance in Songjiang and Shanghai* (*Songhu kangzhan jishi*), 231
Lai Manwai–*Minxin* (*New People*): founded by, 54; mobility and combat featured in, 54; Sun Yat-Sen's activities filmed by, 54
Lai Manwai–*War on Sea, Land, and Air* (*Guominjun hailukong dazhan ji*): etiquette during exhibitions of, 56; footage included in *Chronicle of the Modern Era* (1984–1989), 232; footage included in *River Elegy* (1988), 241; photographic portraits, 57; political leadership of the Nationalist Party articulated in, 53; screening of, 266n102
Lardy, Nicholas, 158
Laughlin, Charles, on Chinese reportage literature, 72
LBGTQ activism: Beijing Queer Film Festival, 248; Cui Zi'en's *Queer China, "Comrade" China* (*Zhi tongzhi*), 252
Lee, Haiyan, 285n68–69
Lenin: educational films ordered for labor retraining, 154–55; on newspaper as the "starting point" toward revolutionary organization, 12; *Three Songs of Lenin* (1934), 228, 287–88n23
Li, Jie, 279n56, 281n95, 285n69, 290–91n3
Li, Jinying, 290n1
Li Hong, 248
Li Minwei. See Lai Manwai
Li Xianting Film fund, 248–49
Li Xiaoping, 217
Liang Cheng, "On Small-Scale Cinema" (*Xiaoxing dianying lun*), 83–84
Liang Qichao: circulation of information by newspapers compared with the blood and pulse in the body, 12, 32–33; on the need for modern media and a free press, 33, 38, 62
Liao Weici, 49, 264n83
Liberated China (*Jiefangle de Zhongguo*, 1951, dir. Sergei Gerasimov), 17, 135, 142
Ling He, 78
Liu, Deyuan: *The Customers' Troubles* (*Guke de fannao*, 1956), 193; background in Man-ei, 193
Liu, Lydia, 166

Liu Na'ou: autobiographical amateur filmmaking of, 85–86, 96–97, 100; biographical details, 100; *Spring Silkworm* criticized by, 78–79

Liu Na'ou–*Man Who Holds a Movie Camera*: "City Symphony" sequence from, 97, 98; filming and water related in, 92–93, 94–95; Pathé Baby camera used for filming of, 84, 87; reel 1, "Light of the Human" (*Ningen no hikari*), 87–92, 89, 92, 94; reel 2, "Tokyo," 92–93; reel 3, "Guangzhou," 92, 93–94, 95; reel 4, "Scenery" reel, 92, 97; reel 5, unnamed carnival in colonial Taiwan documented in, 99–100; Vertov, Dziga-Man with a Movie Camera (1929) compared with, 84, 89–90, 89

Liu Na'ou-theoretical writing on film: "Camera Apparatus: On the Functions of Position and Angle, 96; "cinematic reality" (*yingxi de shizai*) and "actual reality" (*zhen de shizai*) distinguished by, 95–96; "On the Attitude of the Author," 97, 99

Liu Shaoqi: death of, 225; rehabilitation ceremony, 225–27, 226, 233; self-criticism for mistakes of the Great Leap Forward (1962), 196; state visit to Indonesia. See *Chairman Liu Shaoqi Visits Indonesia* (*Liu Shaoqi zhuxi fangwen Yindunixiya*, 1963)

Liu Shaoqi-downfall in 1967: *Criminal Liu Visits Indonesia* (*Liuzei fangwen yindunixiya*, 1967), 201–5; documentary films offering guides on staging an anti-Liu rally, 210–11; Liu compared with Khrushchev, 202–5; photographs of Liu removed from Chinese media and public spaces, 226–27; Qi Benyu, "Patriotism or National Betrayal: On the Reactionary Film *Inside Story of the Qing Court*," 202, 210

Liu Tielin, 224, 225

Liu, Xiao, 244

Long Live the Nation(s) (*Minzu wansui*, dir. Zheng Junli, 1941): avoiding war images, 113; clouds, 114–5; documentary dramaturgy, 115–6; filmmaking process according to Zheng Junli, 110, 111–12, 115–17; Kumbum Monastery featured in, 117, 119; music, 113–14; phenomenological approach of, 21; process of logging by Miao men featured in, 121–22, 122; "winning reality" of national unity staged, 112–17

Lumiére brothers: *The Arrival of a Train* (1895), 55, 152; Workers Leaving the Lumiére Factory in Lyon (1895), 51

Lu, Xun: biographical documentary made of, 230; in Japan during the Russo-Japanese war, 37–38, 39, 40

Lü Xinyu, 256n8, 290n2

McGrath, Jason, 22, 208–9

The May Thirtieth Shanghai Movement (*Wusa Huchao*, 1925). See Chen Jianran–*The May Thirtieth Shanghai Movement*

Man-ei (Manchurian Film Company), 103

Mao Dun (Shen Yanbing), novella *Spring Silkworm*, 75, 80; reportage, 79

Mao-era documentaries: availability of, 4, 256n7; dismissed as reified political propaganda by 1980s filmmakers, 256n8

Mao Zedong: call to "never forget class struggle" (Sept. 1962), 207; death in 1976 of, 213, 242; revolutionary romanticism, 157; end of his tenure as head of the state, 196; friends and enemies identified in "The Analysis of Social Classes in China," 178; funeral films of, 287–88n23; Moscow visit and the Moscow Declaration of 1957, 194, 195, 206, 276n4, 283n31; politics of the mass line articulated by, 13–14, 179; Red Guards inspected in Tiananmen Square during the Cultural Revolution, 216; Yan'an talks on literature an art, 12–13, 106, 127–28, 144, 158

Marcus, Daniel, 11

mass line, 13–14, 179

mediation and the work of media: documentary's mediating role in the digital age, 11; Liang Qichao on the need for modern media and a free press, 12, 32–33, 38, 62; mediation as a process, 10–11. See also events and eventfulness

Mei Lanfang, 266n108
Ming Tombs Reservoir: *State Leaders at Work with Us* (*Lingxiu he women tong laodong*), 159, 161. See also *The Caprice of the Ming Tombs Reservoir* (*Shisanling shuiku changxiangqu*, dir. Jin Shan, 1958); M. Pathé. See Umeya Shōkichi–M. Pathé

Nanniwan (dir. Wu Yinxian, 1943): enacted scenes in, 136; CCP's first campaign film, 16; formal qualities of a solidarity film suited for Yan'an, 106, 129; production of, 129–32; mediating between the Communist army and the local population, 16; as a socialist process film, 19, 169
Nazarov, I., 140–41
Nichols, Bill: "discourses of sobriety" associated with documentary, 18; documentaries evaluated via "ethical accounting," 11, 104–5; on documentary as a concept, 5
Nornes, Abé Markus, 41, 47, 262n48
Northeastern Film Studio (*Dongbei dianying zhipian chang*): battlefront filmmaking by, 106, 132–33, 134, 135; and Beijing Film studio, 141, 149; Changchun Film Studio as its name (1955), 149; *Harvest* (*Fengshou*, 1953), 184; training of Communist documentary filmmakers, 103, 133, 274n73; Yuan Muzhi as its director, 132, 187–88

Ouyang Yuqian, 59, 110

Pang, Kaikwan, 32, 62, 71–72, 80–81
Pathé Frères, films and newsreels produced by, 46, 63
Perry, Elizabeth J., 13
Plum Flowers, Spring Rain, and Jiangnan (*Xinghua chunyu Jiangnan*, 1957, codirected by Gao Zhongming and Zhang Mengqi). See Gao Zhongming–*Plum Flowers, Spring Rain, and Jiangnan*
political leadership on film: contribution of cinema to, 28, 52–53; images of Sun Yat-Sen, 53; warlords featured, 53, 65, 265–66n101. See also Feng Yuxiang's Northern Expedition; Lai Manwai–*War on Sea, Land, and Air* (*Guominjun hailukong dazhan ji*)
popular education associations: founding after the 1911 revolution, 48; visual aids (including lantern slides and cinema) used by, 43; Yuan Xitao's founding of the Popular Education Association in Baoshan County, 43
process films: the basic narrative of industrial capitalism enacted by, 18–19; industrial films from the West shown in China, 49, 264n89; on production techniques for silk and cotton, 50; subversion by left-wing filmmakers in the 1930s, 19. See also Cheng Bugao–*Spring Silkworm* (*Chun chan*, 1933); *Nanniwan* (dir. Qian Xiaozhang, 1943); Great Leap Forward
Proletarian Film League (Prokino), 3, 125
propaganda: dissemination of information associated with the Chinese term *xuanchuan*, 102–3; eventful approach to evaluating propaganda, 16, 104–5, 143; Japanese propaganda during the First Sino-Japanese War, 31–32; Japanese propaganda during the Russo-Japanese War, 39; pejorative connotations of the English term *propaganda*, 103; "winning realities" presented in wartime propaganda documentaries, 104, 107–9, 175, 195; Zheng Yongzhi on the wartime need for, 107–8

Qi Benyu, "Patriotism or National Betrayal: On the Reactionary Film Inside Story of the Qing Court," 202, 210

Raise Your Eyebrows and Draw Your Sword (*Yangmei jian chujiao*, 1978): accountability of the filmmaking process, 220, 221; amateur photographs from People's Mourning (*renmin de huainian*) included in, 217–18, 218, 219, 219; commemoration of the death of Zhou Enlai, 214–15; image-making and records-keeping in the square highlighted, 219, 219; inclusion of footage in *River Elegy* (*He shang*, 1988),

Raise Your Eyebrows and Draw Your Sword (Yangmei jian chujiao, 1978) *(continued)* 241; protest in Tianamen Square between late March and early April 1976 chronicled in, 215, 216–17, 218, 221; secret filming by Xinying filmmakers, 14, 216–17, 218, 220, 221

Ramsaye, Terry, on newsreel production in the *Battle of Shanghai*, 66–67, 268n17

Rancière, Jacques, 22, 171

A Record of the National Revolutionary Army's War on Sea, Land, and Air (Guominjun hailukong dazhan ji, 1927). See Lai Manwai–*War on Sea, Land, and Air (Guominjun hailukong dazhan ji)*

Rehabilitation (*pingfan*): archival materials used to build biographies, 213–14, 224–25, 226–27, 231–32; CCP's reversal of unjust verdicts between 1978 and 1982, 214–15; films used to "give form to rehabilitation" (*shi "pingfan" xingxianghua*), 215; of the party-people relationship by 1980s documentaries, 22–23, 215, 230, 239, 250. See also *Raise Your Eyebrows and Draw Your Sword (Yangmei jian chujiao)*

Renov, Michael, 180

reportage literature: as a critical alternative to mainstream journalism, 72; sketch (*sumiao*) as a type of, 79; *Songs on the Reservoir* as an adaptation from, 159, 278n8; Xia Yan's reportage writing, 79–80

Resist America and Aid Korea (1951): cartographic value of, 24, 182, 183, 189; "concrete events" (*shizai de shi*) depicted in, 184; influence of, 183–84

reform and opening, 231, 242–43

revolution: documentary as a revolutionary media, 2–5, 12–14; Antonio Gramsci on revolutionary hegemony, 18; processual understanding of revolutions, 2; knowledge formation in, 17–18

Ricciardi, Alessia, 246

River Elegy (*He shang*, 1988): aesthetics of, 240–47; inclusion of historical footage, 241; viewer correspondence, 243–44

Rosen, Philip, 6

Rotha, Paul, 116

Rouch, Jean, on "film trances" induced by filmmakers, 123

Rouch, Jean and Edgar Morin, *Chronicle of a Summer* (1961), 239

Russo-Japanese War (1904–1905): Chinese visitors to Japan in the wake of, 33–34; as the first "war of light," 29; war films as the new media for, 2, 39, 45–46

Ruttmann, Walter, *Berlin: Symphony of a Great City*, 55, 92

Second Sino-Japanese War: documentary filmmaking during, 14, 31, 103, 143; Japanese propaganda during, 31–32, 39, 104; misinformation in Qing government reports, 32; reconfiguration of power dynamics in East Asia in the wake of, 2, 26, 27; relocation of the capital from Nanjing to Chongqing, 110, 112;

Schmalzer, Sigrid, 162

Scholtz, Sally J., 105

Selden, Mark, 130

Sewell, William H., Jr., 14

Shanghai Document (1928), 16, 143–44

Shen Zhihua, 283n31

Shi Mei: on bourgeois tendencies in documentary filmmaking, 186–87; criticism of films made at Xinying, 191; criticism of *Plum Flowers, Spring Rain*, and *Jiangnan*, 188–89, 191; Great Leap documentaries on building backyard furnaces, 168–69, 186, 280n76

Siegert, Bernhard, 258n29

Silk Road (*Sichou zhilu*, 1980), 214, 234–35

situated aesthetics, 4, 16

Skvirsky, Salomé Aguilera, on the "process genre," 19, 131, 169

Snow, Edgar, 138

Socialist Education Movement: documentary filmmaking during, 208, 217; increased emphasis on class struggle, 207–8, 209–10

Socialist Education Movement–documentaries made during: *Forget Not Class Bitterness and Remember a Blood Ocean of Grievances* (*Buwang jieji ku, yongji xuehaichou*, 1965), 208; *Collection Courtyard* (*Shouzu yuan*, 1966), 208

Society for Aiding and Reinvigorating the Navy: film about the Imperial Chinese Navy, 38–41; filmmaking as the group's

prioritized activity, 39, 42–43; founding of, 38–39
soft aesthetic. *See* hard (Marxist) versus soft (modernist) cinema debate
solidarity film: China a locus in Soviet solidarity filmmaking, 16–17; definitions of, 16, 105–6; Joris Ivens's films as, 9, 16; Nanniwan as a, 106; political relationality underlying, 16, 106–7, 142; Soviet solidarity filmmaking in China, 16, 143–44; Thomas Waugh on, 16, 105; *Long Live the Nation(s)* as a, 106, 112–17; Sino-Soviet coproduction, 106–7, 136, 142. *See also Victory of the Chinese People*
Songs on the Reservoir (*Shuiku shang de gesheng*, dir. Yu Yanfu, 1958), 159–60
The Songs of the Pioneers (*Xianquzhe zhe ge*, 1981), 230
socialist realism, 17, 136, 139–42
Spanish Civil War: Joris Iven's documentary *The Spanish Earth* (1937), 105, 125; Roman Karmen's documentary on, 126
Spring Silkworm. *See* Cheng Bugao–*Spring Silkworm* (*Chun chan*, 1933)
Su Xiaokang, 242, 243
Sun Yat-sen: interest in cinema's educational value, 49; Revolutionary Alliance of, 2, 45, 54; and Umeya Shōkichi, 1–2, 8, 23, 44, 45. *See also* Lai Manwai–*War on Sea, Land, and Air* (*Guominjun hailukong dazhan ji*)

Taylor, Frederick Winslow, scientific management developed by, 153
Taylorism (scientific management): cinema use in Taylorist management, 153–54; Lenin's interest in Taylorism, 154; resisted by unions, 155. *See also Inch of Time*
television: associated with first-generation independent documentary, 248; approximated by mobile cinema, 165; broadcast of Gang of Four trials and Liu Shaoqi's rehabilitation, 222, 225; coproduction with Japan, 234–5; exchange with overseas television producers, 214, 232, 234; first broadcast in 1958, 164; in *Caprice of the Ming Tombs Reservoir*, 162, 164, *164*; as infrastructure, 214, 233; intellectuals' interest in television, 245; television aesthetics, 234. *See also Silk Road*; *Yangtze*; *Grand Canal*; *Today in History*; *River Elegy*
Thompson, E. P., 155
Thornton, Patricia, 207
Tian Han, 110; *The Caprice of the Ming Tombs Reservoir* adapted by, 160; review of *Songs on the Reservoir*, 278n45
Tiananmen Movement (1976). *See* April 5 Movement
Tiananmen Movement (1989): independent documentary arising in the aftermath of, 23, 248, 250; market reforms leading up to, 243; party-people relationship disrupted by the suppression of protests, 250
Today in History (*Lishishang de jintian*): images of events during the Cultural Revolution excluded from, 241; popular interest in history stimulated by, 232–33, 289n45; shutting down of, 289n45
Trial by Nine Hundred Million People (*Jiuyi renmin de shenpan*, 1980). *See* Gang of Four trials
Trotsky, Leon, 13, 144
Tyerman, Edward, 143–44

Umeya Shōkichi: background of, 44–45; and Sun Yat-sen, 1–2, 8, 23, 27, 44, 45
Umeya Shōkichi–*The Chinese Revolution*: premiere in Japan (1911), 1–2; as a solidarity film, 16; the making of, 46–47
Umeya Shōkichi-M. Pathé: founding of, 1–2, 45–46; scientific and educational films from Europe imported to Japan, 46; *The Chinese Revolution* produced by, 1, 44

Varlamov, Leonid, *Victory of the Chinese People* directed by, 135, 141, 142–43
Veg, Sebastian, 291n7
Vertov, Dziga: "documentalism" of, 139, 275n88; documentary form created by, 125; kino-eye of, 55, 140; *kinopravda* (film truth), 139, 206; *Leninskaia Kinopravda* (Lenin's film-truth, 1925), 287–88n23; *Three Songs of Lenin* (1934), 228, 287–88n23

Vertov, Dziga–*Man with a Movie Camera* (1929): Liu Na'ou on, 86–87; Liu Na'ou's *A Man Who Holds a Movie Camera* compared with, 84, 89–90, 89

Victorious Song of Life (*Shenghuo de kaige*, 1958), 169–70, 170

Victory of the Chinese People (*Zhongguo renmin de shengli*, 1950): aesthetics of victory, 136–37; as the CCP's first-ever documentary in color, 135, 136; mediation role of, 143; *Millon Heroes Crossing the Yangtze* (1949) compared with, 136, 138; reenactments of major battles in, 15, 17, 106–7; as a Sino-Soviet coproduction, 17, 106–7, 135, 137, 140, 142, 183

Vietnam: Liu Shaoqi's visit to, 176; *Vietnam in Resistance* (*Kangzhan de Yuenan*, 1952), 184

village memory project, 252. See also Wu Wenguang

Virilio, Paul, 29

Wagner, Rudolf, on funerary rites and films, 287–8n23

Wang, Ban, 282n8

Wang, David Der-wei, 262n38

Wang, Jing. 244, 245

Wang Guangmei: denunciation of, 175–76, 177, 201, 206, 210; as a "diplomatic wife" in *Chairman Liu Shaoqi Visits Indonesia* (*Liu Shaoqi zhuxi fangwen Yindunixiya*, 1963), 21, 176–77, 180, 199–201, 281n1; in *Long Live the Memory of Comrade Liu Shaoqi*, 229, 229; Socialist Education Movement spearheaded by, 207, 209

Wang Hui, 243

Wang Jiyan, 234–35

Wang Zhiping, 217

water and liquidity: association with capital and commodity exchange in Cheng Bugao's *Spring Silkworm*, 94; documentary series *Grand Canal*, 236–39, 241; documentary series *Yangtze*, 235–38, 241; filming and water related in Liu's *Man Who Holds a Movie Camera*, 92–93, 94–95; labor mobilization for rural construction of irrigation infrastructure, 158–59; in modernist cinema, 92; waterways as sites of historical and cultural sedimentation, 214. See also Cheng Bugao–*Torrent* (*Kuangliu*, 1933); Liu Na'ou–*Man Who Holds a Movie Camera* (1932); *River Elegy* (*He shang*, 1988)

Waugh, Thomas, 115, 120; on solidarity films, 16, 105

Wei Jingsheng, essay "The Fifth Modernization," 222

"wife diplomacy": building relationship with nonrevolutionary states, 21, 211; Deng Yingchao's consideration of, 197–98; ending of, 209–10; Jiang Qing's public appearance as Mao's wife, 199; the party's patriarchal tendencies demonstrated by, 198–99; Wang Guangmei as a "diplomatic wife" in *Chairman Liu Shaoqi Visits Indonesia*, 21, 176–77, 180, 199–201, 281n1

Wilcox, Emily, 198

Williams, Raymond, 18

Winston, Brian, 11

Workers' Film and Photo League, 3, 125

Workers International Relief (WIR), 125

Wu, Yiching, 206

Wu Hung, 217

Wu Peifu, 53, 65, 265–66n101

Wu Wenguang: association with a state-run television station, 248; *Bumming in Beijing* (*Liulang Beijing*, 1990), 252; *Fuck Cinema* (*Cao tamade dianying*, 2005), 252; Village Memory Project, 252

Wu Yinxian, see also *Nanniwan* (dir. Wu Yinxian, 1943),

Xia Yan: collaboration with Cheng Bugao on *Spring Silkworm* (*Chun chan*, 1933), 71, 75; reportage writing by, 79–80; response to criticism of *Spring Silkworm*, 79

Xinying (Central Newsreel and Documentary Film Studio, Zhongyang Xinwen jilu dianying zhipianchang): Ding Jiao on documenting tomorrow, 157; experimentation with documentary form in the mid-1950s, 21, 151, 194, 195, 196; filmmaking infrastructure, 149–51; the founding of, 149; impact of the rise of television documentary on, 233; the making of instructional documentaries for backyard furnaces during the Great Leap Forward, 168–70; presence at international events and domestic political events, 14, 149; Shi Mei's criticism of the "bourgeois line" at Xinying, 191; Zhong Dianfei's guidance of, 20, 180

Xu Suling, call for filmmakers to get out of the studio in wartime, 102, 108, 117

Yan'an: blockade and economic difficulties, 16, 129–30; documentary mediating local relationships,16, 22, 129–32; Edgar Snow's footage of Yan'an's revolutionary culture, 126; founding of the CCP's own film unit in, 81, 126–27; Mao's Yan'an talks, 127–28; Roman Karmen filming in Yan'an, 126; Wu Benli, 135; Yan'an and the Eighth Route Army (*Yan'an yu Balujun*, 1940), 128–29; Yan'an Forum on Literature and Art (1942), 13; See also *Nanniwan* (dir. Wu Yinxian, 1943); Northeastern Film Studio (*Dongbei dianying zhipian chang*)

Yangtze (Stories of the Yangtze, *Huashuo changjiang*, 1983), 214, 235–36

Yan Ruisheng (dir. Ren Pengnian, 1921), 52

Ye Mai, 167

Yeh, Emilie Yueh-Yu, 29, 257n24

Yu, Sabrina Qiong, 290n1–2

Yuan Muzhi: collaboration with Wu Yinxian on *Yan'an and the Eighth Routh Army* (*Yan'an yu Balujun*, 1940), 128–29; documentary envisioned as the foundation of new cinema, 124–26, 128, 149; filmmaking equipment arranged for by the Communist Party, 81, 128; and Joris Ivens, 81, 124–26; Northeastern Film Studio directed by, 9, 132, 187–88

Yuan Xiluo: background of, 42; cinema's educational value exploited by, 49; film about the Imperial Chinese Navy, 38, 39–41; Society for Aiding and Reinvigorating the Navy founded by, 38, 39

Yuan Xitao: background of, 42; cinema's educational value exploited by, 42, 43, 49

Zhang Mengqi, 188, 252
Zhang Tongdao, 191, 193
Zhang Yingjin, 29, 257n23, 260n10
Zhang Yuan, 252
Zhang Zhen, 100
Zheng Junli: background of, 110–11; dramatization staged for the camera by, 116; on the making of *Long Live the Nation(s)*, 110, 111–12, 115–17; wartime drama, 112. See also *Long Live the Nation(s)* (*Minzu wansui*, dir. Zheng Junli, 1941)
Zheng Yongzhi: on China Motion Picture Studio' production capacity, 107; on the wartime need for propaganda, 108, 127
Zhong Dafeng, 28–29
Zhong Dianfei: condemning as a "Rightest," 187, 195; critical documentaries produced in Xinying guided by, 20, 180; "The Gongs and Drums of Cinema," 191
Zhou, Chenshu, 38
Zhou Enlai: activities at the Bandung Conference (1955), 185, 186; artistic documentary (*yishuxing jilupian*) suggested by, 157; death in 1976, 216; funeral film, *Long Live the Memory of Premier Zhou Enlai* (*Jing'aide Zhou Enlai Zongli yongchui buxiu*, 1977), 228–29, 287n23; interest in drama and cinema, 185; "peaceful coexistence" mediated by, 185; self-criticism for mistakes of the Great Leap Forward (1962), 196; Yuan Muzhi encouraged by, 128. See also *Raise Your Eyebrows and Draw Your Sword* (*Yangmei jian chujiao*)
Zhou Yang, 157, 167
Zimmermann, Patricia: on amateur and avant-garde filmmaking, 85; on digital participatory documentary, 11; on "reverse engineering," 23
Zou Xueping, 252

STUDIES OF THE WEATHERHEAD EAST ASIAN INSTITUTE, COLUMBIA UNIVERSITY

Selected Titles
(Complete list at: weai.columbia.edu/content/publications)

A Third Way: The Origins of China's Current Economic Development Strategy, by Lawrence Chris Reardon. Harvard University Asia Center, 2020.
Disruptions of Daily Life: Japanese Literary Modernism in the World, by Arthur M. Mitchell. Cornell University Press, 2020.
Recovering Histories: Life and Labor after Heroin in Reform-Era China, by Nicholas Bartlett. University of California Press, 2020.
Figures of the World: The Naturalist Novel and Transnational Form, by Christopher Laing Hill. Northwestern University Press, 2020.
Arbiters of Patriotism: Right Wing Scholars in Imperial Japan, by John Person. Hawaii University Press, 2020.
The Chinese Revolution on the Tibetan Frontier, by Benno Weiner. Cornell University Press, 2020.
Making It Count: Statistics and Statecraft in the Early People's Republic of China, by Arunabh Ghosh. Princeton University Press, 2020.
Tea War: A History of Capitalism in China and India, by Andrew B. Liu. Yale University Press, 2020.
Revolution Goes East: Imperial Japan and Soviet Communism, by Tatiana Linkhoeva. Cornell University Press, 2020.
Vernacular Industrialism in China: Local Innovation and Translated Technologies in the Making of a Cosmetics Empire, 1900–1940, by Eugenia Lean. Columbia University Press, 2020.
Fighting for Virtue: Justice and Politics in Thailand, by Duncan McCargo. Cornell University Press, 2020.
Beyond the Steppe Frontier: A History of the Sino-Russian Border, by Sören Urbansky. Princeton University Press, 2020.
Learning to Rule: Court Education and the Remaking of the Qing State, 1861–1912, by Daniel Barish. Columbia University Press, 2022.
Common Ground: Tibetan Buddhist Expansion and Qing China's Inner Asia, by Lan Wu. Columbia University Press, 2022.

GPSR Authorized Representative: Easy Access System Europe, Mustamäe tee
50, 10621 Tallinn, Estonia, gpsr.requests@easproject.com